HENRY VAUGHAN

POETRY AND SELECTED PROSE

Oxford University Press, Amen House, London E.C.4
GLASGOW NEW YORK TORONTO MELBOURNE WELLINGTON
BOMBAY CALCUTTA MADRAS KARACHI LAHORE DACCA
CAPE TOWN SALISBURY NAIROBI IBADAN ACCRA
KUALA LUMPUR HONG KONG

HENRY VAUGHAN

POETRY AND SELECTED PROSE

EDITED WITH AN
INTRODUCTION BY

L. C. MARTIN

LONDON
OXFORD UNIVERSITY PRESS
NEW YORK TORONTO
1963

HENRY VAUGHAN

Born, Newton, Breconshire, 1621 or 1622
Died, Scethrog, Breconshire, 23 April 1695

The Oxford Standard Authors edition of Henry Vaughan, Poetry and Selected Prose, *edited by L. C. Martin from his edition of* The Works of Henry Vaughan *for the Oxford English Texts (Clarendon Press, 1957), was first published in 1963*

PRINTED IN GREAT BRITAIN
O.S.A.

CONTENTS

THALIA REDIVIVA

TRANSLATIONS

INTRODUCTION

I. SHORT BIOGRAPHY

HENRY VAUGHAN came of a well-established Welsh family, the Vaughans of Tretower, and lived for nearly the whole of his life in the country parish of Llansantffread, on the Usk, between the Brecon Beacons and the Black Mountains, where his parents, Thomas and Denise, had a small property called Trenewydd or Newton. Henry and his younger twin brother Thomas were born at Newton in 1621 or early in the following year. They had their schooling from the Reverend Matthew Herbert, Rector of Llangattock, near Crickhowell, to whom they both later addressed Latin verses, recording their gratitude and affection.

Both boys went to Oxford, but only Thomas graduated (February 1641/2), afterwards taking orders and holding the living of Llansantffread until he was evicted from it in 1650, and thenceforward devoting himself to theosophy and science. Henry, after about two years at Oxford, 'in Logicals under a noted Tutor', went to London to study law, but was summoned home to Llansantffread on the outbreak of the Civil War in 1642. Like his brother he appears to have served in the war, on the king's side, but no very clear details are available; Henry's references (published during the Commonwealth) are generally vague, perhaps by intention. About 1646 he married Catherine Wise, of Coleshill, Warwickshire, and on her death some years later he married her sister, Elizabeth. There were four children by each marriage.

With the exception of *Thalia Rediviva*, 1678, all Vaughan's published writings belong to the eleven years 1646–57. Section II of this Introduction contains a list of all the volumes, and Section III some observations on those included in the present edition.

On the death of his father in 1658 Vaughan became heir-apparent to Newton, which was his mother's property, and lived there for thirty years more. In 1689 an agreement was made whereby he was to evacuate the property in favour of his elder son, Thomas, and remove to a cottage in the neighbouring village of Scethrog.

In 1673 he supplied his kinsman, John Aubrey, with information about himself and his brother which was made the basis of their lives as recounted in Wood's *Historia et Antiquitates Universitatis Oxoniensis*, 1674, and *Athenae Oxonienses*, 1692 and (amended) 1721. Vaughan's letter includes the statement that his profession was physic, 'which I have practised now for many years with good successe (I thank god!) & a repute big enough for a person of greater parts than my selfe'. What medical training he had is unknown. He was still practising in 1693, less than two years before his death on 23 April 1695. He was buried in the churchyard at Llansantffread, where the gravestone shows that, as on some of his title-pages, he continued to call himself 'Silurist', after the local British tribe whose name is given as 'Silures' by Tacitus:

HENRICUS | VAUGHAN | SILURIS | M · D · OBIIT AP · 23 ANO | SAL · 1695 · ÆTAT · SUÆ · 73 | [Arms] | QUOD IN SEPULCHRUM | VOLUIT | SERVUS INUTILIS: | PECCATOR MAXIMUS | HIC IACEO | + | GLORIA MISERERE · |

For a fuller account of Vaughan's life see F. E. Hutchinson, *Henry Vaughan, a Life and an Interpretation*, 1947 (referred to below as '*Life*').

II. LIST OF PUBLISHED WORKS

Vaughan's works appeared in the following order:

1. *Poems, with the tenth Satyre of Iuvenal*, 1646.

2. *Silex Scintillans*, 1650 (the first part).

3. *Olor Iscanus*, 1651. Dedication dated 1647. Poems with four short prose translations:

(*a*) *Of the Benefit wee may get by our Enemies* (Plutarch);
(*b*) *Of the Diseases of the Mind and the Body* (Plutarch);
(*c*) *Of the Diseases of the Mind, and the Body* (Maximus Tyrius);
(*d*) *The Praise and Happinesse of the Countrie-life* (Antonio de Guevara).

4. *The Mount of Olives: or, Solitary Devotions*, 1652. Prose, in two sections, of which *Man in Darkness* is the second. This is followed by *Man in Glory*, translated from *De felicitate sanctorum*, attributed to Anselm.

5. *Flores Solitudinis*, 1654. Translations:

(*a*) *Of Temperance and Patience*;
(*b*) *Of Life and Death*. Both (*a*) and (*b*) by I. E. Nieremberg, S.J.;
(*c*) *The World Contemned*. By Eucherius, Bishop of Lyons;
(*d*) *Primitive Holiness, Set forth in the Life of blessed Paulinus* (partly translated).

6. *Silex Scintillans*, 1655. The unsold sheets of the 1650 edition, save for two leaves replaced by cancels, make up part i, to which part ii is added. This volume may have been preceded by *Hermetical Physick* (7), which was registered two months earlier.

7. *Hermetical Physick*, 1655. Translated from Heinrich Nolle, *Systema medicinae Hermeticae generale*, 1613.

8. *The Chymists Key*, 1657. Translated from Heinrich Nolle, *De generatione rerum naturalium*, 1613.

9. *Thalia Rediviva*, 1678. A collection of miscellaneous poems by both Henry and Thomas Vaughan.

Of these the present volume contains, in the following order:

(*a*) the whole of *Poems* (1);
(*b*) all the poems in *Olor Iscanus* (3);
(*c*) *The Mount of Olives* (4), excluding the translation, *Man in Glory*;
(*d*) *Primitive Holiness*, from *Flores Solitudinis* (5);
(*e*) *Silex Scintillans*, (2) and (6) together;
(*f*) *Thalia Rediviva* (Henry Vaughan's part).

The present text is that of Vaughan's *Works* in Oxford English Texts (2nd edition, 1957) with the following exceptions: p. 205, l. 35 *tangam*] *tanquam* 1957; p. 335, l. 1 O, do not] I, do not *1957*; p. 344, l. 33 rare] rare; *1957*; p. 428, l. 24 descent.] descent *1957*; p. 435, l. 3 mole] mule *1957*; p. 449, l. 8 will] wilt *1957*.

In his book *On the Poems of Henry Vaughan* (Cobden-Sanderson, 1927) Professor Edmund Blunden included his verse-translations of seven Latin poems by Vaughan, and has kindly given permission for these translations to reappear in the present volume. (See pp. 456–9.)

III. PREFACES

(*a*) *Poems, with the tenth Satyre of Iuvenal*, 1646

In this volume of apprentice work Vaughan experiments in several of the lyrical modes favoured at about the time when he was in London (*c.* 1640–2). Some evidence of his tastes and ambitions can also be gathered from his reverent allusion to Jonson, his mention of two plays by Randolph, and his willingness to borrow phrases from Donne, Randolph, and Habington. Already he is thinking about the moral integrity of his work; 'You have here a *Flame*, bright only in its own Innocence'; and there are hints of the other-worldly strain which was soon to pervade his poetry. Already also his craftsmanship appears, especially in his management of rhythms and cadences. The translation of Juvenal, x (The Vanity of Human Wishes), is often very free and initiates Vaughan's habit of expanding translations by inserting his own comments. Thus ll. 159–65 are his, not Juvenal's.

(*b*) *Olor Iscanus*, 1651

This volume, or something like it, was apparently ready in December 1647, when the dedication was dated. How it differed from what was finally published is not known, but there is reason to believe that it contained war poems of a kind which it would no longer be safe to acknowledge (*Life*, pp. 74–75); and this may have been the chief reason why it was suppressed. Another reason might be that Vaughan was beginning to have serious doubts about the worth of non-religious literature and the propriety of contributing to it. This could hardly yet have been a settled disposition in him because *Olor Iscanus*, as finally published 'by a Friend', contained secular poems written both in and after 1647, including a poem in enthusiastic praise of Davenant's *Gondibert* (1651). Vaughan also eulogizes the plays of Fletcher (1647) and the plays and poems of Cartwright (1651). In what degree, if at all, the publication of *Olor Iscanus* had his approval can only be conjectured, but he was certainly justified later in claiming that his published secular poems were not licentious, and that any lightness in them was redeemed 'by many virtuous and some pious mixtures'. He may have been thinking especially of the verse translations from Boethius, *De consolatione philosophiae*, and from the Christian poetry of Casimire Sarbiewski.

(*c*) *The Mount of Olives*, 1652. Dedication 1 October 1651

This work, as distinct from *Man in Glory*, the translation appended to it, is Vaughan's nearest approach to an original prose work, although it contains many quoted or translated passages.

As observed by Hutchinson (*Life*, 136–7), the main purpose of the book was to encourage the practice of Christian devotion and meditation at a time when the ordinary services of the Episcopal Church had been banned; and there are various references to what was happening in 'these times of persecution and triall', to the death of Charles I ('We have seen Princes brought to their graves by a new way'), and to the Act for the Propagation of the Gospel in Wales of 1650 (whereby Thomas Vaughan was evicted from his incumbency of Llansantffread).

The allusion (p. 132, ll. 7–8) to those who have 'washed their hands in the blood of my . . . dearest and nearest relatives' is less certain, as no close relative of Vaughan is known to have died in the violent way indicated. Probably, however, Vaughan refers to the death in 1648 of his younger brother, William, which is likely to have resulted from wounds or illness incurred during military service (*Life*, 95–97).

In these ways *The Mount of Olives* helps to explain the moods of depression and austerity reflected in Vaughan's writings of 1650–5. He tries to meet the new conditions in a spirit of Christian forgiveness, occasionally letting it appear how much he thought there was to forgive.

It is characteristic of one who was always ready to idealize the past (as in his poems on childhood) that he could describe the Puritan régime in terms of degeneration from a former age of relative sinlessness, here typified by the innocent lives and simple piety of the early Christian fathers.

(*d*) *Primitive Holiness*, from *Flores Solitudinis*, 1654. Dedication dated 1653

The first three works contained in *Flores Solitudinis* are translations freely interspersed with Vaughan's own comments (usually brief). The fourth, *Primitive Holiness*, is more largely original although it also comprises a fairly large amount of translated material. In the present volume this work is preceded by the dedication and the address 'To the Reader' introducing *Flores Solitudinis* as a whole. The poem which follows this prefatory matter ('O doe not goe') is omitted here as it reappears in *Silex Scintillans* (p. 335).

Primitive Holiness is a biography of Paulinus, who was born *c.* A.D. 353, was a pupil of Ausonius, became a convert to Christianity, and was afterwards made Bishop of Nola. As Vaughan states on the title-page, he draws a good deal on Paulinus's own writings (letters and poems) and 'other Primitive Authors'. He also uses a Latin life of Paulinus by the Jesuit Francesco Sacchini, published in 1621 and 1622.

Among the many passages in this work apparently by Vaughan himself the following are specially worth noting:

165.1–166.7; 172.9–22; 179.1–180.8; 180.12–25; 180.37–181.10; 181. 11–18; 182.36–183.27; 189.11–20; 189.35–190.23; 192.33–193.27; 196.40–197.4; 198.27–199.3; 201.5–40; 206.35–207.19.

In these places and elsewhere Vaughan again (as in *The Mount of Olives*) contrasts 'primitive holiness' with modern degeneracy, as where he observes that Paulinus, derided by the multitude for his conversion, 'would not buy their friendship with the losse of Heaven, nor call those Saints and propagators who were Devills and destroyers'; or where he deplores the prohibition of the time-honoured Christmas and Easter festivals. But there are also in this work many passages of serenely ordered prose which would probably be much better known and appreciated if the best of Vaughan's poetry had not excelled it.

(*e*) *Silex Scintillans*, 1650 and 1655. Preface dated 1654

The first edition consisted of the poems which in 1655 form the first part or section (pp. 226–314), now supplemented by the second part (pp. 315–84). The edition of 1650 alone has the engraved title-page and the accompanying 'Emblema'. The edition of 1655 replaces these by a new printed title-page (p. 216) and a Preface. The 1655 edition also enlarges the Dedication by adding ll. 15–46 and the quotation from Revelation i. Further, it adds the prefatory verses 'Vain Wits and eyes', &c. (p. 225).

The personal and political afflictions from which Vaughan had been suffering since 1646 seem to have culminated somewhere about the year 1653, when he had a serious illness. He alludes to this both towards the end of the Preface and in the concluding poems of part ii, having already mentioned a state of ill health on the title-page of *Flores Solitudinis* and also in the Dedication thereto; and this illness as much as anything may account for the mood of extreme austerity pervading the Preface, wherein Vaughan deprecates the writing and reading of all 'idle books'.

His own concentration on religious writing he explains as resulting from the example of George Herbert, 'whose holy life and *verse* gained many pious *Converts*, (of whom I am the least)'; and although this is probably too great a simplification of a complex issue yet without any doubt the influence of Herbert was both powerful and far-reaching, confirming Vaughan in his religious orthodoxy, stimulating him to explore the possibilities of devotional poetry, and supplying him with countless ideas, phrases, and formal patterns which he sometimes took over with little or no modification. But often he transforms what he borrows; and in his most arresting poems, such as 'The Retreat', 'The Night', 'The Waterfall', 'My soul, there is a Country', 'I saw Eternity the other night', the debt to Herbert is usually slighter and Vaughan's native abilities reach their fullest expansion. He never acquired all Herbert's sense of form and finish, but he had the advantage in visionary power and in range and enterprise of imagination, gifts which enabled him not only, with Herbert, to enhance the poetic value of ancient Christian doctrines, but sometimes rewardingly to go outside them. It was easier for him than for Herbert to proceed from thoughts of immortality to thoughts of pre-existence; to hold acquaintance with a transcendent world, 'the world of light', which was yet connected with the world of common experience by strange affiliations and correspondences; and thus to entertain beliefs or half-beliefs that all created things are unified and held together by a single world-spirit, that there is no death, only change, and that the whole of nature is alive and conscious, adoring and praising the Creator and joyfully awaiting the day of consummated Revelation.

For ideas such as these, variously introduced and combined in *Silex Scintillans*, there were many precedents and analogies in the Neoplatonic traditions, and in the writings of those who, like Thomas Vaughan, were enthusiastic about the benefits, physical or spiritual, to be obtained from knowledge of the 'Hermetic' writings, from the study of nature, or from alchemical experiments. Henry Vaughan's own translations of two Latin medical treatises of an allegedly 'Hermetic' character did not appear until

1655 and 1657; but as this kind of influence is distributed through both books of *Silex Scintillans*, 1650 as well as 1655, it may well have affected him at least as early as did his reading of George Herbert.

(*f*) *Thalia Rediviva*, 1678

When Vaughan wrote to Aubrey in 1673 giving some biographical facts about his brother and himself he mentioned *Thalia Rediviva* as 'a peece now ready for the presse'. After five years it appeared without his name on the title-page but with several sets of commendatory verse addressed to him; so that he must have overcome in some degree his objections to being known as a secular poet. The volume represents a salvaging of poems written at various times, some possibly as early as those published in 1646. Some are occasional, with dates attached or assignable from their subjects. The 'Pious Thoughts and Ejaculations' have characteristic titles such as 'Looking Backward', 'Retirement', and 'The Recovery'; and practically all of these can be regarded as addenda to *Silex Scintillans*. The volume as a whole gives a fair illustration of Vaughan's poetic interests and abilities at different stages of his career. One of the best poems, 'Daphnis, An Elegiac Eclogue', laments the death in 1666 of Thomas Vaughan ('Eugenius Philalethes'), who is also represented in *Thalia Rediviva* by a collection of his poems.

POEMS,
WITH
The tenth SATYRE of
IUVENAL
ENGLISHED.

By *Henry Vaughan*, Gent.

—— *Tam nil, nullâ tibi vendo*
Illiade ————

LONDON,
Printed for *G. Badger*, and are to be ſold at his
ſhop under Saint *Dunſtans* Church in
Fleet-ſtreet. 1646.

To all Ingenious Lovers of POESIE

Gentlemen,

To you alone, whose more refined Spirits *out-wing these dull Times, and soare above the drudgerie of durty* Intelligence, *have I made sacred these* Fancies: *I know the yeares, and what course entertainment they affoord* Poetry. *If any shall question that* Courage *that durst send me abroad so late, and revell it thus in the* Dregs *of an Age, they have my silence: only,*

Languescente seculo, liceat ægrotari;

My more calme Ambition, *amidst the common noise, hath thus exposed* 10 *me to the World: You have here a* Flame, *bright only in its owne* Innocence, *that kindles nothing but a generous* Thought; *which though it may warme the Bloud, the fire at highest is but* Platonick, *and the* Commotion, *within these limits, excludes* Danger: *For the* Satyre, *it was of purpose borrowed, to feather some slower Houres; And what you see here, is but the* Interest: *It is one of his, whose* Roman *Pen had as much true* Passion, *for the infirmities of that state, as we should have* Pitty, *to the distractions of our owne: Honest (I am sure) it is, and offensive cannot be, except it meet with such* Spirits *that will quarrell with* Antiquitie, *or purposely* Arraigne 20 *themselves; These indeed may thinke, that they have slept out so many* Centuries *in this* Satyre, *and are now awaked; which, had it been still* Latine, *perhaps their Nap had been Everlasting: But enough of these,—It is for you only that I have adventured thus far, and invaded the Presse with* Verse; *to whose more noble* Indulgence, *I shall now leave it; and so am gone.*——

H. V.

To my Ingenuous Friend, *R. W.*

When we are dead, and now, no more
Our harmles mirth, our wit, and score
Distracts the Towne; when all is spent
That the base niggard world hath lent
Thy purse, or mine; when the loath'd noise
Of Drawers, Prentises, and boyes
Hath left us, and the clam'rous barre
Items no pints i'th' Moone, or Starre;
When no calme whisp'rers wait the doores,
To fright us with forgotten scores; 10
And such aged, long bils carry,
As might start an Antiquary;
When the sad tumults of the Maze,
Arrests, suites, and the dreadfull face
Of Seargeants are not seene, and wee
No Lawyers Ruffes, or Gownes must fee:
When all these Mulcts are paid, and I
From thee, deare wit, must part, and dye;
Wee'le beg the world would be so kinde,
To give's one grave, as wee'de one minde; 20
There (as the wiser few suspect,
That spirits after death affect)
Our soules shall meet, and thence will they
(Freed from the tyranny of clay)
With equall wings, and ancient love
Into the Elysian fields remove,
Where in those blessed walkes they'le find,
More of thy Genius, and my mind:
First, in the shade of his owne bayes,
Great *BEN* they'le see, whose sacred Layes, 30
The learned Ghosts admire, and throng,
To catch the subject of his Song.
Then *Randolph* in those holy Meades,
His Lovers, and *Amyntas* reads,
Whilst his Nightingall close by,
Sings his, and her owne Elegie;

From thence dismiss'd by subtill roades,
Through airie paths, and sad aboads;
They'le come into the drowsie fields
Of Lethe, which such vertue yeelds, 40
That (if what Poets sing be true)
The streames all sorrow can subdue.
Here on a silent, shady greene,
The soules of Lovers oft are seene,
Who in their lifes unhappy space,
Were murther'd by some perjur'd face.
All these th' inchanted streames frequent,
To drowne their Cares, and discontent,
That th' inconstant, cruell sex
Might not in death their spirits vex: 50
  And here our soules bigge with delight
Of their new state will cease their flight:
And now the last thoughts will appeare,
They'le have of us, or any here;
But on those flowry banks will stay,
And drinke all sense, and cares away.
  So they that did of these discusse,
  Shall find their fables true in us.

Les Amours

Tyrant farewell: This heart, the prize
And triumph of thy scornfull eyes,
I sacrifice to Heaven, and give
To quit my sinnes, that durst believe
A Womans easie faith, and place
True joyes in a changing face.
  Yet e're I goe; by all those teares,
And sighs I spent 'twixt hopes, and feares;
By thy owne glories, and that houre
Which first inslav'd me to thy power; 10
I beg, faire One, by this last breath,
This tribute from thee after death.
If when I'm gone, you chance to see
That cold bed where I lodged bee:

Let not your hate in death appeare,
But blesse my ashes with a teare:
This influxe from that quickning eye,
By secret pow'r, which none can spie,
The cold dust shall informe, and make
Those flames (though dead) new life partake. 20
Whose warmth help'd by your tears shall bring,
O're all the tombe a sudden spring
Of Crimson flowers, whose drooping heads
Shall curtaine o're their mournfull beds:
And on each leafe by Heavens command,
These Emblemes to the life shall stand:
  Two Hearts, the first a shaft withstood;
The second, shot, and washt in bloud;
And on this heart a dew shall stay,
Which no heate can court away; 30
But fixt for ever witnesse beares,
That hearty sorrow feeds on teares.
  Thus Heaven can make it knowne, and true,
  That you kill'd me, 'cause I lov'd you.

To Amoret

The Sigh

Nimble Sigh on thy warme wings,
    Take this Message, and depart,
Tell *Amoret*, that smiles, and sings,
At what thy airie voyage brings,
    That thou cam'st lately from my heart.

Tell my lovely foe, that I
Have no more such spies to send,
    But one or two that I intend
Some few minutes ere I dye,
    To her white bosome to commend. 10

Then whisper by that holy Spring
    Where for her sake I would have dyed,
Whilst those water Nymphs did bring
    Flowers to cure what she had tryed;
And of my faith, and love did sing.

That if my *Amoret*, if she
    In after-times would have it read,
How her beauty murther'd mee,
With all my heart I will agree,
    If shee'le but love me, being dead. 20

To his Friend

Being in Love

Aske Lover, ere thou dyest; let one poor breath
Steale from thy lips, to tell her of thy Death;
Doating Idolater! can silence bring
Thy Saint propitious? or will *Cupid* fling
One arrow for thy palenes? leave to trye
This silent Courtship of a sickly eye;
Witty to tyranny: She too well knowes
This but the incense of thy private vowes,
That breaks forth at thine eyes, and doth betray
The sacrifice thy wounded heart would pay; 10
Aske her, foole, aske her, if words cannot move,
The language of thy teares may make her love:
  Flow nimbly from me then; and when you fall
On her breasts warmer snow, O may you all,
By some strange Fate fixt there, distinctly lye
The much lov'd Volume of my Tragedy.
  Where if you win her not, may this be read,
The cold that freez'd you so, did strike me dead.

Song

Amyntas *goe, thou art undone,*
    Thy faithfull heart is crost by fate;
That Love is better not begunne,
    Where Love is come to love too late;
Had she professed hidden fires,
    Or shew'd one knot that tyed her heart:
I could have quench'd my first desires,
    And we had only met to part;

But Tyrant, thus to murther men,
And shed a Lovers harmles bloud, 10
And burne him in those flames agen,
Which he at first might have withstood:
Yet, who that saw faire Chloris *weep*
Such sacred dew, with such pure grace;
Durst thinke them fained teares, or seeke
For Treason in an Angels face:
This is her Art, though this be true,
Mens joyes are kil'd with griefes and feares;
Yet she like flowers opprest with dew,
Doth thrive and flourish in her teares: 20
This Cruell thou hast done, and thus,
That Face hath many servants slaine.
Though th' end be not to ruine us,
But to seeke glory by our paine.

To Amoret

Walking in a Starry Evening

If *Amoret*, that glorious Eye,
In the first birth of light,
And death of Night,
Had with those elder fires you spye
Scatter'd so high
Received forme, and sight;

We might suspect in the vast Ring,
Amidst these golden glories,
And fierie stories;
Whether the Sunne had been the King, 10
And guide of Day,
Or your brighter eye should sway;

But, *Amoret*, such is my fate,
That if thy face a Starre
Had shin'd from farre,
I am perswaded in that state
'Twixt thee, and me,
Of some predestin'd sympathie.

For sure such two conspiring minds,
Which no accident, or sight, 20
Did thus unite;
Whom no distance can confine,
Start, or decline,
One, for another, were design'd.

To Amoret gone from him

Fancy, and I, last Evening walkt,
And, *Amoret*, of thee we talkt;
The West just then had stolne the Sun,
And his last blushes were begun:
We sate, and markt how every thing
Did mourne his absence; How the Spring
That smil'd, and curl'd about his beames,
Whilst he was here, now check'd her streames:
The wanton Eddies of her face
Were taught lesse noise, and smoother grace; 10
And in a slow, sad channell went,
Whisp'ring the banks their discontent:
The carelesse ranks of flowers that spread
Their perfum'd bosomes to his head,
And with an open, free Embrace,
Did entertaine his beamy face;
Like absent friends point to the West,
And on that weake reflection feast.
If Creatures then that have no sence,
But the loose tye of influence, 20
(Though fate, and time each day remove
Those things that element their love)
At such vast distance can agree,
Why, *Amoret*, why should not wee.

A Song to *Amoret*

If I were dead, and in my place,
Some fresher youth design'd,
To warme thee with new fires, and grace
Those Armes I left behind;

Were he as faithfull as the Sunne,
    That's wedded to the Sphere;
His bloud as chaste, and temp'rate runne,
    As Aprils mildest teare;

Or were he rich, and with his heapes,
    And spacious share of Earth, 10
Could make divine affection cheape,
    And court his golden birth:

For all these Arts I'de not believe,
    (No though he should be thine)
The mighty Amorist could give
    So rich a heart as mine.

Fortune and beauty thou mightst finde,
    And greater men then I:
But my true resolved minde,
    They never shall come nigh. 20

For I not for an houre did love,
    Or for a day desire,
But with my soule had from above,
    This endles holy fire.

An Elegy

'Tis true, I am undone; Yet e're I dye,
I'le leave these sighes, and teares a legacye
To after-Lovers; that remembring me,
Those sickly flames which now benighted be,
Fann'd by their warmer sighs may love; and prove
In them the Metempsuchosis of Love.
'Twas I (when others scorn'd) vow'd you were fair,
And sware that breath enrich'd the courser aire,
Lent Roses to your cheekes, made *Flora* bring
Her Nymphs with all the glories of the Spring 10
To waite upon thy face, and gave my heart
A pledge to *Cupid* for a quicker dart,
To arme those eyes against my selfe; to me
Thou owest that tongues bewitching harmonye:

I courted Angels from those upper joyes,
And made them leave their spheres to heare thy voice:
I made the Indian curse the houres he spent
To seeke his pearles, and wisely to repent
His former folly, and confesse a sinne
Charm'd by the brighter lustre of thy skinne. 20
I borrow'd from the winds, the gentler wing
Of *Zephirus*, and soft soules of the Spring:
And made (to ayre those cheeks wth fresher grace)
The warme Inspirers dwell upon thy face.

Oh! jam satis————

A Rhapsodie

Occasionally written upon a meeting with some of his friends at the Globe Taverne, in a Chamber painted over head with a Cloudy Skie, and some few dispersed Starres, and on the sides with Land-scapes, Hills, Shepheards, and Sheep

Darknes, & Stars i' th' mid day! they invite
Our active fancies to beleeve it night:
For Tavernes need no Sunne, but for a Signe,
Where rich Tobacco, and quick tapers shine;
And royall, witty Sacke, the Poets soule,
With brighter Suns then he doth guild the bowl;
As though the Pot, and Poet did agree,
Sack should to both Illuminator be.
That artificiall Cloud with it's curl'd brow,
Tels us 'tis late; and that blew space below 10
Is fir'd with many Stars; Marke, how they breake
In silent glaunces o're the hills, and speake
The Evening to the Plaines; where shot from far,
They meet in dumbe salutes, as one great Star.
The roome (me thinks) growes darker; & the aire
Contracts a sadder colour, and lesse faire:
Or is't the Drawers skill, hath he no Arts
To blind us so, we cann't know pints from quarts?

No, no, 'tis night; looke where the jolly Clowne
Musters his bleating heard, and quits the Downe. 20
Harke! how his rude pipe frets the quiet aire,
Whilst ev'ry Hill proclaimes *Lycoris* faire.
Rich, happy man! that canst thus watch, and sleep,
Free from all cares; but thy wench, pipe & sheep.
But see the Moone is up; view where she stands
Centinell o're the doore, drawn by the hands
Of some base Painter, that for gaine hath made
Her face the Landmarke to the tipling trade.
This Cup to her, that to *Endymion* give;
'Twas wit at first, and wine that made them live: 30
Choake may the Painter! and his Boxe disclose
No other Colours then his fiery Nose;
And may we no more of his pencill see,
Then two Churchwardens, and Mortalitie.
Should we goe now a wandring, we should meet
With Catchpoles, whores, & Carts in ev'ry street:
Now when each narrow lane, each nooke & Cave,
Signe-posts, & shop-doors, pimp for ev'ry knave,
When riotous sinfull plush, and tell-tale spurs
Walk Fleet street, & the Strand, when the soft stirs 40
Of bawdy, ruffled Silks, turne night to day;
And the lowd whip, and Coach scolds all the way;
When lust of all sorts, and each itchie bloud
From the Tower-wharfe to Cymbelyne, and Lud,
Hunts for a Mate, and the tyr'd footman reeles
'Twixt chaire-men, torches, & the hackny wheels:
Come, take the other dish; it is to him
That made his horse a Senatour: Each brim
Looke big as mine; The gallant, jolly Beast
Of all the Herd (you'le say) was not the least. 50
Now crown the second bowle, rich as his worth,
I'le drinke it to; he! that like fire broke forth
Into the Senates face, crost Rubicon,
And the States pillars, with their Lawes thereon:
And made the dull gray beards, & furr'd gowns fly
Into *Brundusium* to consult, and lye:
This to brave *Sylla*! why should it be sed,
We drinke more to the living, then the dead?

Flatt'rers, and fooles doe use it: Let us laugh
At our owne honest mirth; for they that quaffe 60
To honour others, doe like those that sent
Their gold and plate to strangers to be spent:
Drink deep; this Cup be pregnant; & the wine
Spirit of wit, to make us all divine,
That big with Sack, and mirth we may retyre
Possessours of more soules, and nobler fire;
And by the influxe of this painted Skie,
And labour'd formes, to higher matters flye;
So, if a Nap shall take us, we shall all,
After full Cups have dreames Poeticall. 70

Lets laugh now, and the prest grape drinke,
Till the drowsie Day-Starre winke;
And in our merry, mad mirth run
Faster, and further then the Sun;
And let none his Cup forsake,
Till that Starre againe doth wake;
So we men below shall move
Equally with the gods above.

To Amoret, *of the difference 'twixt him, and other Lovers, and what true Love is*

Marke, when the Evenings cooler wings
Fanne the afflicted ayre, how the faint Sunne,
Leaving undone,
What he begunne,
Those spurious flames suckt up from slime, and earth
To their first, low birth,
Resignes, and brings.

They shoot their tinsill beames, and vanities,
Thredding with those false fires their way;
But as you stay 10
And see them stray,
You loose the flaming track, and subt'ly they
Languish away,
And cheate your Eyes.

Just so base, Sublunarie Lovers hearts
Fed on loose prophane desires,
May for an Eye,
Or face comply:
But those removed, they will as soone depart,
And shew their Art, 20
And painted fires.

Whil'st I by pow'rfull Love, so much refin'd,
That my absent soule the same is,
Carelesse to misse,
A glaunce, or kisse,
Can with those Elements of lust and sence,
Freely dispence,
And court the mind.

Thus to the North the Loadstones move,
And thus to them th' enamour'd steel aspires: 30
Thus, *Amoret*,
I doe affect;
And thus by winged beames, and mutuall fire,
Spirits and Stars conspire,
And this is LOVE.

To Amoret Weeping

Leave, *Amoret*, melt not away so fast
Thy Eyes faire treasure, Fortunes wealthiest Cast
Deserves not one such pearle; for these well spent,
Can purchase Starres, and buy a Tenement
For us in Heaven; though here the pious streames
Availe us not; who from that Clue of Sun-beams
Could ever steale one thread? or with a kinde
Perswasive Accent charme the wild, lowd winde?
Fate cuts us all in Marble, and the Booke
Forestalls our glasse of minutes; we may looke, 10
But seldome meet a change; thinke you a teare
Can blot the flinty Volume? shall our feare,
Or griefe adde to their triumphes? and must wee
Give an advantage to adversitie?

Deare, idle Prodigall! is it not just
We beare our Stars? What though I had not dust
Enough to cabinett a worme? nor stand
Enslav'd unto a little durt, or sand?
I boast a better purchase, and can shew
The glories of a soule that's simply true. 20
 But grant some richer Planet at my birth
Had spyed me out, and measur'd so much earth
Or gold unto my share; I should have been
Slave to these lower Elements, and seen
My high borne soul flagge with their drosse, & lye
A pris'ner to base mud, and Alchymie;
I should perhaps eate Orphans, and sucke up
A dozen distrest widowes in one Cup;
Nay further, I should by that lawfull stealth,
(Damn'd Usurie) undoe the Common-wealth; 30
Or Patent it in Soape, and Coales, and so
Have the Smiths curse me, and my Laundres too;
Geld wine, or his friend Tobacco; and so bring
The incens'd subject Rebell to his King;
And after all (as those first sinners fell)
Sinke lower then my gold; and lye in Hell.
 Thanks then for this deliv'rance! blessed pow'rs,
You that dispence mans fortune, and his houres,
How am I to you all engag'd! that thus
By such strange means, almost miraculous, 40
You should preserve me; you have gone the way
To make me rich by taking all away.
For I (had I been rich) as sure as fate,
Would have bin medling with the King, or State,
Or something to undoe me; and 'tis fit
(We know) that who hath wealth, should have no wit.
But above all, thanks to that providence,
That arm'd me with a gallant soule, and sence
'Gainst all misfortunes; that hath breath'd so much
Of Heav'n into me, that I scorne the touch 50
Of these low things; and can with courage dare
What ever fate, or malice can prepare:
I envy no mans purse, or mines; I know,
That loosing them, I've lost their curses too;

And, *Amoret*, (although our share in these
Is not contemptible, nor doth much please)
Yet whilst Content, and Love we joyntly vye,
  We have a blessing which no gold can buye.

UPON THE PRIORIE GROVE

His usuall Retyrement

Haile sacred shades! coole, leavie House!
Chaste Treasurer of all my vowes,
And wealth! on whose soft bosome layd
My loves faire steps I first betrayd:
  Henceforth no melancholy flight,
No sad wing, or hoarse bird of Night,
Disturbe this Aire, no fatall throate
Of Raven, or Owle, awake the Note
Of our laid Eccho, no voice dwell
Within these leaves, but *Philomel.* 10
The poisonous Ivie here no more
His false twists on the Oke shall score,
Only the Woodbine here may twine,
As th' Embleme of her Love, and mine;
The Amorous Sunne shall here convey
His best beames, in thy shades to play;
The active ayre, the gentlest show'rs,
Shall from his wings raine on thy flowers;
And the Moone from her dewie lockes
Shall decke thee with her brightest drops: 20
What ever can a fancie move,
Or feed the eye; Be on this Grove;
  And when at last the Winds, and Teares
Of Heaven, with the consuming yeares,
Shall these greene curles bring to decay,
And cloathe thee in an aged Gray:
(If ought a Lover can foresee;
Or if we Poets, Prophets be)
From hence transplanted, thou shalt stand
A fresh Grove in th' Elysian Land; 30
Where (most blest paire!) as here on Earth
Thou first didst eye our growth, and birth;

So there againe, thou 'lt see us move
In our first Innocence, and Love:
And in thy shades, as now, so then,
Wee'le kisse, and smile, and walke agen.

FINIS

IVVENALS
TENTH
SATYRE
TRANSLATED.

Nèc verbum verbo curabit reddere fidus
Interpres———

LONDON,
Printed for *G. B.* and are to be ſold at his Shop
under Saint *Dunſtans* Church. 1646.

IVVENALS tenth Satyre
TRANSLATED

In all the parts of Earth, from farthest West,
And the Atlanticke Isles, unto the East
And famous Ganges; Few there be that know
What's truly good, and what is good in show
Without mistake: For what is't we desire,
Or feare discreetly? to what e're aspire,
So throughly blest; but ever as we speed,
Repentance seales the very Act, and deed.
The easie gods mov'd by no other Fate,
Then our owne pray'rs whole Kingdomes ruinate, 10
And undoe Families, thus strife, and warre
Are the swords prize, and a litigious barre
The Gownes prime wish; vain confidence to share
In empty honours, and a bloudy care,
To be the first in mischiefe, makes him dye
Fool'd 'twixt ambition, and credulitie;
An oilie tongue with fatall, cunning sence,
And that sad vertue ever, Eloquence,
Are th' others ruine; but the common curse,
And each dayes ill waits on the rich mans purse: 20
He, whose large acres, and imprison'd gold
So far exceeds his Fathers store of old,
As Brittish Whales the Dolphins doe surpasse.
In sadder times therefore, and when the Lawes
Of *Nero's fiat* raign'd; an armed band
Ceas'd on *Longinus*, and the spacious Land
Of wealthy *Seneca*, besieg'd the gates
Of *Lateranus*, and his faire estate
Divided as a spoile; In such sad Feasts,
Souldiers (though not invited) are the guests. 30
Though thou small peeces of the blessed Mine
Hast lodg'd about thee; travelling in the shine
Of a pale Moone, if but a Reed doth shake,
Mov'd by the wind, the shadow makes thee quake.
Wealth hath its cares, and want hath this reliefe,
It neither feares the Souldier, nor the Thiefe;

Thy first choyce vowes, and to the Gods best knowne,
Are for thy stores encrease, that in all towne
Thy stocke be greatest, but no poyson lyes
I'th' poore mans dish, he tasts of no such spice: 40
Be that thy care, when with a Kingly gust,
Thou suck'st whole Bowles clad in the guilded dust
Of some rich minerall; whilst the false Wine
Sparkles aloft, and makes the draught Divine.
Blam'st thou the Sages then? because the one
Would still be laughing, when he would be gone
From his owne doore, the other cryed to see
His times addicted to such vanity?
Smiles are an easie purchase, but to weep
Is a hard act, for teares are fetch'd more deep; 50
Democritus his nimble Lungs would tyre
With constant laughter, and yet keep entire
His stocke of mirth, for ev'ry object was
Addition to his store; though then (Alas!)
Sedans, and Litters, and our Senat Gownes,
With Robes of honour, fasces, and the frownes
Of unbrib'd Tribunes were not seene; but had
He lived to see our *Roman Prætor* clad
In *Ioves* owne mantle, seated on his high
Embroyder'd Chariot 'midst the dust and Crie 60
Of the large Theatre, loaden with a Crowne
Which scarse he could support, (for it would downe,
But that his servant props it) and close by
His page a witnes to his vanitie:
To these his Scepter, and his Eagle adde
His Trumpets, Officers, and servants clad
In white, and purple; with the rest that day,
He hir'd to triumph for his bread, and pay;
Had he these studied, sumptuous follies seene,
'Tis thought his wanton, and effusive spleene 70
Had kill'd the Abderite, though in that age
(When pride & greatnes had not swell'd the stage
So high as ours) his harmles, and just mirth
From ev'ry object had a suddaine birth;
Nor wast alone their avarice, or pride,
Their triumphs, or their cares he did deride;

Their vaine contentions, or ridiculous feares;
But even their very poverty, and teares.
He would at fortunes threats as freely smile
As others mourne; nor was it to beguile 80
His crafty passions; but this habit he
By nature had, and grave Philosophie.
He knew their idle and superfluous vowes,
And sacrifice, which such wrong zeale bestowes,
Were meere Incendiaries; and that the gods
Not pleas'd therewith, would ever be at ods;
Yet to no other aire, nor better place
Ow'd he his birth, then the cold, homely *Thrace*;
Which shewes a man may be both wise, & good,
Without the brags of fortune, or his bloud. 90
  But envy ruines all: What mighty names
Of fortune, spirit, action, bloud, and fame,
Hath this destroy'd? yea, for no other cause
Then being such; their honour, worth, and place,
Was crime enough; their statues, arms & crowns;
Their ornaments of Triumph, Chariots, Gowns,
And what the Herauld with a learned care,
Had long preserv'd, this madnes will not spare.
  So once *Sejanus* Statue Rome allow'd
Her Demi-god, and ev'ry Roman bow'd 100
To pay his safeties vowes; but when that face
Had lost *Tyberius* once, it's former grace
Was soone eclips'd; no diff'rence made (Alas!)
Betwixt his Statue then, and common Brasse;
They melt alike, and in the Workmans hand
For equall, servile use, like others stand.
  Goe now fetch home fresh Bayes, and pay new vowes
To thy dumbe Capitoll gods! thy life, thy house,
And state are now secur'd; *Sejanus* lyes
I'th' Lictors hands; ye gods! what hearts, & eyes 110
Can one dayes fortune change? the solemne crye
Of all the world is, Let *Sejanus* dye:
They never lov'd the man they sweare, they know
Nothing of all the matter; when, or how,
By what accuser, for what cause, or why,
By whose command, or sentence he must dye.

But what needs this? the least pretence will hit,
When Princes feare, or hate a Favourite.
A large Epistle stuff'd with idle feare,
Vaine dreames, and jealousies, directed here 120
From *Caprea* does it; And thus ever dye
Subjects, when once they grow prodigious high.
'Tis well, I seeke no more; but tell me how
This tooke his friends? no private murmurs now?
No teares? no solemne mourner seene? must all
His Glory perish in one funerall?
O still true Romans! State-wit bids them praise
The Moone by night; but court the warmer rayes
O' th' Sun by day; they follow fortune still,
And hate, or love discreetly, as their will 130
And the time leades them; This tumultuous fate
Puts all their painted favours out of date:
And yet this people that now spurne, & tread
This mighty Favourites once honour'd head,
Had but the Tuscaine goddesse, or his Stars
Destin'd him for an Empire, or had wars,
Treason, or policie, or some higher pow'r
Opprest secure *Tyberius*; that same houre
That he receiv'd the sad Gemonian doome,
Had crown'd him Emp'ror of the world, & Rome. 140
But Rome is now growne wise, & since that she
Her Suffrages, and ancient Libertie,
Lost in a Monarchs name; she takes no care
For Favourite, or Prince; nor will she share
Their fickle glories, though in *Cato's* dayes
She rul'd whole States, & Armies with her voice,
Of all the honours now within her walls,
She only doats on Playes, and Festivalls:
Nor is it strange; for when these Meteors fall,
They draw an ample ruine with them; All 150
Share in the storm; each beame sets with the Sun,
And equall hazard friends, and flatt'rers run.
This makes, that circled with distractive feare
The livelesse, pale Sejanus limbes they teare,
And least the action might a witnesse need,
They bring their servants to confirme the deed,

Nor is it done for any other end,
Then to avoid the title of his friend.
So fals ambitious man, and such are still
All floating States built on the peoples will: 160
Hearken all you! whom this bewitching lust
Of an houres glory, and a little dust
Swels to such deare repentance! you that can
Measure whole kingdoms with a thought or span
Would you be as *Sejanus*? would you have
So you might sway as he did, such a grave?
Would you be rich as he? command, dispose,
All Acts, and Offices? All friends, and foes?
Be Generalls of Armies, and Colleague
Unto an Emperour? breake, or make a league? 170
No doubt you would; for both the good, and bad,
An equall itch of honour ever had:
But O what State can be so great, or good,
As to be bought with so much shame, and bloud!
Alas! *Sejanus* will too late confesse
'Twas only pride, and greatnes made him lesse:
For he that moveth with the lofty wind
Of Fortune, and ambition, unconfin'd
In act, or thought; doth but increase his height,
That he may loose it with more force, & weight; 180
Scorning a base, low ruine, as if he
Would of misfortune, make a Prodigie.
  Tell mighty *Pompey*, *Crassus*, and O thou
That mad'st Rome kneele to thy victorious brow,
What but the weight of honours, and large fame
After your worthy Acts, and height of name,
Destroy'd you in the end? the envious Fates
Easie to further your aspiring States,
Us'd them to quell you too; pride, and excesse
In ev'ry Act did make you thrive the lesse: 190
Few Kings are guiltie of gray haires, or dye
Without a stab, a draught, or trecherie:
And yet to see him, that but yesterday
Saw letters first, how he will scrape, and pray;
And all her Feast-time tyre *Minervaes* eares
For Fame, for Eloquence, and store of yeares

To thrive and live in; and then lest he doates,
His boy assists him with his boxe, and notes;
Foole that thou art! not to discerne the ill
These vows include; what, did Rom's Consull kill 200
Her *Cicero*? what, him whose very dust
Greece celebrates as yet; whose cause though just,
Scarse banishment could end; nor poyson save
His free borne person from a forraigne grave:
All this from Eloquence! both head, and hand,
The tongue doth forfeit; pettie wits may stand
Secure from danger, but the nobler veine,
With losse of bloud the barre doth often staine.

* * * * *
O fortunatam natam me Consule Romam. } *Carmen Ciceronianum.*
* * * * *

Had all been thus, thou might'st have scorn'd the sword
Of fierce *Antonius*, here is not one word 211
Doth pinch, I like such stuffe; 'tis safer far
Then thy Philippicks, or Pharsalia's war:
What sadder end then his, whom Athens saw
At once her Patriot, Oracle, and Law?
Unhappy then is he, and curs'd in Stars,
Whom his poore Father, blind with soot, & scars
Sends from the Anviles harmles chime, to weare
The factious gowne, and tyre his Clients eare,
And purse with endles noise; Trophies of war 220
Old rusty armour, with an honour'd scar;
And wheeles of captiv'd Chariots, with a peece
Of some torne Brittish Galley, and to these
The Ensigne too, and last of all the traine
The pensive pris'ner loaden with his Chaine,
Are thought true Roman honors; these the Greek
And rude Barbarians equally doe seeke.
Thus aire, and empty fame, are held a prize
Beyond faire vertue; for all vertue dyes
Without reward; And yet by this fierce lust 230
Of Fame, and titles to ovtlive our dust,
And Monuments; (though all these things must dye
And perish like our selves) whole Kingdomes lye

Ruin'd, and spoil'd: Put *Hannibal* i'th' scale,
What weight affords the mighty Generall?
This is the man, whom Africks spacious Land
Bounded by th' Indian Sea, and Niles hot sand,
Could not containe; (Ye gods! that give to men
Such boundles appetites, why state you them
So short a time? either the one deny, 240
Or give their acts, and them Eternitie)
All Æthiopia, to the utmost bound
Of *Titans* course, (then which no Land is found
Lesse distant from the Sun) with him that ploughs
That fertile soile where fam'd Iberus flowes,
Are not enough to conquer; past now o're
The Pyrene hills, The Alps with all its store
Of Ice, and Rocks clad in eternall snow
(As if that Nature meant to give the blow)
Denyes him passage; straight on ev'ry side 250
He wounds the Hill, and by strong hand divides
The monstrous pile, nought can ambition stay,
The world, and nature yeeld to give him way:
And now past o're the Alps, that mighty bar
'Twixt France, and Rome, feare of the future war
Strikes Italy; successe, and hope doth fire
His lofty spirits with a fresh desire.
All is undone as yet (saith he) unlesse
Our Pænish forces we advance, and presse
Upon Rome's selfe; break downe her gates, & wall, 260
And plant our Colours in *Suburra's* Vale.
O the rare sight! if this great souldier wee
Arm'd on his Getick Elephant might see!
But what's the event? O glory! how the itch
Of thy short wonders doth mankinde bewitch!
He that but now all Italy, and Spaine,
Had conquer'd o're, is beaten out againe;
And in the heart of Africk, and the sight
Of his owne Carthage, forc'd to open flight.
Banish'd from thence, a fugitive he posts 270
To Syria first, then to Bythinia's Coasts;
Both places by his sword secur'd; though he
In this distresse must not acknowledg'd be;

Where once a Generall he triumphed, now
To shew what Fortune can, he begs as low.
  And thus that soule, which through all nations hurl'd
Conquest, and warre, and did amaze the world;
Of all those glories rob'd at his last breath,
Fortune would not vouchsafe a souldiers death,
For all that bloud the field of Cannæ boasts, 280
And sad Apulia fill'd with Roman ghoasts:
No other end (freed from the pile, and sword)
Then a poore Ring would Fortune him afford.
  Goe now ambitious man! new plots designe,
March o're the snowie Alps, and Apennine;
That after all, at best thou mayst but be
A pleasing story to posteritie!
  The *Macedon* one world could not containe,
We heare him of the narrow Earth complaine,
And sweat for roome, as if Seryphus Ile, 290
Or Gyara had held him in Exile:
But Babylon this madnes can allay,
And give the great man but his length of clay;
The highest thoughts, and actions under Heaven,
Death only with the lowest dust layes even.
It is believed (if what Greece writes be true)
That *Xerxes* with his Persian Fleet did hewe
Their waies throgh mountains, that their sails full blowne,
Like clouds hung over Athos, and did drowne
The spacious Continent, and by plaine force 300
Betwixt the Mount, and it made a divorce;
That Seas exhausted were, and made firme land,
And Sestos joyned unto Abidos Strand;
That on their march, his Meades but passing by,
Dranke thee Scamander, and Melenus dry;
With what soe're incredible designe
Sostratus sings inspired with pregnant Wine:
But what's the end? He that the other day
Divided Hellespont, and forc'd his way
Through all her angry billowes; that assigned 310
New punishments unto the waves, and wind:
No sooner saw the Salaminian Seas,
But he was driven out by *Themistocles*,

And of that Fleet (suppos'd to be so great,
That all mankinde shar'd in the sad defeate)
Not one Sayle sav'd, in a poore Fishers boat,
Chas'd o're the working surge, was glad to float,
Cutting his desp'rate course through the tyr'd floud,
And fought againe with Carkasses, and bloud.
O foolish mad ambition! these are still 320
The famous dangers that attend thy will.
Give store of dayes, good *Iove*, give length of yeares,
Are the next vowes; these with religious feares,
And Constancie we pay; but what's so bad,
As a long, sinfull age? what crosse more sad
Then misery of yeares? how great an Ill
Is that, which doth but nurse more sorrow still?
It blacks the face, corrupts, and duls the bloud,
Benights the quickest eye, distasts the food,
And such deep furrowes cuts i'th' Checker'd skin 330
As in th'old Okes of Tabraca are seene.
Youth varies in most things; strength, beauty, wit,
Are severall graces; but where age doth hit,
It makes no diff'rence; the same weake voice,
And trembling ague in each member lyes:
A generall, hatefull baldnes, with a curst
Perpetuall pettishnes; and which is worst,
A foule, strong fluxe of humors, and more paine
To feed, then if he were to nurse again.
So tedious to himselfe, his wife, and friends, 340
That his owne sonnes, and servants, wish his end,
His tast, and feeling dyes; and of that fire
The am'rous Lover burnes in, no desire:
Or if there were, what pleasure could it be,
Where lust doth raigne without abilitie?
Nor is this all, what matters it, where he
Sits in the spacious Stage? who can nor see,
Nor heare what's acted, whom the stiller voice
Of spirited, wanton ayres, or the loud noise
Of Trumpets cannot pierce; whom thunder can 350
But scarse informe who enters, or what man
He personates, what 'tis they act, or say?
How many Scænes are done? what time of day?

Besides that little bloud, his carkasse holds,
Hath lost its native warmth, & fraught wth colds,
Catarrhs, and rheumes, to thick, black jelly turns,
And never but in fits, and feavers burns;
Such vast infirmities, so huge a stock
Of sicknes, and diseases to him flock,
That *Hyppia* ne're so many Lovers knew, 360
Nor wanton *Maura*; Phisick never slew
So many Patients, nor rich Lawyers spoile
More Wards, and Widowes; it were lesser toile
To number out what Mannors, and Demaines,
Licinius razer purchas'd: One complaines
Of weaknes in the back, another pants
For lack of breath, the third his eyesight wants;
Nay some so feeble are, and full of paine,
That Infant like they must be fed againe.
These faint too at their meales; their wine they spill, 370
And like young birds, that wait the Mothers Bill
They gape for meat; but sadder far then this
Their senslesse ignorance, and dotage is;
For neither they, their friends, nor servants know,
Nay those themselves begot, and bred up too
No longer now they'le owne; for madly they
Proscribe them all, and what on the last day,
The Misers cannot carry to the Grave
For their past sinnes, their prostitutes must have.
But grant age lack'd these plagues; yet must they see
As great, as many: Fraile Mortalitie 381
In such a length of yeares, hath many falls,
And deads a life with frequent funerals.
The nimblest houre in all the span, can steale
A friend, or brother from's; there's no Repeale
In death, or time; this day a wife we mourne,
To morrowes teares a sonne, and the next Urne
A Sister fills; Long-livers have assign'd
These curses still: That with a restles mind,
An age of fresh renewing cares they buye, 390
And in a tide of teares grow old and dye.
Nestor, (if we great *Homer* may believe)
In his full strength three hundred yeares did live:

Happy (thou'lt say) that for so long a time
Enjoy'd free nature, with the grape, and Wine
Of many Autumnes; but I prethee, heare
What *Nestor* sayes himselfe, when he his deare
Antilochus had lost, how he complaines
Of life's too large Extent, and copious paines?
Of all he meets, he askes what is the cause 400
He lived thus long; for what breach of their Laws
The gods thus punish'd him? what sinne had he
Done worthy of a long lifes miserie?
Thus *Peleus* his *Achilles* mourned, and he
Thus wept that his *Vlysses* lost at Sea.
Had *Priam* dyed, before *Phereclus* Fleet
Was built, or *Paris* stole the fatall Greeke,
Troy had yet stood, and he perhaps had gone
In peace unto the lower shades; His sonne
Saved with his plenteous offspring, and the rest 410
In solemne pompe bearing his fun'rall Chest;
But long life hinder'd this: Unhappy he,
Kept for a publick ruine; lived to see
All Asia lost, and e're he could expire,
In his owne house saw both the sword, and fire;
All white with age, and cares, his feeble arme
Had now forgot the warre; but this Allarme
Gathers his dying spirits; and as wee
An aged Oxe worne out with labour, see,
By his ungratefull Master, after all 420
His yeares of toyle, a thankles victime fall:
So he by *Ioves* owne Altar; which shewes, wee
Are no where safe from Heaven, and destinie:
Yet dyed a man; but his surviving Queene,
Freed from the Greekish sword was barking seen.
  I haste to Rome, and Pontus King let passe,
With Lydian *Crœsus*, whom in vaine (Alas!)
Just *Solons* grave advice bad to attend,
That happines came not before the end.
  What man more blest in any age to come 430
Or past, could Nature shew the world, or Rome,
Then *Marius* was? if 'midst the pompe of war,
And triumphs fetch'd with Roman bloud from far

His soule had fled; Exile, and fetters then,
He ne're had seen, nor known *Mynturna's* fenne;
Nor had it, after Carthage got, been sed,
A Roman Generall had beg'd his bread.
Thus *Pompey* th' envious gods, & Romes ill stars
(Freed from *Campania's* feavers, and the Wars)
Doom'd to *Achilles* sword: Our publick vowes 440
Made *Cæsar* guiltles; but sent him to loose
His head at Nile; This curse *Cethegus* mist;
This *Lentulus*, and this made him resist
That mangled by no Lictors axe, fell dead
Entirely *Catiline*, and saved his head.
The anxious Matrons, with their foolish zeale,
Are the last Votaries, and their Appeale
Is all for beauty; with soft speech, and slow,
They pray for sons, but with a louder vow
Commend a female feature: All that can 450
Make woman pleasing now they shift, and scan:
And why reprov'd they say, *Latona's* paire
The Mother never thinks can be too faire.
But sad *Lucretia* warnes to wish no face
Like hers; *Virginia* would bequeath her grace
To Crooke-backe *Rutila* in exchange; for still
The fairest children do their Parents fill
With greatest cares; so seldome Chastitie
Is found with beauty; though some few there be
That with a strict, religious care contend 460
Th' old, modest, Sabine Customes to defend:
Besides, wise nature to some faces grants
An easie blush, and where shee freely plants,
A lesse Instruction serves; but both these joyn'd,
At *Rome* would both be forc'd or else purloyn'd.
So steel'd a forehead vice hath, that dares win,
And bribe the Father to the Childrens sin;
But whom have gifts defiled not? what good face
Did ever want these tempters? pleasing grace
Betraies it selfe; what time did *Nero* mind 470
A course, maim'd shape? what blemish'd youth confin'd
His goatish Pathick? whence then flow these joies
Of a faire issue? whom these sad annoies

Waite, and grow up with; whom perhaps thou'lt see
Publick Adulterers, and must be
Subject to all the Curses, Plagues, and awe
Of jealous mad men, and the *Iulian* Law;
Nor canst thou hope they'le find a milder Starre,
Or more escapes then did the God of Warre;
But worse then all, a jealous braine confines 480
His furie to no Law; what rage assignes,
Is present justice: Thus the rash Sword spils
This Lechers bloud, the scourge another kils.
But thy spruce boy must touch no other face
Then a *Patrician*? Is of any race
So they be rich; *Servilia* is as good
With wealth, as shee that boasts *Iulus* blood:
To please a servant all is cheape; what thing
In all their stocke to the last suite, and Ring
But lust exacts? the poorest whore in this, 490
As generous as the *Patrician* is.
  But thou wilt say what hurt's a beauteous skin
With a chaste soule? aske *Theseus* sonne, and him
That *Stenobœa* murther'd; for both these
Can tell how fatall 'twas in them to please;
A womans spleene then carries most of fate,
When shame and sorrow aggravate her hate:
Resolve me now, had *Silius* been thy sonne,
In such a hazzard what should he have done?
Of all *Romes* youth, this was the only best, 500
In whom alone beauty, and worth did rest:
This *Messalina* saw, and needs he must
Be ruin'd by the Emp'rour, or her lust,
All in the face of *Rome*, and the worlds eye,
Though *Cesars* wife, a publicke Bigamie
Shee dares attempt; and that the act might beare
More prodigie, the notaries appeare,
And Augures to't; and to compleat the sin
In solemne forme, a dowrie is brought in;
All this (thou'lt say) in private might have past, 510
But shee'le not have it so; what course at last?
What should he doe? If *Messaline* be crost
Without redresse thy *Silius* will be lost;

If not, some two daies length is all he can
Keep from the grave; just so much as will span
This newes to *Hostia*, to whose fate he owes
That *Claudius* last his owne dishonour knowes.
  But he obeyes, and for a few houres lust,
Forfeits that glory should outlive his dust,
Nor was it much a fault; for, whether he 520
Obey'd, or not; 'twas equall destinie:
So fatall beauty is, and full of wast,
That neither wanton can be safe, nor chast.
What then should man pray for? what is't that he
Can beg of Heaven, without Impiety?
Take my advice: first to the Gods commit
All cares; for they things competent, and fit
For us foresee; besides man is more deare
To them, then to himselfe: we blindly here
Led by the world, and lust, in vaine assay 530
To get us portions, wives, and sonnes; but they
Already know all that we can intend,
And of our Childrens Children see the end.
  Yet that thou may'st have something to commend
With thankes unto the Gods for what they send;
Pray for a wise, and knowing soule; a sad
Discreet, true valour, that will scorne to adde
A needlesse horrour to thy death; that knowes
'Tis but a debt which man to nature owes;
That starts not at misfortunes, that can sway, 540
And keep all passions under locke and key;
That couets nothing, wrongs none, and preferres
An honest want before rich injurers;
All this thou hast within thy selfe, and may
Be made thy owne, if thou wilt take the way;
What boots the worlds wild, loose applause? what can
Fraile, perillous honours adde unto a man?
What length of years, wealth, or a rich faire wife?
Vertue alone can make a happy life.
To a wise man nought comes amisse: but we 550
Fortune adore, and make our Deity.

FINIS

Ad Posteros

Diminuat ne sera *dies* præsentis *honorem*,
Quis, qualisq; *fui*, *percipe* Posteritas.
CAMBRIA *me genuit*, patulis *ubi* vallibus *errans*
Subjacet aeriis montibus ISCA pater.
Inde sinu placido *suscepit maximus arte*
HERBERTUS, Latiæ *gloria prima* Scholæ,
Bis ternos, *illo me Conducente*, *per* annos
Profeci, & geminam *Contulit unus opem*,
Ars & amor, mens *atq;* manus *certare solebant*,
Nec lassata Illi mensve, manusve *fuit*. 10
Hinc qualem cernis crevisse: Sed ut mea Certus
Tempora Cognoscas, dura *fuere*, *scias*.
Vixi, *divisos cum* fregerat *hæresis Anglos*
Intèr Tysiphonas *presbyteri* & *populi*.
His *primùm* miseris *per* amæna *furentibus* arva
Prostravit sanctam *vilis avena* rosam,
Turbârunt fontes, & *fusis* pax *perit undis*,
Mæstaq; Cœlestes *obruit umbra* dies.
Duret ut Integritas *tamen*, & pia gloria, *partem*
Me nullam in tantâ strage *fuisse*, *scias*; 20
Credidimus nempè insonti vocem *esse Cruori*,
Et vires *quæ post funera* flere *docent*.
Hinc Castæ, fidæq; *pati me more* parentis
Commonui, & *Lachrymis* fata *levare meis*;
Hinc nusquàm horrendis violavi Sacra *procellis*,
Nec mihi mens *unquàm*, *nec* manus *atra fuit*.
Si pius *es*, *ne plura petas*; Satur *Ille recedat*
Qui sapit, & *nos non Scripsimus* Insipidis.

OLOR ISCANUS.

A COLLECTION OF SOME SELECT POEMS, AND TRANSLATIONS,

Formerly written by

Mr. Henry Vaughan *Silurist.*

Published by a Friend.

Virg. Georg.
Flumina amo, Sylvasq; Inglorius——

LONDON,
Printed by *T.W.* for *Humphrey Moseley*,
and are to be sold at his shop, at the
Signe of the Prince's Arms in St. *Pauls*
Church-yard, 1651.

——O quis me gelidis in vallibus ISCÆ
Sistat, & Ingenti ramorum protegat umbrâ!

TO

The truly Noble, and most Excellently accomplish'd, the Lord KILDARE DIGBY

MY LORD,

It is a Position *anciently* known, and *modern Experience* hath allowed it for a *sad truth*, that *Absence* and *time*, (like *Cold weather*, and an *unnaturall dormition*) will *blast* and *wear* out of memorie the most *Endearing obligations*; And hence it was that some *Politicians* in *Love* have lookt upon the *former* of these *two* as a main remedy against the *fondness* of that *Passion*. But for my own part (my Lord) I shall deny this *Aphorisme* of the *people*, and beg leave to assure your *Lordship*, that, though these *reputed obstacles* have lain long in my way, yet neither of them could *work* upon me: for I am 10 now (without adulation) as *warm* and *sensible* of those *numerous* favours, and *kind Influences* receiv'd sometimes from your Lordship, as I really was at the *Instant* of *fruition*. I have no *plott* by *preambling* thus, to set any *rate* upon this present *addresse*, as if I should presume to value a *Return* of this nature equall with your Lordships *Deserts*, but the *designe* is, to let you see that this *habit* I have got of being *troublesome* flowes from two *excusable principles*, Gratitude, and Love. These inward *Counsellours* (I know not how discreetly) perswaded me to this *Attempt* and *Intrusion* upon your *name*, which if your Lordship will vouchsafe to own as the *Genius* 20 to these *papers*, you will *perfect* my *hopes*, and place me at my full *height*. This was the *Ayme*, my Lord, and is the *End* of this work, which though but a *Pazzarello* to the *voluminosè Insani*, yet as *Jezamin* and the *Violet* find room in the *bank* as well as *Roses* and *Lillies*, so happily may this, and (if *shin'd* upon by your *Lordship*) please as much. To whose *Protection*, Sacred as your *Name*, and those eminent *Honours* which have alwayes attended upon't through so many *generations*, I humbly offer it, and remain in all *numbers* of *gratitude*,

My honour'd Lord, 30

Your most affectionate,
humblest Servant
VAUGHAN

Newton by *Usk*
this 17. of
Decemb. 1647

The Publisher to the Reader

It was the glorious Maro, *that referr'd his* Legacies *to the* Fire, *and though* Princes *are seldome* Executors, *yet there came a* Cæsar *to his* Testament, *as if the* Act *of a* Poet *could not be* repeal'd *but by a* King. *I am not Reader* Augustus vindex: *Here is no* Royall Rescue, *but here is a* Muse *that* deserves *it. The* Author *had long agoe condemn'd these* Poems *to* Obscuritie, *and the* Consumption *of that* Further Fate, *which* attends *it. This* Censure *gave them a* Gust *of* Death, *and they have* partly *known that* Oblivion, *which our* Best Labours *must* come to *at* Last. *I present thee then not onely with* 10 *a* Book, *but with a* Prey, *and in this* kind *the first* Recoveries *from* Corruption. *Here is a* Flame *hath been sometimes* extinguished: *Thoughts that have been* lost *and* forgot, *but now they* break out *again like the* Platonic Reminiscencie. *I have not the Author's* Approbation *to the* Fact, *but I have* Law *on my* Side, *though never a* Sword: *I hold it no man's* Prærogative *to* fire *his* own House. *Thou seest how* Saucie *I am* grown, *and if thou doest expect I should* Commend *what is* published, *I must tell thee*, I crie no Sivill Oranges. *I will not say*, *Here is* Fine *or* Cheap: *that were an* Injurie *to the* Verse *it selfe*, *and to the* Effects *it can* produce. *Read on*, *and* 20 *thou wilt find thy* Spirit ingag'd: *not by the* Deserts *of what wee call* Tolerable, *but by the* Commands *of a* Pen, *that is* Above it.

Vpon the most Ingenious *pair* of Twins, *Eugenius Philalethes*, and the *Authour* of these *Poems*

What *Planet* rul'd your *birth*? what *wittie star*?
That you so like in *Souls* as *Bodies* are!
So like in *both*, that you seem *born* to free
The *starrie art* from *vulgar* Calumnie.
My *doubts* are solv'd, from hence my *faith* begins,
Not only your *faces*, but your *wits* are *Twins*.

When this bright *Gemini* shall from earth ascend,
They will *new light* to dull-ey'd mankind lend,
Teach the *Star-gazers*, and delight their *Eyes*,
Being fixt a *Constellation* in the Skyes. 10

T. Powell Oxoniensis

To my friend the Authour upon these his *Poems*

I call'd it once my *sloth*: In such an age
So many *Volumes deep*, I not a *page*?
But I recant, and vow 'twas thriftie Care
That kept my *Pen* from spending on *slight ware*,
And breath'd it for a *Prize*, whose pow'rfull *shine*
Doth both *reward* the striver, and *refine*;
Such are thy *Poems*, friend: for since th'hast writ,
I cann't reply to any *name*, but *wit*;
And lest amidst the *throng* that make us *grone*,
Mine prove a groundless *Heresie* alone, 10
Thus I dispute, Hath there not rev'rence bin
Pay'd to the *Beard* at doore, for *Lord* within?
Who notes the *spindle-leg*, or *hollow eye*
Of the *thinne Usher*, the *faire Lady* by?
Thus I *sinne* freely, *neighbour* to a *hand*
Which while I aime to *strengthen*, gives *Command*
For my *protection*, and thou art to me
At once my *Subject* and *Securitie*.

I. Rowlandson Oxoniensis

Vpon the following *Poems*

I write not here, as if thy *last* in store
Of learned *friends*, 'tis known that thou hast *more*;
Who, were they told of this, would find a way
To rise a guard of *Poets* without *pay*,
And bring as many *hands* to thy *Edition*,
As th'*City* should unto their *May'rs* Petition,
But thou wouldst none of this, lest it should be
Thy *Muster* rather, than our *Courtesie*,
Thou wouldst not beg as *Knights* do, and appeare
Poet by *Voice*, and *suffrage* of the *Shire*, 10
That were enough to make thy *Muse* advance
Amongst the *Crutches*, nay it might enhance
Our *Charity*, and we should think it fit
The *State* should build an *Hospital* for wit.

But here needs no *reliefe*: Thy richer *Verse*
Creates all *Poets*, that can but *reherse*,
And they, like *Tenants* better'd by their *land*,
Should pay thee *Rent* for what they understand,
Thou art not of that *lamentable Nation*,
Who make a blessed *Alms* of *approbation*, 20
Whose *fardel-notes* are *Briefes* in ev'ry thing,
But, that they are not licens'd *By the King*.
Without such *scrape-requests* thou dost come forth
Arm'd (though I speak it) with thy *proper worth*,
And needest not this *noise* of friends, for wee
Write out of *love*, not thy *necessitie*;
And though this *sullen age* possessed be
With some strange *Desamour* to Poetrie,
Yet I suspect (thy fancy so delights)
The *Puritans* will turn thy *Proselytes*, 30
And that thy *flame* when once abroad it *shines*,
Will bring thee as many *friends*, as thou hast *lines*.

EUGENIUS PHILALETHES *Oxoniensis*

Olor Iscanus

To the River *Isca*

When *Daphne*'s Lover here first wore the *Bayes*,
Eurotas secret streams heard all his *Layes*.
And holy *Orpheus*, Natures *busie* Child
By headlong *Hebrus* his deep *Hymns* Compil'd.
Soft *Petrarch* (thaw'd by *Laura*'s flames) did weep
On *Tybers* banks, when she (*proud fair!*) cou'd sleep;
Mosella boasts *Ausonius*, and the *Thames*
Doth murmure *SIDNEYS Stella* to her *streams*,
While *Severn* swoln with *Joy* and *sorrow*, wears
Castara's smiles mixt with fair *Sabrin*'s tears. 10
Thus *Poets* (like the *Nymphs*, their *pleasing themes*)
Haunted the *bubling Springs* and *gliding streams*,
And *happy banks*! whence such *fair flowres* have sprung,
But happier those where they have *sate* and *sung*!
Poets (like *Angels*) where they once appear
Hallow the *place*, and each succeeding year
Adds *rev'rence* to't, such as at length doth give
This aged faith, *That there their Genii live.*
Hence th'*Auncients* say, That, from this *sickly aire*
They passe to *Regions* more *refin'd* and *faire*, 20
To *Meadows* strow'd with *Lillies* and the *Rose*,
And *shades* whose *youthfull green* no *old age* knowes,
Where all in *white* they walk, discourse, and Sing
Like Bees *soft murmurs*, or a *Chiding Spring.*
  But *Isca*, whensoe'r those *shades* I see,
And thy *lov'd Arbours* must no more *know* me,
When I am layd to *rest* hard by thy *streams*,
And my *Sun sets*, where first it *sprang* in beams,
I'le leave behind me such a *large*, *kind light*,
As shall *redeem* thee from *oblivious night*, 30
And in these *vowes* which (living yet) I pay
Shed such a *Previous* and *Enduring Ray*,

As shall from age to age thy *fair name* lead
'Till *Rivers* leave to *run*, and *men* to *read.*
First, may all *Bards* born after me
(When I am *ashes*) sing of thee!
May thy *green banks* and *streams* (or none)
Be both their *Hill* and *Helicon*;
May *Vocall Groves* grow there, and all
The *shades* in them *Propheticall*, 40
Where (laid) men shall more *faire truths* see
Than *fictions* were of *Thessalie.*
May thy gentle *Swains* (like *flowres*)
Sweetly spend their *Youthfull houres*,
And thy *beauteous Nymphs* (like *Doves*)
Be *kind* and *faithfull* to their *Loves*;
Garlands, and *Songs*, and *Roundelayes*,
Mild, dewie *nights*, and Sun-shine *dayes*,
The *Turtles voyce*, *Joy* without *fear*,
Dwell on thy *bosome* all the year! 50
May the *Evet* and the *Tode*
Within thy Banks have no abode,
Nor the *wilie*, *winding Snake*
Her *voyage* through thy *waters* make.
In all thy *Journey* to the *Main*
No *nitrous Clay*, nor *Brimstone-vein*
Mixe with thy *streams*, but may they passe
Fresh as the *aire*, and cleer as *Glasse*,
And where the *wandring Chrystal* treads
Roses shall *kisse*, and *Couple* heads. 60
The *factour-wind* from far shall bring
The *Odours* of the *Scatter'd* Spring,
And *loaden* with the rich *Arreare*,
Spend it in *Spicie whispers* there.
No *sullen heats*, nor *flames* that are
Offensive, and *Canicular*,
Shine on thy *Sands*, nor *pry* to see
Thy *Scalie*, *shading familie*,
But *Noones* as mild as *Hesper's* rayes,
Or the first *blushes* of fair dayes. 70
What *gifts* more *Heav'n* or *Earth* can adde
With all those *blessings* be thou *Clad*!

Honour, *Beautie*,
Faith and *Dutie*,
Delight and *Truth*,
With *Love*, and *Youth*
Crown all about thee! And what ever *Fate*
Impose else-where, whether the graver state,
Or some toye else, may those *lowd*, *anxious Cares*
For *dead* and *dying things* (the Common *Wares* 80
And *showes* of time) ne'r break thy *Peace*, nor make
Thy *repos'd Armes* to a new warre *awake*!
But *Freedome*, *safety*, *Joy and blisse*
United in one loving *kisse*
Surround thee quite, and *stile* thy borders
The Land redeem'd from all disorders!

The Charnel-house

Blesse me! what damps are here? how stiffe an aire?
Kelder of mists, a second *Fiats* care,
Frontspeece o'th' grave and darkness, a Display
Of ruin'd man, and the disease of day;
Leane, bloudless shamble, where I can descrie
Fragments of men, Rags of Anatomie;
Corruptions ward-robe, the transplantive bed
Of mankind, and th'Exchequer of the dead.
How thou arrests my sense? how with the sight
My *Winter'd* bloud growes stiffe to all delight? 10
Torpedo to the Eye! whose least glance can
Freeze our wild lusts, and rescue head-long man;
Eloquent silence! able to Immure
An *Atheists* thoughts, and blast an *Epicure*.
Were I a *Lucian*, Nature in this dresse
Would make me wish a Saviour, and Confesse.
Where are you shoreless thoughts, vast tenter'd hope,
Ambitious dreams, *Aymes* of an Endless scope,
Whose stretch'd Excesse runs on a string too high
And on the rack of self-extension dye? 20
Chameleons of state, Aire-monging band,
Whose breath (like Gun-powder) blowes up a land,

Come see your dissolution, and weigh
What a loath'd nothing you shall be one day,
As th' Elements by Circulation passe
From one to th'other, and that which first was
Is so again, so 'tis with you; The grave
And Nature but Complott, what the one gave,
The other takes; Think then, that in this bed
There sleep the Reliques of as proud a head 30
As stern and subtill as your own, that hath
Perform'd, or forc'd as much, whose tempest-wrath
Hath levell'd Kings with slaves, and wisely then
Calme these high furies, and descend to men;
Thus *Cyrus* tam'd the *Macedon*, a tombe
Checkt him, who thought the world too straight a Room.
 Have I obey'd the *Powers* of a face,
A beauty able to undoe the Race
Of easie man? I look but here, and strait
I am Inform'd, the lovely Counterfeit 40
Was but a smoother Clay. That famish'd slave
Begger'd by wealth, who starves that he may save,
Brings hither but his sheet; Nay, th'*Ostrich-man*
That feeds on *steele* and *bullet*, he that can
Outswear his *Lordship*, and reply as tough
To a kind word, as if his tongue were *Buffe*,
Is *Chap*-faln here, wormes without wit, or fear
Defie him now, death hath disarm'd the *Bear*.
Thus could I run o'r all the pitteous score
Of erring men, and having done meet more, 50
Their shuffled *Wills*, abortive, vain *Intents*,
Phantastick *humours*, perillous *Ascents*,
False, empty *honours*, traiterous *delights*,
And whatsoe'r a blind Conceit Invites;
But these and more which the weak vermins swell,
Are Couch'd in this Accumulative Cell
Which I could scatter; But the grudging Sun
Calls home his beams, and warns me to be gone,
Day leaves me in a double night, and I
Must bid farewell to my sad library. 60
Yet with these notes. Henceforth with thought of thee
I'le season all succeeding Jollitie,

Yet damn not mirth, nor think too much is fit,
Excesse hath no *Religion*, nor *Wit*,
But should wild bloud swell to a lawless strain
One Check from thee shall *Channel* it again.

In Amicum fœneratorem

Thanks mighty *Silver*! I rejoyce to see
How I have spoyl'd his thrift, by spending thee.
Now thou art gone, he courts my wants with more,
His *Decoy* gold, and bribes me to restore.
As lesser lode-stones with the *North* consent
Naturally moving to their Element,
As bodyes swarm to th' Center, and that fire
Man stole from heaven, to heav'n doth still aspire,
So this vast crying summe drawes in a lesse,
And hence this bag more Northward layd I guesse, 10
For 'tis of *Pole-star* force, and in this sphere
Though th'least of many rules the master-bear.
Prerogative of debts! how he doth dresse
His messages in *Chink*? not an Expresse
Without a fee for reading, and 'tis fit,
For gold's the best restorative of wit,
O how he gilds them o'r! with what delight
I read those lines, where Angels doe Indite?
  But wilt have money *Og*? must I dispurse?
Will nothing serve thee but a *Poets* curse? 20
Wilt rob an Altar thus? and sweep at once
What *Orpheus*-like I forc'd from stocks and stones?
'Twill never swell thy *Bag*, nor ring one peale
In thy dark *Chest*. Talk not of *Shreeves*, or gaole,
I fear them not. I have no land to glutt
Thy durty appetite, and make thee strutt
Nimrod of acres; I'le no Speech prepare
To court the *Hopefull Cormorant*, thine heire.
Yet there's a Kingdome, at thy beck, if thou
But kick this drosse, *Parnassus* flowrie brow 30
I'le give thee with my *Tempe*, and to boot
That horse which struck a fountain with his foot.

A Bed of Roses I'le provide for thee,
And Chrystal Springs shall drop thee melodie;
The breathing shades wee'l haunt, where ev'ry leafe
Shall *Whisper* us asleep, though thou art deafe;
Those waggish *Nymphs* too which none ever yet
Durst make love to, wee'l teach the Loving fit,
Wee'l suck the *Corall* of their lips, and feed
Upon their spicie breath, a meale at need, 40
Rove in their *Amber-tresses*, and unfold
That glist'ring grove, the Curled wood of gold,
Then peep for babies, a new Puppet-play,
And riddle what their *pratling Eyes* would say.
But here thou must remember to dispurse,
For without money all this is a Curse,
Thou must for more bags call, and so restore
This Iron-age to gold, as once before;
This thou must doe, and yet this is not all,
For thus the Poet would be still in thrall, 50
Thou must then (if live thus) my neast of honey,
Cancell old bonds, and beg to lend more money.

To his friend——

I wonder, *James*, through the whole Historie
Of ages, such *Entailes* of povertie
Are layd on Poets; Lawyers (they say) have found
A trick to cut them, would they were but bound
To practise on us, though for this thing wee
Should pay (if possible) their bribes and fee.
Search (as thou canst) the old and moderne store
Of *Rome* and ours, in all the wittie score
Thou shalt not find a rich one; Take each Clime
And run o'r all the pilgrimage of time 10
Thou'lt meet them poor, and ev'ry where descrie
A thredbare, goldless genealogie.
Nature (it seems) when she meant us for Earth
Spent so much of her treasure in the birth
As ever after niggards her, and Shee,
Thus stor'd within, beggers us outwardly.

Wofull profusion! at how dear a rate
Are wee made up? all hope of thrift and state
Lost for a verse: When I by thoughts look back
Into the wombe of time, and see the Rack 20
Stand useless there, untill we are produc'd
Unto the torture, and our soules infus'd
To learn afflictions, I begin to doubt
That as some tyrants use from their chain'd rout
Of slaves to pick out one whom for their sport
They keep afflicted by some lingring art,
So wee are meerly thrown upon the stage
The mirth of fooles, and Legend of the age.
When I see in the ruines of a sute
Some nobler brest, and his tongue sadly mute 30
Feed on the *Vocall silence* of his Eye,
And knowing cannot reach the remedie,
When soules of baser stamp shine in their store,
And he of all the throng is only poore,
When *French* apes for forraign fashions pay,
And *English* legs are drest th'outlandish way,
So fine too, that they their own shadows wooe,
While he walks in the *sad* and *Pilgrim-shooe*,
I'm mad at Fate, and angry ev'n to sinne,
To see deserts and learning clad so thinne: 40
To think how th'earthly Usurer can brood
Upon his bags, and weigh the pretious food
With palsied hands, as if his soul did feare
The Scales could rob him of what he layd there;
Like Divels that on hid Treasures sit, or those
Whose jealous Eyes trust not beyond their nose
They guard the durt, and the bright Idol hold
Close, and Commit adultery with gold.
A Curse upon their drosse! how have we sued
For a few scatter'd *Chips*? how oft pursu'd 50
Petitions with a blush, in hope to squeeze
For their souls health, more than our wants a peece?
Their steel-rib'd Chests and Purse (rust eat them both!)
Have cost us with much paper many an oath,
And Protestations of such solemn sense,
As if our soules were sureties for the Pence.

Should we a full nights learned cares present,
They'l scarce return us one short houres Content,
'Las! they're but quibbles, things we Poets feign,
The short-liv'd Squibs and Crackers of the brain. 60
  But wee'l be wiser, knowing 'tis not they
That must redeem the hardship of our way,
Whether a Higher Power, or that starre
Which neerest heav'n, is from the earth most far
Oppresse us thus, or angel'd from that Sphere
By our strict Guardians are kept luckless here,
It matters not, wee shall one day obtain
Our native and Celestiall scope again.

To his retired friend, an Invitation to *Brecknock*

Since last wee met, thou and thy horse (my dear,)
Have not so much as drunk, or litter'd here,
I wonder, though thy self be thus deceast,
Thou hast the spite to Coffin up thy beast;
Or is the *Palfrey* sick, and his rough hide
With the penance of *One Spur* mortifide?
Or taught by thee (like *Pythagoras's Oxe*)
Is then his master grown more *Orthodox*?
What ever 'tis, a sober cause't must be
That thus long bars us of thy Companie. 10
The Town believes thee lost, and didst thou see
But half her suffrings, now distrest for thee,
Thou'ldst swear (like *Rome*) her foule, polluted walls
Were sackt by *Brennus*, and the salvage *Gaules*.
Abominable face of things! here's noise
Of bang'd Mortars, blew Aprons, and Boyes,
Pigs, Dogs, and Drums, with the hoarse hellish notes
Of politickly-deafe Usurers throats,
With new fine *Worships*, and the old cast *teame*
Of Justices vext with the *Cough*, and *flegme*. 20
Midst these the *Crosse* looks sad, and in the *Shire-*
-Hall furs of an old *Saxon Fox* appear,
With brotherly Ruffs and Beards, and a strange sight
Of high Monumentall Hats ta'ne at the fight

Of *Eighty eight*; while ev'ry *Burgesse* foots
The mortall *Pavement* in eternall boots.
  Hadst thou been batc'lour, I had soon divin'd
Thy Close retirements, and Monastick mind,
Perhaps some Nymph had been to visit, or
The beauteous Churle was to be waited for, 30
And like the *Greek*, e'r you the sport would misse
You stai'd, and stroak'd the *Distaffe* for a kisse.
But in this age, when thy coole, settled bloud
Is ty'd t'one flesh, and thou almost grown good,
I know not how to reach the strange device,
Except (*Domitian* like) thou murther'st flyes;
Or is't thy pietie? for who can tell
But thou may'st prove devout, and love a Cell,
And (like a Badger) with attentive looks
In the dark hole sit rooting up of books. 40
Quick Hermit! what a peacefull Change hadst thou
Without the noise of *haire-cloth*, *Whip*, or *Vow*?
But is there no redemption? must there be
No other penance but of liberty?
Why two months hence, if thou continue thus
Thy memory will scarce remain with us,
The Drawers have forgot thee, and exclaim
They have not seen thee here since *Charles* his raign,
Or if they mention thee, like some old man
That at each word inserts—Sir, *as I can* 50
Remember—So the *Cyph'rers* puzzle mee
With a dark, cloudie character of thee.
That (certs!) I fear thou wilt be lost, and wee
Must ask the *Fathers* e'r 't be long for thee.
  Come! leave this sullen state, and let not Wine
And precious Witt lye dead for want of thine,
Shall the dull *Market-land-lord* with his *Rout*
Of sneaking Tenants durtily swill out
This harmlesse liquor? shall they knock and beat
For Sack, only to talk of *Rye*, and *Wheat*? 60
O let not such prepost'rous tipling be
In our *Metropolis*, may I ne'r see
Such *Tavern-sacrilege*, nor lend a line
To weep the *Rapes* and *Tragedy* of wine!

Here lives that *Chimick*, quick fire which betrayes
Fresh Spirits to the bloud, and warms our layes,
I have reserv'd 'gainst thy approach a Cup
That were thy Muse stark dead, shall raise her up,
And teach her yet more Charming words and skill
Than ever *Cœlia*, *Chloris*, *Astrophil*, 70
Or any of the Thredbare names Inspir'd
Poore riming lovers with a *Mistris* fir'd.
Come then! and while the slow Isicle hangs
At the stiffe thatch, and Winters frosty pangs
Benumme the year, blith (as of old) let us
'Midst noise and War, of Peace, and mirth discusse.
This portion thou wert born for: why should wee
Vex at the times ridiculous miserie?
An age that thus hath fool'd it selfe, and will
(Spite of thy teeth and mine) persist so still. 80
Let's sit then at this *fire*, and while wee steal
A Revell in the Town, let others seal,
Purchase or Cheat, and who can, let them pay,
Till those black deeds bring on the darksome day;
Innocent spenders wee! a better use
Shall wear out our short Lease, and leave th'obtuse
Rout to their *husks*; They and their bags at best
Have cares in *earnest*, wee care for a *Jest*.

Monsieur Gombauld

I 'ave read thy Souls fair night-peece, and have seen
Th'*Amours* and Courtship of the *silent Queen*,
Her stoln descents to Earth, and what did move her
To Juggle first with *Heav'n*, then with a *Lover*,
With *Latmos* lowder rescue, and (alas!)
To find her out a *Hue and Crie* in Brasse,
Thy Journall of deep Mysteries, and sad
Nocturnall Pilgrimage, with thy dreams clad
In fancies darker than thy *Cave*, Thy *Glasse*
Of sleepie draughts, and as thy soul did passe 10
In her calm voyage what discourse she heard
Of Spirits, what dark Groves and ill-shap'd guard

Ismena lead thee through, with thy proud flight
O'r *Periardes*, and deep, musing night
Neere fair *Eurotas* banks, what solemn *green*
The neighbour shades weare, and what forms are seen
In their large Bowers, with that sad path and seat
Which none but light-heeld *Nymphs* and *Fairies* beat;
Their solitary life, and how exempt
From Common frailtie, the severe contempt 20
They have of Man, their priviledge to live
A *Tree*, or *Fountain*, and in that *Reprieve*
What ages they consume, with the sad *Vale*
Of *Diophania*, and the mournfull tale,
Of th' bleeding vocall *Myrtle*; These and more
Thy richer thoughts we are upon the score
To thy rare fancy for, nor doest thou fall
From thy first Majesty, or ought at all
Betray Consumption, thy full vig'rous *Bayes*
Wear the same *green*, and scorn the lene decayes 30
Of *stile*, or *matter*; Just so have I known
Some *Chrystal* spring, that from the neighbour down
Deriv'd her birth, in gentle murmurs steal
To their next Vale, and proudly there reveal
Her streams in lowder accents, adding still
More noise and waters to her Channell, till
At last swoln with Increase she glides along
The Lawnes and Meadows in a wanton throng
Of frothy billows, and in one great name
Swallows the tributary brooks drown'd fame. 40
Nor are they meere Inventions, for we
In th' same peece find scatter'd *Philosophie*
And hidden, disperst truths that folded lye
In the dark shades of deep *Allegorie*,
So neatly weav'd, like *Arras*, they descrie
Fables with *Truth*, *Fancy* with *Historie*.
So that thou hast in this thy curious mould
Cast that commended mixture wish'd of old,
Which shall these Contemplations render far
Lesse mutable, and lasting as their star, 50
And while there is a *People*, or a *Sunne*,
Endymions storie with the *Moon* shall runne.

An Elegie on the death of Mr. *R. W.* slain in the late unfortunate differences at *Routon* Heath, neer *Chester*, 1645

I am Confirm'd, and so much wing is given
To my wild thoughts, that they dare strike at heav'n.
A full years griefe I struggled with, and stood
Still on my sandy hopes uncertain good,
So loth was I to yeeld, to all those fears
I still oppos'd thee, and denyed my tears.
But thou art gone! and the untimely losse
Like that one day, hath made all others Crosse.
Have you seen on some Rivers flowrie brow
A well-built *Elme*, or stately *Cedar* grow, 10
Whose Curled tops gilt with the Morning-ray
Becken'd the Sun, and whisperd to the day,
When unexpected from the angry *North*
A fatall sullen whirle-wind sallies forth,
And with a full-mouth'd blast rends from the ground
The *Shady twins*, which rushing scatter round
Their sighing leafes, whilst overborn with strength,
Their trembling heads bow to a prostrate length;
So forc'd fell he; So Immaturely Death
Stifled his able heart and active breath. 20
The world scarce knew him yet, his early Soule
Had but new-broke her day, and rather stole
A sight, than gave one; as if subt'ly she
Would learn our stock, but hide his treasurie.
His years (should time lay both his *Wings* and *glasse*
Unto his charge) could not be summ'd (alas!)
To a full *score*; Though in so short a span
His riper thoughts had purchas'd more of man
Than all those worthless livers, which yet quick,
Have quite outgone their own *Arithmetick*. 30
He seiz'd perfections, and without a dull
And mossie *gray* possess'd a solid skull,
No Crooked knowledge neither, nor did he
Wear the friends name for Ends and policie,

And then lay't by; As those *lost Youths* of th'stage
Who only flourish'd for the *Play's* short age
And then retir'd, like *Jewels* in each part
He wore his friends, but chiefly at his heart.
  Nor was it only in this he did excell,
His equall valour could as much, as well. 40
He knew no *fear* but of his *God*; yet durst
No injurie, nor (as some have) e'r purs't
The sweat and tears of others, yet would be
More forward in a royall gallantrie
Than all those vast pretenders, which of late
Swell'd in the ruines of their King and State.
He weav'd not *Self-ends*, and the *Publick* good
Into one piece, nor with the peoples bloud
Fill'd his own veins; In all the doubtfull way
Conscience and *Honour* rul'd him. O that day 50
When like the *Fathers* in the *Fire* and *Cloud*
I mist thy face! I might in ev'ry *Crowd*
See Armes like thine, and men advance, but none
So neer to lightning mov'd, nor so fell on.
Have you observ'd how soon the nimble *Eye*
Brings th' *Object* to *Conceit*, and doth so vie
Performance with the *Soul*, that you would swear
The *Act* and *apprehension* both lodg'd there,
Just so mov'd he: like *shott* his active hand
Drew bloud, e'r well the foe could understand. 60
But here I lost him. Whether the last turn
Of thy few sands call'd on thy hastie urn,
Or some fierce rapid fate (hid from the Eye)
Hath hurl'd thee Pris'ner to some distant skye
I cannot tell, but that I doe believe
Thy Courage such as scorn'd a base Reprieve.
What ever 'twas, whether that day thy breath
Suffer'd a *Civill* or the *Common* death,
Which I doe most suspect, and that I have
Fail'd in the *glories* of so known a grave, 70
Though thy lov'd ashes misse me, and mine Eyes
Had no acquaintance with thy Exequies,
Nor at the last farewell, torn from thy sight
On the *Cold sheet* have fix'd a *sad delight*,

Yet what e'r pious hand (in stead of mine)
Hath done this office to that dust of thine,
And till thou rise again from thy low bed
Lent a Cheap pillow to thy quiet head,
Though but a private *turffe*, it can do more
To keep thy name and memory in store 80
Than all those *Lordly fooles* which lock their bones
In the dumb piles of Chested brasse, and stones.
Th'art rich in thy own fame, and needest not
These *Marble-frailties*, nor the *gilded blot*
Of posthume honours; There is not one sand
Sleeps o'r thy grave, but can outbid that hand
And pencill too, so that of force wee must
Confesse their *heaps* shew lesser than thy *dust*.
And (blessed soule!) though this my sorrow can
Adde nought to thy perfections, yet as man 90
Subject to Envy, and the common fate
It may redeem thee to a fairer date;
As some blind Dial, when the day is done,
Can tell us at mid-night, *There was a Sun*,
So these perhaps, though much beneath thy fame,
May keep some weak remembrance of thy name,
And to the faith of better times Commend
Thy loyall upright life, and gallant End.

Nomen & arma locum servant, te, amice, nequivi
Conspicere, —— 100

Upon a Cloke lent him by Mr. *J. Ridsley*

Here, take again thy *Sack-cloth*! and thank heav'n
Thy Courtship hath not kill'd me; Is't not Even
Whether wee dye by peecemeale, or at once
Since both but ruine, why then for the nonce
Didst husband my afflictions, and cast o're
Me this forc'd *Hurdle* to inflame the score?
Had I neer *London* in this *Rug* been seen
Without doubt I had executed been
For some bold *Irish* spy, and crosse a sledge
Had layn mess'd up for their *foure gates* and *bridge*. 10

When first I bore it, my oppressed feet
Would needs perswade me, 'twas some *Leaden sheet*;
Such deep Impressions, and such dangerous holes
Were made, that I began to doubt my soals,
And ev'ry step (so neer necessity)
Devoutly wish'd some honest Cobler by,
Besides it was so short, the *Jewish* rag
Seem'd Circumcis'd, but had a *Gentile* shag.
Hadst thou been with me on that day, when wee
Left craggie *Biston*, and the fatall *Dee*, 20
When beaten with fresh storms, and late mishap
It shar'd the office of a *Cloke*, and *Cap*,
To see how 'bout my clouded head it stood
Like a thick *Turband*, or some Lawyers *Hood*,
While the stiffe, hollow pletes on ev'ry side
Like *Conduit-pipes* rain'd from the *Bearded hide*,
I know thou wouldst in spite of that day's fate
Let loose thy mirth at my new shape and state,
And with a shallow smile or two professe
Some *Sarazin* had lost the *Clowted Dresse*. 30
Didst ever see the *good wife* (as they say)
March in her short cloke on the *Christning* day,
With what soft motions she salutes the Church,
And leaves the Bedrid Mother in the lurch;
Just so Jogg'd I, while my dull horse did trudge
Like a Circuit-beast plagu'd with a goutie Judge.
But this was Civill. I have since known more
And worser pranks: One night (as heretofore
Th' hast known) for want of change (a thing which I
And *Bias* us'd before me) I did lye 40
Pure *Adamite*, and simply for that end
Resolv'd, and made this for my bosome-*friend*.
O that thou hadst been there next morn, that I
Might teach thee new *Micro-cosmo-graphie*!
Thou wouldst have ta'ne me, as I naked stood,
For one of th' *seven pillars* before the floud,
Such *Characters* and *Hierogliphicks* were
In one night worn, that thou mightst justly swear
I'd slept in *Cere-cloth*, or at *Bedlam* where
The mad men lodge in straw, I'le not forbear 50

To tell thee all, his wild *Impress* and *tricks*
Like *Speeds* old *Britans* made me look, or *Picts*;
His villanous, biting, *Wire-embraces*
Had seal'd in me more strange formes and faces
Than *Children* see in dreams, or thou hast read
In *Arras*, *Puppet-playes*, and *Ginger-bread*,
With *angled Schemes*, and *Crosses* that bred fear
Of being handled by some *Conjurer*,
And neerer thou wouldst think (such *strokes* were drawn)
I'd been some rough statue of *Fetter-lane*, 60
Nay, I believe, had I that instant been
By *Surgeons* or *Apothecaries* seen,
They had Condemned my raz'd skin to be
Some walking *Herball*, or *Anatomie*.
  But (thanks to th'day!) 'tis off. I'd now advise
Thee friend to put this peece to Merchandize;
The *Pedlars* of our age have business yet,
And gladly would against the *Fayr-day* fit
Themselves with such a *Roofe*, that can secure
Their *Wares* from *Dogs and Cats* rain'd in showre, 70
It shall performe; or if this will not doe
'Twill take the *Ale-wives* sure; 'Twill make them *two*
Fine Roomes of *One*, and spread upon a stick
Is a partition without Lime or Brick.
Horn'd obstinacie! how my heart doth fret
To think what *Mouthes* and *Elbowes* it would set
In a wet day? have you for two pence e're
Seen King *Harryes* Chappell at *Westminster*,
Where in their dustie gowns of *Brasse* and *Stone*
The Judges lye, and markt you how each one 80
In sturdie Marble-plets about the knee
Bears up to shew his legs and symmetrie?
Just so would this; That I think't weav'd upon
Some stiffneckt *Brownists* exercising loome.
O that thou hadst it when this Jugling fate
Of Souldierie first seiz'd me! at what rate
Would I have bought it then, what was there but
I would have giv'n for the *Compendious hutt*?
I doe not doubt but (if the weight could please,)
'Twould guard me better than a *Lapland-lease*, 90

Or a *German* shirt with Inchanted lint
Stuff'd through, and th'devils *beard* and *face* weav'd in't.
But I have done. And think not, friend, that I
This freedome took to Jeere thy Courtesie,
I thank thee for't, and I believe my Muse
So known to thee, thou'lt not suspect abuse;
She did this, 'cause (perhaps) thy *love* paid thus
Might with my *thanks* out-live thy *Cloke*, and *Us*.

Upon Mr. *Fletchers* Playes, published, 1647

I knew thee not, nor durst *attendance* strive
Labell to *wit*, *Verser remonstrative*,
And in some *Suburb-page* (scandal to thine)
Like *Lent* before a *Christmasse* scatter mine.
This speaks thee not, since at the utmost rate
Such *remnants* from thy *peece* Intreat their date;
Nor can I *dub* the *Coppy*, or afford
Titles to *swell* the *reare* of *Verse* with Lord,
Nor politickly big to *Inch* low fame
Stretch in the *glories* of a strangers name, 10
And Clip those *Bayes* I Court, weak *striver* I,
But a faint *Echo* unto *Poetrie*.
I have not *Clothes* t'adopt me, nor must sit
For *Plush* and *Velvets* sake *Esquire* of wit,
Yet *Modestie* these *Crosses* would improve,
And *Rags* neer thee, some *Reverence* may move.
I did believe (great *Beaumont* being dead,)
Thy *Widow'd Muse* slept on his *flowrie bed*;
But I am *richly* Cosen'd, and can see
Wit *transmigrates*, his *Spirit* stayd with thee, 20
Which *doubly* advantag'd by thy *single* pen
In *life* and *death* now treads the *Stage* agen;
And thus are wee freed from that *dearth* of wit
Which *starv'd* the Land since into *Schismes* split,
Wherein th'hast done so much, wee must needs guesse
Wits last *Edition* is now i'th' *Presse*,
For thou hast *drain'd* Invention, and he
That writes hereafter, doth but *pillage* thee.

But thou hast *plotts*; and will not the *Kirk* strain
At the *Designes* of such a *Tragick brain*? 30
Will they themselves think safe, when they shall see
Thy most *abominable policie*?
Will not the *Eares* assemble, and think't fit
Their *Synod fast*, and *pray*, against thy wit?
But they'le not *tyre* in such an *idle Quest*,
Thou doest but *kill*, and *Circumvent* in *Jest*,
And when thy anger'd Muse *swells* to a blow
'Tis but for *Field*'s, or *Swansteed*'s overthrow.
Yet shall these *Conquests* of thy *Bayes* outlive
Their *Scotish zeale*, and *Compacts* made to grieve 40
The *Peace* of *Spirits*, and when such deeds fayle
Of their foule Ends, a *faire name* is thy *Bayle*.
But (happy thou!) ne'r saw'st these *stormes*, our *aire*
Teem'd with even in thy time, though *seeming faire*;
Thy gentle *Soule* meant for the *shade*, and *ease*
Withdrew betimes into the *Land* of *Peace*;
So *neasted* in some Hospitable shore
The *Hermit-angler*, when the *mid-Seas* roare
Packs up his *lines*, and (ere the tempest *raves*,)
Retyres, and leaves his *station* to the *waves*. 50
Thus thou diedst almost with our *peace*, and wee
This *breathing time* thy last fair *Issue* see,
Which I think such (if *needless Ink* not soyle
So *Choice a Muse*,) others are but thy *foile*;
This, or that *age* may write, but never see
A *Wit* that dares run *Paralell* with thee.
True, *BEN* must live! but bate *him*, and thou hast
Undone all *future wits*, and match'd the *past*.

Upon the *Poems* and *Playes* of the ever memorable Mr. *William Cartwright*

I did but *see* thee! and how *vain* it is
To *vex* thee for it with *Remonstrances*,
Though *things* in fashion, let those *Judge*, who sit
Their *twelve-pence* out, to *clap* their *hands* at *wit*;

I fear to *Sinne* thus *neer* thee; for (*great Saint!*)
'Tis known, *true beauty* hath no need of *paint*.
  Yet, since a *Labell* fixt to thy fair *Hearse*
Is all the *Mode*, and *tears* put into *Verse*
Can teach *Posterity* our present *griefe*
And their own *losse*, but never give *reliefe*; 10
I'le tell them (and a *truth* which needs no *passe*,)
That *wit* in *Cartwright* at her *Zenith* was,
Arts, *Fancy*, *Language*, all *Conven'd* in thee,
With those *grand Miracles* which *deifie*
The old worlds *Writings*, kept yet from the *fire*,
Because they *force* these worst times to *admire*.
Thy matchless *Genius*, in all thou didst write,
Like the *Sun*, wrought with such *stayd heat*, and *light*,
That not a *line* (to the most *Critick* he)
Offends with *flashes*, or *obscuritie*. 20
  When thou the *wild* of *humours* trackst, thy *pen*
So Imitates that *Motley stock* in men,
As if thou hadst in all their *bosomes* been,
And seen those *Leopards* that lurk within.
The am'rous *Youth* steals from thy *Courtly page*
His *vow'd Addresse*, the *Souldier* his *brave rage*;
And those *soft beauteous Readers* whose *looks* can
Make some men *Poets*, and make any man
A *Lover*, when thy *Slave* but *seems* to dye,
Turn all his *Mourners*, and melt at the *Eye*. 30
Thus, thou thy *thoughts* hast *drest* in such a *strain*
As doth not only *speak*, but *rule* and *raign*,
Nor are those *bodyes* they assum'd, *dark Clouds*,
Or a *thick bark*, but *clear*, *transparent shrouds*,
Which who *lookes* on, the *Rayes* so strongly beat
They'l *brushe* and *warm* him with a *quickning heat*,
So *Souls* shine at the *Eyes*, and *Pearls* display
Through the *loose-Chrystal-streams* a *glaunce of day*.
But what's all this unto a *Royall Test*?
Thou art the *Man*, whom great *Charles* so exprest! 40
Then let the *Crowd* refrain their *needless humme*,
When *Thunder* speaks, then *Squibs* and *Winds* are *dumb*.

To the best, and most accomplish'd Couple

Blessings as rich and fragrant crown your heads
As the mild heav'n on *Roses* sheds,
When at their Cheeks (like Pearls) they weare
The Clouds that court them in a teare,
And may they be fed from above
By him which first ordain'd your love!

Fresh as the *houres* may all your pleasures be,
And healthfull as *Eternitie*!
Sweet as the flowres *first breath*, and Close
As th'*unseen spreadings* of the Rose, 10
When he unfolds his Curtain'd head,
And makes his bosome the *Suns bed.*

Soft as *your selves* run your whole lifes, and cleare
As your own *glasse*, or *what shines* there;
Smooth as heav'ns *face*, and bright as he
When without *Mask*, or *Tiffanie*,
In all your time not one *Jarre* meet
But peace as silent as his *feet.*

Like the dayes *Warmth* may all your Comforts be,
Untoil'd for, and *Serene* as he, 20
Yet free and full as is that *sheafe*
Of Sun-beams gilding ev'ry leafe,
When now the *tyrant-heat* expires
And his Cool'd locks breath milder fires.

And as those *parcell'd glories* he doth shed
Are the *faire Issues* of his head,
Which ne'r so distant are soon known
By th' *heat* and *lustre* for his own,
So may each branch of yours wee see
Your *Coppyes*, and our *Wonders* be! 30

And when no more on Earth you must remain
Invited hence to heav'n again,

Then may your vertuous, virgin-flames
Shine in those *Heires* of your fair names,
And teach the world that mysterie
Your selves in your Posteritie!

So you to both worlds shall *rich presents* bring,
And *gather'd* up to heav'n, leave here a *Spring*.

An Elegie on the death of Mr. *R. Hall*, slain at *Pontefract*, 1648

I knew it would be thus! and my Just fears
Of thy great spirit are Improv'd to tears.
Yet flow these not from any base distrust
Of a fair name, or that thy honour must
Confin'd to those cold reliques sadly sit
In the same Cell an obscure Anchorite.
Such low distempers *Murther*, they that must
Abuse thee so, *weep* not, but *wound* thy dust.
But I past such dimme Mourners can descrie
Thy fame above all Clouds of obloquie, 10
And like the Sun with his victorious rayes
Charge through that darkness to the last of dayes.
'Tis true, fair *Manhood* hath a *female* Eye,
And tears are beauteous in a Victorie,
Nor are wee so high-proofe, but griefe will find
Through all our guards a way to wound the mind;
But in thy fall what addes the brackish summe
More than a blott unto thy *Martyrdome*,
Which scorns such wretched suffrages, and stands
More by thy single worth, than our whole bands. 20
Yet could the puling tribute rescue ought
In this sad losse, or wert thou to be brought
Back here by tears, I would in any wise
Pay down the summe, or quite Consume my Eyes.
Thou fell'st our double ruine, and this rent
Forc'd in thy life shak'd both the *Church and tent*,
Learning in others steales them from the *Van*,
And basely wise *Emasculates* the man,

But lodged in thy brave soul the *bookish feat*
Serve'd only as the light unto thy *heat*; 30
Thus when some quitted action, to their shame,
And only got a *discreet Cowards* name,
Thou with thy bloud mad'st purchase of renown,
And diedst the glory of the *Sword* and *Gown*,
Thy bloud hath hallow'd *Pomfret*, and this blow
(Prophan'd before) hath Church'd the Castle now.
  Nor is't a Common valour we deplore,
But such as with *fifteen* a *hundred* bore,
And lightning like (not coopt within a wall)
In stormes of *fire* and *steele* fell on them all. 40
Thou wert no *Wool-sack* souldier, nor of those
Whose Courage lies in *winking* at their foes,
That live at *loop-holes*, and consume their breath
On *Match* or *Pipes*, and sometimes *peepe* at death;
No, it were sinne to number these with thee,
But that (thus poiz'd) our losse wee better see.
The fair and open valour was thy *shield*,
And thy known station, the *defying field*.
  Yet these in thee I would not *Vertues* call,
But that this age must know, that thou hadst all. 50
Those richer graces that adorn'd thy mind
Like stars of the *first magnitude*, so shin'd,
That if oppos'd unto these lesser lights
All we can say, is this, *They were fair nights*.
Thy *Piety* and *Learning* did unite,
And though with *Sev'rall beames* made up *one light*,
And such thy Judgement was, that I dare swear
Whole *Counsels* might as soon, and *Synods* erre.
  But all these now are out! and as some *Star*
Hurl'd in Diurnall motions from far, 60
And seen to droop at night, is vainly sed
To fall, and find an *Occidentall bed*,
Though in that other world what wee Judge *West*
Proves *Elevation*, and a new, fresh *East*.
So though our weaker sense denies us sight
And bodies cannot trace the *Spirits* flight,
Wee know those graces to be still in thee,
But wing'd above us to eternitie.

Since then (thus flown) thou art so much refin'd,
That we can only reach thee with the mind, 70
I will not in this *dark* and *narrow glasse*
Let thy scant *shadow* for *Perfections* passe,
But leave thee to be read more high, more queint,
In thy own bloud a *Souldier* and a *Saint*.

—— *Salve æternum mihi maxime Palla!*
Æternumq; vale!——

To my learned friend, Mr. *T. Powell*, upon His Translation of *Malvezzi's* *Christian Politician*

Wee thank you, worthy Sir, that now we see
Malvezzi languag'd like our Infancie,
And can without suspition entertain
This forraign States-man to our brest or brain,
You have enlarg'd his praise, and from your store
By this Edition made his worth the more.
Thus by your learned hand (amidst the *Coile*)
Outlandish plants thrive in our thankless soile,
And wise men after death, by a strange fate,
Lye *Leiguer* here, and beg to serve our *State*. 10
Italy now, though *Mistris* of the *Bayes*,
Waits on this *Wreath*, proud of a forraign praise,
For, wise *Malvezzi*, thou didst lye before
Confin'd within the language of one shore,
And like those *Stars* which neer the *Poles* doe steer
Wer't but in one part of the *Globe* seen cleer,
Provence and *Naples* were the best and most
Thou couldst shine in, fixt to that single Coast,
Perhaps some *Cardinal* to be thought wise
And honest too, would ask, *what was thy price?* 20
Then thou must pack to *Rome*, where thou mightst lye
E'r thou shouldst have new cloathes eternally,
For though so neer the *seav'n hills*, ne'rthelesse
Thou cam'st to *Antwerp* for thy *Roman* dresse;

But now thou art come hither, thou mayst run
Through any Clime as well known as the *Sun*,
And in thy *sev'rall dresses* like the *year*
Challenge acquaintance with each peopled Sphere.
  Come then rare Politicians of the time,
Brains of some standing, Elders in our Clime, 30
See here the method: A wise, solid state
Is quick in acting, friendly in debate,
Ioynt in advice, in resolutions just,
Mild in successe, true to the Common trust.
It cements ruptures, and by gentle hand
Allayes the heat and burnings of a land,
Religion guides it, and in all the Tract
Designes so twist, that heav'n confirms the act;
If from these lists you wander as you steere,
Look back, and *Catechise* your actions here, 40
These are the *Marks* to which true States-men tend,
And *greatness* here with *goodness* hath one End.

To my worthy friend Master *T. Lewes*

Sees not my friend, what a deep snow
Candies our Countries wooddy brow?
The yeelding branch his load scarse bears
Opprest with snow, and *frozen tears*,
While the *dumb* rivers slowly float,
All bound up in an *Icie Coat*.
  Let us meet then! and while this world
In wild *Excentricks* now is hurld,
Keep wee, like nature, the same *Key*,
And walk in our forefathers way; 10
Why any more cast wee an Eye
On what *may come*, not what is *nigh*?
Why vex our selves with *feare*, or *hope*
And cares beyond our *Horoscope*?
Who into future times would peere
Looks oft beyond his terme set here,
And cannot goe into those grounds
But through a *Church-yard* which them bounds;

Sorrows and sighes and searches spend
And draw our bottome to an end, 20
But discreet Joyes lengthen the lease
Without which life were a disease,
And who this age a Mourner goes,
Doth with his tears but feed his foes.

To the most Excellently accomplish'd, Mrs. *K. Philips*

Say wittie fair one, from what Sphere
Flow these rich numbers you shed here?
For sure such *Incantations* come
From thence, which strike your Readers dumbe.
A strain, whose measures gently meet
Like *Virgin-lovers*, or times *feet*,
Where language *Smiles*, and accents rise
As quick, and pleasing as your *Eyes*,
The *Poem* smooth, and in each line
Soft as *your selfe*, yet *Masculine*; 10
Where no Coorse trifles blot the page
With matter borrow'd from the age,
But thoughts as Innocent, and high
As *Angels* have, or *Saints* that dye.
These Raptures when I first did see
New miracles in Poetrie,
And by a hand, their God would misse
His *Bayes* and *Fountaines* but to kisse,
My weaker *Genius* (crosse to fashion)
Slept in a silent admiration, 20
A Rescue, by whose grave disguise
Pretenders oft have past for wise,
And yet as *Pilgrims* humbly touch
Those *Shrines* to which they bow so much,
And Clouds in Courtship flock, and run
To be the Mask unto the Sun,
So I concluded, It was true
I might at distance worship you

A *Persian* Votarie, and say
It was your light shew'd me the way. 30
So *Lodestones* guide the duller *Steele*,
And high perfections are the *Wheele*
Which moves the lesse, for gifts divine
Are strung upon a *Vital line*
Which touch'd by you, Excites in all
Affections *Epidemicall.*
And this made me (a truth most fit)
Adde my weak *Eccho* to your wit,
Which pardon, Lady, for Assayes
Obscure as these might blast your Bayes, 40
As Common hands soyle *Flowres*, and make
That dew they wear, *weepe* the mistake.
But I'le wash off the *staine*, and vow
No *Lawrel* growes, but for your *Brow.*

An Epitaph upon the Lady *Elizabeth*, Second Daughter to his late Majestie

Youth, Beauty, Vertue, Innocence
Heav'ns royall, and select Expence,
With Virgin-tears, and sighs divine,
Sit here the *Genii* of this shrine,
Where now (thy fair soule wing'd away,)
They guard the *Casket* where she lay.
Thou hadst, e'r thou the light couldst see,
Sorrowes layd up, and stor'd for thee,
Thou suck'dst in woes, and the *brests* lent
Their *Milk* to thee, but to lament; 10
Thy portion here was *griefe*, thy years
Distilld no other rain, but tears,
Tears without noise, but (understood)
As lowd, and shrill as any bloud;
Thou seem'st a *Rose-bud* born in *Snow*,
A flowre of purpose sprung to bow
To headless tempests, and the rage
Of an Incensed, stormie Age.

Others, e're their afflictions grow,
Are tim'd, and season'd for the blow, 20
But thine, as *Rhumes* the tend'rest part,
Fell on a *young* and *harmless* heart.
And yet as *Balm-trees* gently spend
Their tears for those, that doe them rend,
So mild and pious thou wert seen,
Though full of *Suffrings*, free from *spleen*,
Thou didst nor murmure, nor revile,
But drank'st thy *Wormwood* with a *smile*.
As envious Eyes blast, and Infect
And cause misfortunes by aspect, 30
So thy sad stars dispens'd to thee
No Influxe, but Calamitie,
They view'd thee with *Ecclypsed* rayes,
And but the *back-side* of bright dayes.

* * *

These were the Comforts she had here,
As by an unseen hand 'tis cleer,
Which now she reads, and smiling wears
A Crown with him, who wipes off tears.

To Sir *William D'avenant*, upon his *Gondibert*

Well, wee are rescued! and by thy rare Pen
Poets shall live, when *Princes* dye like men.
Th'hast cleer'd the prospect to our harmless *Hill*,
Of late years clouded with imputed Ill,
And the *Soft*, *youthfull Couples* there may move
As chast as *Stars* converse and smile above.
Th'hast taught their *Language*, and their *love* to flow
Calme as *Rose-leafes*, and coole as *Virgin-snow*,
Which doubly feasts us, being so refin'd
They both *delight*, and *dignifie* the mind, 10
Like to the watrie Musick of some Spring,
Whose pleasant flowings at once *wash* and *sing*.
And where before *Heroick Poems* were
Made up of *Spirits*, *Prodigies*, and *fear*,

And shew'd (through all the *Melancholy flight*,)
Like some dark Region overcast with night,
As if the Poet had been quite dismay'd,
While only *Giants* and *Inchantments* sway'd,
Thou like the *Sun*, whose Eye brooks no disguise
Hast Chas'd them hence, and with Discoveries 20
So rare and learned fill'd the place, that wee
Those fam'd *Grandeza's* find out-done by thee,
And under-foot see all those *Vizards* hurl'd,
Which bred the wonder of the former world.
'Twas dull to sit, as our fore-fathers did,
At *Crums* and *Voyders*, and because unbid
Refrain wise appetite. This made thy *fire*
Break through the *ashes* of thy aged *Sire*
To lend the world such a Convincing light
As shewes his *fancy* darker than his sight. 30
Nor was't alone the *bars* and *length* of dayes
(Though those gave *strength* and *stature* to his *bayes*,)
Encounter'd thee, but what's an old Complaint
And kills the fancy, a *forlorn Restraint*;
How couldst thou mur'd in solitarie stones
Dresse *BIRTHA'S smiles*, though well thou might'st her *grones*?
And, strangely Eloquent, thy self divide
'Twixt *Sad misfortunes*, and a *Bloomie Bride*?
Through all the tenour of thy ample Song
Spun from thy own rich store, and shar'd among 40
Those fair *Adventurers*, we plainly see
Th' *Imputed* gifts, *Inherent* are in thee.
Then live for ever (and by high desert)
In thy own *mirrour*, matchless *Gondibert*,
And in *bright Birtha* leave thy *love* Inshrin'd
Fresh as her *Emrauld*, and *fair* as her *mind*,
While all Confesse thee (as they ought to doe)
The Prince of *Poets*, and of *Lovers* too.

Tristium Lib. 5°. *Eleg*. 3ª.
To his fellow-Poets at *Rome*, upon the birth-day of *Bacchus*

This is the day (blith god of *Sack*) which wee
If I mistake not, Consecrate to thee,
When the soft *Rose* wee marry to the *Bayes*,
And warm'd with thy own wine reherse thy praise,
'Mongst whom (while to thy *Poet* fate gave way)
I have been held no small part of the day,
But now, dull'd with the Cold *Bears* frozen seat,
Sarmatia holds me, and the warlike *Gete*.
My former life, unlike to this my last,
With *Romes* best wits of thy full Cup did tast, 10
Who since have seen the savage *Pontick* band,
And all the *Choler* of the Sea and Land:
Whether sad Chance, or heav'n hath this design'd,
And at my birth some fatall Planet shin'd,
Of right thou shouldst the *Sisters* knots undoe,
And free thy *Votarie* and *Poet* too.
Or are you Gods (like us) in such a state
As cannot alter the decrees of fate?
I know with much adoe thou didst obtain
Thy *Jovial godhead*, and on earth thy pain 20
Was no whit lesse, for wandring thou didst run
To the *Getes* too, and Snow-weeping *Strymon*,
With *Persia*, *Ganges*, and what ever streams
The thirsty *Moore* drinks in the mid-day beames.
But thou wert twice-born, and the Fates to thee
(To make all sure) doubled thy miserie,
My suffrings too are many: if it be
Held safe for me to boast adversitie,
Nor was't a Common blow, but from above
Like his, that died for Imitating *Jove*, 30
Which when thou heardst, a ruine so divine
And *Mother*-like, should make thee pitty mine.
And on this day, which *Poets* unto thee
Crown with full bowles, ask, *What's become of me?*

Help bucksome God then! so may thy lov'd *Vine*
Swarm with the num'rous grape, and *big* with Wine
Load the kind *Elm*, and so thy *Orgyes* be
With priests lowd showtes, and *Satyrs* kept to thee!
So may in death *Lycurgus* ne'r be blest,
Nor *Pentheus* wandring ghost find any rest! 40
And so for ever bright (thy Chiefe desires,)
May thy *Wifes Crown* outshine the lesser fires!
If but now, mindfull of my love to thee,
Thou wilt, in what thou canst, my helper be.
You *Gods* have Commerce with your selves, try then
If *Cæsar* will restore me *Rome* agen.
And you my trusty friends (the Jollie Crew
Of careless *Poets*!) when, without me, you
Perform this dayes glad Myst'ries, let it be
Your first Appeal unto his Deitie, 50
And let one of you (touch'd with my sad name)
Mixing his wine with tears, lay down the same,
And (sighing) to the rest this thought Commend,
O! Where is Ovid *now our banish'd friend?*
This doe, if in your brests I e'r deserv'd
So large a share, nor spitefully reserv'd,
Nor basely sold applause, or with a brow
Condemning others, did my selfe allow.
And may your happier wits grow lowd with fame
As you (my best of friends!) preserve my name. 60

De Ponto, *Lib*. 3°.
To his friends (after his many sollicitations) refusing to petition *Cæsar* for his releasement

You have Consum'd my language, and my pen
Incens'd with begging scorns to write agen.
You grant, you knew my sute: My Muse, and I
Had taught it you in frequent Elegie,
That I believe (yet seal'd) you have divin'd
Our *Repetitions*, and *forestal'd* my mind,

So that my thronging Elegies, and I
Have made you (more then *Poets*) prophesie.
  But I am now awak'd; forgive my dream
Which made me Crosse the *Proverb* and the *Stream*, 10
And pardon, friends, that I so long have had
Such good thoughts of you, I am not so mad
As to continue them. You shall no more
Complain of troublesome *Verse*, or write o're
How I endanger you, and vex my *Wife*
With the sad legends of a banish'd life.
I'le bear these plagues my selfe: for I have past
Through greater ones, and can as well at last
These pettie Crosses. 'Tis for some young beast
To kick his bands, or wish his neck releast 20
From the sad Yoke. Know then, That as for me
Whom Fate hath us'd to such calamitie,
I scorn her spite and yours, and freely dare
The highest ills your malice can prepare.
  'Twas Fortune threw me hither, where I now
Rude *Getes* and *Thrace* see, with the snowie brow
Of Cloudie *Æmus*, and if she decree
Her sportive pilgrims *last bed* here must be
I am content; nay more, she cannot doe
That Act which I would not consent unto. 30
I can delight in vain hopes, and desire
That state more then her *Change* and *Smiles*, then high'r
I hugge a strong *despaire*, and think it brave
To *baffle* faith, and give those hopes a *grave*.
Have you not seen cur'd wounds enlarg'd, and he
That with the first wave sinks, yielding to th'free
Waters, without th'Expence of armes or breath
Hath still the easiest, and the quickest death.
Why nurse I sorrows then? why these desires
Of Changing *Scythia* for the *Sun* and *fires* 40
Of some calm kinder aire? what did bewitch
My frantick hopes to flye so vain a pitch,
And thus out-run my self? Mad-man! could I
Suspect fate had for me a Courtesie?
These errours grieve: And now I must forget
Those pleas'd *Idœa's* I did frame and set

Unto my selfe, with many fancyed *Springs*
And *Groves*, whose only losse new sorrow brings.
And yet I would the worst of fate endure,
E're you should be repuls'd, or lesse secure, 50
But (base, low soules!) you left me not for this,
But 'cause you durst not. *Cæsar* could not misse
Of such a trifle, for I know that he
Scorns the *Cheap triumphs* of my miserie.
Then since (degen'rate friends) not he, but you
Cancell my hopes, and make afflictions new,
You shall Confesse, and fame shall tell you, I
At *Ister* dare as well as *Tyber* dye.

De Ponto, *Lib*. 4°. *Eleg*. 3ª.
To his Inconstant friend, translated for the use of all the *Judases* of this touch-stone-Age

Shall I complain, or not? Or shall I mask
Thy hatefull name, and in this bitter task
Master my just Impatience, and write down
Thy crime alone, and leave the rest unknown?
Or wilt thou the succeeding years should see
And teach thy person to posteritie?
No, hope it not; for know, most wretched man,
'Tis not thy base and weak detraction can
Buy thee a *Poem*, nor move me to give
Thy name the honour in my Verse to live. 10
Whilst yet my *Ship* did with no stormes dispute
And temp'rate winds *fed* with a calme salute
My prosp'rous sailes, thou wert the only man
That with me then an equall fortune ran,
But now since angry heav'n with Clouds and night
Stifled those *Sun*-beams, thou hast ta'ne thy flight,
Thou know'st I want thee, and art meerly gone
To shun that rescue, I rely'd upon;
Nay, thou dissemblest too, and doest disclame
Not only my *Acquaintance*, but my name; 20

Yet know (though deafe to this) that I am he
Whose *years* and *love* had the same *Infancie*
With thine, Thy *deep familiar*, that did share
Soules with thee, and partake thy *Joyes* or *Care*,
Whom the same *Roofe* lodg'd, and my *Muse* those nights
So solemnly endear'd to her delights;
But now, perfidious traitour, I am grown
The *Abject* of thy brest, not to be known
In that *false Closet* more; Nay, thou wilt not
So much as let me know, I am forgot. 30
If thou wilt say, thou didst not love me, then
Thou didst dissemble: or, if love agen,
Why now Inconstant? came the Crime from me
That wrought this Change? Sure, if no Justice be
Of my side, thine must have it. Why dost hide
Thy reasons then? for me, I did so guide
My selfe and actions, that I cannot see
What could offend thee, but my miserie.
'Las! if thou wouldst not from thy store allow
Some rescue to my wants, at least I know 40
Thou couldst have writ, and with a line or two
Reliev'd my *famish'd Eye*, and eas'd me so.
I know not what to think! and yet I hear,
Not pleas'd with this, th'art *Witty*, and dost Jeare;
Bad man! thou hast in this those tears kept back
I could have shed for thee, shouldst thou but lack.
Know'st not that *Fortune* on a *Globe* doth stand,
Whose *upper* slipprie part without command
Turns *lowest* still? the sportive leafes and wind
Are but dull *Emblems* of her fickle mind, 50
In the whole world there's nothing I can see
Will throughly parallel her wayes, but thee.
All that we hold, hangs on a slender twine
And our best states by sudden chance decline;
Who hath not heard of *Crœsus* proverb'd gold
Yet knowes his foe did him a pris'ner hold?
He that once aw'd *Sicilia*'s proud Extent
By a poor art could famine scarse prevent;
And mighty *Pompey* e'r he made an end
Was glad to beg his slave to be his friend; 60

Nay, he that had so oft *Romes* Consull bin,
And forc'd *Jugurtha*, and the *Cimbrians* in,
Great *Marius*! with much want, and more disgrace
In a foul Marsh was glad to hide his face.
A divine hand swayes all mankind, and wee
Of one short houre have not the certaintie;
Hadst thou one day told me, the time should be
When the *Getes* bowes, and th'*Euxine* I should see,
I should have check'd thy madness, and have thought
Th' hadst need of all *Anticira* in a draught; 70
And yet 'tis come to passe! nor though I might
Some things foresee, could I procure a sight
Of my whole destinie, and free my state
From those eternall, higher *tyes* of fate.
Leave then thy pride, and though now *brave* and *high*,
Think thou mayst be as *poore* and *low* as *I*.

Tristium Lib. 3°. *Eleg*. 3ª.
To his Wife at *Rome*, when he was sick

Dearest! if you those fair Eyes (wondring) stick
On this strange Character, know, *I am sick*.
Sick in the *skirts* of the lost world, where I
Breath hopeless of all Comforts, but to dye.
What heart (think'st thou?) have I in this sad seat
Tormented 'twixt the *Sauromate* and *Gete*?
Nor *aire* nor *water* please; their very *skie*
Looks strange and unaccustom'd to my Eye,
I scarse dare breath it, and I know not how
The Earth that bears me shewes unpleasant now. 10
Nor *Diet* here's, nor *lodging* for my Ease,
Nor any one that *studies* a disease;
No friend to comfort me, none to defray
With smooth discourse the Charges of the day.
All tir'd alone I lye, and (thus) what e're
Is absent, and at *Rome* I fancy here,
But when thou com'st, I blot the *Airie Scrowle*,
And give thee full possession of my soule,

Thee (absent) I embrace, thee only *voice*,
And night and day *bely* a Husbands Joyes; 20
Nay, of thy name so oft I mention make
That I am thought distracted for thy sake;
When my tir'd Spirits faile, and my sick heart
Drawes in that *fire* which actuates each part,
If any say, th'art come! I force my pain,
And hope to see thee, gives me life again.
Thus I for thee, whilst thou (perhaps) more blest
Careless of me doest breath all peace and rest,
Which yet I think not, for (*Deare Soule!*) too well
Know I thy griefe, since my first woes befell. 30
But if strict heav'n my stock of dayes hath spun
And with my life my errour wilbe gone,
How easie then (*O Cæsar!*) wer't for thee
To pardon one, that now doth cease to be?
That I might yeeld my native aire this breath,
And banish not my ashes after death;
Would thou hadst either spar'd me untill dead,
Or with my bloud redeem'd my absent head,
Thou shouldst have had both freely, but O! thou
Wouldst have me live to dye an *Exile* now. 40
And must I then from *Rome* so far meet death,
And double by the place my losse of breath?
Nor in my last of houres on my own bed
(In the sad Conflict) rest my dying head?
Nor my soules *Whispers* (the last pledge of life,)
Mix with the tears and kisses of a wife?
My last words none must treasure, none will rise
And (with a teare) seal up my vanquish'd Eyes,
Without these *Rites* I dye, distrest in all
The *splendid sorrowes* of a Funerall, 50
Unpittied, and unmourn'd for, my sad head
In a strange Land goes friendless to the dead.
When thou hear'st this, O how thy faithfull soule
Will sink, whilst griefe doth ev'ry part controule!
How often wilt thou look this way, and Crie,
O where is't yonder that my love doth lye!
Yet spare these tears, and mourn not now for me,
Long since (*dear heart!*) have I been dead to thee,

Think then I dyed, when *Thee* and *Rome* I lost
That death to me more griefe then this hath Cost; 60
Now, if thou canst (but thou canst not) *best wife*
Rejoyce, my Cares are ended with my life,
At least, yeeld not to sorrowes, frequent use
Should make these miseries to thee no newes.
And here I wish my Soul died with my breath
And that no part of me were free from death,
For, if it be Immortall, and outlives
The body, as *Pythagoras* believes,
Betwixt these *Sarmates ghosts*, a *Roman* I
Shall wander, vext to all Eternitie. 70
But thou (for after death I shall be free,)
Fetch home these bones, and what is left of me,
A few *Flowres* give them, with some *Balme*, and lay
Them in some *Suburb-grave* hard by the way,
And to Informe posterity, who's there,
This sad Inscription let my marble weare,
,*Here lyes the soft-soul'd Lecturer of Love*,
,*Whose envy'd wit did his own ruine prove*.
But thou, (who e'r thou beest, that passing by
Lendst to this *sudden stone* a *hastie* Eye,) 80
If e'r thou knew'st of *Love* the sweet disease,
Grudge not to say, *May* Ovid *rest in peace!*
This for my tombe: but in my books they'l see
More strong and lasting Monuments of mee,
Which I believe (though fatall) will afford
An Endless name unto their ruin'd Lord.
And now thus gone, It rests for love of me
Thou shewst some sorrow to my memory;
Thy Funerall offrings to my ashes beare
With Wreathes of *Cypresse* bath'd in many a teare, 90
Though nothing there but dust of me remain,
Yet shall that *Dust* perceive thy pious pain.
But I have done, and my tyr'd sickly head
Though I would fain write more, desires the bed;
Take then this word (perhaps my last to tell)
Which though I want, I wish it thee, *Fare-well*.

Ausonii Cupido, Edyl. 6

In those blest fields of *Everlasting aire*
(Where to a *Myrtle*-grove the soules repaire
Of deceas'd *Lovers*,) the sad, thoughtfull ghosts
Of *Injur'd Ladyes* meet, where each accoasts
The other with a sigh, whose very breath
Would break a heart, and (*kind Soules!*) love in death.
A thick wood clouds their *walks*, where day scarse peeps,
And on each hand Cypresse and Poppey *sleepes*,
The drowsie Rivers *slumber*, and *Springs* there
Blab not, but softly melt into a teare, 10
A sickly dull aire *fans* them, which can have
When most in force scarce breath to *build* a wave.
On either bank through the still shades appear
A *Scene* of pensive flowres, whose bosomes wear
Drops of a *Lover's* bloud, the *Emblem'd* truths
Of deep despair, and Love-slain *Kings* and *Youths*.
The *Hyacinth*, and self-enamour'd Boy
Narcissus flourish there, with *Venus* Joy
The spruce *Adonis*, and that *Prince* whose flowre
Hath sorrow languag'd on him to this houre; 20
All sad with love they hang their heads, and grieve
As if their passions in each leafe did *live*;
And here (*alas!*) these soft-soul'd Ladies stray,
And (oh! too late!) treason in love betray.
  Her blasted birth sad *Semele* repeats,
And with her *tears* would quench the thund'rers *heats*
Then shakes her bosome, as if fir'd again,
And fears another lightnings *flaming train*.
The lovely *Procris* (here) bleeds, sighes, and swounds
Then wakes, and kisses him that gave her wounds. 30
Sad *Hero* holds a torch forth, and doth light
Her lost *Leander* through the waves and night.
Her *Boateman* desp'rate *Sapho* still admires,
And nothing but the *Sea* can quench her *fires*.
Distracted *Phœdra* with a restless Eye
Her disdain'd Letters reads, then casts them by.
Rare, faithfull *Thysbe* (sequestred from these)
A silent, unseen sorrow doth best please,

For her *Loves* sake, and last *good-night*, poor she
Walks in the shadow of a *Mulberrie*. 40
Neer her young *Canace* with *Dido* sits
A lovely Couple, but of desp'rate wits,
Both dy'd alike, both pierc'd their tender brests,
This with her *Fathers* Sword, that with her *Guests*.
Within the thickest *textures* of the Grove
Diana in her *Silver-beams* doth rove,
Her Crown of stars the *pitchie aire* Invades,
And with a faint light *gilds* the silent shades,
Whilst her sad thoughts fixt on her *sleepie Lover*
To *Latmos*-hill, and his retirements move her. 50
A thousand more through the wide, darksome wood
Feast on their cares, the *Maudlin-Lovers* food,
For *griefe* and *absence* doe but *Edge* desire,
And Death is *fuell* to a Lovers *fire*.
To see these *Trophies* of his wanton bow
Cupid comes in, and all in triumph now
(Rash, unadvised Boy!) disperseth round
The sleepie Mists, his *Wings* and *quiver* wound
With noise the quiet aire. This sudden stirre
Betrayes his *godship*, and as we from far 60
A clouded, sickly *Moon* observe, so they
Through the *false Mists* his *Ecclyps'd torch* betray.
A hot pursute they make, and though with care,
And a slow wing he softly *stems* the aire,
Yet they (as subtill now as he) surround
His silenc'd course, and with the thick night bound
Surprize the *Wag*. As in a dream we strive
To voyce our thoughts, & vainly would revive
Our Entraunc'd tongues, but can not speech enlarge
'Till the Soule wakes and reassumes her Charge, 70
So joyous of their *Prize*, they flock about
And vainly *Swell* with an *Imagin'd* shout.
Far in these shades, and melancholy Coasts
A *Myrtle* growes, well known to all the ghosts,
Whose stretch'd top (like a *great man* rais'd by Fate)
Looks big, and scorns his neighbours low estate;
His *leavy arms* into a *green Cloud* twist,
And on each Branch doth *sit* a lazie mist.

A fatall tree, and luckless to the gods,
Where for *disdain* in life (loves *worst* of *Ods*,) 80
The *Queen* of shades, fair *Proserpine* did rack
The sad *Adonis*, hither now they pack
This little *God*, where, first disarm'd, they *bind*
His skittish wings, then both his hands behind
His back they tye, and thus secur'd at last
The *peevish wanton* to the tree make fast.
Here at adventure without *Judge* or Jurie
He is condemn'd, while with united furie
They all assaile him; As a thiefe at Bar
Left to the Law, and mercy of his Star, 90
Hath *Bills* heap'd on him, and is question'd there
By all the men that have been rob'd that year,
So now what ever *Fate*, or their own *Will*
Scor'd up in life, *Cupid* must pay the bill.
Their *Servants* falshood, Jealousie, disdain,
And all the plagues that *abus'd Maids* can feign,
Are layd on him, and then to heighten spleen
Their own deaths crown the summe. Prest thus between
His faire accusers, 'tis at last decreed,
He by those weapons, that they died, should bleed. 100
One grasps an *airie Sword*, a second holds
Illusive *fire*, and in *vain*, wanton folds
Belyes a flame; Others lesse kind appear
To let him bloud, and from the purple tear
Create a *Rose*. But *Sapho* all this while
Harvests the aire, and from a thicken'd pile
Of Clouds like *Leucas-top*, spreads underneath
A *Sea* of *Mists*, the peacefull billowes breath
Without all noise, yet so exactly move
They seem to *Chide*, but distant from above 110
Reach not the eare, and (thus prepar'd) at once
She doth o'rwhelm him with the *airie Sconce*.
Amidst these tumults, and as fierce as they
Venus steps in, and without thought, or stay
Invades her *Son*; her old disgrace is cast
Into the *Bill*, when *Mars* and *Shee* made *fast*
In their Embraces were expos'd to all
The *Scene* of gods stark naked in their *fall*.

Nor serves a *verball* penance, but with hast
From her fair brow (O happy flowres so plac'd!) 120
She tears a *Rosie garland*, and with this
Whips the *untoward Boy*, they gently kisse
His *snowie skin*, but she with angry hast
Doubles her strength, untill bedew'd at last
With a thin bloudie sweat, their *Innate Red*,
(As if griev'd with the Act) grew pale and dead.
This *layd* their spleen: And now (*kind soules!*) no more
They'l punish him, the torture that he bore,
Seems greater then his crime; with joynt Consent
Fate is made guilty, and *he* Innocent. 130
As in a dream with dangers we contest,
And *fictious pains* seem to afflict our rest,
So frighted only in these shades of night
Cupid (got loose) stole to the upper light,
Where ever since (for malice unto these)
The *spitefull Ape* doth either *Sex* displease.
But O that had these *Ladyes* been so wise
To keep his *Arms*, and give him but his *Eyes*!

Boet. Lib. 1. *Metrum* 1

I whose first year flourish'd with youthfull verse,
In slow, sad numbers now my griefe reherse;
A broken stile my sickly lines afford,
And only tears give weight unto my words;
Yet neither fate nor force my Muse cou'd fright
The only faithfull Consort of my flight;
Thus what was once my green years greatest glorie,
Is now my Comfort, grown decay'd and hoarie,
For killing Cares th'Effects of age spurr'd on
That griefe might find a fitting Mansion; 10
O'r my young head runs an untimely gray,
And my loose skin shrinks at my bloods decay.
Happy the man! whose death in prosp'rous years
Strikes not, nor shuns him in his age and tears.
But O how deafe is she to hear the Crie
Of th' opprest Soule, or shut the weeping Eye!

While treacherous Fortune with slight honours fed
My first estate, she almost drown'd my head,
But now since (clouded thus) she hides those rayes,
Life adds unwelcom'd length unto my dayes; 20
Why then, my friends, Judg'd you my state so good?
He that may fall once, never firmly stood.

Metrum 2

O in what haste with Clouds and Night
Ecclyps'd, and having lost her light,
The dull Soule whom distraction rends
Into outward Darkness tends!
How often (by these mists made blind,)
Have earthly cares opprest the mind!
This Soule sometimes wont to survey
The spangled *Zodiacks firie way*
Saw th'early Sun in Roses drest
With the Coole Moons unstable Crest, 10
And whatsoever wanton Star
In various Courses neer or far
Pierc'd through the orbs, he cou'd full well
Track all her Journey, and would tell
Her Mansions, turnings, Rise and fall,
By Curious Calculation all.
Of sudden winds the hidden Cause,
And why the Calm Seas quiet face
With Impetuous waves is Curld,
What spirit wheeles th'harmonious world, 20
Or why a Star dropt in the *West*
Is seen to rise again by *East*,
Who gives the warm Spring temp'rate houres
Decking the Earth with spicie flowres,
Or how it Comes (for mans recruit)
That Autumne yeelds both Grape and fruit,
With many other Secrets, he
Could shew the Cause and Mysterie.
But now that light is almost out,
And the brave Soule lyes Chain'd about 30

With outward Cares, whose pensive weight
Sinks down her Eyes from their first height,
And clean Contrary to her birth
Poares on this vile and foolish Earth.

Metrum 4

Whose calme soule in a settled state
Kicks under foot the frowns of Fate,
And in his fortunes bad or good
Keeps the same temper in his bloud,
Not him the flaming Clouds above,
Nor *Ætna's* fierie tempests move,
No fretting seas from shore to shore
Boyling with Indignation o're
Nor burning thunderbolt that can
A mountain shake, can stirre this man. 10
Dull Cowards then! why should we start
To see these tyrants act their part?
Nor hope, nor fear what may befall
And you disarm their malice all.
But who doth faintly fear, or wish
And sets no law to what is his,
Hath lost the buckler, and (poor Elfe!)
Makes up a Chain to bind himselfe.

Metrum 5

O thou great builder of this starrie frame
Who fixt in thy eternall throne dost tame
The rapid Spheres, and lest they jarre
Hast giv'n a law to ev'ry starre!
Thou art the Cause that now the Moon
With full orbe dulls the starres, and soon
Again growes dark, her light being done,
The neerer still she's to the Sun.
Thou in the early hours of night
Mak'st the coole Evening-star shine bright, 10

And at Sun-rising ('cause the least)
Look pale and sleepie in the East.
Thou, when the leafes in Winter stray,
Appointst the Sun a shorter way,
And in the pleasant Summer-light
With nimble houres doest wing the night.
Thy hand the various year quite through
Discreetly tempers, that what now
The North-wind tears from ev'ry tree
In Spring again restor'd we see. 20
Then what the *winter-starrs* between
The furrowes in meer seed have seen
The Dog-star since (grown up and born)
Hath burnt in stately, full-ear'd Corn.
 Thus by Creations law controll'd
All things their proper stations hold
Observing (as thou didst intend)
Why they were made, and for what end.
Only humane actions thou
Hast no Care of, but to the flow 30
And Ebbe of Fortune leav'st them all,
Hence th' Innocent endures that thrall
Due to the wicked, whilst alone
They sit possessours of his throne,
The Just are kill'd, and Vertue lyes
Buried in obscurities,
And (which of all things is most sad)
The good man suffers by the bad.
No perjuries, nor damn'd pretence
Colour'd with holy, lying sense 40
Can them annoy, but when they mind
To try their force, which most men find,
They from the highest sway of things
Can pull down great, and pious Kings.
 O then at length, thus loosely hurl'd
Look on this miserable world
Who e'r thou art, that from above
Doest in such order all things move!
And let not man (of divine art
Not the least, nor vilest part) 50

By Casuall evills thus bandied, be
The sport of fates obliquitie.
But with that faith thou guid'st the heaven,
Settle this Earth, and make them even.

Metrum 6

When the Crabs fierce Constellation
Burns with the beams of the bright Sun,
Then he that will goe out to sowe,
Shall never reap where he did plough,
But in stead of Corn may rather
The old worlds diet, Accorns gather.
Who the Violet doth love
Must seek her in the flowrie grove,
But never when the *Norths* cold wind
The *Russet* fields with frost doth bind. 10
If in the Spring-time (to no end)
The tender Vine for Grapes we bend,
Wee shall find none, for only (still)
Autumne doth the Wine-presse fill.
Thus for all things (in the worlds prime)
The wise God seal'd their proper time,
Nor will permit those seasons he
Ordain'd by turns, should mingled be
Then whose wild actions out of season
Crosse to nature, and her reason, 20
Would by new wayes old orders rend,
Shall never find a happy End.

Metrum 7

Curtain'd with Clouds in a dark night
The Stars cannot send forth their light.
And if a sudden Southern blast
The Sea in rolling waves doth cast,
That angrie Element doth boile,
And from the deep with stormy Coile

Spues up the Sands, which in short space
Scatter, and puddle his Curl'd face;
Then those Calme waters, which but now
Stood clear as heavens unclouded brow, 10
And like transparent glasse did lye
Open to ev'ry searchers Eye,
Look foulely stirr'd, and (though desir'd)
Resist the sight, because bemir'd,
So often from a high hills brow
Some Pilgrim-spring is seen to flow,
And in a straight line keep her Course
'Till from a Rock with headlong force
Some broken peece blocks up her way
And forceth all her streams astray. 20
Then thou that with inlightned Rayes,
Wouldst see the truth, and in her wayes
Keep without *Errour*; neither fear
The future, nor too much give ear
To present Joyes; And give no scope
To griefe, nor much to flatt'ring hope.
For when these Rebels raign, the mind
Is both a Pris'ner, and stark blind.

Lib. 2. *Metrum* I

Fortune (when with rash hands she quite turmoiles
The state of things, and in tempestuous foiles
Comes whirling like *Euripus*,) beats quite down
With headlong force the highest Monarchs crown
And in his place unto the throne doth fetch
The despis'd looks of some mechanick wretch.
So Jests at tears and miseries, is proud,
And laughs to hear her vassals grone aloud.
These are her sports, thus she her wheele doth drive
And plagues man with her blind prerogative; 10
Nor is't a favour of Inferiour strain,
If once kickt down, she lets him rise again.

Metrum 2

If with an open, bounteous hand
(Wholly left at Mans Command)
Fortune should in one rich flow
As many heaps on him bestow
Of massie gold, as there be sands
Tost by the waves and winds rude bands,
Or bright stars in a Winter-night
Decking their silent Orbs with light,
Yet would his lust know no restraints,
Nor cease to weep in sad Complaints. 10
Though heaven should his vowes reguard,
And in a prodigall reward
Return him all he could implore,
Adding new honours to his store,
Yet all were nothing. Goods in sight
Are scorn'd, and lust in greedy flight
Layes out for more; What measure then
Can tame these wild desires of men?
Since all wee give both last and first
Doth but inflame, and feed their thirst; 20
For how can he be rich, who 'midst his store
Sits sadly pining, and believes he's poore.

Metrum 3

When the Sun from his Rosie bed
The dawning light begins to shed,
The drowsie sky uncurtains round,
And the (but now bright) stars all drown'd
In one great light, look dull and tame,
And homage his victorious flame.
Thus, when the warm *Etesian* wind
The Earth's seald bosome doth unbind,
Straight she her various store discloses,
And purples every Grove with Roses; 10
But if the Souths tempestuous breath
Breaks forth, those blushes pine to death.

Oft in a quiet sky the deep
With unmov'd waves seems fast asleep,
And oft again the blustring North
In angrie heaps provokes them forth.
If then this world, which holds all Nations,
Suffers it selfe such alterations,
That not this mighty, massie frame,
Nor any part of it can Claime 20
One certain course, why should man prate,
Or Censure the designs of Fate?
Why from fraile honours, and goods lent
Should he expect things permanent?
Since 'tis enacted by divine decree
That nothing mortall shall eternall be.

Metrum 4

Who wisely would for his retreat
Build a secure and lasting seat,
Where stov'd in silence he may sleep
Beneath the *Wind*, above the *Deep*;
Let him th' high hils leave on one hand,
And on the other the false sand;
The first to winds lyes plain and even
From all the blustring points of heaven;
The other hollow and unsure,
No weight of building will endure. 10
Avoyding then the envied state
Of buildings bravely situate,
Remember thou thy selfe to lock
Within some low neglected Rock;
There when fierce heaven in thunder Chides,
And winds and waves rage on all sides,
Thou happy in the quiet fense
Of thy poor Cell with small Expence
Shall lead a life serene and faire,
And scorn the anger of the aire. 20

Metrum 5

Happy that first white age! when wee
Lived by the Earths meere Charitie,
No soft luxurious Diet then
Had Effeminated men,
No other meat, nor wine had any
Then the Course Mast, or simple honey,
And by the Parents care layd up
Cheap *Berries* did the Children sup.
No pompous weare was in those dayes
Of gummie Silks, or Skarlet bayes, 10
Their beds were on some flowrie brink
And clear Spring-water was their drink.
The shadie Pine in the Suns heat
Was their Coole and known Retreat,
For then 'twas not cut down, but stood
The youth and glory of the wood.
The daring Sailer with his slaves
Then had not cut the swelling waves,
Nor for desire of forraign store
Seen any but his native shore. 20
No stirring Drum had scarr'd that age,
Nor the shrill Trumpets active rage,
No wounds by bitter hatred made
With warm bloud soil'd the shining blade;
For how could hostile madness arm
An age of love to publick harm?
When Common Justice none withstood,
Nor sought rewards for spilling bloud.
O that at length our age would raise
Into the temper of those dayes! 30
But (worse then *Ætna's* fires!) debate
And Avarice inflame our state.
Alas! who was it that first found
Gold hid of purpose under ground,
That sought out Pearles, and div'd to find
Such pretious perils for mankind!

Metrum 6

He that thirsts for glories prize,
    Thinking that the top of all
Let him view th'Expansed skies,
    And the Earths Contracted ball,
'Twill shame him then, the name he wan
Fils not the short *walk* of one man.

2

O why vainly strive you then
    To shake off the bands of Fate,
Though fame through the world of men
    Should in all tongues your names relate, 10
And with proud titles swell that storie
The Darke grave scorns your brightest glorie.

3

There with Nobles beggers sway,
    And Kings with Commons share one dust,
What newes of *Brutus* at this day,
    Or *Fabricius* the Just?
Some rude *Verse* Cut in stone, or led
    Keeps up the names, but they are dead.

4

So shall you, one day (past reprieve)
    Lye (perhaps) without a name, 20
But if dead you think to live
    By this aire of humane fame,
Know, when time stops that posthume breath,
You must endure a second death.

Metrum 7

That the world in constant *force*
Varies her *Concordant course*;
That *seeds* jarring *hot* and *cold*
Doe the *breed* perpetuall hold;

That in his golden Coach the *Sun*
Brings the *Rosie day* still on;
That the *Moon* swayes all those *lights*
Which *Hesper* ushers to *dark nights*
That *alternate tydes* be found
The Seas *ambitious* waves to bound, 10
Lest o'r the wide Earth without End
Their *fluid Empire* should extend;
All this frame of *things* that *be*,
Love which rules *Heaven*, *Land*, and *Sea*,
Chains, keeps, orders as we see.
This, if the raines he once cast by,
All things that now by turns comply,
Would fall to discord, and this frame
Which now by sociall faith they tame,
And comely orders in that fight 20
And jarre of things would perish quite.
This in a holy league of peace
Keeps King and People with Increase;
And in the sacred nuptiall bands
Tyes up chast hearts with willing hands,
And this keeps firm without all doubt
Friends by his bright Instinct found out.
O happy Nation then were you
If love which doth all things subdue,
That rules the spacious heav'n, and brings 30
Plenty and Peace upon his wings,
Might rule you too! and without guile
Settle once more this floting Ile!

Casimirus, *Lib*. 4. *Ode* 28

All-mighty *Spirit*! thou that by
Set *turns* and *changes* from thy high
And glorious *throne*, dost here below
Rule all, and all things dost *foreknow*;
Can those *blind plots* wee here discusse
Please thee, as thy *wise Counsels* us?

When thou thy *blessings* here dost strow,
And poure on *Earth*, we flock and flow
With *Joyous strife*, and *eager care*
Strugling which shall have the best share 10
In thy *rich gifts*, just as we see
Children about *Nuts* disagree.
Some that a *Crown* have got and foyl'd
Break it; Another sees it *spoil'd*
E're it is *gotten*: Thus the *world*
Is all to *peece-meals* cut, and hurl'd
By *factious hands*, It is a *ball*
Which *Fate* and *force* divide 'twixt all
The *Sons* of *men*. But ô good God!
While these for *dust* fight, and a *Clod*, 20
Grant that poore I may *smile*, and be
At rest, and *perfect peace* with thee.

Casimirus, Lib. 2. *Ode* 8

It would lesse vex *distressed man*
If *Fortune* in the same *pace* ran
To *ruine* him, as he did *rise*;
But highest *states* fall in a trice.
No *great Successe* held ever *long*:
A restless *fate* afflicts the throng
Of *Kings* and *Commons*, and lesse dayes
Serve to *destroy* them, then to *raise*.
Good luck *smiles* once an age, but *bad*
Makes *Kingdomes* in a *minute* sad, 10
And ev'ry *houre* of *life* wee drive,
Hath o're us a *Prerogative*.
Then leave (by *wild Impatience* driv'n,
And *rash resents*,) to rayle at *heav'n*,
Leave an *unmanly*, *weak complaint*
That *Death* and *Fate* have no restraint.
In the same houre that gave thee *breath*,
Thou hadst ordain'd thy houre of *death*,
But *he* lives *most*, who here will *buy*
With a few tears, *Eternitie*. 20

Casimirus, *Lib*. 3. *Ode* 22

Let not thy *youth* and *false delights*
Cheat thee of *life*; Those *headdy flights*
But wast thy *time*, which posts away
Like *winds* unseen, and swift as they.
Beauty is but meer *paint*, whose *die*
With times *breath* will *dissolve* and *flye*,
'Tis *wax*, 'tis *water*, 'tis a *glasse*
It *melts*, *breaks*, and *away* doth *passe*
'Tis like a *Rose* which in the *dawne*
The *aire* with gentle breath doth *fawne* 10
And *whisper* too, but in the houres
Of *night* is sullied with smart showres.
Life spent, is wish'd for but in vain,
Nor can past *years* come back again.
Happy the *Man*! who in this *vale*
Redeems his time, shutting out all
Thoughts of the *world*, whose *longing Eyes*
Are ever *Pilgrims* in the *skyes*,
That views his *bright home*, and desires
To *shine* amongst those *glorious fires*. 20

Casimirus Lyric. *Lib*. 3. *Ode* 23

'Tis not *rich furniture* and *gems*
With *Cedar-roofes*, and ancient *stems*,
Nor yet a *plenteous*, *lasting floud*
Of *gold*, that makes man *truly good*.
Leave to Inquire in what *faire fields*
A *River* runs which *much gold* yeelds,
Vertue alone is the *rich prize*
Can purchase *stars*, and buy the *skies*.
Let others build with *Adamant*,
Or pillars of *carv'd Marble* plant, 10
Which *rude* and *rough* sometimes did dwell
Far under *earth*, and neer to *hell*.
But *richer* much (from *death* releast)
Shines in the *fresh groves* of the *East*

The *Phœnix*, or those *fish* that dwell
With *silver'd scales* in *Hiddekel.*
Let others with rare, various *Pearls*
Their *garments* dresse, and in *forc'd Curls*
Bind up their *locks*, look *big* and *high*,
And shine in *robes* of *Scarlet-die.* 20
But in my thoughts more *glorious* far
Those *native stars*, and *speckles* are
Which *birds* wear, or the *spots* which wee
In *Leopards* dispersed see.
The harmless *sheep* with her warm *fleece*
Cloathes *man*, but who his *dark heart* sees
Shall find a *Wolfe* or *Fox* within
That kills the *Castor* for his *skin.*
Vertue alone, and nought else can
A diffrence make 'twixt *beasts* and *man*, 30
And on her *wings* above the *Spheres*
To the *true light* his *spirit* bears.

Casimirus, *Lib.* 4. *Ode* 15

Nothing on *Earth*, nothing at all
Can be exempted from the *thrall*
Of peevish *weariness*! The *Sun*
Which our *fore-fathers* Judg'd to run
Clear and *unspotted*, in our dayes
Is tax'd with *sullen*, *Ecclips'd rayes.*
What ever in the *glorious skie*
Man sees, his rash, *audacious Eye*
Dares Censure it, and in meer *spite*
At *distance* will condemn the *light.* 10
The *wholsome mornings*, whose *beams* cleer
Those *hills* our *fathers* walkt on here
Wee fancy not, nor the *Moons* light
Which through their *windows* shin'd at *night*,
Wee change the *Aire* each year, and scorn
Those *Seates*, in which we first were *borne.*
Some nice, affected *wand'rers* love
Belgia's mild winter's, others remove

For want of *health* and *honestie*
To *Summer* it in *Italie*; 20
But to no end: The *disease* still
Sticks to his *Lord*, and kindly will
To *Venice* in a *Barge* repaire,
Or *Coach* it to *Vienna's* aire,
And then (too late with *home* Content,)
They leave this *wilfull banishment*.
But he, whose *Constancie* makes sure
His *mind* and *mansion*, lives secure
From such *vain tasks*, can *dine* and *sup*
Where his *old parents* bred him up. 30
Content (no doubt!) most times doth dwell
In *Countrey-shades*, or to some *Cell*
Confines it selfe, and can alone
Make simple *straw*, a Royall *Throne*.

Casimirus, *Lib*. 4. *Ode* 13

If *weeping Eyes* could wash away
Those *Evills* they mourn for *night and day*,
Then gladly I to *cure* my *fears*
With my best *Jewells* would buy *tears*.
But as *dew* feeds the growing *Corn*,
So *Crosses* that are grown *forlorn*
Increase with *griefe*, *teares* make *teares* way,
And *cares* kept up, keep *cares* in *pay*.
That *wretch* whom *Fortune* finds to *feare*,
And *melting* still into a *teare*, 10
She *strikes* more *boldly*, but a *face*
Silent and *drie* doth her *amaze*.
Then leave thy *teares*, and tedious *tale*
Of what thou doest *misfortunes* call,
What thou by *weeping* think'st to *ease*,
Doth by that *Passion* but *Increase*;
Hard things to *Soft* will never yield,
'Tis the *drie Eye* that wins the field;
A noble *patience* quells the *spite*
Of *Fortune*, and *disarms* her quite. 20

The Praise of a Religious life by *Mathias Casimirus.* In Answer to that Ode of *Horace*, *Beatus Ille qui procul negotiis*, &c.

Flaccus not so: That worldly *He*
Whom in the Countreys *shade* we see
Ploughing his own *fields*, seldome can
Be justly stil'd, *The Blessed man.*
  That title only fits a *Saint*,
Whose free thoughts far above restraint
And weighty Cares, can gladly part
With *house* and *lands*, and leave the smart
Litigious troubles, and lowd strife
Of this world for a better life. 10
He fears no *Cold*, nor *heat* to blast
His *Corn*, for his *Accounts* are cast,
He *sues* no man, nor stands in Awe
Of the *devouring Courts* of Law;
But all his time he spends in *tears*
For the *Sins* of his youthfull years,
Or having tasted those *rich Joyes*
Of a Conscience without *noyse*
Sits in some fair *shade*, and doth give
To his *wild thoughts* rules how to live. 20
  He in the *Evening*, when on high
The *Stars* shine in the *silent skye*
Beholds th'*eternall flames* with mirth,
And *globes* of *light* more large then *Earth*,
Then weeps for *Joy*, and through his tears
Looks on the *fire-enamel'd* Spheres,
Where with his *Saviour* he would be
Lifted above mortalitie.
Mean while the *golden stars* doe set,
And the *slow-Pilgrim* leave all wet 30
With his own tears, which flow so fast
They make his *sleeps* light, and soon past.
By this, the *Sun* o're night *deceast*
Breaks in *fresh Blushes* from the *East*,

When mindfull of his former *falls*
With *strong Cries* to his *God* he calls,
And with such *deep-drawn sighes* doth move
That he turns *anger* into *love.*
  In the Calme *Spring*, when the Earth *bears*,
And feeds on *Aprils breath*, and *tears*, 40
His Eyes accustom'd to the *skyes*
Find here *fresh objects*, and like *spyes*
Or busie *Bees* search the soft *flowres*
Contemplate the *green fields*, and *Bowres*,
Where he in *Veyles*, and *shades* doth see
The *back Parts* of the *Deitye.*
Then sadly sighing sayes, ,*O how*
,*These flowres With hasty, stretch'd heads grow*
,*And strive for heav'n, but rooted here*
,*Lament the distance with a teare!* 50
,*The Honey-suckles Clad in white,*
,*The Rose in Red point to the light,*
,*And the Lillies hollow and bleak*
,*Look, as if they would something speak,*
,*They sigh at night to each soft gale,*
,*And at the day-spring weep it all.*
,*Shall I then only* (*wretched I!*)
,*Opprest with Earth, on Earth still lye?*
Thus speaks he to the neighbour trees
And many sad *Soliloquies* 60
To *Springs*, and *Fountaines* doth impart,
Seeking God with a longing heart.
  But if to ease his busie breast
He thinks of *home*, and taking rest,
A *Rurall Cott*, and *Common fare*
Are all his *Cordials* against *Care.*
There at the *doore* of his low *Cell*
Under some *shade*, or neer some *Well*
Where the *Coole Poplar* growes, his *Plate*
Of Common *Earth*, without more *state* 70
Expect their *Lord. Salt* in a *shell*,
Green *Cheese*, thin *beere*, *Draughts* that will *tell*
No *Tales*, a *hospitable Cup*,
With some *fresh berries* doe make up

His healthfull feast, nor doth he wish
For the fatt *Carp*, or a rare dish
Of *Lucrine Oysters*; The swift *Quist*
Or *Pigeon* sometimes (if he list)
With the *slow Goose* that loves the *stream*,
Fresh, various *Sallads*, and the *Bean* 80
By Curious *Pallats* never sought,
And to Close with, some Cheap unbought
Dish for *digestion*, are the most
And Choicest *dainties* he can *boast*.
Thus feasted, to the *flowrie Groves*,
Or pleasant *Rivers* he removes,
Where neer some *fair Oke* hung with Mast
He shuns the *Souths* Infectious blast.
On shadie *banks* sometimes he lyes,
Sometimes the open *Current tryes*, 90
Where with his *line* and *feather'd flye*
He sports, and takes the *Scaly frie*.
Mean-while each *hollow wood* and *hill*
Doth ring with *lowings* long and shrill,
And shadie *Lakes* with *Rivers* deep,
Eccho the *bleating* of the *Sheep*.
The *Black-bird* with the pleasant *Thrush*
And *Nightingale* in ev'ry Bush
Choice *Musick* give, and *Shepherds* play
Unto their *flocks* some loving *Lay*; 100
The thirsty *Reapers* in thick throngs
Return home from the *field* with Songs,
And the *Carts* loden with ripe *Corn*
Come groning to the well-stor'd *Barn*.
Nor passe wee by as the least good,
A *peacefull*, *loving neighbourhood*,
Whose *honest Wit*, and *Chast discourse*
Make none (by hearing it) the *worse*,
But *Innocent* and *merry* may
Help (without *Sin*) to spend the day. 110
Could now the *Tyrant-usurer*
Who *plots* to be a *Purchaser*
Of his poor neighbours *seat*, but taste
These *true delights*, ô with what haste

And hatred of his wayes would he
Renounce his *Jewish Crueltie*,
And those *Curs'd summes* which poor men borrow
On *use* to day, *remit* to morrow!

Ad fluvium Iscam

Isca *parens florum, placido qui spumeus ore*
Lambis lapillos aureos,
Qui mœstos hyacinthos, & picti ἄνθεα *tophi*
Mulces susurris humidis,
Dumq; novas *pergunt* menses *Consumere* Lunas
Cœlumq; mortales *terit,*
Accumulas cum Sole *dies, œvumq; per omne*
Fidelis *Induras* latex,
O quis Inaccessos & quali murmure lucos
Mutumq; *Solaris* nemus! 10
Per te discerpti credo Thracis *ire querelas*
Plectrumq; divini senis.

Venerabili viro, præceptori suo olim & semper Colendissimo Mro. Mathæo Herbert

Quod vixi, Mathæe, *dedit* Pater, *hæc tamen olim*
Vita fluet, nec erit fas meminisse datam.
Ultrà Curâsti Solers, perituraq; mecum
Nomina post Cineres *das resonare* meos.
Divide discipulum: brevis hæc & lubrica nostri
Pars vertat Patri, *Posthuma vita* tibi.

Præstantissimo viro, Thomæ Poëllo *in suum de Elementis opticæ libellum*

Vivaces *oculorum* Ignes & lumina dia
Fixit in angusto *maximus* orbe *Deus,*
Ille Explorantes radios *dedit*, & vaga lustra
In quibus Intuitûs *lexq; modusq; latent.*

Hos tacitos Jactus, lususq; volubilis orbis
Pingis in Exiguo, *magne Poëlle*, libro,
Excursusq; situsq;, *ut* Lynceus opticus, *edis*
Quotq; modis fallunt, *quotq; adhibenda* fides.
Æmula naturæ manus*!* & mens *Conscia cœli!*
Illa videre dedit, *vestra videre* docet. 10

Ad Echum

O Quæ frondosæ per amœna Cubilia *sylvæ*
Nympha volas, *lucoq;* loquax *spatiaris in alto*,
Annosi numen *nemoris*, *saltusq; verendi*
Effatum, *cui sola placent* postrema *relatu!*
Te per Narcissi *morientis verba*, *precesq;*
Per pueri Lassatam animam, & Conamina *vitæ*
Ultima, *palantisq; precor* suspiria *linguæ.*
Da quo secretæ hæc Incædua devia *sylvæ*,
Anfractusq; *loci dubios*, & lustra *repandam.*
Sic tibi perpetuâ (*meritoq;*) *hæc regna* Juventâ 10
Luxurient, *dabiturq; tuis*, *sinè fine*, viretis
Intactas *Lunæ* lachrymas, & *lambere* rorem
Virgineum, *Cæliq;* animas *haurire tepentis.*
Nec cedant ævo stellis, *sed* lucida *sempèr*
Et satiata sacro *æterni* medicamine *veris*
Ostendant longè vegetos, *ut Sydera*, vultus*!*
Sic spiret Muscata Comas, & Cynnama *passim!*
Diffundat levis umbra, *in funere qualia spargit*
Phœnicis rogus *aut Pancheæ* nubila *flammæ!*

THE
MOUNT of OLIVES:
OR,
SOLITARY DEVOTIONS.

By

HENRY VAUGHAN *Silurist.*

With

An excellent Discourse of the blessed state of MAN in GLORY, written by the most Reverend and holy Father ANSELM Arch-Bishop of *Canterbury*, and now done into English.

LUKE 21. v. 39, 37.

Watch ye therefore, and pray always, that ye may be accompted worthy to escape all these things that shall come to passe, and to stand before the Sonne of Man.

And in the day time he was teaching in the Temple, and at night he went out, and abode in the Mount that is called the Mount of Olives.

LONDON, Printed for WILLIAM LEAKE at the Crown in Fleet-street between the two Temple-Gates 1652.

TO THE

Truly Noble and Religious
Sr. CHARLES EGERTON
KNIGHT

SIR,

Though I should have no other *defence*, that near *relation* by which my *dearest friend* laies claime to your *person*, might in some measure excuse this otherwise *unhansome adventure* of publishing these *weake productions* under the *shelter* of your *name*. But I was not so much induced to *it* by that *Tye*, though very deare unto me, as by your *love* to *Religion* and *Learning*, and the *respects* due from my selfe to your *person*, and those *reverend years*, which by a *faire* and *virtuous disposal* of your *time* you have happily attained to, 10 and wherein you *safely* are,

—— *Cœlo dignus canente senectâ*
Consilioque deûm, ——

I know, *Sir*, you will be pleased to accept of this poore *Olive-leafe* presented to you, so that I shall not be driven to put forth my hand to take in my *Dove* againe. And indeed (considering how *fast* and how *soone* men degenerate), It must be counted for a great *blessing*, that there is yet any left which dares *look* upon, and *commiserate* distressed Religion. *Good men* in *bad times* are very scarce; They are like the *standing eares of Corne escaped out of the* 20 *Reapers hands*, or the *Vine-dressers last gleanings after the first ripe fruits have been gathered.* Such a *precious generation are the Just* in the *day of trouble*, and their *names* are like to *afflicted truth*, like the *shadow of a great rock in a weary land*, or a *wayfaring mans lodge in the waste and howling Wildernesse.* The *Sonne* of *God* himselfe (when *he* was *here*,) had no place to put his head in; And his *Servants* must not think the *present measure* too hard, seeing their *Master* himself took up his *nights-lodging* in the cold *Mount* of *Olives*.

By this time, *Sir*, you may see the *reason* which moved me to 30 take *Sanctuary* at your *name*, and now I will acquaint you with my *designe*. To be short, *Sir*, It is no other, but that your *name* (like the *royall stamp*) may make *current* and commend this *poore mite* to posterity: And that the unfained *lover* of your *Person* may in these few and *transitory sheets* waite upon your memory in the ages to come; when your immortal and precious *soule* shall be bound up in the bundle of the living, in the *ever-lasting book* of life; which is devoutly desired by

SIR,

Newton by *Usk*
this first of
October
1651

Your very affectionate
and faithful Servant

VAVGHAN 10

TO THE
Peaceful, humble, and pious READER

I know the world abounds with these Manuals, and triumphs over them. It is not then their scarsity that call'd this forth, nor yet a desire to crosse the age, nor any in it. I envie not their frequent Extasies, *and raptures to the third heaven; I onely wish them real, and that their actions did not tell the world, they are rapt into some other place. Nor should they, who assume to themselves the glorious stile of Saints, be uncharitably moved, if we that are yet in the body, and carry our treasure in earthen vessels, have need of these helps.*

It is for thy good, and for his glory, who in the dayes of his flesh 10 *prayed here himselfe, and both taught and commanded us to pray, that I have published this. Thou hast here sound directions and wholsome words, and if thou wilt enquire of the Lord and say,* If the Lord will, I shall live, and do this or that, *thou mayest. Here are* Morning *and* Evening *sacrifices, with holy and apposite* Ejaculations *for most times and occasions. And lastly, here are very faithful and necessary Precepts and Meditations before we come to the Lords Table. To which last part I have added a short and plaine Discourse of Death, with a Prayer in the houre thereof. And for thy comfort after thou hast past through that* Golgotha, *I have annexed a Dissertation of* 20 *the blessed state of the righteous after this life, written originally by holy* Anselme *sometimes Arch-Bishop of* Canterbury.

I *have purposely avoided to leade thee into this little Book with a large discourse of Devotion, what it is, with the severall Heads, Divisions, and sub-divisions of it, all these being but so many fruitlesse curiosities of Schoole-Divinity,* Cui fumus est pro fundamento. *Neither did I thinke it necessary that the ordinary Instructions for a regular life (of which theere are infinite Volumes already extant) should be inserted into this small Manuall, lest instead of Devotion, I should trouble thee with a peece of Ethics. Besides, thou hast them* 30 *already as briefly delivered as possibly I could, in my* Sacred Poems.

And thus, Christian Reader, do I commend it to thy practise, and the benefit thou shalt finde thereby. Onely I shall adde this short Exhortation: That thou wouldest not be discouraged in this way, because very many are gone out of it. Think not that thou art alone upon this Hill, there is an innumerable company both before and behinde thee. Those with their Palms in their hands, and these expecting them. If therefore the dust of this world chance to prick thine eyes, suffer it not to blinde them; but running thy race with patience, look to JESUS the Authour and finisher of thy faith, who when he was reviled, reviled not againe. Presse thou towards the mark, *and let the people and their Seducers rage*; be faithful unto the death, and he will give thee a Crowne of life. *Look not upon transitorie, visible things, but upon him that is eternal, and invisible. Choose the better part, yea, that part with Saint* Hierome, *who preferred the poore Coate of* Paul *the Hermite to the purple and pride* 10 *of the world. Thus with my simple Advise unto thee, I bid thee farewel.*

Thy Christian friend

Henry Vaughan.

The Table

FINIS

ADMONITIONS
FOR *Morning-Prayer*

The night (saith *Chrysostome*) was not therefore made, that either we should sleep it out, or passe it away idly; and Chiefly because we see many worldly persons to watch out whole nights for the Commodities of this life. In the *Primitive* Church also the *Saints* of God used to rise at midnight to praise the *Rock of their salvation* with *Hymns and Spiritual Songs*. In the same manner shouldst thou do now, and Contemplate the *Order* of the Stars, and how they all in their several stations praise their Creator. When all the world is asleep, thou shouldst watch, weep and pray and propose unto thy self that *Practise* of the Psalmist, *I am weary of my groaning*, *every night wash I my bed*, *and water my Couch with my tears;* for as the *Dew* which falls by night is most fructifying, and tempers the heat of the *Sun*; so the tears we shed in the night, make the soul fruitful, quench all Concupiscence, and supple the hardnesse we got in the day. *Christ* himself in the day-time taught and preach'd, but continued all night in prayer, sometimes in a Mountain apart, sometimes amongst the wild beasts, and sometimes in solitary places. 10

They, whose Age or Infirmity will not give them way to do thus, should use all Convenient means to be up before the Sun-rising, for *we must prevent the Sunne to give God thanks*, *and at the day-spring pray unto him*, Wisd. 16. It was in the morning that the Children of *Israel* gathered the *Manna*; and of the Just man it is said, *That He will give his heart to resort early to the Lord that made him*, *and will pray before the most high*, Eccl. 39. So soon therefore as thou dost awake, shut thy door against all prophane and worldly thoughts, and before all things let thy God be first admitted, offer unto him thy first fruits for that day, and commune with him after this manner. 20

When thou dost awake 30

O God the Father! who saidst in the beginning, *Let there be light*, and it was so; *Inlighten my Eyes that I never sleepe in death:* lest at any time my Enemy should say, *I have prevailed against him*.

O God the Sonne! light of light; the most true and perfect light, from whom this light of the Sun, and the day had their beginning; thou, that art the light shining in darknesse, Inlightning every one that cometh into this world, expell from me all Clouds of Ignorance, and give me true understanding, that in thee, and by thee I may know the *Father*; whom to know is to live, and to serve is to reigne.

O God the Holy Ghost! the fire that inlightens, and warms our hearts, shed into me thy most sacred light, that I may know the 10 true Joyes of Heaven, and see to escape the illusions of this world. Ray thy selfe into my soul that I may see what an Exceeding weight of glory my Enemy would bereave me of for the meer shadowes and painting of this world. Grant that I may know those things which belong unto thee, and nothing else; Inflame me with thy divine love that with a true Christian Contempt I may tread upon all transitory Pleasures, and seek only those things which are eternal.

Most blessed Trinity! and one eternal God! as thou hast this day awaked me from this bodily sleep, so awake my soule from 20 the sleep of sin, and as thou hast given me strength after sleep, now again to watch, so after death give me life, for what is death to me, is but sleep with thee, to whom be ascribed all glory, wisdome, majesty, dominion and praise now and for Ever, Amen.

When thou dost arise

Arise O my soul that sleepest, arise from the dead, and Christ shall give thee light. Arise O daughter of *Sion*, O my soul redeemed with the blood of Christ! sit no more in the dust of thy sins, but arise, and rest in that peace which is purchas'd by thy Saviours 30 merits.

Christ Jesus! my most merciful and dear Redeemer! as it is thy meer goodness that lifts up this mortal and burthensome body, so let thy grace lift up my soul to the true knowledge and love of thee; grant also that my body may this day be a helper and servant to my soul in all good works, that both *body* and *soul* may be partakers of those Endlesse Joyes, where thou livest and reignest with the Father and the Holy Ghost, one true God world without End, *Amen*.

As soone as thou art drest, before thou comest forth from thy Chamber, kneel down in some convenient place, and in this, or the like Prayer commend thy self for that day unto thy Creator's Protection.

Almighty, eternal God, the Father of our Lord *Jesus Christ*, I blesse and praise thy holy name, and with my whole heart give thee all possible thanks, that out of thine infinite goodness thou wert pleased to watch over me this night, to resist my adversary, and to keep me from all perils of body and soul; O thou! that never slumbrest nor sleepest, how careful hast thou been of me! how 10 hast thou protected me, and with thy holy angels, thy ministring spirits sent forth to minister for the heirs of salvation, incompast me about! yea, with what unmeasurable love hast thou restored unto me the light of the day, and rais'd me from sleep and the shadow of death, to look up to thy holy hill; Justly mightst thou, O God, have shut the gates of death upon me, and laid me for ever under the barres of the Earth, but thou hast redeemed me from Corruption, and with thy *Everlasting armes* enlarged my time of Repentance.

And now O Father of mercies, and God of all Consolation, hear 20 the voyce of thy Supplicant, and let my cry be heard in thy highest heavens: As I do sincerely love thee, and beg for thy Protection, so receive thou me under the shadow of thy wings, watch over me with the Eyes of thy mercy, direct me in the wayes of thy Law, and enrich me with the gifts of thy Spirit, that I may passe through this day, to the glory of thy great name, the good of others, and the comfort of my own soul. Keep me, O my God, from the great offence; quench in me all vain Imaginations, and sensual desires; sanctifie and supple my heart with the dew of thy divine Spirit, refresh it with the streams of thy grace, that I may bring forth 30 fruit in due season, and not cumber the ground, nor be cut off in thy anger. And to this end I do here resigne my body and my soul, with all the faculties thou hast bestowed upon both, into thy Almighty hands; Guide thou them in the works of thy Law, turne my eyes from all transitory objects, to the things which are eternal, and from the *Cares* and *Pride* of this world to the *fowles of the aire* and the *Lillies of the field*; And now, O my God, seeing I am but Dust and Ashes, and my Righteousnesse a filthy Rag, having no deserts in my self but what should draw Everlasting vengeance, and the Vials of thy bitter wrath upon my body and soul; behold, 40

I have brought with me thy first-born and onely begotten, the propitiation for my sins, the *Incense* I offer up with my prayers, *Rev.* 8. 3. my Redeemer and Mediatour in whom thou art well-pleased, hear thou him. O look not upon my Leprosie, but on his beauty and perfection! and for the righteousnesse of thy *Son*, forgive the sins of thy *Servant*. Grant this for his sake, to whom with thee and the Holy Ghost, be all glory and majesty, Dominion and power now and for ever. Amen.

Admonitions when we prepare for any farre Journey

10 When thou art to go from home, remember that thou art to come forth into the *World*, and to Converse with an Enemy; And what else is the World but a Wildernesse? A darksome, intricate wood full of *Ambushes* and dangers; A Forrest where spiritual hunters, principalities and powers spread their nets, and compasse it about; wouldst thou then escape these ghostly snares; this *wickednes in high places*, and return home if not better and holier, yet not worse then at thy setting out? Wouldst thou with *Jacob* passe over these *Waters* with thy staffe onely, and in thy return become two bands? *Gen.* 32. 10. Why then, do as he did, begin 20 thy Journey with prayer, and say, *If God will be with me*, *and keep me in this way that I go*, *and will give me bread to eate*, *and raiment to put on*, *so that I come again to my fathers house in peace: then shall the Lord be my God*, Gen. 28. 20, 21. This was his practise, and the practise of his fathers; *The Lord God of heaven* (saith *Abraham*) *who took me from my fathers house*, *and from the land of my kindred*, *&c. he shall send his Angel before thee*. Nor must thou pray only at thy setting forth, but all the way, and at all times; Thus *Eliezer* prayed at the Well, *Isaac* in the field, and *Elias* (in his journey to *Mount Horeb*) under a *Juniper* tree in the Wildernesse. 30 This also (if thou wilt imitate these holy men) thou may'st do, and for that pious purpose thou hast here these following Prayers.

When we go from home

Almighty and everlasting God, who art the *Way*, the *Life* and the *Truth*; look down from heaven, and behold me now betwixt the Assaults of the Devil, the allurements of the World, and my own inclinations; I cannot look abroad, but these flock about me; But O thou that leadest *Joseph* like a sheep, thou most faithful and Almighty guide, lend me thy hand, open mine Eyes, direct my steps, and cause me to walk in thy fear; Thou that didst go out with *Jacob* from *Beer-she-ba* unto *Padan-aran*, guiding him in the *waste plaines*, and watching over him on his *Pillow of stones*, be not now farre from me; Leade me, O Lord, in thy righteousnesse, make my paths straight, and strengthen my goings, that having finished my Course here, I may sit down in thy Kingdome, an Inheritance undefiled, purchased for me with the blood of my Saviour, and thy beloved Son *Jesus Christ*, Amen.

II

O thou, that art every where! *Thou that sittest upon the Circle of the Earth, and all the Inhabitants thereof are as Grashoppers before thee! Whose Eyes discover the deep things of the night, before whom Hell is naked, and all the Devices of my spirituall Enemies!* Thou that didst leade *Abraham* thy chosen from *Ur* of the *Chaldees* into a land flowing with milk and honey, favour I beseech thee the present harmlesse Enterprise and innocent purpose of thy servant, be unto me in my Journey a Comfort, in the heate a shadow, in stormes a shelter, and in adversity my protection; That having finished my intended course, I may return in peace full of thy praises, who art near to all those that call upon thee; Grant this for *Christ Jesus* his sake, *Amen*.

Meditate in the way upon the sojournings and travels of the Patriarchs and Prophets, the many weary journeys of *Jesus Christ* in the flesh, the travels of his Apostles by sea and land, with the pilgrimage and peregrinations of many other precious Saints that wandred in Deserts and Mountains, of whom the world was not worthy.

Admonitions how to carry thy self in the Church

Holinesse (saith the Royall Prophet) *becometh thy house for ever*. When thou art going thither then, carry not the world with thee.

Let vain or busie thoughts have there no part,
Bring not thy *Plough*, thy *Plots*, thy *Pleasures* thither,
Christ purg'd his Temple; so must thou thy heart.
All worldly thoughts are but Theeves met together
To Cousin thee. Look to thy actions well,
For *Churches* are either our Heav'n or Hell.

These reverend and sacred buildings (however now vilified and shut up) have ever been, and amongst true Christians still are the solemne and publike places of meeting for Divine Worship: There the *flocks feed at noon-day*, there the great *Shepherd* and *Bishop* of their souls is *in the midst of them*, and where he is, that *Ground is holy*; Put off thy shoes then, thy worldly and carnall affections, and when thou beginnest to enter in, say with *Jacob*, *How dreadful is this place! sure this is none other then the house of God, and this is the gate of heaven!* Such reverence and religious affection hath 10 in all ages been shew'd towards these places, that the holy men of God detain'd either by Captivity, or other necessary occasions, when they could not remedy the distance, yet to testifie their *desire and longing for the Courts of the Lord*, Psal. 84. they would always worship towards them. Thus *Daniel* upon the Idolatrous Decree signed by *Darius*, *goes into his house, and his windows being open in his Chamber towards Jerusalem, he kneeled upon his knees, and prayed and gave thanks before his God as he did afore-time*, Dan. 6. 10. which fully proves it to have been his Constant manner of Devotion. And of *Judith* we read *that about the time that the* 20 *Incense of that Evening was offered up in* Hierusalem, *she cried unto the Lord*, *Iud.* 9. 1. But above all, most pathetical and earnest is that crie of King *David* in the 85. *Psalm*.

How amiable are thy Tabernacles O Lord of Hosts!

My soul longeth, yea even fainteth for the Lord, my heart and my flesh cryeth out for the living God.

Yea the Sparrow hath found an house, and the Swallow a nest for her selfe, where she may lay her young, even thine Altars, O Lord of Hosts, my God and my King!

Blessed are they that dwell in thy house, they will be still praising 30 *thee.*

For one day in thy Courts is better than a thousand; I had rather be a doore-keeper in the House of my God, than to dwell in the tents of wickednesse.

Let it be thy Care then, when thou art there present to carry thy self like a true worshipper; Give none offence, neither outwardly to thy *Brethren*, nor the *Angels*, 1 Cor. 11. 10. Nor inwardly to thy God, whose Eyes shine within thee, and discern thy reins and thy heart. Look seriously about thee, and Consider with thy self how many beauteous, wittie, and hopeful personages in their time lie now under thy feet; thou canst not tell but thy turn may be next. Humble thy self in this dust, and all vain Imaginations will flie from thee. Consider that thou art now in the *Cave of Macpelah*, in a sacred *Repositorie* where the Bodies of Saints are asleep, expecting that hour, *when those that are in the grave shall hear his voyce*. Do not then stop thy eares against the *Charmer*, but give diligent attention, and hear him while it is yet to day, that in the day of thy death thou mayst rest there in the same hope. When thy vessell is fill'd with this *Manna*, and thy soul satisfied, go not off without Thanksgiving; Be not like those nine *Leapers* who never returned 10 to give glory to God; but come back with the thankfull *Samaritane*, and receive another blessing, *Go in peace*. Saint *Luke* in the *Acts* of the Apostles making mention of the *Ethiopian Eunuch*, who came up to *Jerusalem* for to worship, tells us, that in his returne he was reading in *Isaiah* the Prophet; This blessed *Convert* I would have thee to imitate: When thou hast fill'd thy *Hin* with this living water, leave it not behinde thee at the Fountain; spill not thy *Milk* and thy *Wine*, because thou hast it without *money and without price*, but carry it home and use it. Thou mayest have need of it in six dayes, and perhaps shalt not come to draw again, untill thou 20 drinkest it anew with thy Saviour in *his Fathers Kingdom*.

A Prayer before thou goest to Church

Lord *Jesus Christ*, who out of thy Fathers bosome wert sent into this world to reveal his will unto sinners, and to instruct them in the way of salvation; behold, I am now going to hear thy blessed word, and these many yeers have so done, expecting still thy good pleasure and the Consummation of thy sacred will in me. I have come unto the bread of life, and yet am hungry; into the light, and yet am blind; unto the great Physician, and yet my Issue runs: The former and the later rain of thy heavenly Doctrine falls still 30 without intermission upon my heart, but this bad ground yeelds nothing but Thornes and Briers. Many dayes, many moneths, and many yeers hast thou expected fruit, and found nothing but leaves. It is thy Infinite mercy, O Lord, that thou hast left unto us the seed of thy word, and sendest into thy harvest such upright and faithful labourers; but in vain, O Lord, shall they cry in our Ears, unlesse thou openest and renewest our hearts. Open then, I beseech thee (O blessed Jesu!) the eares of my heart, that not onely the outward hearing, but the inward also may be stirr'd up in me, and what I hear with the eare, I may understand with the spirit. O thou most mild and merciful *Lamb of God!* the onely, and the Almighty sower! grant, I beseech thee, that the seed which falls this day upon my heart, may never be choak'd with the Cares of this world, nor be devoured by the fowles of the aire, nor wither away in these times of persecution and triall: but so Cherish it with the Dew of thy divine spirit, that (as in a good and faithful ground) it may bring forth fruit unto eternal life, to the glory of thy great name, and the Comfort of my poor soul, which 10 thou hast bought with thy most precious and saving blood. *Amen.*

Another when thou art come home, or in the way if thou beest alone

Lord *Jesus Christ*, my ever mercifull, and most loving Redeemer! I give unto thee most hearty thanks for this thy heavenly, spiritual provision wherewith thou hast fed and refreshed my soul. Grant I beseech thee that this Celestial seed may take root in me, and be effectual to my salvation; Watch over my heart, O Lord, and hedge it in with thy grace, that the fowles which descend in the shadows 20 of the Evening may not pick it out; But so prepare and fit me for thy love, that I may never forget thy gracious words, thy blessed and saving advice, but may know in *this my day what belongs unto my peace*. It is thy promise by thy holy Prophet, *That as the rain cometh down, and the snow from heaven, and returneth not thither, but watereth the earth, and maketh it bring forth and bud, that it may give seed to the sower, and bread to the eater: So thy word that goeth forth out of thy mouth, shall not return unto thee void, but shall accomplish that which thou pleasest, and prosper in the thing whereto thou sendest it*, Isai. 55. 10, 11. Even so, Lord *Jesus*, let it be as 30 thou hast promised. Let the words I have heard this day out of the mouth of thy servant, the *Dispenser*, and *Steward* of thy Mysteries prosper in me, and make my life answerable to his Doctrine; that I may not onely know what thy blessed will is, but performe also and fulfill it; so that at last by thy mediation and mercies I may attain to thy eternal and most glorious Kingdom. *Amen.*

Admonitions for Evening-Prayer

Remember that in the *Levitical* Law there is a frequent Commemoration and Charge given of the two daily Sacrifices, the one to be offer'd up in the morning and the other in the Evening, *Exod.* 30. 7, 8. These offerings by *Incense*, our holie, harmlesse and undefiled High-Priest hath taken away, and instead of them every devout *Christian* is at the appointed times to offer up a Spiritual Sacrifice, namely that of *Prayer*; for *God is a Spirit, and they that worship him, must worship him in spirit and in truth*, John 4. 24. At these prescribed times (if thou wilt have thy Prayers to ascend up before God) thou must with-draw from all outward occupations to prepare for the inward and divine. To which end thou hast here this following Meditation, that thou maiest therewith season and invite thy soul from thy worldlie imployments to her proper vocation, and so come not altogether undrest into the presence of the *King of glory*.

A Meditation at the setting of the Sun, or the Souls Elevation to the true light

The path of the Just (O my God) is as the shining light, that shineth more and more unto a perfect day of eternity, *Prov.* 4. But the wicked neither know, nor understand, they walk in darknesse, and from the inward darknesse of their minds passe at last into the outward, eternal darknesse. O most miserable and undone soul! to whom thy *Sunne* is set; that everlasting glorious *Sun*! which in thy holy Elects never setteth, but is alwaies at the height, full of brightnesse and Consolation. A heavie night sits in the noone-day upon those souls that have forsaken thee; They look for light, and behold darknesse; for brightnesse, and they walk in obscurity. They grope for the wall like the blind, as if they had no Eyes; They stumble at noone-day as in the night, they are in desolate places as dead men. But on those that walk with thee an everlasting day shines; This *Sun* of the firmament hath his Course; it riseth, setteth, comes up again, and again goes down: But thou Lord, knowest no vicissitudes, thou art the *Ancient of dayes*, thou art the *Rock of ages from Everlasting to Everlasting*. O thou, *the same to day and yesterday, and for evermore! Thou bright and morning Starre springing from on high*, illuminate me, who am now sitting in darknesse and in the shadow of death. *O light of light, the brightnesse of thy Fathers glory*, inlighten all inward obscurities in me, that after this life I may never be cast into the outward darknesse. O most blessed, most merciful, and Almighty *Jesu*! abide I beseech thee with me, *for it is towards Evening, and the day*

is far spent, Luke 24. As long as thou art present with me, I am in the light, but when thou art gone, I am in the shadows of death, and amongst the stones of emptinesse. When thou art present, all is brightnesse, all is sweetnesse, I am in my Gods bosome, I discourse with him, watch with him, walk with him, live with him, and lie down with him. All these most dear and unmeasurable blessings I have with thee, and want them without thee. Abide then with me, O thou whom my soul loveth! Thou Sun of righteousnesse with healing under thy wings arise in my heart; refine,
10 quicken, and cherish it; make thy light there to shine in darknesse, and a perfect day in the dead of night.

A Prayer for the Evening

Most gracious, Almighty God! full of loving kindnesse, and long-suffering, whose mercy is above all thy works, and thy glory above the heavens; whose truth reacheth unto the Clouds, and whose words shall never passe away, forgive me, I beseech thee, my transgressions this day, my vain thoughts, idle words, and loose conversation; my exceeding neglect and forgetfulnesse of thee, my head-long inclinations and lusting after the world, preferring
20 this land of *Cabul* before the snow of *Lebanon*, and a broken Cistern before the Well of life. Justly, O Lord, might'st thou have shewed me thy back this day, and cut me off from amongst thy people, *Jer*. 18. 17. but thou hast had mercy, and not sacrifice; thou hast shed upon me the light of thy Countenance, and removed my sins farre out of thy sight. I know, O my God, it is not in man to establish his own ways, it is thy Almighty arme must do it; It is thou alone that hast led me through this day, and kept me both from doing and from suffering evill. And now, O thou preserver of men! What shall I do unto thee? What shall I render unto my Lord for
30 all the mercies and loving kindnesses shewed unto thy servant this day, and all the dayes of my life hitherto? *I will offer unto thee the sacrifice of thanksgiving, and call upon the name of the Lord.* I will ever love thee, fear thee, praise thee, and trust in thee; My song shall be of thee in the night season, and in the day time I will be speaking of thy wondrous works, thy most merciful and liberal arme; I will make thee my *Delight* in the house of my pilgrimage, and I shall alwayes with all my strength, with all my heart, and with all my soul ascribe unto thee, all glory, wisdome, majesty, dominion, and honour this day and for evermore. *Amen.*

A Prayer when thou art going into bed

Most glorious, and onely wise God! to whom the light and the darknes are the same, whose dwellings are eternal, and in whose Kingdome there is no need of Candles, nor of the light of the Sunne; look, I beseech thee, upon thy servant, who tarries in this *place all night*, Gen. 28. 11. And forasmuch as thou (out of thy tender love and Compassion on thy Creatures) hast ordained this time for their repose and refreshing, that having past through the Cares and dangers of the day, they might under the shadow of thy wings finde rest and security; keep me, I most humbly beseech thee, from the 10 hours and the powers of darknesse; watch over me this night in thy Almighty providence, and scatter all the rebellions and devices of my Adversaries. Inlighten my soul, sanctifie my body, govern my affections, and guide my thoughts, that in the fastest closures of my eyelids my spirit may see thee, and in the depth of sleep be Conversant with thee. Suffer me not, O my God, to forget thee in the dark, or to say, *The Lord seeth me not*, *The Lord hath forsaken the earth*, Ezek. 8. 12. but so keep me in thy fear, and sanctifie me with thy grace, that all the words of my mouth, and the meditations of my heart may be alwayes of thee. Make my soul to thirst for thee, and my flesh also 20 to long after thee. And at what time soever thou shalt awake me from this bodily sleep, awake also my soul in me, make thy morning-star to arise in my heart, and let thy spirit blow upon my garden, that the spices thereof may flow out. Quicken me O Lord, according to thy wonted kindnesse, so shall I seek thee early, and make my prayer unto thee with joyful lips. And now O my most loving and faithful Creatour, take me, I beseech thee, into thy Almighty protection, stretch over me the *Arme* of thy mercy, let thine Eye be towards the work of thine own hands, and the purchased possession of thy onely begotten, and my most merciful Redeemer *Jesus Christ*, Amen. 30

¶ As often as thou dost awake in the night, be sure to lift up thy heart unto God in this or the like short *Ejaculation*. *Holy*, *holy*, *holy*, *Lord God of Sabbath! heaven and earth are full of the majesty of thy glory*. By resorting thus unto God, thou shalt finde a great furtherance and cheerfulnesse in thy spiritual exercises, and besides it will keep always about thee the *savour of life*. And because thou shalt not be unfurnished upon any incident occasions, I have strowed here this handful of savoury herbs, which thou mayest take up as thou findest them in thy way.

EJACULATIONS

When the Clock strikes.

Blessed be the houre in which my Lord Jesus was borne, and the houre in which he died! O Lord Remember me in the houre of death!

When thou intendest any businesse, or Journey.

O do well unto thy servant! that I may live and keep thy Word.

When thou art persecuted.

Haste thee, O God, to deliver me, make haste to help me, O Lord!

Upon some suddaine fear.

10 *O set me upon the Rock that is higher then I, for thou art my hope, and a strong tower for me against my enemy.*

Upon any disorderly thoughts.

Make me a clean heart, O God, and renew a right spirit within me.

Upon any occasions of sadnesse.

Thy rebuke hath broken my heart, I am full of heavinesse, but thou, O Lord, shalt lift me up again.

Upon any Diffidence.

Thou art my hope, O Lord, even from my youth, through thee have I been holden up ever since I was borne; though thou shouldst 20 *kill me, yet will I trust in thee.*

When thou dost any good work.

Not unto me, O Lord, not unto me, but unto thy name give the praise.

When thou art provoked to anger.

Give thy peace unto thy servant, O God, let no man take away my Crown; In patience, O Lord, let me possesse my soul.

For thine Enemies.

Lord, lay not this sinne to their Charge; they know not what they do.

Upon any gracious deliverance, or other mercies conferr'd upon thee.

The Lord is my Shepherd, I shall not want. He maketh me to lie down in green pastures, he leadeth me besides the still waters. He hath prevented me with the blessings of goodnesse, he hath granted me my hearts desire, and not with-holden the request of my lips. Surely goodnesse and mercy shall follow me all the dayes of my life: And I will dwell in the house of my God for ever.

Upon any losses, or other adversities.

Shall we receive good at the hand of God, and shall we not receive evill? Naked came I out of my mothers womb, and naked shall I return thither; the Lord gave, and the Lord hath taken away, blessed be the name of the Lord. 10

When thou hearest that any is dead.

Teach me, O Lord, to number my dayes, that I may apply my heart unto wisdome.

Upon thought of thy sins.

Turn away thy face from my sins, O Lord, and blot out all mine offences.

Praise the Lord, O my soul, and forget not all his benefits, who forgiveth all thy sins, and healeth all thine Infirmities. 20

When thou art weary of the cares and vanities of this world.

Like as the Hart brayeth for the water-brooks, so thirsteth my soul after thee O God.

O who will give me the wings of a Dove, that I may flie, and be at rest.

¶ *Admonitions, with Meditations and Prayers to be used before we come to the Lords Supper*

All the Sacraments of the New Testament, in those that come to participate them, require a most Exquisite and sincere preparation. But this Sacrament of the Lords Table, because in *Institution* and *Effect* it is the highest of all, requires the most perfect and purest Accomplishments. Our preparation to this Sacrament is not perfected by Contrition onely and Confession of sins, (both which are unavoidably requisite) but if we will be worthy receivers 30 and partake of those graces which are exhibited unto us in this heavenly banquet, there are many other duties we must necessarily performe, for this Sacrament is of an infinite vertue, having in it the *Wel-spring* of all graces, even *Jesus Christ* with all the merits of his most bitter passion, which admit neither number nor measure. Wherefore such as our pre-disposition is, such also shall our proportion be of this spiritual *Manna*; for as he that cometh to a Well to draw water, takes no more thence, then what his vessel contains; which yet he cannot impute unto the Well, but unto his Pitcher 10 which could hold no more; so they that come unto this glorious Sacrament, receive onely so much grace as their preparation and holines makes them capable of. Now there are required of us, before we presume to lay hands upon this bread of life, three things.

1. Purity of Conscience.
2. Purity of Intention.
3. Fervent and effectual Devotion.

We must (as far as it lies in us) refrain from all actual sins in thought, word, and deed. Secondly, We must do it to a good end, 20 not for any private benefit; not by compulsion, or for fear of Censure, or any other Ecclesiastical correction; not out of Custome, nor for any sensual devotion or joy because of the confluence and company at these love-feasts. Thirdly and lastly, we must watch over our owne souls, and take heed that no wind blows upon our garden but the spiritual and eternal; we must labour for an heavenly setlednesse, sanctified affections, holy hopes, new garments, a clean heart, and a right spirit. *Cant.* 2. The soul must be sick of love, she must long for the banqueting house, nothing now must appear but flowers, nothing must be heard but the singing of birds, and 30 the voice of the Turtle. Lord God (saith S. *Ambrose*) with what contrition of heart, with what fountains of tears, with what reverence & fear, with what chastity of body and purity of mind should this divin mystery be celebrated! where thy flesh is the meat, where thy blood is the drink, where the creature feeds upon the Creatour, and the Creatour is united unto the creature, where Angels are spectators, and God himself both the Priest and the Sacrifice, what holinesse and humility should we bring thither?

O what pure things, most pure, must those hands be
which bring my God to me!

As therefore some rich, odoriferous water is distill'd out of many and several sorts of fragrant herbs and flowers, so our devotion at this soveraigne Sacrament should be composed of many spiritual, acceptable affections with God, as (amongst others) are profound humility, unmeasurable reverence, ardent love, firme faith, actuall charity, impatient hunger, and an intollerable longing after this heavenly banquet.

And because we may not touch these white robes with dirty hands, nor come neer the Rose of *Sharon* with ill sents and offensive fumes, it hath been ever the Custom of Gods Church to injoyn and set apart a certain limited time of purification before this mysterious solemnity, wherein all religious and worthy Communicants addressed and prepared themselves in some measure for this unmeasurable mercy. Such was in our Church, that more strict and holy season, called *Lent*, and such still are the preparation-dayes before this glorious Sabbath in all true Churches. Two dayes were given the *Israelites* to sanctifie themselves, and to wash their clothes, that they might be ready against the third day, upon which the Lord was to come downe (in the sight of all the people) upon Mount *Sinai*; And this onely at the reception of the Law which was given by Angels; much more then ought we to wash and cleanse our vessels from all vaine affections, idle words and actions, and to separate our selves from the world for three dayes at least, that we may be ready against that great and blessed day, wherein we are to come, not to a mountain that might not be touched, nor to the sound of a Trumpet, nor to the voice of words spoken to us out of the midst of fire, but to the general assembly, and Church of the first-borne, which are written in heaven, and to *Jesus the Mediatour of the new Covenant, and to the blood of sprinkling, that speaketh better things then that of Abel.* See then that thou refuse not to come to this great marriage of the Kings Son with thy soul, and see withall, that thou comest not without a wedding garment, that is to say, unprepared. *For, whosoever shall eate this bread, and drink this cup of the Lord unworthily, shall be guilty of the body and blood of the Lord; But let a man examine himselfe, and so let him eate of that bread, and drink of that cup of the Lord, for he that eateth and drinketh unworthily, eateth and drinketh damnation to himselfe, not discerning the Lords body*, 1 Cor. 11. 27, 28, 29. These are the words of a faithful witnesse, and thou maiest beleeve them.

When therefore thou doest intend to be a partaker of this merciful and mysterious Sacrament, be sure for three daies at least not to intermeddle with any worldly businesse, but all that time redeeme those many daies which were vainly spent by thee; enter into thine owne bosome, examine what thou hast there, and if thou findest any sons of darknesse lurking under those fig-leaves, conceal them not, but turne them out of doors, and wash their Couch with thy teares; have a care that in the Bridegroomes bed, instead of myrrhe and flowers, thou strowest not thornes and thistles. 10 The Evening before thou art to communicate, feed but moderately, and after supper use no corrupt communication, but converse inwardly with thine own heart, and meditate what an Almighty guest thou art to entertaine there next day. Consider seriously thine own unworthinesse, and desire of him that he would sanctifie and furnish the roome where he is to eate the Passeover with thee. Intreat him to defend thee that night from all sinful Illusions and temptations, and to keep the house cleane and garnished for himself. When thou hast thus commended thy self into his hands, let thy sleep that night be shorter then usual, be up with the day, or 20 rather with thy Saviour, who rose up early, while it was yet dark. Meditate with thy self what miracles of mercy he hath done for thee. Consider how he left his Fathers bosome to be lodged in a manger, and laid by his robes of glory to take upon him the seed of *Abraham*, that he might cloath thee with Immortality. Call to minde his wearisome journeys, continual afflictions, the malice and scorne he underwent, the persecutions and reproaches laid upon him, his strong cries and teares in the days of his flesh, his spiritual agony and sweating of blood, with the Implacable fury of his Enemies, and his own unspeakable humility, humbling him- 30 self to the death of the Crosse, a death accursed by Gods own mouth. Consider againe (if thou canst) of what unmeasurable love was he possessed, who having designed and spent his time of life here for thy salvation, did not onely leave thee those divine Oracles and Instructions to be guided by, but to seale up the summe and make heaven sure unto thee, did by his last Testament give himself with all the merits of his life and death to be wholly thine, and instead of them took upon him all thy transgressions, bore all thine iniquities, and to appease the anger, and satisfie the Justice of his Father, became the holy, harmlesse, and undefiled sacrifice 40 and perfect satisfaction for the sins of the world, reconciling all things unto his Father, whether they be things in earth, or things in heaven.

When thou hast thus considered him in his acts of love and humility, consider him again in his glory, take thine Eyes off from *Bethlehem* and *Golgotha*, and look up to the mount of *Olives*, yea, to heaven where he sits now upon the right hand of his Father, Angels, principalities and powers being made subject unto him. Call to minde his Joyful resurrection, his most accomplished conquest, and triumph over the world, death and hell; his most gracious and familiar conversation with his Apostles before his 10 Ascension, with his most loving and comfortable carriage towards them at his departure, *leading them out as farre as* Bethanie, *and lifting up his hands, and blessing them.* Lastly, close up these thoughts with a serious and awful meditation of that great and joyful, though dreadful day of his second coming to judgement, promised by himself, and affirmed at the time of his Ascension by the two men in white apparel. *Ye men of Galilee, why stand ye gazing up into heaven? this same Jesus which is taken up from you into heaven, shall so come in like manner as ye have seen him go into heaven.*

Behold! he cometh with clouds, and every eye shall see him, and 20 *they also which pierced him, and all kindreds of the earth shall waile because of him. Amen! even so, come quickly, Lord Jesus!*

¶ These are the duties required of thee, and which thou must faithfully and punctually performe, if thou wouldst be a worthy Communicant, and receive those sacred and mystical Elements to that blessed end for which they were ordained. But when I speak of three dayes preparation, I do not impose that proportion of time, nor conclude it sufficient, as if it were enough for thee to recede from thy corrupt inclinations, and the myre of thy sins for such a terme, with an intention to returne and wallow in it again, 30 when that holy season is over, for our whole life (had we the purity of Angels, and the innocence of infants,) bears no proportion at all, nor can it (without an immediate sanctification from God himself) any way qualifie, or make us fit for the reception of this unmeasurable mercy. But when I spoke of such a proportion of time, I did onely propose it to my Readers for the performing of those holy and necessary duties, which have particular relation to this solemne Feast, and which (indeed) are required then from every Christian. And as for a regular, sober, and holy life; we should in all places, and at all times labour for it, for *without holinesse no man shall see the face of God*, much lesse be partaker of his merits, and by this spiritual eating and drinking become a member of that body, whose life and head he is.

A Prayer for the grace of repentance, together with a Confession of sins

O holy, blessed and glorious Trinity! three persons, and one eternal God, have mercy upon me a miserable sinner.

O who will give mine head waters, and mine eyes a fountain of 10 tears! that I may weep night and day for my infinite transgressions, ingratitude and rebellion against my most milde and merciful Creatour! O God my God be not farre from me! hide not thy face from the work of thine hands, reject not my sighing and mournful spirit, nor the earnest endeavours and desires of mine undone and miserable soul! O thou that breakest not the bruised Reede, nor quenchest the smoking Flax, quench not in me these weak sparks, this dawne and beginnings of the promised earnest. Take away, O my God! this heart of stone, and give me a heart of flesh, renew a right spirit within me; cloath me with white 20 raiment, and anoint mine Eyes with Eye-salve, that I may know and see how wretched, and miserable, and poore, and blinde, and naked I am, and may be zealous therefore and repent! O thou that didst cause the waters to flow out of the stonie rock, and gavest to *Magdalen* such store of teares that she washed thy feet with them, give to me true remorse, and such a measure of repentance as may become a most miserable sinner! I confesse dear God, that I am not worthy of the least of thy mercies, much lesse to appear at this great and solemne Feast, this Feast of mercy and miracles, where none but with holy hands, pure intentions, crucified affections, 30 and renewed spirits should presume to enter. But as for me I am all uncleannesse, a polluted, vile creature, and nothing belongs unto me at this great day, but confusion of face, and an utter separation from this glorious and saving Communion. I have wasted thy stock, consumed thy talents, and destroyed thy goods. I was restlesse, and unquiet till I had found out wayes to offend thee. I have broken thy Commandments, laid open thine Inclosures, and most grievously trespassed against thy truth, and against the light of mine own Conscience. I have preferred rottennesse and dust to the treasure of thy word, and mine own voluptuousnesse to thy revealed will. And now *O thou preserver of men! What shall I do unto thee? Against thee onely have I sinned, and my transgressions are ever in thy sight.* Lord God! I lay me down at thy footstoole, *and if thou wilt be extreme to mark what is amisse*, I shall from my very heart acknowledge and adore thy Justice. But O my dear Creatour, for Christ Jesus his sake have mercy upon me! look not on my deserts, but on thy glory; O Lord do not refuse me, but reforme and restore me! O Lord hearken, and do, and deferre not, but speak peace to my troubled soul, and send thy loving spirit to strengthen and confirme me in the way of holinesse, bring me home, O Lord, and leade me now unto these living waters, incorporate me into the saving vine, and purge me, that I may bear more fruit. O cast me not away like an abominable and withered branch, but make me to flourish in the Courts of thy house, where thy Children are like Olive-branches round about thy table! O Lord hear, and have mercy, and forgive me, and be reconciled unto me for *Christ Jesus* his sake! To whom with thee and the holy Ghost be glory in the Church through all ages world without end, *Amen.*

A Meditation before the receiving of the holy Communion

Holy, *holy*, *holy*, is the Lord God of Hosts, the whole earth is full of his glory! Behold to the Moone, and it shineth not, and the Starres are darknesse in his sight. The Pillars of heaven do tremble, and are astonished at his reproof. O who then am I, that I should appear before thee, or *what is man that thou shouldest regard him*? O light of light, the all-seeing light that shineth in darknesse, and the darknesse comprehendeth it not, what will become of me, when I shall appear before thy glorious and searching Eye! What an habitation of darknesse and death wilt thou finde within me? What abominable desolations and emptinesse? What barrennesse and disorders wilt thou see there? Many a time hast thou knockt, and I have shut the doors against thee, thou hast often called, and I would not answer. Sleeping and waking, early and late, day and night have I refused instruction, and would not be healed. And now, O my God, after all this rebellion and uncleannesse, wilt thou come and lodge with me? O Lord, where shall I prepare, and make ready for thee? *What communion can there be betwixt light and darknesse*, purity and pollution, perfection and deformity?

O Rose of *Sharon*! thou undefiled and everlasting flower, the glory of the fields, and the first fruits of the dead, shall the wilde Asses and the beasts of the wildernesse feed now upon thee? Wilt thou give the bread of life unto dogs, and cast thy pearls before swine? O *Jesus Christ*, the lover and the redeemer of all humble and penitent souls! Thou that feedest among the Lilies untill the day breaks and the shadows flee, what is there in my heart where onely tares and thistles grow, that thou canst feed upon? Thy blessed body was wrapt in fine and white linen, (which is the righteousnesse of 10 the Saints.) It was laid in a new and undefiled grave, hewen out of a rock, wherein never man was laid before. But all my righteousnesse is a filthy rag, my heart neither new nor undefiled, but a nest of unclean birds, where they have not onely laine, but hatched and brought forth their viperous young ones.

I confesse, dear God, I confesse with all my heart mine own extrem unworthyness, my most shameful and deplorable condition. But with thee, O Lord, there is mercy and plenteous redemption. Thou dost not use to reject and cast off those that unfeignedly repent and return unto thee; the great design and end 20 of thine Incarnation was to save sinners: Thou hadst never come into this world, but for thy love to thy lost sheep, and those thou didst then love, thou dost love still unto the end. Thou didst not come unto the whole, but to the sick. The first (had there been any such,) had no need of a *Physician*, and the last (hadst not thou come to restore them,) had perished for ever. It was thy gracious pleasure (while thou wert here in the world) to receive Publicans and sinners, and though thou art now ascended to thy Father, yet hast not thou changed thy nature. Thou art the same yesterday, to day, and for evermore. Thy life here was nothing else but a 30 pilgrimage and laborious search after sinners, that thou mightst finde them out and make them whole. And how willingly (O blessed Jesus!) didst thou lay down thy robes of glory, and cloath thy self with flesh, that thou mightst afterwards lay down thy life a propitiation for our sins! How many scorching and wearisome journeys didst thou undergo for our sakes! How many cold and tedious nights didst thou watch and spend abroad in prayer, when the birds of the aire lay warme in their nests, and thou hadst not a place to put thy head in! In the day time I finde thee preaching in the Temple, and all night praying in the Mount of *Olives*; a little 40 after on thine own Sabbath travelling for me in the corne-field;

Another time (wearied with thy journey) sitting on the Well of *Jacob*, and begging a draught of that cold water from the woman of *Samaria*; Now again I meet thee on the Asse, made infinitely happy by so glorious a rider, by *the God of Jeshurun who rideth on the heavens, and in his excellencie on the skies.* Sure, it was his simplicity and ordinary contempt with man, that made him so acceptable in thy sight. But (Oh!) with what language shall I attempt thy passion? thy bloody sweat, thy deep and bitter agony, thy lingring peece-mealed death, with all the lively anguishments, and afflictions of thy martyr'd Spirit? O my most loving and merciful Saviour! It is onely thy own Spirit, that can fully character thy own sufferings. 10

These miracles of love and most comfortable circumstances encourage me (O my God) to draw neer unto thee: for it is not probable that thou wouldst have subjected thy self to such bitter reproaches, blasphemies, and torments, had not thy love to man (for whose redemption thou didst suffer them,) been as infinite as thy self; *And greater love then this hath no man, that a man lay down his life for his friends.* And lay it down thou didst, for *no man could take it from thee.* Thou couldst have commanded twelve legions of Angels from thy Father, and when thou wentest forth to meet thy murtherers, they went backwards and fell to the ground, and without thy permission (in whose hand their breath was) they could have done nothing. These merciful passages, together with thy own voice and frequent invitation much encourage me to draw neer unto thee. 20

Come unto me all ye that labour, and are heavy laden, and I will give you rest. Matth. 11. 28.

If any man thirst, let him come unto me, and drink, John 7. 37.

These, with many more, are thy loving Invitations: This is the voyce of the great Shepherd, and thy sheep hear thy voyce. Thus thou didst cry, and these were the words thou didst speak while thou wert here upon earth, and shall I then turn away from thee, *that speakest now from heaven? Thou art a Priest for ever after the order of Melchisedech*, and thy preaching and Intercession shall last untill the heavens be no more, and woe unto them that refuse to hear thee. 30

Wherefore, most holy *Jesus*, seeing thou dost invite sinners to thee, and didst die to redeem them, and *art able to save them to the uttermost, that come to God by thee, and dost live for ever to make intercession for them*, Heb. 7. 25, 26. I the most wretched and the worst of sinners in full assurance of thy mercies, and that *thou art touched with the feeling of mine infirmities*, Heb. 4. 15. and wilt have compassion upon my penitent soul, draw neer to thy throne of grace, that I may obtaine mercy, and finde grace to help in time of need.

O Lord be merciful unto me, forgive all my sins, and heal all mine infirmities. Cleanse my heart, sanctifie my affections, renew my spirit, and strengthen my faith, that I may at this great Feast discerne thy blessed body, and eate and drink salvation to my self, to the glory of thy great name, and the comfort of my poor and sorrowful soul, *Amen.*

Now unto him that hath loved us, and washed us from our sins in his own blood, and hath made us Kings and Priests unto God and his Father, to him be glory and dominion for ever, and ever. *Amen.*

A Prayer when thou art upon going to the Lords Table

In the name of the Father, and of the Son, and of the holy Ghost, *Amen!*

Jesus Christ, the Lamb, the Branch, the bright and morning-Starre, the bread of life that came down from heaven, have mercy upon me! It is thy promise, that whosoever eateth thy flesh, and drinketh thy blood, he shall have eternal life in him, and thou wilt raise him up at the last day. Behold, O God, I am now coming to thee; O thou fountain of purgation! thou Well of living waters wash me cleane! be unto me the bread of life to strengthen me in my pilgrimage towards heaven! grant that I may suck salvation from thy *heart, that spring of the blood of God, which flowes into all believers. Thy flesh is meat indeed, and thy blood is drink Indeed. O give me grace to receive both worthily, that I may never incurre thy anger, and eternal condemnation! Lord *Jesus Christ*! I beleeve all that thou hast said, and all that thou hast promised, helpe thou mine unbelief; thou art the Author, be thou the finisher of my faith; And for thy glories sake, for thine own names sake, leade me in the right way to this great mercy and mystery, *Amen!*

* *Cyprian* de cænâ domini. Cruci hæremus, sanguinem fugimus, & inter ipsa redemptoris nostri vulnera figimus linguam.

Immediately before the receiving, say,

O Lord I am not worthy of the least of all the mercies, and of all the truth which thou hast shewed unto thy servant, all my life long unto this very day; much lesse am I worthy thou shouldst come now under my roof but seeing it is thy institution and free mercy that will have it so, be jealous, O God, of the place of thine honour, cause me to remember whose Temple I am, and suffer not my last state to be worse then the first. Even so, Lord Jesus, come quickly, *Amen!*

¶ *Admonitions after receiving the holy Communion* 10

When you have received the Sacred Elements, you should not presently after spit, nor eate and drink, but refraine untill they are perfectly digested and resolved. You must lay aside all worldly communication, and humane discourses, though never so serious; for judge of your self, what an uncivil part it will be in you, when you have received so great a guest as *Jesus Christ* with all his merits, to turne your back upon him presently, and neither to meditate of him, nor to discourse with him, and keep him company. Wherefore you should all that day be instant in prayer, meditations, thanksgiving, and good works; you should consider and 20 think upon the love of God, who so loved the world, that he gave his onely begotten Son to redeeme it. You should meditate upon his birth, life, doctrine and passion, his death and buriall, resurrection and ascension, and his second coming to judgement. You should pray, that you may be found blamelesse and without spot of him, and so much the more, because you see the day approaching. Tread not under foot the Son of God, and his precious blood wherewith you are sanctified and saved, by returning again to your former sins, like the dog to his vomit, but be sure that you walk warily, and fall not wilfully into the myre. Be not regular and holy 30 for a day or two, but all the dayes of thy life, and number thy dayes, that thou mayst apply thy heart unto wisdome. Cast thy bread upon the waters, (be merciful to the poor) and remember thy Creator, for the dayes of darknesse are many, but the outward darknesse is eternal, and from it there is no redemption.

Instead of printed Meditations which are usually prescribed after communicating, I would advise the pious receiver to read over all these following parcels of Scripture, *John* 6. 22. *to the end*, *John* 17. *Rom.* 8. 2 *Cor.* 5. *Ephes.* 1. & 4. *Heb.* 10. 1 *Pet.* 1. *Rev.* 5.

A Prayer after you have received

Lord Jesus Christ, very God, and very man, made in all things like unto us, sin onely excepted; I blesse and praise thy holy name, and with all my heart, with all my strength, and with all my soul give thee all possible thanks for thy infinite love and pity towards lost man. Blessed be the hour in which thou wert born, and the hour in which thou didst die! Blessed and for ever hallowed be thy most comfortable and glorious name, the name JESUS CHRIST, *at which every knee shall bow*, *of things in heaven*, *and things in earth*, *and things under the earth*; *for thy name is above every name*, *and there is no other name by which we can be saved*. O most holy, most humble and harmlesse Lamb! how didst thou make thy self of no reputation, and becamest obedient to the death of the Crosse for my sake! And when thou wert to drink the cup of thy Fathers anger due to my sins, didst instead of it ordain and bequeath to me the cup of life and everlasting salvation! O Lord give me a heart to understand, and eyes to see what thou hast done for me; O never suffer me to crucifie thee again by returning to my former iniquities and pollutions, but write thy sufferings and the price of my redemption in the tables of my heart, set them for a signet upon mine hand, and for a bracelet upon mine arme, that by a continual and careful remembrance of them, I may in the strength of this bread received to day at thy table travel to thy holy mountain, and that this drink which I drank out of the spiritual rock may become a Well of living waters, springing up in me to eternal life. Grant this, O God, for thy glories sake, and for that love and mercies sake which brought thee hither out of thy Fathers bosome to suffer so many things for his Elects sake, *Amen!*

Worthy is the Lamb that was slaine, *to receive power*, *and riches*, *and wisdome*, *and strength*, *and honour*, *and glory*, *and blessing*; *for he hath redeemed us to God by his blood out of every kindred*, *and tongue*, *and people*, *and nation*, *and hath made us unto our God Kings and Priests*, *and we shall reigne on the earth*.

Now the God of peace that brought again from the dead my Lord

Jesus, that great Shepherd of the sheep, through the blood of the everlasting Covenant,

Make me perfect in every good work, to do his will, working in me that which is well-pleasing in his sight through Jesus Christ, to whom be glory for ever and ever, Amen!

A Prayer in time of persecution and Heresie

Most glorious and Immortall God, the Prince of peace, unity and order, which makest men to be of one mind in a house, heale I beseech thee these present sad breaches and distractions! Consider, O Lord, the teares of thy Spouse which are daily upon her cheeks, whose adversaries are grown mighty, and her enemies prosper. The wayes of *Zion* do mourne, our beautiful gates are shut up, and the Comforter that should relieve our souls is gone far from us. Thy Service and thy Sabbaths, thy own sacred Institutions and the pledges of thy love are denied unto us; Thy Ministers are trodden down, and the basest of the people are set up in thy holy place. O Lord holy and just! behold and consider, and have mercy upon us, for thy own names sake, for thy promise sake suffer not the gates of hell to prevaile against us; but return and restore us, that joy and gladnesse may be heard in our dwellings, and the voyce of the Turtle in all our land. *Arise O God, and let thine enemies be scattered, and let those that hate thee flee before thee. Behold, the robbers are come into thy Sanctuary, and the persecuters are within thy walls. We drink our own waters for money, and our wood is sold unto us. Our necks are under persecution, we labour and have no rest. Yea, thine own Inheritance is given to strangers, and thine own portion unto aliens. Wherefore dost thou forget us for ever, and forsake us for so long a time? Turne thou us unto thee, O Lord, and we shall be turned, renew our dayes as of old. Lord hear, and have mercy, and be jealous for the beloved of thine own bosome, for thy truth, and for the words of thine own mouth. Help us, O God of our salvation, and for thine own honours sake deal Comfortably with us*, Amen, Amen.

A Prayer in adversity, and troubles occasioned by our Enemies

O holy and almighty God, full of goodness and compassion, look I beseech thee with thine Eye of mercy upon my present sad sufferings and most bitter afflictions! Behold, O God, I put my mouth in the dust, and confess I have deserv'd them. I despise not thy Chastenings, but begge grace of thee that I may not faint, and that they may yeild the fruits of righteousnesse unto me, who am now exercised by them. Thou seest, O God, how furious and Implacable mine Enemies are, they have not only rob'd me of that portion and provision which thou hadst graciously given me, but they have also washed their hands in the blood of my friends, my dearest and nearest relatives. I know, O my God, and I am daily taught by that disciple whom thou did'st love, that no murderer hath eternal life abiding in him. Keep me therefore, O my God, from the guilt of blood, and suffer me not to stain my soul with the thoughts of recompense and vengeance, which is a branch of thy great prerogative, and belongs wholly unto thee. Though they persecute me unto death, and pant after the very dust upon the heads of thy poore, though they have taken the bread out of the childrens mouth, and have made me a desolation, yet Lord, give me thy grace, and such a measure of charity as may fully forgive them. Suffer me not to open my mouth in Curses, but give me the spirit of my Saviour, who reviled not again, but was dumb like a Lamb before his shearers. O Lord, sanctifie all these afflictions unto thy servant, and let no man take away my crown. Remember those that are in troubles for thy truth, and put their tears into thy bottle. Grant this, O merciful Father, for my dear Saviours sake, and bring me quickly into thy Kingdom, where I shall have all these tears wiped away from mine eyes, Amen, Amen!

MAN IN Darkneſs,

OR, A DISCOURSE OF *DEATH*

Eccles. 11. 7, 8, 9, & 10

Truly the light is sweet, and a pleasant thing it is to behold the Sun.

But if a man live many dayes and rejoyce in them all, yet, let him remember the dayes of darknesse, for they are many.

Rejoyce, O young man, in thy youth, and let thy heart cheere thee in the dayes of thy youth, and walk in the wayes of thy heart, and in the sight of thine eyes, but know thou, that for all these things God will bring thee into judgement.

Therefore remove sorrow from thy heart, and put away evil from thy flesh, for childhood and youth are vanity. 10

¶

Draw neer, fond man, and dresse thee by this glasse,
Mark how thy bravery and big looks must passe
Into corruption, rottennesse and dust;
The fraile Supporters which betray'd thy trust.
O weigh in time thy last and loathsome state,
To purchase heav'n for tears is no hard rate.
Our glory, greatnesse, wisdome, all we have,
If misimploy'd, but adde hell to the grave:
Onely a faire redemption of evill Times
Finds life in death, and buryes all our Crimes. 20

It is an observation of some *spirits*, that **the night is the mother of thoughts*. And I shall adde, that those thoughts are *Stars*, the *Scintillations* and *lightnings* of the soul strugling with *darknesse*. This *Antipathy* in her is *radical*, for being descended from the *house of light*, she hates a contrary *principle*, and being at that time a prisoner in some measure to an enemy, she becomes pensive, and full of thoughts. Two great *extremes* there are, which she equally abhors, *Darkness* and *Death*. And 'tis observable, that in the *second death*, when she shall be wholly mancipated to her 30 enemies, those two are united. For those furious and unquenchable burnings of hell (which the *Scripture* calls *the lake of fire*, *&c.*)

* A Proverb in *Italy*, La notte é madre de pensieri.

though they be of such an insuperable *intense heat*, as to work upon *spirits*, and the most subtile Essences, yet do they give no light at all, but burn blacker then *pitch*, *Cremationem habet*, *lumen verò non habet*. (Greg. Mor. c. 46.) The Contemplation of *death* is an obscure, melancholy *walk* an Expatiation in *shadows* & *solitude*, but it leads unto *life*, & he that sets forth at *midnight*, will sooner meet the *Sunne*, then he that sleeps it out betwixt his curtains. Truly, when I consider, how I came first into this world, and in what condition I must once again go out of it, and compare my ap-
10 pointed time here with the *portion* preceding it, and the *eternity* to follow, I can conclude my present *being* or *state* (in respect of the *time*) to be nothing else but an *apparition*. The first man that appeared thus, came from the *East*, and the *breath* of *life* was received there. Though then we travel *Westward*, though we embrace *thornes* and swet for *thistles*, yet the businesse of a *Pilgrim* is to *seek his Countrey*. But the *land* of *darknesse* lies in our way, and how few are they that study this *region*, that like holy *Macarius* walk into the wildernesse, and discourse with the skull of a dead man? We run all after the present world, and the Primitive
20 Angelical life is quite lost.

It is a sad perversnesse of *man*, to preferre warre to peace, cares to rest, grief to joy, and the vanities of this narrow Stage to the true and solid comforts in heaven. *The friends of this world* (saith a holy father) *are so fearful to be separated from it, that nothing can be so grievous to them as to think of death. They put farre away the evill day, and cause the seate of violence to come neer; They lie upon beds of Jvory, and stretch themselves upon their Couches; they eat the lambs out of the flock, and the calves out of the midst of the stall; They chant*
30 *to the sound of the viol, they drink wine in bowls, and anoint themselves with the chief ointments; they account the life of the righteous to be madnesse, and his end to be without honour*, Amos 6. In this desperate and senselesse state they cast away their precious souls, and make their brightest dayes but *dayes of darknesse and gloominesse*, *dayes of clouds and of thick mists*. They consider not the day that *shall burne like an Oven*, *when the heavens being on fire shall be dissolved*, *and the Elements shall melt with a fervent heat; when the wicked shall be stubble*, *and all the workers of iniquity shall be burnt up*. Miserable men! that knowing their masters pleasure, will not
40 do it, that refuse Oyle and balsame to make way for poyson and

—Contempsit mori Qui non concupiscit—

corrasives. And why will they call him *Master*, *Master*, whose precepts they trample on, and whose members they crucifie? It is a sad observation for true Christians to see these men who would seem to be Pillars, to prove but reeds and specious dissemblers. For what manner of livers should such *professors* be, seeing they expect and beleeve the dissolution of all things? With what constant holinesse, humility and devotion should they watch for it? How should they *passe the time of their sojourning here in fear, and be diligent that they may be found of him in peace, without spot, and blamelesse*? What preparation should they make against the evill 10 day? What comforts and treasures should they lay up for that long voyage? For what a day of terrors and indignation is the day of death to the unprepared? How will they lie on their last beds, *like wilde Buls in a net, full of the fury of the Lord*? When *their desolation shall come like a flood, and their destruction like a whirle-wind; How will they say in the morning, would God it were Even, and at night, would God it were Morning! for the fear of their heart wherwith they shal fear, and for the sight of their Eyes wherewith they shall see?* This is a truth they will not believe, untill death tells it them, and then it will be too late; It is therefore much to be wished, that they 20 would yet, while it is life-time with them, remember their last ends, and seriously question with themselves, what is there under the Sun, that can so justly challenge their thoughts as the contemplation of their own mortality? We could not have lived in an age of more instruction, had we been left to our own choice. We have seen such vicissitudes and examples of humane frailty, as the former world (had they happened in those ages) would have judged prodigies. We have seen Princes brought to their graves by a new way, and the highest order of humane honours trampled upon by the lowest. We have seene Judgement beginning at Gods 30 Church, and (what hath beene never heard of, since it was redeem'd and established by his blessed Son,) *we have seen his Ministers cast out of the Sanctuary, & barbarous persons without *light* or *perfection*, usurping holy offices. A day, an hour, a minute (saith *Causabone*) is sufficient to over-turn and extirpate the most settled Governments, which seemed to have been founded and rooted in Adamant. Suddenly do the high things of this world come to an end, and their delectable things passe 40

* There is extant a little book called *Speculum Visionis* printed at *Norimberge* 1508, wherein this fearful desolation and destruction of the Church by Lay-men is expressely foretold.

away, for when they seem to be in their *flowers* and full strength, they perish to astonishment; And sure the ruine of the most goodly peeces seems to tell, that the dissolution of the whole is not far off. It is the observation of a known Statesman, (Sir *Water Rawleigh*) *That to all dominions God hath set their periods, who though he hath given to man the knowledge of those wayes, by which Kingdoms rise and fall, yet he hath left him subject unto the* **affections which draw on these fatal mutations in their appointed time.* Vain therefore and deceitful is all the pomp of this world, which though it flatters us with a seeming permanency, will be sure to leave us even then, when we are most in chase of it. And what comfort then, or what security can poor man promise to himself? whose breath is in the hand of another, and whose few dayes are most commonly out-lived by every creature, and sometimes by a *flower* of his own *setting*. Or what benefit can these *humane delights though blest with successe, and a large time of fruition, afford him at his death? for satisfaction in this point, let us but have recourse to the ages that are past, let us aske the *Fathers*, & they will tell us. If we insist upon eminent persons, the rulers of this world, & the Counsellors of the earth who built *sumptuous Palaces for themselvs and filled their houses with silver*; we shall have no better account from them, then if we enquired of the *prisoners* & the oppressed. They are gone all the same way, *their pomp & the noise of their viols is brought down to the grave, the worms cover them, and the worms are spread under them. Riches* and *power* travel not beyond this life; they are like *Jobs* friends, *deceitful as a brook, and as the stream of brooks they passe away, which vanish when it is hot, and are consumed out of their place.* Hast thou found riches (saith one) then, thou hast lost thy rest. Distractions & cares come along with them, and they are seldome gotten without the worme of conscience. It was an act of *Anacreon* becoming the royalty of a *Poets* spirit: *Policrates* rewards him with five talents; but he, after he had been troubled with the keeping of them for two nights, carries them back to the owner, telling him, that, *if he had been accustomed to such companions he had never made any verses.* Certainly there is so much of

* N. *Marcellus* de doctorum indagine. Potest fatum morum mutabilitate converti, ut ex iis celeriùs vel tardiùs aut bonum fiat, aut pessimum.

* Non est, falleris, hæc beata non est,
Quam vos creditis esse, vita non est.
Fulgentes manibus videre gemmas,
Aut auro bibere, & cubare cocco:
Qui vultus Acherontis atri,
Qui Styga tristem non tristis videt,
Audétque vitæ ponere finem,
Par ille regi, par superis erit.

Mammon and *darknesse* in them, as sufficeth to shew their *parentage* is low, and not very far from *hell.* Some such thing we may gather from that exclamation of S. *James* against the rich men; *Your gold and your silver is canker'd, and the rust of them shall be a witnesse against you, and shall eate your flesh as it were fire, you have heaped treasure together for the last dayes.* But to return thither from whence we are digrest: What is become now of these great *Merchants of the earth*, and where is the fruit *of all their labours under the Sun*? Why, truly they are *taken out of the way as all others, and they are cut off as the tops of the eares of corn.* Their dwelling is in the dust, and as for their place here, it lies wast, & is not known: *Nettles and Brambles come up in it, and the Owle and the Raven dwell in it.* But if you will visit them at their *long homes*, and knock at those *desolate doors*, you shall find some remains of them, a heap of loathsomness and corruption. O miserable and sad mutations! (*Petrarch. de otio Rel.*) Where is now their *pompous* & *shining train*? Where are their *triumphs, fire-works, and feasts*, with all the *ridiculous tumults* of a *popular, prodigious pride*? Where is their *purple* and *fine linen*, their chains of *massie gold*, and sparkling ornaments of *pearls*? Where are their *Cooks* and *Carvers*, their **fowlers* and *fishers*? Where are their curious *Utensils*, their *Cups* of *Agate, Chrystal*, and *China-earth*? Where are their sumptuous *Chambers*, where they inclosed themselvs in *Cedar, Ivory*, and *Ebeny*? Where is their *Musick*, their *soft* and *delicate dressings, pleasing motions*, and *excellency of looks*? Where are their rich *perfumes*, costly *Conserves*, with their precious and various store of *forreign* and *domestick* wines? Where are their *sons* and their *daughters* fair as the *flowers*, strait as the *Palm-trees*, and *polish'd as the corners of the Temple*? O pittiful and astonishing transformations! all is gone, all is dust, deformity, and desolation. *Their bones are scatter'd in the pit, and instead of well-set hair, there is baldnesse, and loathsomnesse instead of beauty.* This is the state of their *bodies*, and (O blessed *Jesus*!) who knowes the state of their *souls*? To have a sad guesse at this, it will not be much out of our way, if we step and visit a *Roman Emperour* upon his death-bed. If you desire his name, it is *Hadrianus*, the most

* Ingeniosa gula est: siculo scarus æquore mersus
Ad mensam vivus perducitur, inde lucrinis
Eruta littoribus vendunt conchylia cænas
Ut renovent per damna famem. Jam Phasidos unda,
Orbata est avibus; mutoque in littore tantum
Solæ desertis aspirant frondibus auræ.

— mors sola fatetur
Quantula sunt hominum corpuscula.——

ingenious and learned that ever sate upon the throne of *Cæsar*. You may beleeve, he was royally accommodated, and wanted nothing which this world could afford; but how farre he was from receiving any comfort in his death from that pompous and fruitlesse abundance, you shall learn from his own mouth, consider (I pray) what he speaks, for they are the words of a dying man, and spoken by him to his departing soul,

Animula vagula, blandula,
Hospes comésque corporis,
10 Quæ nunc abibis in loca?
Pallidula, querula, nudula,
Nec, ut soles, dabis jocos.

My soul, my pleasant soul and witty,
The guest and consort of my body,
Into what place now all alone
Naked and sad wilt thou be gone?
No mirth, no wit, as heretofore,
Nor Jests wilt thou afford me more.

Certainly, this is the saddest *poetrie*, that ever I met with; and 20 what he thought of his soul in that last *agonie*, when the *pangs* of *death* came *thick* upon him, is enough to draw tears and commiseration from a heart of flint. O happy then, yea Infinitly happy is that religious liver, who is ever meditating upon the houre of death before it comes, that when it is come, he may passe through it with joy, and speak to his soul in the language of old *Hilarion*, **Go forth, O my soul, go forth; what is it that thou art afraid of? Seventy yeers almost hast thou serv'd Christ, and art thou now afraid of death?*

* Egredere, quid times? egredere anima mea; Septuaginta propèannis Christo servisti, & mortem times? *Hieron.* in vitâ *Hilar.*

30 Alas! what is *life* if truly and throughly considered, that we should trust to it, and promise to our selves a multitude of years, as if we held *time* by the *wings*, and had the *spirit* of life in our own *hands*? *Our present life* (saith *Chrysostome*) *is a meere apparition, and differs but very little from a dreame; therefore that minde which is proud of a shadow, and relies upon a dreame, is very idle and childish.* Natural histories tell us of a bird called *Hemerobios* by the river *Hypanis*, which receives his life in the *morning*, sings at *noon*, and dyes at *night*. This *bird* may very well signifie our *life*, and by the *river* we may understand *time*, upon whose brink we are always

pearching. *Time* runs faster then any *streame*, and our *life* is swifter than any *bird*, and oft-times all the pomp of it comes to an end in one *day*, yea sometimes in an *houre*. There is no *object* we can look upon, but will do us the kindnesse to put us in minde of our mortality, if we would be so wise as to make use of it. The *day* dyes into *night*, the *spring* into *winter*, *flowers* have their *rootes* ever in their *graves*, *leaves* loose their *greenenesse*, and drop under our feete where they *flye* about and *whisper* unto us. The *beasts* run the Common lott with *us* and when they dye by our hands to give us *nourishment*, they are so kinde as to give us *Instruction* also. And if from these *frailer objects* we turne our Eyes to things that are more *permanent*, we may by the doctrine of *contrarieties* make them as useful as any of the former; And this is elegantly done by the *poet*, who was then *serious* and *stayed* enough, though somewhat *passionate*.

Nam mihi quid prodest quod longo flumina cursu
Semper inexhaustis prona feruntur aquis?
Ista manent: nostri sed non mansêre parentes,
Exigui vitam temporis hospes ago.

What is't to me that spacious rivers run
Whole ages, and their streams are never done?
Those still remain: but all my fathers di'd,
And I my self but for few dayes abide.

Thus he of the *water-course*, which he saw would out-run him, and will do so with all that come after him. But the quick *tyde* of mans life, when it is once turned and begins to *ebbe*, will never *flow* again. The *Spring* comes constantly once a yeere, and *flowers*, when the *frosts* are past, keep *house* no longer under *ground*, but feel the *Sun*, and come *abroad*. The *leaves* come again to *whisper* over our heads, and are as *green* and as *gay* as ever, *but man dieth and wasteth away*, *yea man giveth up the ghost*, *and where is he?* In these sad contemplations was the *Brittish Bard*, when he broke out into this Eloquent complaint

Mis mawrddh rhyddhig Adar,
Pob peth y ddhaw trwʒ ddhayar,
Ond y marw maur vy garchar.

In March birds couple, a new birth
Of herbs and flowers breaks through the earth,
But in the grave none stirs his head;
Long is th' Impris'ment of the dead.

The dayes of darknesse are many, and he that *goeth down to the grave shall not come up, his place shall not know him, nor shall he returne to his house; he shall not be awaked nor raised out of his sleep, untill the heavens be no more.* These last words were put in for our *comfort*, and imply the *resurrection* or the time of restoring all things. This was manifested to *Ezekiel* by the vision of dry bones with a noise and a shaking amongst them, and they came together bone to bone, and were clothed with sinews, flesh and skin, and the breath of life entered into them, and they stood upon 10 their feet an exceeding great army. We have it also confirmed out of the mouth of *Jesus Christ* himself, *John* 5. 28, 29. his words are these, *Marvel not at this, for the hour is coming, in the which all that are in the grave shall hear his voyce; And they shall come forth that have done good unto the resurrection of life; but they that have done evill unto the resurrection of condemnation.* The *Scripture* is every where full of these *proofs*: But I shall insist only upon *three.*

1. *For I know that my Redeemer liveth, and that he shall stand at the later day upon the earth. And though after my skin worms* 20 *destroy this body, yet in my flesh shall I see God. Whom I shall see for my self, and mine eyes shall behold and not another, though my reins be consumed within me.* Job. 19. 25, 26, 27.

2. *Thy dead men shall live, together with my dead body shall they arise; Awake and sing ye that dwell in the dust, for thy dew is as the dew of herbs, and the earth shall cast out the dead.* Isa. 26. 19.

3. *Behold* (*O my people*) *I will open your graves; and cause you to come up out of your graves; And ye shall know that I am the Lord when I have opened your graves, O my people, and brought you up out of your graves, and shall put my spirit in you, and yee shall live.* 30 Ezek. 37. 12, 13, 14.

And thus have we most full and absolute promises from the *divine spirit*, and from *Jesus Christ*, who is *the life of the world*, for the redemption of our bodies. Nor are we left destitute of very clear and inexcusable demonstrations of it in *nature*. We see mortal men when the *body* and *substance* of *vegetables* is consumed in the *fire*, out of their very *ashes* to make *glasse*, which is a very bright and noble *body*, how much more shall the Immortal and Almighty God (who created all things of nothing) out of dust and corruption, raise us up incorrupt and glorious bodies? *Thou fool*, (saith St.

Paul) *that which thou sowest is not quickened*, *except it die first; and that which thou sowest*, *thou sowest not that body which shall be*, *but bare grain; but God giveth it a body as he pleaseth*. There are in *nature* many *creatures* which at certain *seasons*, that their *spirit* is inconsistent with, fall into a *dormition*, or *dead sleep* which differs little from *death*, and convey themselves into *secret places*, as *hollow trees*, or some *desolate ruines*, where they may rest in safety during that *season*, as being taught by some *secret informant* that they shall *awake* again. Here have we a clear type of the *resurrection*, for what else is *death* but *sleep*, as the *Apostle* calls it? A great *Philosopher* and *Secretary* to *nature* discoursing of the *resurrection* of the *dead*, tells us, *that he oftentimes lighted upon some of those creatures in that dark state of dormition*, *and did dissect some of them*, *and cut off the limbs of others*, *and yet* (saith he) *could I perceive no signe of life at all in them*, *their arteries and flesh being as hard and as dry as a stick*, *but casting them into a pot of seething water*, *they would soften by degrees*, *and shortly after stir about*, *and those very parts which were dissected*, *would give very clear and satisfactory Indications of life*. This is so strong a *Symboll* of the resurrection, that I think it needlesse to make any application. Onely this I shall adde, that the curious observers of nature reckon these creatures amongst those of the *lunar order*; And indeed if we consider well the nature of that *planet* (whose *sphere* is the *veil* or **partition* drawn betwixt *us* and *Immortality*) and whose *relation* to this lower world is more *intimate*, and of a *greater tye* then any of the other *six*, we shall finde that she exactly typifies and demonstrates unto us those two famous *states* of terrestrial bodies, *viz.* their state of *darknesse* and their state of *glory*, their *dissolution* and *restoration*; for she doth *agonizare*, and suffers a monethly *recession* of *light*, and in a short time becomes *full* again. And I pray, are not *light* and *life* compatriots? What else is *death* but the recession and absence of *life*? or *darknesse* but the absence of *light*?

* Omne quod est suprà lunam æternumque bonúmque
Esse scias nec triste aliquid cœlestia tangit.
Quippe ultra fines lunæ illætabile nil est;
Cuncta mala in terris posuit Deus, illáque clausit
In medio, & vetuit sacrum contingere cœlum.
Supra autem lunam lucis sunt omnia plena
Nec non lætitiæ & pacis; non tempus & error
Et senium & mors est illîc, nec inutile quicquam. *Mar. Pal.*

Sic nostros casus solatur mundus in astris.
So our decays God comforts by
The Stars concurrent state on high.

Do not we see divers birds of this *regiment* such as are commonly known to us, with other meaner Creatures as *silk-worms* and the *humble-bee*, which yet are not so contemptible, but they may serve us for noble instances in this point, seeing there is in them a *living spirit*, and that creatures of the same *rank* with them are recorded in Gods own *word*, yea, and are own'd by him as *memorable* and *select Instruments* of his service, as Joshuah *Cap.* 24. *ver.* 12. *And I sent the hornet before you*, *which drove them out from before you*, *even the two kings of the Amorites*, *but not with thy sword*, *nor with* 10 *thy bowe*. And Isaiah Chap. 6 ver. 18, 19. *And it shall come to passe in that day*, *that the Lord shall hisse for the flye that is in the uttermost parts of the river of Egypt*, *and for the Bee that is in the land of Assyria ; And they shall come*, *and shall rest all of them in the desolate valleys*, *and in the holes of the rocks*, *and upon all thornes*, *and upon all bushes*. I say then, do not we see that these *birds* and inferiour *creatures* which in the *spring* and *summer* continue here very merry and *musical*, do on a sudden leave us, and all *winter*-long suffer a kind of *death*, and with the *Suns* warmth in the *youth* of the year *awake* again, and *refresh* the world with their *reviv'd notes*? For the 20 singing of birds is *naturalis musica mundi*, to which all *arted strains* are but *discord* and *hardnesse*; How much more then shall *Jesus Christ* the *Sun of righteousnesse rising with healing under his wings*, awake those that sleep in him, and bring them again with a joyful resurrection?

Having then these *prolusions* and strong *proofs* of our *restoration* laid out in *nature*, besides the promise of the *God* of nature, who cannot faile, let us so dispose of this short time of our sojourning here, that we may with joy and sure comforts expect that day of refreshing. Let us number our dayes, and apply our hearts unto 30 wisdome. What ever happens here under our feet, let it not draw down our eyes from the *hill*, whence cometh our help. Let not these sudden and prodigious mutations (like violent *earth-quakes*) shake our foundation; let us hold fast the *faith*, and presse towards the *mark*, that whether absent or present we may be accepted of him; for many are already gone astray, and have slipt into the same damnable estate with those *wretches*, whom a very *Heathen* could reprove,

> Sunt qui in fortunæ jam casibus omnia ponunt,
> Et nullo credunt mundum rectore moveri,
> 40 Naturâ volvente vices & lucis & anni.

There are that do believe all things succeed
By chance or fortune, & that nought's decreed
By a divine, wise will; but blindly call
Old time and nature rulers over all.

Let us consider him that is *invisible*, and *those that are righteous, let them be righteous still; let them have respect into the recompence of the reward, for he comes quickly, and his reward is with him. Let us endure unto the end, and overcome, that we may have right unto the tree of life, and may enter in through the gates into the City*: for, *Ex hoc momento pendet æternitas.* Upon our little inch of time in this life, depends the length and breadth, the height and depth of Immortality in the world to come: even two eternities, the one infinitely accursed, the other infinitely blessed. I remember (saith a reverend Author) that I have read (and not without admiration) of some Primitive *Christian*, that considered with himself the eternity of the torments to be endured in hell, after this manner. '*What man living* (said he) *that were in his right minde and reason,* '*if he were offered the most spacious and flourishing Kingdoms of* 'France, Spain *and* Polonia, *onely for lying continually upon any* '*one part of his body in a bed of roses for the space of forty yeers,* '*would accept of them upon that condition? And though perhaps* '*such a mad man could be found, as would accept of the offer, yet, it* '*is a thing most certain, that before three yeers would come about, he* '*would get him up, and beg to have the conditions cancell'd. And* '*what madnesse then is it, for the enjoying of one minutes pleasure,* '*for the satisfaction of our sensual, corrupt appetite, to lie for ever in* '*a bed of burning brasse, in the lake of eternal and unquenchable fire?* '*Suppose* (saith the same Writer) *that this whole Globe of earth* '*were nothing else but a huge masse, or mountain of sand, and that* '*a little Wren came but once in every thousand yeers to fetch away* '*but one grain of that huge heap; what an innumerable number of* '*yeers would be spent, before that world of sand could be so fetcht* '*away? And yet (alas!) when the damned have laine in that fiery* '*lake so many yeers as all those would amount to, they are no nearer* '*coming out, then the first houre they entered in.* To the same purpose is this *Hymne* of the *Ancients.*

Ex quo poli sunt perfecti
Aude numero complecti
Stellas cœli, stillas roris,
Undas aquei fluoris,

Guttas imbris pluvialis,
Floccos velleris nivalis.
Quot sunt vere novo flores,
Quot odores, quot colores,
Quot vinacios Autumnus,
Poma legit & vertumnus;
Quot jam grana tulit æstas,
Frondes hyemis tempestas,
Totus orbis animantes,
10 *Aër atomos volantes,*
Pilos feræ, pecus villos,
Vertex hominum capillos;
Adde littoris arenas,
Adde graminis verbenas,
Tot myriades Annorum,
Quot momenta sæculorum:
Heus adhuc æternitatis
Portus fugit à damnatis!
Æternum, æternum! quanta hæc duratio, quanta!
20 Quàm speranda bonis, quámque tremenda malis!

From the first hour the heav'ns were made
Unto the last, when all shall fade,
Count (if thou canst) the drops of dew,
The stars of heav'n and streams that flow;
The falling snow, the dropping showres,
And in the moneth of *May* the flowres,
Their sents and colours, and what store
Of grapes and apples Autumne bore;
How many grains the Summer beares,
30 What leaves the wind in Winter tears;
Count all the creatures in the world,
The motes which in the air are hurl'd,
The haires of beasts and mankind, and
The shores innumerable sand,
The blades of grasse, and to these last
Adde all the yeers which now are past,
With those whose course is yet to come,
And all their minutes in one summe.
When all is done, the damneds state
40 Out-runs them still, and knows no date.

O Eternity, eternity (saith a holy *Father*) *whose strength is able to bear out thy torments! And the smoke of their torments ascendeth up for ever & ever! & they have no rest day nor night! O what is this same for ever and ever! Gladly would I speak something of it, but I know not what to speak. All that I know, is this; That it is that, which onely the infinitenesse of the Almighty God doth compasse about and comprehend.* Seeing then it is so, that eternal pleasures or eternal pains do inavoidably and immediately overtake us after our dissolution, with what unwearied care and watchfulnesse should we continue in well-doing, and *work out our salvation with fear and trembling?* How should we *as strangers and pilgrims abstain from fleshly lusts, which warre against the soul? What manner of persons* 10 *ought we to be in all holy conversation and godlinesse?* With what Christian thrift and diligence should we dispose of every minute of our time that we might make *our calling and election sure?* It is a fearful thing to die without reconciliation; And with what confusion of face and horrour of spirit (if we die in that state,) shall we appear before the *Judge of all the world?* when he shall come in the *Clouds of heaven* with his *holy Angels*, and all mankind from the *first* man created, unto the *last* that shall be borne upon the earth shall appear before his Judgement-seate. Me thinks I see the remisse, lukewarme *professour*, and the *hypocritical*, *factious* 20 *pretender* of *sanctity* looking up to the *Clouds*, and crying out, *O that throne! that flaming, white, and glorious throne! and he that sits thereon, with the sharp sickle in his hand and the crown of pure gold upon his head!* Revel. 14. 14, *from whose face the heaven and the earth flye away, and the foundations of the world are brought to nothing. Oh! is he the Lamb that was slain whose blood was poured out like water upon the earth to save his people from their sins? Is he the Prince of life that was crown'd with thornes, scourged, spit upon, crucified, pierced through, and murthered, and comes he now to judge the world? Oh! It is he! It is he! miserable wretch that* 30 *I am! What shall I do, or whither shall I go?*

Such will be the *dreadful agonies* and *concertations* in that *day* betwixt the *Hypocrite* and his *conscience*, betwixt the *enemies* of Gods truth and their *gasping undone souls. When the people that forget God shall go down quick into hell, and the secrets of all hearts shall be disclosed and laid open before Angels and men;* For in that day all their dark and private *lusts*, their *closet-sins*, *bosome-councels*, *specious pretences*, and *bloody machinations*, which now (like so many *foul spirits*) lurk in their *gloomy breasts*, shall be forced out, and will appear as visible to all *mankind*, as if they were written with the 40 *beams* of the *Sun* upon the pure and unclouded *firmament*. In the *mean while the very *fowles of the aire*, and their own *horrid guilt* either in time of *distraction* (which they are alwayes subject to) or in their *sleep* (which is alwayes fraught with *penal visions* and *spiritual tumults*) may make a *full discovery* of their most *secret villanies* before the appointed time.

* Est pœna præsens consciæ mentis pavor, Animúsque culpâ plenus, & semet timens. Scelus aliquis tutum, nullus securum tulit.

It was a blessed and a glorious age the Primitive *Christians* lived 10 in, *when the wildernesse and the solitary places were glad for them, and the desert rejoyced and blossom'd as the rose*. When the blood of *Christ* was yet warme, and the memory of his *miracles* and *love* fresh and vigorous; what *Zeale*, what powerful *faith*, what perfect *charity*, hearty *humility*, and true *holinesse* was then to be found upon the earth? If we compare the *shining* and *fervent piety* of those Saints, with *the painted* and *illuding appearance* of it in *these of our times*, we shall have just cause to fear that our *Candlestick* (which hath been now of a long time under a Cloud) is at this very instant upon removing. But I had rather you should be informed 20 of their true *holinesse* and *love* to *Christ*, by an *Eye-witnesse* that was conversant with them, *and went in and out amongst them*, then by a bare relation from my pen. Heare therefore what he saith. *Vidi ego, & verè vidi thesaurum Christi in humanis absconditum vasculis, &c. vidi enim apud eos multos Patres in terra positos cœlestem vitam agentes, & novos quosdam Prophetas tam virtutibus animi, quàm vaticinandi officio imbutos, &c. Nonnullos namque eorum ità ab omni malitia, cogitatione & suspicione vidimus alienos, ut nec si aliquid mali adhuc in seculo gereretur, meminissent, tanta in eis erat tranquillitas* 30 *animi, tantúsque in eis inoleverat bonitatis affectus, &c. Commanent autem per eremum dispersi & separati cellulis, sed charitatis vinculo connexi. Ob hoc autem dirimuntur habitaculis, ut silentii sui quietem & intentionem mentis nec vox aliqua, nec occursus ullus, aut sermo aliquis otiosus obturbet. Intentis ergo in suo quisque loco animis velut fideles servi adventantem dominum expectant. Omnes hi nullam cibi, aut indumenti, aut ullius horum sollicitudinem gerunt. Justitiam & regnum Dei requirunt, armis orationum pugnant, & scuto fidei ab inimico insidiante protecti patriam sibi cœlestem conquirunt.* 'I have 'seen (saith he,) and I was not deceived, the treasure of Christ laid 40 'up in earthen vessels; for amongst those Christians in *Egypt* I have

Hieron. in vit. Pat.

'seen many Fathers who had here upon earth already begun the 'heavenly life; and regenerate Prophets who were indued not onely 'with holy habits, but had received therewith the Spirit of promise: 'for I have known many of them that were so free from malice, 'perverse thoughtfulnesse and suspition, as if they had never 'known that there were such evill wayes to be followed in the world, 'Such a great tranquillity of mind, and such a powerful love or 'longing after goodnesse had wholly possessed them. They lived 'dispersed up and down the wildernesse, and separated from one 'another in several Cells or Cots, but knit all together in the perfect 10 'bond of Charity. The reason of their distinct and distant habita- 'tions, was, because they would not have the silence of their retire- 'ments disturbed, nor their minds diverted from the contemplation 'of heavenly things by any noyse, sudden occurrence, or idle dis- 'course; for this cause they have every one their particular mansion, 'where with intentive or earnest minds they do (like faithful 'servants) expect and look for the coming of their Master. They 'take no thought for meat and drink and cloathing, nor for any 'such accommodations; they seek onely the Kingdome of God 'and the righteousnesse thereof, they fight with the weapons of 20 'prayer, & being guarded with the shield of faith from the devices 'of their spiritual enemies, so travel on towards their heavenly 'countrey. This was the *old way*, and whether we are *in it*, or *out* of it, is not hard to be decided. A pretended *sanctity* from the teeth outward, with the frequent *mention* of the *Spirit*, and a pre- sumptuous assuming to our selves of the stile of *Saints*, when we are within full of *subtilty*, *malice*, *oppression*, *lewd opinions*, and *diverse lusts*, is (I am sure) a convincing argument that we are not onely *out* of it, but that we have no mind to returne *into* it. The *way* to heaven is *wet* and *slippery*, but it is made so with *teares* 30 and not with *blood*; it is through the *vale of miseries*, *and the raine filleth the pooles*, Psal. 85. There is no *voyce* in those *shades of Palme*, but the *voyce* of the *Turtle*, which is alwayes *groning*, and *Naturalists* say, *she hath no gall.* It is ill coming to the *Lamb* of God in a *Wolfes* skin; They that do so, must be taught that he hath another *attribute*, and they shall finde him a *Lion.* It is strange that (after the experience of almost *six thousand yeares*) men will hazard so highly, as to purchase a few dayes false honours, with the losse of eternal and true glory. In what a horrid darknesse and agony will the pleasures of this world leave us, after we have cast away 40 our bodies and souls in the acquisition of them? how suddenly must the *rich man* leave his *barnes*, and the *oppressour* his ill-gotten *power*? how do they labour under the load of their private guilt, and feele the flames of hell while they are yet alive? With what gloomy and despairing looks do they passe from hence, as if that eternal darknesse they are going into, were already in their faces? It was a sad and a dark reply that *Henry* the *fourth* made to his *hasty son*, when he had taken away the *Crowne*; *God knowes* (said he and sighed) *what right I had unto it*. Tyrants and oppressors may very well be compared to the *Hyæna*; while they prosper, and devoure the *prey*, there is nothing to be seene amongst them but *mirth* and *triumphs*; but when they have drank *blood* enough, when they are full and cloyed, *then they *weepe*. The onely difference is this, that the *Hyæna's* teares are deceitful, but the teares of Tyrants springing from their inward guilt and horrour, are wofully true, though (like *storms* in *harvest*) they are unprofitable and prodigious.

* Sinnes are not felt, till they are acted.

The difference betwixt the *righteous* and the *wicked* is to be seen in their *death*. The good man goes hence like the *Sunne* in the *summers evening* chearful and unclouded, his memory is precious here with men, and his spirit is received into the *joy of his Master*. This Saint *Hierome* saw in the death of *Paul* the *Heremite*, whose *coate* of *Palm-leaves* he preferr'd to the *purple robes* of the proud. *Let me now* (saith he) *aske the great men of this world, whose possessions are numberlesse, and whose dwellings are of marble, what was it, that was ever wanting to this poor old man? They drink rich wines out of gold, and he drank clean water out of the fountains. They have silk and gold weav'd into their coates, and he had not so much as the coursest wooll. But then is he out of that simple habit carried into Paradise, and they out of their silk and gold into hell.* Paul *the Heremite hath no covering but the *common earth; Their karkasses are laid up in ¶costly Sepulchres of marble and brasse; but* Paul *shall be raised to glory, and they to condemnation.* And presently after directing his speech to the Reader, he concludes thus: *Who ever thou art, that shalt reade this Book, I beseech thee to remember* Hieronymus *the **sinner, who (if God would grant him his desire) had rather be*

* Cœlo tegitur, qui non habet urnam.

¶ Jam ruet & bustum, titulúsque in marmore sectus,
— tumulis autem morientibus, ipse
Occumbes etiam, sic mors tibi tertia restat.

** Non sanctum dixit, sed peccatorem.

master of Paul *the Heremites coate with his rewards then of the purple robes of Princes with their punishments.* A *dinner of herbes* with a *good conscience* is *heavenly fare*, and *godlinesse is great gaine*, *if we would be contented therewith.* I do not so much admire *Apitius* his feasts, and *Cleopatra's* banquets of *dissolved pearles*, as I do the *Raven* of *Elias*, and *Hilarion's Crow.* Neither can I in this place passe by that *old Cilician* and Countreyman to Saint *Paul*, who (I verily beleeve,) for a reward of his contented and harmlesse life, had the *honor* and the *happinesse* to have it described and left for ever upon record to posterity, by that inimitable *Prince* and *Patriarch* of *Poets*;

—O quantum bonum est obstare nulli, carpere securas dapes!

Humi ejacentem scelera non intrant casam.

Virg. lib. 4. *Georgic.*

Namque sub Oebaliæ memini me turribus altis
Corycium vidisse senem: cui pauca relicti
Jugera ruris erant, nec fertilis illa juvencis,
Nec pecori opportuna seges, nec commoda Baccho.
Hic rarum tamen in dumis holus, albáque circum
Lilia, verbenásque premens, vescúmque papaver,
Regum æquabat opes animo, serâque revertens
Nocte domum, dapibus mensas onerabat inemptis.
Primus vere rosam, atque Autumno carpere poma:
Et cum tristis hyems etiamnum frigore saxa
Rumperet, & glacie cursus frænaret aquarum,
Ille comam mollis jam tum tondebat Acanthi
Æstatem increpitans seram, Zephirósque morantes.

Englished thus

I saw beneath Tarentum's *stately towers*
An old Cilician *spend his peaceful houres:*
Some few bad acres *in a waste*, *wild* field,
Which neither Grasse, *nor* Corne, *nor* Vines *would yield*,
He did possesse; There (*amongst* thorns *and* weeds)
Cheap Herbs and Coleworts, *with the common* Seeds
Of Chesboule *or* tame poppeys *he did sowe*,
And Verveyne *with* white Lilies *caus'd to grow.*
Content he was, *as are successeful* Kings,
And late at night come home (for long work brings
The night still home,) *with* unbought messes *layd*
On his low table, *he his* hunger *stayd.*

Roses *he gather'd in the* youthful Spring;
And Apples *in the* Autumn *home did bring;*
And when the sad, cold winter *burst with frost*
The stones, *and the* still streams *in* Ice *were lost,*
He would soft leaves of Beares-foot *crop, and chide*
The slow West-winds, and lingring Summer tyde!

Saint *Hierome* in the life of *Antonius*, (who was nobly borne and as tenderly bred) tells us, that about the age of *eighteen* (his parents being then dead,) he gave away all his possessions, & resolving
10 upon a strict, religious life betook himself to the *wildernesse*; where having erected for himself a poore narrow *Cottage*, he digg'd hard by it, and found a *well*, with whose streams he watered a small piece of *ground*, which he did sowe and set with some ordinary *herbs* for his own provision. To this place thus furnished by his industrie, the *wild asses* would in great numbers very often resort, and not contented to borrow of his *water*, they would some times trespasse upon his *garden*, and make bold with his *sallads*. But he upon a time comming amongst them, commanded the *leader* of them, which he had observed to *guide* the *rest*, to stand still, and
20 beating him upon the sides with his hand, reproved him in these words, *What is the reason that thou com'st to eat that which thou hast not sowen? Et exinde* (saith my Author) *acceptis aquis ad quas potandas ventitabant, nec arbusculam, nec holera unquam contigebant.* We see by these Examples how safe it is to rely upon our *Masters* promise, and how needlesse and superfluous in the Christian state this worldly abundance is. This our Saviour himself hath admonished us of, and upraids our diffidence with the examples of the *birds* and the *lilies* of the *field*. Certainly it is dangerous medling with the *world*; It is like the **Torpedo*, he that
30 catcheth it, comes to lose his life by the bargain. *Love not the world* (saith St. *John*) *neither the things that are in the world, if any man love the world, the love of the Father is not in him.* We should therefore be very cautious how we deal with it, or with the followers and favourites of it. *Condescend to men of low estate*, saith the *chosen vessel*; This is good counsel, but it lies so low that most men tread upon it, & very few are they that will stoop to take it up. There is nothing can bring us sooner to it then the serious consideration of our own frailty. This is the
40 *Catharma* that turns away the plague; and as *Physicians* say of

* *A fish that* (*as soon as ever he is struck*,) *so benums the Angler, that he dies.*
Arcanas hyemes & cæca papavera ponti Abdo sinu, & celerem frigida vincla necem.

fasting, that it cures almost all bodily diseases: So may I say of this, that it prevents (if timely applyed) all the *depravations and diseases* of the mind. It will bring down every *high thought* & set us upon even ground, where we shall be in no danger of soul or body. Our Saviour was buried in a Rock, and he that builds upon his grave, he that mortifies his affections, and hides his life in him, needs feare no *stormes*. What beauty is there in a *deaths-head* crownd with *roses*? If we carry the *one* about us, we shall be safe enough from the temptations of the *other*. Let sensual *natures* judge as they please, but for my part, I shall hold it no *Paradoxe* to affirme, *there are no pleasures in this world*. Some *coloured griefes* and *blushing woes* there are, which look so clear as if they were *true complexions*; but it is a very sad and a tryed truth that they are but *painted*. To draw then to an end, let us looke alwayes upon this *Day-Lilie* of life, as if the *Sun* were already *set*. Though we *blossome* and *open* many *mornings*, we shall not do so always, *Soles occidere & redire possunt*; but *man* cannot. *He hath his time appointed him upon earth, which he shall not passe, and his days are like the days of an hireling*. Let us then so husband our time, that when the *flower* falls, the *seed* may be preserved. We have had many blessed Patterns of a holy life in the *Brittish Church*, though now trodden under foot, and branded with the title of *Antichristian*. I shall propose but *one to you, the most obedient *Son* that ever his *Mother* had, and yet a most glorious true *Saint* and a *Seer*. Heark how like a *busie Bee* he *hymns* it to the *flowers*, while in a handful of *blossomes* gather'd by himself, he foresees his own *dissolution*.

Qui jacet in terra, non habet undè cadat.

Omnem crede diem tibi diluxisse supremum.

* Mr. *George Herbert* of blessed memory; See his incomparable prophetick Poems, and particularly these, *Church-musick*, *Church-rents, and schisms*, *The Church militant*.

I made a Posie while the day ran by:
Here will I smell my remnant out, and tye
My life within this band,

But time did becken to the flowers, and they
By noon most cunningly did steal away,
And wither'd in my hand.

My hand was next to them, and then my heart:
I took, without more thinking, in good part
Times gentle admonition;

Who did so sweetly death's sad taste convey,
Making my mind to smell my fatal day;
Yet sugring the suspition.

Farewel dear flowers! sweetly your time ye spent,
Fit, while ye liv'd, for smell or ornament,
And after death for cures.

I follow strait without complaint or grief,
Since if my sent be good, I care not if
It be as short as yours.

10 As often therefore as thou seest the *full* and *ripe corne*, to succeed the *tender* and *flowery Spring*, the *Autumne* again to succeed the *Summer*, and the *cold* and *snowie Winter* to succeed the *Autumne*, say with thy self, *These seasons passe away, but will returne againe: but when I go, I shall returne no more.*

Petrar. *de Contemp. mundi.*
Immortalia ne speres monet annus, & almum
Quæ rapit hora diem.
Frigora mitescunt Zephyris,
ver proterit æstas
Interitura simul
Pomifer Autumnus fruges effuderit, & mox
Bruma recurrit iners.

When thou seest the *Sun* to set, and the melancholy *shadowes* to prevaile and increase, meditate with thy selfe, *Thus when my life is* 20 *done, will the shadowes of death be stretched over me; And yet this Sun which now leaves me, will be here againe to morrow: but when the Sun of my life sets, it shall not returne to me, until the heavens be no more.*

When the *night* is drawn over thee, and the whole world lies slumbring under it, do not thou sleep it out; for as it is a *portion* of time much abused by wicked livers, so is it of all others the most powerful to excite thee to *devotion*; be stirring therefore, and make special use of that *deepest* and *smoothest current* of *time*, like that vigilant *Pilot* who alwayes mistrusted the *greatest calms*,

30 Sydera cuncta notat tacito labentia cœlo. *And rising at midnight the Stars espi'd*
All posting Westward in a silent glide.

When thou also seest those *various, numberles, and beautiful luminaries* of the night to move on in their *watches*, and some of them to *vanish* and *set*, while all the rest do *follow after*, consider that *thou* art carried on with *them* in the *same motion*, and that there is no hope of subsisting for thee, but in *him who never moves, and never sets.*

Consider thy own *posterity* (if thou hast any) or those that are *younger then thy self*, and say, *These are travelling up the hill of life, but I am going head-long down.* Consider thy own *habitation*, how many have been there before thy *time*, whom that place must never know again, and that there is no help, but *thou* must follow. Consider the *works of thine own hands*, the *flowers*, *trees* and *arbours* of thine own planting, for all those must survive thee; Nay, who knows but thou mayst be gone, before thou canst enjoy those pleasures thou dost expect from them; for the *Poet* in that point proves oftentimes a *Prophet*,

The trees, we set, grow slowly, and their shade 10
Stays for our sons, while (we the Planters) fade.

Virg. Georg.

Tarda venit, serísque futura nepotibus umbra.

To be short, acquit thee *wisely* and *innocently* in all thy Actions, live a *Christian*, and die a *Saint*. Let not the *plurality* of *dayes*, with the numerous *distinctions* and *mincings* of thy *time* into *moneths*, *weeks*, *houres* and *minutes* deceive thee, nor be a means to make thee misspend the *smallest portion* of it; let not the *empty honours* and *pompous nothing* of this world keep thee back from the *grapes* of the *brook* of *Eshcol*. Remember that we must account for 20 every idle *word*, much more for our *actions*. If thou hast lost any *dear friends*, have them alwayes before thine eyes, visit their *graves* often, and be not unkind to a *Jonathan* though in the *dust*. Give eare to *heaven*, and forget not what is spoken to thee from thence. *Behold, I come as a thief; blessed is he that watcheth and keepeth his garments, lest he walk naked, and they see his shame.* The time of life is short, and *God* (when he comes to see us) *comes without a bell. Let us therefore gird up the loynes of our minds, and be sober, and hope to the end. Let us keep our selves in the love of God as obedient children, not grieving his holy Spirit, by which we are sealed unto* 30 *the day of redemption. And let us not give place to the devil, nor be weary of well-doing; but let us be renewed daily in the spirit of our mind that when he comes (who will not tarry) we may be found faithful, and about our masters businesse.*

Let us feare God, and forgive men, blesse those that persecute us, and lay up treasure for our selves in heaven, that where our treasure is, there our hearts may be also, and this (if God permits) will we do, and then

—We can go die as sleep, and trust
Half that we have
Unto an honest, faithful grave
Making our pillows either down or dust.

Now unto him, who shall change our vile bodies, that they may be fashioned like unto his glorious body, according to the working whereby he is able to subdue all things unto himselfe, even unto *Jesus Christ* the Prince of the Kings of the earth, and the first begotten of the dead, be glory and dominion for ever and ever. *Amen.*

10 *A Prayer when thou findest thy self sickly, or when thou art visited with any Disease*

Most merciful, and wise God, who *bringest light out of darknesse*, and true *comforts* out of the greatest *afflictions*, I do in all humility and with all my soule resigne my selfe unto thy divine pleasure, and give thee most hearty and unfeined thanks for this thy present *visitation*, an infallible argument of thy fatherly love, and that tender care which thou hast of my salvation. Thou gavest me health, and I took no notice of thy *gift*, and but very little of the *Giver*: Thou gavest me dayes of gladnesse and I *numberd them not.* 20 Wherefore with most true sorrow for my unthankfulnesse, and with all the *sad Resentments* of a most penitent heart I do acknowledge thy *justice*, adore thy *providence*, and beg thy *mercy.* O *righteous Father!* Though I have gone astray, do not thou cast me off: though *I am no more worthy to be called thy son*, yet have *thou a minde to the work of thine own hands.* Confirme my *faith*, sanctifie my *affections*, give me a lively and enduring *hope*, with an unwearied *patience*; And strengthen me in all my *Agonies* with the *celestial assistance* and *inexpressible refreshments* of thy *overcoming spirit.* Thou that didst give to thy blessed and faithful 30 *Martyrs* such a glorious *measure* of thy Almighty *spirit*, as encouraged them for thy sake to be *sawed* asunder, to be *burnt*, *stoned and beheaded*, give unto me now such a gracious *portion* of the same *Comforter* as may leade me through *death* unto *life*. Or if thou wilt in mercy restore me again, and enlarge my time, give me, I beseech thee, a thankful *heart*, holy *resolutions*, and a stedfast *spirit* to performe them; And for *Jesus Christ* his sake never suffer me to forget thy *tender and fatherly compassion*, or to fall again into my old sins, and *heap* up for my self thy eternal anger and most just indignation.

For what end soever thou hast sent this present *sicknesse*, whether for my *dissolution*, or for a temporal *correction* of my sinful life, grant I beseech thee, that both may be for thy *glory*, and the salvation of my poore soule, purchased with the *precious blood* of thine only *Sonne* and my dear *Redeemer*, to whom with thee and the *holy Ghost* be ascribed by *Angels* and *men*, all wisdome, dominion and majesty for ever and ever, *Amen!*

A Prayer in the hour of Death

O my most blessed and glorious *Creatour* that *hast fed me all my life long*, and *redeemed me from all evil*, seeing it is thy merciful pleasure to take me out of this fraile body, and to *wipe away all teares from mine eyes*, and all sorrowes from my heart, I do with all humility and willingnesse consent and submit my self wholly unto thy sacred will. *I desire to be dissolved and to be with my Saviour.* I blesse and praise thy holy name for all thy great mercies conferred upon me, from the first day of my life unto this present hour. I give thee all possible thanks for this gracious & kind *visitation*, in which thou art mercifully pleased to order this *last act* of thy *poor creature* to thy *glory*, and the *fruition* of those *heavenly comforts* which have already *swallowed* up my whole *spirit*. O let *all* that come after me speak of thy *wondrous mercies*, and the *generations* which are yet unborn give praise unto thy *name*.

Lord *Jesus Christ* my most loving Redeemer, into thy saving and *everlasting Armes* I commend my *spirit*, I am ready my *dear Lord*, and earnestly expect and long for thy good pleasure; *Come quickly*, and receive the soul of thy *servant* which trusteth in thee.

Blessing, and honour, and glory and power be unto him that sitteth upon the throne, and unto the Lamb and to the holy Ghost for ever and ever Amen.

Glory be to God on high, and on earth peace, good will towards men!

Blessed be God alone!
Thrice blessed three in one!

Flores Solitudinis.

Certaine Rare and Elegant

PIECES;

Viz.

Two Excellent Diſcourſes

Of { 1. *Temperance, and Patience*; 2. *Life and Death.* }

BY

I. E. NIEREMBERGIUS.

THE WORLD

CONTEMNED;

BY

EUCHERIUS, Bp of LYONS.

And the Life of

PAULINUS,

Bp of *NOLA.*

Collected in his Sickneſſe and Retirement

BY

HENRY VAUGHAN, Siluriſt.

Tantus Amor Florum, & generandi gloria Mellis.

London, Printed for *Humphrey Moſeley* at the
Princes Armes in St *Pauls* Church-yard. 1654.

TO

THE TRUELY NOBLE
And Religious
Sir *CHARLES EGERTON*
Knight

SIR,

If, when you please to looke upon these Collections, *you will find them to lead you from the Sun into the* shade, *from the open* Terrace *into a private* grove, *& from the* noyse *and* pompe *of this world into a silent and solitary* Hermitage*: doe not you thinke then, that you have descended* (*like the* dead) in Occidentem & tenebras, *for in this* withdrawing-roome (*though secret and seldome frequented,*) *shines that happy* starre, *which will directly lead you to the* King *of* light. *You have long since quitted the* Publick, *& to present you now with some thing of solitude* and the contempt of the world, *would looke like a* designe *to Flatter you, were not my* Name, *argument enough for the contrary. Those few that know me, will* (*I am sure*) *be my* Compurgators*; and I my selfe dare assert this,* you have no cause to suspect it. *But what ever the thoughts of men will be, I am already sure of this advantage, that we live in an age, which hath made this very* Proposition (*though suspected of* Melancholie,) *mighty pleasing, and even* meane witts *begin to like it; the* wiser sort *alwaies did, for what* (*I beseech you,*) *hath this world, that should make a wise man in love with it? I will take the boldnesse to describe it in the same character which* Bisselius *did the hansome concubine of* Mahomet *the great:*

> *Puella tota quanta, nil erat aliud*
> *Quàm Illecebra picta, delicatus harpago, &c.*

> *The whole* wench (*how compleat soe'r*) *was but*
> *A specious* baite*; a soft, sly, tempting* slut*;*
> *A pleasing witch; a living* death*; a faire,*
> *Thriving* disease*; a fresh,* infectious aire*;*
> *A pretious* plague*; a* furie *sweetly drawne;*
> Wild fire *laid up and finely drest in* Lawne.

This delicate, admir'd Inchantresse (even to those who enjoy her after their owne lusts, and at their owne rate,) will prove but a very sad bargaine; she is all deception and sorrow. This world *and the* prince *of it are the* Canker-Rose *in the mouth of the* fox*:* Decipit, arefit, pungit. *But those future, supreme* fruitions *which God hath in store for those that love him are neither* Phantasmes, *nor* fallacies*; they are all substantiall and certaine, and in the Apostles phrase, Καθ' ὑπερβολὴν εἰς ὑπερβολὴν αἰώνιον Βάρος δόξης*, a far more exceeding and eternall weight of glory. *Nothing can give that, which it hath not, this transitory, changeable and corrupt world cannot afford permanent treasures. All it gives, and all it shewes us, is but* trash & illusion. *The true incorruptible riches dwell above the reach of rust and theeves.*

Man himselfe in his outward part, *which was taken out of the world, feeles the like passions with the world, he is worn, washed, dissolved and changed, he comes hither, he knowes not how, and goes from hence, he knowes not whither.* Nescio quò vado, valete posteri! *was the* Roman's *Epitaph: One generation commeth, and another passeth away.* Properant & decurrunt in absconditum, *they hasten and drive on to their appointed place, untill the great day of accompt. All the severall* shapes *and* gestures *we see in this wild* Masque *of* time *are but so many* disguises *which the* Spirits *that first assumed them, cast off againe when they have acted their* parts. *Most elegantly did* Augurellius *sing to* Peter Lipomanus *upon the death of his sister* Clara*;*

Amæna, Petre, cum vides, &c.

Peter, *when thou this pleasant world dost see,*
Beleeve, thou seest meere Dreames *and* vanitie*;*
Not reall *things, but* false*: and through the* Aire
Each where, an empty, slipp'rie Scene, *though faire.*
The chirping birds, *the fresh* woods *shadie boughes,*
The leaves *shrill whispers, when the* west-wind *blowes.*
The swift, fierce Greyhounds *coursing on the plaines,*
The flying hare *distrest 'twixt feare and paines;*
The bloomy Mayd *decking with* flowers *her head,*
The gladsome, easie youth *by light* love *lead;*
And whatsoe'r heere with admiring eyes
Thou seem'st to see, 'tis but a fraile disguise
Worne by eternall things, *a passive* dresse
Put on by beings *that are passiveles.*

All the gay appearances in this life seeme to me but a swift succession of rising Clouds, *which neither abide in any certaine* forme, *nor continue for any* long time*; And this is that, which makes the* sore travell of the sonnes of men *to be nothing else, but a meere chasing of shadowes.* All is vanity (*said the Royall Philosopher*,) and there is no new thing under the Sun.

I present you therefore with a discourse perswading to a contempt *& a* desertion *of these* old things which (*our Saviour tells us*) shall passe away*; And with an historicall, faithfull relation of the life and* 10 *happinesse of a devout, primitive* father, *who gave all that he had upon earth to the poore, that he* might have treasure in heaven. *Some other* Additions *you will finde, which meeting now in this volume under your name, will in their descent to posterity, carry with them this fairest Testimonie*, I loved you. *This* (*Sir*) *is my maine and my sole designe in this* Addresse, *without* reservation *and without* flattery, *for which respect, and for no other, I beleeve you will accept of what I have done, and looke upon my suddaine and small* Presents, *as upon some forward* flowers *whose kinde hast hath brought them above ground* in cold weather. *The incertainty of life, and a peevish,* 20 *inconstant state of health would not suffer me to stay for greater performances, or a better season; least loosing this, I should never againe have the opportunity to manifest how much and how sincerely I am*

Sir

Your Servant and
well-wisher

Henry Vaughan

Newton by
Uske neare
Sketh-Rock
1653

To the Reader

Candidus & medicans Ignis deus est. *So sings the* Poet, *and so must I affirme, who have been tryed by that* white *and* refining fire, with healing under his wings. *Quarrelling with his* light, *and wandring from that fresh and competent* gourd, *which he had shadowed me with, drew those* Sun-beames *upon my head, whose strong and fervent* vibrations *made me oftentimes beg of him*, that I might dye. *In those sad* Conflicts *I dedicated the* Remissions *to thy* use, *Reader, & now I offer them to thy* view. *If the* title *shall offend thee, because it was found in the* woods *and the* wildernesse, *give mee leave to tell thee, that* Deserts *and* Mountaines *were the* Schooles *of the* Prophets, *and that* Wild-hony *was his* diet, *who by the testimony of the* Sonne *of* God, *was* the greatest amongst those that are borne of women. *It may be thy spirit is such a popular, phantastick* flye, *as loves to gad in the* shine *of this world; if so, this* light *I live by in the* shade, *is too great for thee. I send it abroad to bee a companion of those wise* Hermits, *who have withdrawne from the present generation, to confirme them in their solitude, and to make that rigid* necessity *their pleasant* Choyse. *To leave the* world, *when it leaves us, is both* sordid *and* sorrowfull; *and to quitt our* station *upon discontents, is nothing else, but to be the* Apes *of those Melancholy* Schismaticks, *who having burnt off their owne hands in setting the world on fire, are now fallen out with it*, because they cannot rule it. *They are* Spirits *of a very poore, inferiour* order, *that have so much* Sympathy *with worldlie things, as to weepe at Parting; And of as low a* Parentage *are those, that will be sick of* Leap-yeares & Sublunarie mutations. *I honour that* temper, *which can lay* by *the* garland, *when he may keepe it* on: *which can passe by a* Rosebud, *and bid it* grow, *when he is invited to* crop *it*,

> ———Whose gentle measure
> Complyes and suits with all *estates*;
> Which can let loose to a *Crown*, and yet with pleasure
> Take up within a *Cloyster* gates.
> This Soule doth *Span* the world, and *hang* content
> From either *pole* unto the *center*,
> Where in each *Roome* of the well-furnished *tent*
> He lyes warme and without adventure.

Prince Lewes, *the eldest Son of* Charles *King of* Naples, *at the age of twenty one yeares, and just when he should have been married to the youthfull Princesse of* Majorica, *did suddenly at* Barcellon *put on the rough and severe* habit *of the* Franciscans*: The* Queens *and* Princesses *there met to solemnize the marriage of his sister* Blanch *with* James *King of* Aragon, *imployed all their* Rhetorick *to disswade him from it; but to no purpose, he loved his* Sackcloth *more then their* silks, *and* (*as Mounsier* Mathieu (*alluding to that* young Princesse,) *speakes of him*,) Left Roses to make Conserve of thornes. *Resolution*, Reader, *is the Sanctuary of Man, and Saint* Pauls *content is that famous* Elixir, *which turnes the* rudest mettall *into* smooth *and* ductible gold*: It is the Philosophers* secret fire, *that* stomack *of the* Ostrich *which digests* Iron, *and dissolves the hard flint into bloud and nutriment. It was an honest* Reply *that his* Cook *made unto the Duke of* Millain, *when worsted in a great battell by the* Florentines, *the over passionate resentment of so unexpected a repulse, made him quarrell with his meate:* If the Florentines (*said he*) have spoyled your tast, that is no fault of mine; the meate is pleasant, and well drest, but the good successe of your Enemies hath made your appetite ill.

I protest seriously unto thee, and without Scepticisme, *that there is no such thing in this world, as* misfortune*; the foolish* testinesse *of man arising out of his* misconstruction *and* ignorance *of the wise method of* Providence, *throwes him into many* troubles. *The* Spouse *tells us, that the fingers of the* Bride-groome *are deckt with* Beryll *and* pretious stones*: what ever falls upon us from that Almighty* hand, *it is a* diamond*; It is celestiall* treasure, *and the matter of some new* blessing, *if we abuse it not.* God (*saith the wise King*,) created not Evill, but man (who was created upright) sought out many inventions: *these indeed beget that* monster*; his ill* digestion *of his* punishment (*which is a kinde of* divine diet,) *makes him to pine away in a sinfull discontent. If thou art sick of such an* Atrophie, *the precepts layd down in this little booke* (*if rightly* understood, *and faithfully* practised) *will perfectly cure thee.*

All that may bee objected is, that I write unto thee out of a land of darkenesse, out of that unfortunate region, where the Inhabitants sit in the shadow of death: where destruction passeth for propagation, and a thick black night for the glorious day-spring. If this discourage thee, be pleased to remember, that there are bright starrs under the most palpable clouds, and light is never so beautifull as in the presence of darknes. At least intreat God that the Sun may not goe down upon thy own dwelling, which is hartily desired and prayed for, by

Newton by Usk in
South-wales.
April. 17. 1652

Hen: Vaughan

Primitive Holineſs,

Set forth in the

LIFE

of bleſſed

PAULINUS,

The moſt Reverend, and
Learned BISHOP of
NOLA:

Collected out of his own Works,
and other Primitive Authors by

Henry Vaughan, Siluriſt.

---

2 Kings *cap.* 2. *ver.* 12.
My Father, my Father, the Chariot of
Iſrael, *and the Horſmen thereof.*

LONDON,

Printed for *Humphrey Moſeley* at
the *Prince's Armes* in St. *Paul's*
Church-yard. 1654.

TO THE READER

If thou lovest Heaven, *and the beauty of Immortality, here is a* guide *will lead thee into that* house of light. *The* earth *at present is not worth the enjoying, it is corrupt, and poysoned with the* curse. *I exhort thee therefore to look after a* better country, an inheritance that is undefiled and fadeth not away. *If thou doest this, thou shalt have a portion given thee here, when* all things shall be made new. *In the mean time I commend unto thee the memorie of that* restorer, *and the* reward *he shall bring with him in the* end of this world, *which truely draws near, if it be not* at the door. *Doat not any more* 10 *upon a withered, rotten* Gourd, *upon the seducements and falshood of a most odious, decayed* Prostitute*; but look up to Heaven, where* wealth *without* want, delight *without distast, and* joy *without* sorrow (*like undefiled and incorruptible* Virgins) *sit cloathed with* light, *and crowned with* glory. *Let me incite thee to this* speculation *in the language of* Ferarius*:* Desine tandem aliquando prono in terram vultu, vel præter naturam brutum animal, vel ante diem silicernium videri. Cœlum suspice, ad quod natus, ad quod erectâ staturâ tuendum tenendumque factus es. Immortalia sydera caducis flosculis præfer, aut eadem esse Cœli flores existimato nostratibus 20 Amaranthis diuturniores. *Farewel, and neglect not thy own happiness.*

H. V.

THE LIFE OF HOLY *PAULINUS* THE BISHOP of *NOLA*

Ben Sirach finishing his Catalogue of holy men (to seal up the summe, and to make his list compleat) brings in *Simon* the Sonne of *Onias*: And (after a short narration of his pious care in repairing and fortifying the Temple) hee descends to the particular excellencies, and sacred perfections of his person. Which to render the more fresh and sweet unto posterity, he adornes with these bright and flowrie *Encomiums*.

1. *He was as the Morning-star in the midst of a cloud, and as the Moon at the full.*

2. *As the Sunne shining upon the temple of the most high, and as* 10 *the Rain-bow giving light in the bright clouds.*

3. *As the flower of Roses in the spring of the year, as Lilies by the rivers of waters, and as the branches of the Frankincense-tree in the time of summer.*

4. *As fire and Incense in the Censer, and as a vessel of beaten gold set with all manner of precious stones.*

5. *As a fair Olive-tree budding forth fruit, and as a Cypresse tree which groweth up to the clouds.*

6. *When he put on the robe of honour, and was cloathed with the perfection of glory, when he went up to the holy Altar, he made the* 20 *garment of holinesse honourable.*

Most great (indeed) and most glorious Assimilations, full of life, and full of freshnesse! but in all this beauty of holinesse, in all these spices and flowers of the Spouse, there is nothing too much, nothing too great for our most great and holy *Paulinus*. The Saints of God (*though wandring in sheep-skins, and goat-skins, in caves, and in mountains*) become eminently famous, and leave behind them a more glorious and enduring memory, then the most prosperous tyrants of this world; which like noysome exhalations, moving for a time in the Eye of the Sun, fall afterwards to the 30 earth, where they rot and perish under the *chaines of darkness*. The fame of holy men (like the *Kingdome of God*) is a *seed that grows secretly*; the dew that feeds these plants comes from him, that *sees in secret*, *but rewards openly*. They are those *trees* in the Poet,

> *Which silently*, *and by none seen*,
> *Grow great and green*.

While they labour to conceal, and obscure themselves, they shine the more. And this (saith *Athanasius* in the life of *Antonie* the great) *is the goodnesse of God*, *who useth to glorifie his servants*, *though unwilling*, *that by their examples he may condemn the world*, 10 *and teach men*, *that holinesse is not above the reach of humane nature*. Apposite to my present purpose is all this prolusion, both because this blessed Bishop (whose life I here adventure to publish) was a person of miraculous perfections and holynesse, and because withall he did most diligently endeavour to vilifie his own excellent abilities, and to make himselfe of no account. But Pearls, though set in *lead*, will not lose their brightnesse; and a virtuous life shines most in an obscure livelyhood.

In the explication of his life I shall follow first the method of *Nature*, afterwards of *Grace*: I shall begin with his *Birth*, *Educa-* 20 *tion*, and *Maturitie*; and end with his *Conversion*, *Improvements*, and *Perfection*. To make my entrance then into the work, I finde that he was born in the City of *Burdeaux* in *Gascoyne*, in the year of our Lord three hundred and fifty three, *Constantius* the *Arian* reigning in the East, and *Constans* in the West, and **Liberius* being Bishop of *Rome*: In a Golden Age, when Religion and Learning kissed each other, and equally flourished. So that he had the happines to shine in an age that loved light, and to multiply his own by the light of others. It was the fashion then of 30 the *Roman* Senatours to build them sumptuous houses in their Country-livings, that they might have the pleasure and conveniency of retiring thither from the tumult and noyse of that great City, which sometimes was, and would be yet the head of the World. Upon such an occasion (without doubt) was *Burdeaux* honoured with the birth of *Paulinus*, his Fathers estate lying not far off, about the town of *Embrau*, upon the River *Garumna*, which rising out of the *Pyrene* hils washeth that part of *Guienne* with a pleasant stream, and then runs into the *Aquitane* sea. By this happy accident came *France* to lay claime to *Paulinus*, which she

* *He subscribed to the damnable heresie of* Arius, *as both* Hierome *and* Athanasius *testifie against him.*

makes no small boast of at this day. But his Country indeed (if we follow his descent, which is the right way to find it) is *Italie*, and *Rome* it self; his Ancestors were all *Patricians*, and honour'd (by a long succession) with the Consular *purple*. His Patrimonies were large, and more becomming a Prince then a private man; for besides those possessions in the City of *Burdeaux*, and by the River *Garumna*, he had other most ample Inheritances in *Italy* about *Narbone* and *Nola*, and in *Rome* it self. And for this we have a pregnant testimony out of *Ausonius*, who labouring to disswade him from *Evangelical poverty*, and that obscure course of life (as 10 he is pleased to term it) layes before him (as the most moving arguments) the desolation of his ancient house, with the ruin and *sequestration* (as it were) of his large possessions; his words are these.

Ne raptam sparsamq; domum, &c.

Let me not weep to see thy ravish'd house
All sad & silent, without Lord or Spouse,
And all those vast dominions once thine owne,
Torn 'twixt a hundred slaves to me unknown.

But what account he made of these earthly possessions, will 20 appeare best by his own words in his fifth Epistle to *Severus: Ergo nihil in hunc mundum inferentibus substantiam rerum temporalium quasi tonsile vellus apponit*, &c. 'God (saith he) layes these temporal 'accommodations upon us that come naked into this world, as 'a fleece of wooll which is to be sheared off. He puts it not as a load 'to hinder us, whom it behoves to be born light and active, but as 'a certain matter which rightly used may be beneficial. And when 'he bestoweth any thing upon us, that is either dear or pleasant to 'us, he gives it for this end, that by parting with it, it may be a 'testimonial, or token of our love and devotion towards God, 30 'seeing we neglect the fruition of our best present things for his 'sake, who will amply reward us in the future.

He had conferred upon him all the ornaments of humane life which man could be blest with. He was nobly born, rich, and beautifull, of constitution slender and delicate, but every way fitted for virtuous imployment; of an excellent wit, a happy memory, and, which sweeten'd all these gracious concessions, of a most mild and modest disposition. To bring these seeds to perfection, his Father (having a care of him equall to his degree) caused him to be brought up under the regiment of *Decius magnus Ausonius*, a famous *Poet* and *Oratour*, who at that time kept a School of *Grammar* and *Rhetorick* in the City of *Burdeaux*. The Ingenuity and sweetnesse of *Paulinus* so overcame and ravished *Ausonius*, that he used all possible skill and diligence, to adorne and perfect those natural abilities which he so much loved and admired in this hopefull plant. The effect was, that he exceeded his Master. *Ausonius* upon this being called to the Court by the old Emperor *Valentinian*; *Paulinus* gave himselfe to the study of the *Civill Law*, and the acute and learned pleadings of that age, wherein he was so excellent, that the Emperor taking notice of his Abilities, took order for his Election into the *Senate*, and this a very long time before his *Tutor* attained to that honour. This præcedence of eloquence and honour **Ausonius* himself confesseth; but having a greater witnesse, I shall leave his testimony to the *Margin*, to make room for the other. Take then (if it please you) the Judgement of that glorious and Eloquent Doctour Saint *Hierome*, for thus he writes in his thirteenth Epist. to *Paulinus*, *O si mihi liceret istiusmodi ingenium non per Aonios montes & Heliconis vertices*, *ut poetæ canunt*, *sed per Sion*, &c. 'O that I were able (saith he) to extoll and publish your 'ingenuity and holy learning, not upon the *Aonian* hills, or the 'tops of *Helicon* (as the Poets sing) but upon the Mountaines of '*Sion* and *Sinai*; that I might preach there what I have learnt from 'you, and deliver the sacred mysteries of Scripture through your 'hands; I might then have something to speak, which learned '*Greece* could never boast of. And in another place, A most preg-'nant wit you have, and an infinite treasure of words, which easily 'and aptly flow from you, and both the easinesse and the aptness 'are judiciously mixt.

* *Cedimus ingenio quantum præcedimus ævo, Assurgit Musæ nostra Camæna tuæ. Sic & fastorum titulo prior, & tua Romæ Præcessit nostrum sella curulis ebur.*

To these Divine favours already conferred upon him, God added another great blessing, the Crown of his youth, and the Comfort of his age; I meane *Therasia*, a Noble *Roman* Virgin, whom he tooke to wife in the midst of his honours, and who afterwards (of her owne free will) most joyfully parted with them all, and with her own pleasant possessions to follow *Christ* in the regeneration.

At this height of honours, & growing repute, he was employ'd (upon some concernments of the *Empire*) into *Italy*, *France*, and *Spain*; Where he was detained (together with his dear consort) for the space of almost fifteen years; during which time, he secretly laboured to make himself acquainted with the glorious *Fathers* of that age, and (the Spirit of God now beginning to breath upon him) hee was strongly moved to embrace the *Christian* Faith. In these travells of his, it was his fortune to arrive at *Millaine*, where Saint *Augustine*, and *Alypius*, the Bishop of *Tagasta* in *Africk*, did then Sojourne; here by accident he was known of *Alypius*, though unknown to him; as we see it often fall out, that great persons are known of many, which to them are unknown.

Much about this time (which was the eight and thirtieth year of 10 his age,) he retired privately with his wife into the City of *Burdeaux*. And the hour being now come, that *the singing of birds should be heard, and the lips which were asleep should speak*: Hee was there by the hands of holy *Delphinus* (who then sate Bishop in the *Sea* of *Burdeaux*,) publickly baptized, from which time forward he renounced all his Secular acquaintance, associating himself to the most strict and pious livers in that age, especially to Saint *Ambrose* the Bishop of *Millan*, and Saint *Martin* the Bishop of *Tours*. That he was baptized about the eight and thirtieth yeare of his age, is clear by his owne words in his first Epistle to Saint *Augustine*, 20 *Nolo in me corporalis ortus, magis quam spiritalis exortus ætatem consideres*, &c. 'I would not (saith he) that you consider my tem-'porall age, so much as my spiritual; my age in the flesh is the same 'with that Cripple, who was healed in the beautifull gate by the 'power of Christ working by his Apostles; but my age in the re-'generation is the same with the blessed Infants, who by the 'wounds intended for Christ himself, became the first fruits unto 'Christ, and by the losse of their innocent blood, did foreshew the 'slaughter of the Lamb, and the passion of our Lord. Now for the first, Saint *Luke* tells us, *That the Cripple upon whom this miracle* 30 *of healing was shown, was above forty years of age* (Acts Chap. 4. ver. 22.) and for the Infants, the *Evangelists* words are, that *Herod sent forth his messengers, and slew all the Male Children that were in* Bethlem, *and the Coasts thereof, from two years old and under.* So that considering all the Circumstances which offer themselves for the clearing of this point, it will evidently appear, that he was baptized (as I have said before) in the eight and thirtieth year of his age. The onely Instrument which God was pleas'd to ordain, and imploy upon the Earth for his Conversion, was his dear and Virtuous Wife *Therasia*; Which makes me conjecture, that she 40 was borne of Christian parents, and had received the faith from her infancie. This *Ausonius* his old *Tutor*, (who was scarce a good Christian,) forgat not to upraid him with in most injurious termes, calling her *Tanaquil*, and the *Imperatrix* of her Husband: To which passionate passages (though sadly resented) *Paulinus* replyed with all the humanity and sweetnesse which language could expresse. Thus *Ausonius* barks at him.

Undè istam meruit non fœlix Charta repulsam?
Hostis ab hoste tamen, &c.

——— how could that paper sent,
That luckless paper, merit thy contempt?
Ev'n foe to fo (though furiously) replies;
And the defied, his Enemy defies:
Amidst the swords and wounds ther's a Salute.
Rocks answer man, and though hard, are not mute.
Nature made nothing dumb, nothing unkind:
The trees and leaves speak trembling to the wind.
If thou doest feare discoveries, and the blot
Of my love, *Tanaquil* shal know it not.

To this Poetical fury, *Paulinus* reposeth with that Native mildnesse, which he was wholly composed of.

Continuata meæ durare silentia linguæ,
Te nunquam tacito memoras; placitamq; latebris
Desidiam exprobras; neglectæq; insuper addis
Crimen amicitiæ; formidatamq; Jugalem
Objicis, & durum iacis in mea viscera versum, &c.

Obdurate still, and tongue-tyed you accuse
(Though yours is ever vocall) my dull muse;
You blame my Lazie, lurking life, and adde
I scorne your love, a Calumny most sad;
Then tell me, that I fear my wife, and dart
Harsh, cutting words against my dearest heart.
Leave, learned Father, leave this bitter Course,
My studies are not turn'd unto the worse;
I am not mad, nor idle; nor deny
Your great deserts, and my debt, nor have I
A wife like *Tanaquil*, as wildly you
Object, but a *Lucretia*, chast and true.

To avoid these clamours of *Ausonius*, and the dangerous sollicitations of his great kindred and friends, he left *Burdeaux* and *Nola*, and retyred into the Mountanous and solitary parts of *Spaine*, about *Barcinoe* and *Bilbilis* upon the River *Salo*. Two journeyes he made into *Spain*, this last, and his first (before his baptism) upon the Emperours affairs; he Sojourned then in new *Castile*, in the City of *Complutum* now called *Alcala de henares*, where his wife *Therasia* was delivered of her onely Son *Celsus*, who died upon the eighth day after his birth. Holy *Paulinus* in his *Panegyrick* upon the death of *Celsus* the Son of *Pneumatius*, by his Wife *Fidelis*, takes occasion to mention the early death of this blessed infant, 10

Hoc pignus commune superno in lumine Celsum
Credite vivorum lacte favisq; frui.
Aut cum Bethlæis infantibus in Paradiso
(Quos malus Herodes perculit invidiâ,)
Inter odoratum ludit nemus, &c.

This pledge of your joint love, to Heaven now fled,
With honey-combs and milk of life is fed.
Or with the *Bethlem*-Babes (whom *Herods* rage
Kill'd in their tender, happy, holy age)
Doth walk the groves of Paradise, and make 20
Garlands, which those young Martyrs from him take.
With these his Eyes on the mild lamb are fixt,
A Virgin-Child with Virgin-infants mixt.
Such is my *Celsus* too, who soon as given,
Was taken back (on the eighth day) to Heaven,
To whom at *Alcala* I sadly gave
Amongst the Martyrs Tombes a little grave.
Hee now with yours (gone both the blessed way,)
Amongst the trees of life doth smile and play;
And this one drop of our mixt blood may be 30
A light for my *Therasia*, and for me.

These distant and obscure retirements he made choice of, because he would not be known of any, nor hindred in his course; Which at *Nola*, and the adjacent parts of *Rome* (where his Secular honours and antient descent made all the people obsequious to him) could not possibly be effected. Besides very few in those *Western* parts (especially of the Nobility) had at that time received the *Christian* Faith; for they look'd upon it as a most degenerate, unmanly profession: such a good opinion had those rough times of peace and humility. This made him lesse looked after by the 40

Inhabitants of those parts; and his own friends not knowing what became of him, began to give him over, and not onely to withdraw from him in their care, but in their affections also, giving out that he was mad, and besides himself. But all this moved him not: he was *not ashamed of the Gospel of Christ*, *he counted all things dung that he might gaine* his Saviour, and hee fainted not, but *endured, as seeing him that is invisible*. The first step to Christianity (saith Saint *Hierome*) is to contemne the censures of men. This foundation he laid, and upon this he built; he had given himselfe wholly to *Christ*, and rejected the world; he tooke part with that *man of sorrowes*, and suffered the scoffs and reproaches of these men of mirth. The people are the many waters, he turn'd their froth and fome into pearls, and wearied all weathers with an unimpaired *Superstitie*. Hee was founded upon that Rock, which is not worne with time, but wears all that oppose it. Some dispositions love to stand in raine, and affect wind and showers beyond Musick. *Paulinus* sure was of this temper; he preferred the indignation and hatred of the multitude to their love, he would not buy their friendship with the losse of Heaven, nor call those Saints and propagators, who were Devills and destroyers. What courage he had in such tempests, may be seen in every line almost of his workes; I shal insert one or two out of his 6th Epistle to *Severus*: *Utinam, frater mi, digni habeamur qui maledicamur, & notemur, & conteramur, atque etiam interficiamur in nomine Jesu Christi, dum non ipse occidatur Christus in nobis*. &c. 'I would (saith 'he) my dear brother, that we might be counted worthy to suffer 'reproach, to be branded and troden upon; Yea, and to be killed 'for the name of Christ, so that Christ be not killed in us. Then at 'last should we tread upon the Adder, and the Dragon, and bruise 'the head of the old Serpent. But (alas!) wee as yet relish this 'World, and do but pretend to love Christ; we love indeed to be 'commended and cherished for professing his name, but wee love 'not to be troubled and afflicted for his sake. And in his first 'Epistle to *Aper*; O blessed displeasures (saith he) to displease men 'by pleasing Christ! Let us take heed of the love of such, who will 'be pleased without Christ. It is an observation of the Readers of Saint *Cyprian*, *quod in ejus scriptis singula propè verba Martyrium spirant*, that through all his writings, almost every word doth breath Martyrdome. His expressions are all Spirit and Passion, as if he had writ them with his blood, and conveyed the anguish of his

St. Hierome Ep. 26.

sufferings into his writings. I dare not say so much of *Paulinus*, nor of any other Father of the Church; but I fear not to say that *Paulinus* both durst, and (had he beene called to it) would have laid downe his life for the love of Christ.

Four yeares hee spent in these remote parts of *Spain*, during which time, he did lead a most solitary and austere life, labouring by all meanes to conceale and vilifie himself. *But a City that is built upon a hill cannot be hidden;* his holinesse and humility had so awaked the Common people dwelling about the place of his abode, that they would not rest again till they had him for their Minister. This most honourable and sacred charge he would by no meanes adventure to undergo, judging himselfe a most unworthy vile sinner, not fit to deale in holy Scripture, much lesse to handle and administer the mystical Elements of life. But God, who had ordained him for it, would not suffer this. For the people (not without violence and some rudeness,) carried him away to *Barcinoe*, where holy *Lampius*, then Bishop of that Sea, did upon *Christmasse* day by the laying on of his hands, consecrate him a faithfull steward and learned dispenser of the Mysteries of God. This passage we have fully related in his sixth Epistle to *Severus*, *Nos modo in Barcinonensi* (*ut ante Scripseram*) *civitate consistimus*, &c. 'I live now (saith he) as I formerly writ to you in the City of '*Barcinoe*, where (since the last letters received from you) I was by 'the violence of the people (God, I believe, having foreordained it) 'compell'd to enter into holy Orders upon that day in which our 'Lord was born. I confesse it was done against my will, not for any 'dislike that I have to the place (for Christ is my witnesse, that 'my highest desire was to begin my imployment in his house with 'the office and honour of a door-keeper) but having designed my 'selfe (as you know) *elsewhere, I was much terrified 'with this sudden and unexpected pleasure of the Divine 'will: However I refused it not, but submitted with all humility, 'and have put my necke into the Yoke of Christ, though altogether 'unworthy and unable. I see now that I have medled with things 'that are too wonderful for me; I am made a Steward of the Secrets 'of the Almighty, and honourd with the dispensation of Heavenly 'things, and being called nearer to my Master, I am exercised 'about the Body, about the Spirit, and the glory of Jesus Christ. 'The narrownesse of my understanding cannot comprehend the 'signification of this high and sacred dignity, and I tremble every

* *For Nola.*

'minute (when I consider my own infirmities) to thinke of the great 'burthen that is laid upon me. But he that gives wisedome to his 'little ones, and hath perfected praise out of the mouths of babes 'and sucklings, is able to finish what he begun in me, that by his 'mighty working, I may be made worthy, who was most unworthy 'to be called. The Priesthood is an Office belonging to the Kingdome of Heaven. It is an honour that is ranged upon holy ground, and by it selfe. Worldly dignities, which are but humane inventions, are, and may be acquired (with lesse offence) by humane meanes, as bribery, ambition, and policie. But to take hold of this white robe with such dirty hands, is nothing lesse then to spit in the face of *Christ*, and to dishonour his Ordinance. He that doth it, and he that permits it to be done, agree like *Herod* and *Pilate*, to dispise and crucifie him. They that Countenance and ratifie such disorders, take care to provide so many *Judasses* to betray Christ, and then vote the treason to be lawfull. Every man can speak, but every man cannot preach: Tongues and the gift of tongues are not the same things: The wisdome of God hath *depth* and *riches*, and *things hard to be spoken*, as well as *milk*, and *the first principles of his Oracles*. Wee have amongst us many builders with *hay and stubble*, but let them, and those that hired them, take heed how they build; The tryal will be by fire, and by a consuming fire. The *hidden things of dishonesty*, *the walking in Craftinesse*, and *the handling deceitfully of the word of God* they are well versed in; but true sanctitie, and the Spirit of God (which Saint *Paul* thought he had) I am very sure they have not.

A modest reader would now thinke that *Paulinus* had removed himselfe farre enough from the elaborate temptations, and clamorous pursuits of *Ausonius*; But even in this will he be deceived. For at the fourth years end, did the Incantations of this busie and obstinate Charmer find him out. God (no doubt) providing for the security of his servant all that while, by delaying them in severall regions, or else by concealing the abode of his beloved votary, from this pursuer of Soules. For with all the artifice and strength of wit, did he set upon him in this last letter, which the divine providence suffered not to come into his hand, till he had set both his *hands to the plough*, and seald his conformation with that indelible Character. And now having set a hedge about his beloved, he suffered this *Fowle* of the Evening to fly over, which chattered to him in these melodious numbers.

Vertisti, Pauline, *tuos dulcissime mores?* &c.

Sweet Paulinus, *is thy nature turn'd?*
Have I so long in vaine thy absence mourn'd?
Wilt thou, my glory, and great Romes *delight,*
The Senates prop, their oracle, and light,
In Bilbilis *and* Calagurris *dwel,*
Changing thy Ivorie-chair for a dark Cell?
Wilt bury there thy Purple, and contemn
All the great honours of thy noble stem?

To this *Roman Magick*, and most pernicious Elegancy, *Paulinus* 10
replyed with a certain sacred and serene simplicity, which proved so piercing, and powerful, that he was never after troubled with the Poetry of *Ausonius*.

———*Revocandum me tibi credam,*
Cum steriles fundas non ad divina precatus?
Castalidis supplex averso numine musis, &c.

Shall I beleeve you can make me return,
Who pour your fruitless prayers when you mourn,
Not to your Maker? Who can hear you cry:
But to the fabled Nymphs of *Castalie*? 20
You never shall by such false Gods bring me
Either to *Rome*, or to your company.
As for those former things you once did know,
And which you still call mine, I freely now
Confesse, I am not he, whom you knew then;
I have dyed since, and have been borne agen.
Nor dare I think my sage instructor can
Believe it errour, for redeemed man
To serve his great redeemer. I grieve not,
But glory so to erre. Let the wise knot 30
Of worldlings call me fool; I slight their noise,
And heare my God approving of my choice.
Man is but glass, a building of no trust,
A moving shade, and, without *Christ*, meer dust:
His choice in life concerns the Chooser much:
For when he dyes, his good or ill (just such
As here it was) goes with him hence, and staies
Still by him, his strict Judge in the last dayes.
These serious thoughts take up my soul, and I
While yet 'tis day-light, fix my busie eye 40

Upon his sacred Rules, lifes precious sum,
Who in the twilight of the world shall come
To judge the lofty looks, and shew mankind
The diff'rence 'twixt the ill and well inclin'd.
This second coming of the worlds great King
Makes my heart tremble, and doth timely bring
A saving care into my watchfull soul,
Lest in that day all vitiated and foul
I should be found: That day, times utmost line,
10 When all shall perish, but what is divine.
When the great Trumpets mighty blast shall shake
The earths foundations, till the hard Rocks quake,
And melt like piles of snow, when lightnings move
Like hail, and the white thrones are set above.
That day, when sent in glory by the Father,
The Prince of life his blest Elect shall gather;
Millions of Angels round about him flying,
While all the kindreds of the earth are crying,
And he enthron'd upon the clouds shall give
20 His last just sentence, who must die, who live.
This is the fear this is the saving care,
That makes me leave false honours, and that share
Which fell to mee of this fraile world; lest by
A frequent use of present pleasures I
Should quite forget the future, and let in
Foul Atheism, or some presumptuous sin.
Now by their loss I have secur'd my life,
And bought my peace ev'n with the cause of strife.
I live to him, who gave me life & breath,
30 And without feare expect the houre of death.
If you like this, bid joy to my rich state,
If not, leave me to *Christ* at any rate.

Being now ordained a Minister of holy things, and a feeder of the flock of *Christ*, that he might be enabled to render a joyfull account at the appearance of the great Shepheard, he resolved with all convenient expedition to sell and give away all his large and Princely Possessions in *Italy* and *France*, which hitherto he had not disposed of; for he looked upon his great Patrimonies as matters of distraction and backsliding, the thoughts and solicitousnesse about 40 such vast revenues disturbing his pious affections, and necessarily intruding into his most holy exercitations. Upon this rare resolution he returnes with his faithfull Consort into *France*, leaving

Barcinoe and holy *Lampius* in much sorrow for his departure. For though hee had entred there into the Ministery, yet was he no member of that Diocesse. And here (saith *Uranius*, who was his Presbyter, and wrote a brief narration of his life) did he open his Treasuries to the poor and the stranger. He did not only refresh his neighbours, but sent messengers into other remote parts to summon the naked, and the hungry to this great Feast, where they were both fed and cloathed with his own hands. He eased the oppressed, freed the captives, payd the debts of whole families, and redeemed divers persons that were become bondslaves to their creditors. Briefly, he sold all that he had, and distributed the money amongst the poor, not reserving one penny either for himself, or his dear *Therasia*. Saint *Ambrose* in his thirtieth Epistle to *Sabinus* confirmeth this relation: *Paulinum splendore generis in partibus Aquitaniæ nulli secundum, venditis facultatibus tam suis quam etiam conjugalibus, &c.* '*Paulinus* (saith he) the most eminent for his 'Nobility in all the parts of *Aquitane*, having sold away all his patri- 'monies, together with the goods of his wife, did out of pure love 'to Jesus Christ divide all that vast Summe of Money amongst the 'poor; and he himself from a rich Senator is become a most poor 'man, having cast off that heavy secular burthen, and forsaken his 'own house, his country, and his kindred, that he might with more 'earnestnesse follow Christ. His Wife also, as nobly descended, 'and as zealous for the Faith as himself, consented to all his desires, 'and having given away all her own large possessions, lives with her 'husband in a little thatch'd cottage, rich in nothing but the hidden 'treasures of Religion and holinesse. Saint *Augustine* also in his first book *de Civitate Dei*, and the tenth Chapter, celebrates him with the like testimony: 'Our *Paulinus* (saith hee) from a man most 'splendidly rich, became most poor most willingly, and most richly 'holy. He laboured not to adde field unto field, nor to inclose himself in Cedar and Ivory, and the drossie darke gold of this world, but to enter through the gates into the precious light of that City, which is of *pure gold like unto cleare glasse*. He left some few things in this world, to enjoy all in the world to come. A great performance certainly, and a most fair approach towards the Kingdom of heaven. He that fights with dust, comes off well, if it blinds him not. To slight words, and the names of temptations, is easie, but to deale so with the matter, and substance of them, is a task. Conscience hath Musick, and light, as well as discord and darknesse:

And the triumphs of it are as familiar after good works, as the Checks of it after bad. It is no heresie in devotion to be sensible of our smallest Victories over the World. But how far he was from thinking this a Victory, may be easily gathered out of his owne words in his second Epistle to *Severus*; *Facilè nobis bona*, &c. 'The 'goods (saith he) I carried about me, by the slipping of my skirt 'out of my hand, fell easily from me: And those things which I 'brought not into this World, and could not carry out of it, being 'only lent me for a time, I restored again. I pulled them not as the 'skin off my back, but laid them by, as a garment I had sometimes 'worne. But now comes the difficulty upon me, when those things 'which are truly mine, as my heart, my Soul, and my works must 'be presented and given a living Sacrifice unto God. The abdica-'tion of this World, and the giving of our temporall goods amongst 'the poore, is not the running of the race, but a preparing to run; 'it is not the end, but the beginning, and first step of our Journey. 'Hee that striveth for masteries, shall not be crowned, except he 'first strive lawfully; And he that is to swimme over a River, cannot 'do it by putting off his cloathes onely, he must put his body also 'into the stream, and with the motion of his armes, his hands and 'feete, passe through the violence of the Brook, and then rest upon 'the further side of it. And in his 12th Epistle, he cries out, 'O 'miserable and vaine men! Wee believe that wee bestow something 'upon the poor: wee trade and lend, and would be counted liberall, 'when we are most covetous. The most unconscionable userers 'upon Earth are not so greedy as we are, nor their interest and 'exactions so unreasonable as ours. We purchase Heaven with 'Earth, happinesse with misery, and immortality with rust and 'rottennesse. Such another Divine rapture is that in his Poems.

——— *Et res magna videtur,*
Mercari propriam de re pereunte salutem?
Perpetuis mutare caduca? &c.

——— And is the bargain thought too dear,
To give for Heaven our fraile subsistence here?
To change our mortall with immortall homes,
And purchase the bright Stars with darksome stones?
Behold! my God (a rate great as his breath!)
On the sad crosse bought me with bitter death,
Did put on flesh, and suffer'd for our good,
For ours, (vile slaves!) the losse of his dear blood.

Wee see by these *Manifesto's* what account he made of this great deed; so great, that none now adaies thinke of doing it. *Go thy way, sell whatsoever thou hast, and give to the poor*, is a commandement, as well as, *take up the Crosse and follow me*. This last cannot be done, but by doing the first. Wee sell oftentimes, but seldome give: and happily that is the reason we sell so often. He that keeps all to himselfe, takes not the right way to thrive. The Corn that lies in the Granarie will bring no harvest. It is most commonly the foode of vermine, and some creatures of the night and darknesse. Charity is a relique of Paradise, and pitty is a strong argument that 10 we are all descended from one man: He that carries this rare Jewell about him, will every where meete with some kindred. He is quickly acquainted with distressed persons, and their first sight warmes his blood. I could believe, that the word *stranger* is a notion received from the posterity of *Cain*, who killed *Abel*. The *Hebrewes* in their own tribes, called those of the farthest degree, *brothers*; and sure they erred lesse from the law of pure Nature, then the rest of the Nations, which were left to their owne lusts. The afflictions of man are more moving then of any other Creature; for he onely is a stranger here, where all things else are at home. 20 But the losing of his innocency, and his device of Tyranny have made him unpittied, and forfeited a prerogative, that would have prevailed more by submission, then all his posterity shall do by opposition. Not to give to one that lacks, is a kind of murther: Want and famine are destroyers as well as the sword, and rage very frequently in private, when they are not thought of in the Publick. The blessed *JESUS* who came into the World to rectifie Nature, and to take away the inveterate corruptions of man, was not more in any of his precepts, then in that which bids us *Love one another*. This is the cement not onely of this World, but of that other which 30 is to come. *Blessed are the mercifull;* and, *give to him that asketh thee*, proceeded from the same lips of truth. And in his description of the last judgement, he grounds the sentence of condemnation pronounced against the wicked upon no other fact, but because they did not *cloath the naked*, *feed the hungry*, *and take in the stranger*. *Love covers a multitude of sins*, *and God loves the chearfull giver*. But this is not our whole duty: though we give our bodies to be burnt, and give all our goods unto the poor, yet *without holinesse we shall never see the face of God*. Darknesse cannot stand in the presence of light, and *flesh and blood cannot inherit the Kingdome* 40 *of God*. The great difficulty then (as our holy Bishop here saith) is to become a living sacrifice; and truly the next way to it, is by an Evangelical disposing of these outward incumbrances; this will open and prepare the way before us, though it takes nothing from the length of it. The Hawke *proines* and *rouseth* before she flyes, but that brings her not to the *mark*: Preparations, and the distant flourishes of *Array* will not get the field, but action, and the pursuance of it.

His Estate in *France* being thus disposed of, he retyred into 10 *Italy*; where having done the like to his Patrimonies there, hee came to *Millaine*, and was honourably received by holy *Ambrose*, then Bishop of that *Sea*. But these gay feathers of the World, being thus blown off him, by the breath of that Spirit which makes *the dry tree to become green*, and *tbe spices of the Garden to flow out*, all his kindred and former acquaintance became his deadly Enemies. Flyes of estate follow Fortune, and the Sun-shine; friendship is a thing much talked off, but seldome found; I never knew above two that loved without selfe-ends. That which passeth for love in this age, is the meere counter to it; It is policie in the cloathes of 20 love, or the hands of *Esau* with the tongue of *Jacob*. These smooth Cheats the World abounds with: There is *Clay enough for the potter, but little dust whereof commeth Gold*. The best direction is Religion; find a true Christian, and thou hast found a true friend. He that fears not God, will not feare to do thee a mischiefe.

From *Millaine* he came to *Rome*, where he was honourably entertained by all, but his own kindred, and *Siricius* the great Bishop. It was the ill Fortune of this zealous Pope, to be offended not onely with *Paulinus*, but with that glorious Father Saint 30 *Hierome*. It was a perillous dissolutenesse of some Bishops in that Century, to admit of Lay-men, and unseason'd persons into the Ministry. This rash and impious practice *Siricius* had, by severall strict Sanctions or decrees, condemned and forbidden; and it is probable that the reason of his strange carriage towards *Paulinus* and *Hierome* was, because he would not seem to connive at any persons that were suddenly ordained, though never so deserving, lest he should seeme to offend against his own edicts. It is a sad truth that this pernicious rashnesse of Bishops (fighting *ex diametro* with the Apostolical cautions) hath oftentimes brought boars into 40 the Vineyard, and Wolves into the sheep-fold; which complying afterwards with all manner of Interests, have torne out the bowels of their Mother. Wee need no examples: Wee have lived to see all this our selves. Ignorance and obstinacie make *Hereticks*: And ambition makes *Schismaticks*; when they are once at this passe, they are on the way toward *Atheisme*. I do not say that *Ecclesiastical polity* is an inviolable or sure fense against Church-rents; because there is a necessity that *offences must come*, though *wo to them by whom*; but rules of prevention are given, and therefore they should not be slighted. The Bridegroom adviseth his spouse to *take these foxes while they are litle*. 10

In a pleasant field halfe a mile distant from *Nola* lies the Sepulcher of the blessed Martyr *Felix*. To this place (which from his youth hee was ever devoted to,) did *Paulinus* now retire. It was the custom of holy men in that age, not onely to live near the Tombs of the Martyrs, but to provide also for their buriall in those places; because they were sure, that in the Resurrection, and the terrours of the day of Judgement God would descend upon those places in *the soft voyce*, that is to say in his love and mercies. *Eusebius* in his fourth Book, and the sixth Chapter of the life of *Constantine* tells us, how that great Emperour gave strict order for his buriall 20 amongst the Tombes of the Apostles, and then adds, *Ω'φέλειαν ψυχῆς ὀνησιφὸρον τὴν τῶνδε μνήμην ποιεῖσθαι ἀυτῶ πιστεύων*. Saint *Chrysostome* in that homilie which hee writ to prove that *Christ is God*, gives the same relation, *Καὶ ἐν τῇ Κωνσταντίνου πόλει δε*, &c. The Emperors of *Constantinople* (saith he) esteeme it for a great honour, if they be buried not within the shrines of the Apostles, but at the Gates of their Temple, that they may be the door-keepers of those poor fishers. So *Marcellina*, descended from the consular Nobility of *Rome*, refused to be buried amongst her Ancestors, that she might sleepe at *Millaine* with 30 her great Brother Saint *Ambrose*, where shee lies under this *Epitaph*.

Marcellina, tuos cum vita resolveret artus;
Sprevisti patriis, &c.

Life, *Marcellina*, leaving thy faire frame,
Thou didst contemne those Tombes of costly fame,
Built by thy Roman Ancestours, and lyest
At *Millaine*, where great *Ambrose* sleeps in Christ.
Hope, the deads life, and faith, which never faints,
Made thee rest here, that thou may'st rise with Saints. 40

To this place therefore near *Nola* in *Campania* (a Country lying within the Realm of *Naples*, and called now by the Inhabitants *Terra di Lavoro*,) as to a certain Harbour and recesse from the clamours of their friends, and the temptations of the World, did *Paulinus* and *Therasia* convey themselves. His affection to this holy [a]Martyr was very great: for frequenting *Nola*, when he was yet a youth, he would oftentimes steale privately to visit his Sepulcher: and he loved the possessions which his Father had left him in those parts above any other, because that under pretence of looking to his estate there, he had the convenience of resorting to the Tombe of *Felix*; where he took in his *first love*, and in the seaven and twentieth year of his age, made a private vow to become a Servant of *Jesus Christ*. This *Felix* was by descent a *Syrian*, though born in *Nola*, where his Father (trafficking from the *East* into *Italie*,) had purchased a very fair estate, which he divided afterward betwixt him and his Brother *Hermias*; but *Felix* following *Christ*, gave all to his brother. The frequent miracles manifested at his Tombe, made the place famous, and resorted to from most parts of the world. Saint *Augustine*, upon a Controversie betwixt his Presbyter *Boniface*, and another fellow that accused him, when the truth of either side could not be certainly known, sent them both from *Hippo* to *Nola*, to have the matter decided upon Oath, before the Tombe of *Felix*; and in his 137th Epistle, hee sets down the reason, why he sent them so farre. His words are these: *Multis notissima est sanctitas loci, ubi Felicis Nolensis corpus conditum est, quò volui ut peragrent, quia inde nobis facilius fideliusque scribi potest, quicquid in eorum aliquo divinitus fuerit propalatum.* 'The holinesse (saith he) of that place where the 'body of *Felix* of *Nola* lies interred, is famously knowne to 'many; I have therefore sent them thither, because that from 'thence, I shall be more easily and truly informed about any 'thing that shall be miraculously discovered concerning either of 'them.

[a] *Paulinus calls him a Martyr*, quia multa pro Christo passus, etsi non occisus.

Paulinus had not lived very long in this place, but it pleas'd God to visit him with a very sharpe and tedious sicknesse. Hee had now (upon Earth) no Comforter but *Therasia*; His Estate was gone, and his contempt of that made the World contemne him. In this solitude and poverty, he that tries the reines and the heart, begins to take notice of this his new servant, and the first favour he conferred upon him was a disease. Good Angels doe not appeare without the Ecstasie and passion of the Seere: without afflictions and trialls God will not be familiar with us. Fruit-trees, if they be not pruned, will first leave to beare, and afterwards they will dye. Nature, without she be drest by the hand that made her, will finally perish. He that is not favour'd with visitations, is (in Saint *Pauls phrase*) a bastard, and no Son of the Superiour *Jerusalem*. *Paulinus* had put from him all occasions of worldly sorrowes, but he wanted matter for Heavenly Joyes. Without this disease, hee had not known so soone, how acceptable his first Services were unto his Master. This sicknesse was a pure stratagem of love, God visited him with it for this very purpose, that he himselfe might be his Cordial.

Man and the *Eagle* see best in the day-time, they see by the light of this World: but the [a]*night-Raven* is a bird of Mysterie, and sees in the darke by a light of her own. *Paulinus* thought now (like the servant of *Elisha*) that hee had not a friend in all the World to be of his side; but God removes the mist from his Eyes, and shewed him a glorious Army of *Saints* and *Confessours*, who during the time of his sicknesse, did so throng and fill up his Cottage, and the fields about it, that neither his Palace in *Rome*, nor his house in *Burdeaux* could ever boast of such a number. These Comforters he hath recorded with his own pen in his first Epistle to *Severus*; *viderunt pueri tui*, &c. 'Your men (saith he) 'that were here with me, have seen, and can tell you with what 'constant diligence all the Bishops, and my brethren the Clergy, 'with the common people my neighbours, did minister unto me 'all the time of my sicknesse. Unto you, who are unto me as my 'own soul, I take leave to boast and glory in this mercy of the 'Lord, whose goodnesse it is, that I am so plentifully comforted. 'There is not one Bishop in all *Campania* that did not come 'personally to visit me, and those whom either a farther distance, 'or their own infirmities would not permit to travel, fail'd not 'to visit me by their Presbyters & letters. The Bishops of *Africk* 'allso with the beginning of the spring, sent their particular 'letters and messengers to comfort me. Thus *he that forsakes houses and brethren*, *and lands to follow Christ*, *shall receive an*

a *Paulinus will have the word which is commonly used in the Latin, to be* Nicticora, *from* νυξ *and* χορὴ, *which signifies the apple or candle of the eye, and not from* χοραξ. *And this he saith was told him by a holy man, that had lived a long time in the deserts of* Egypt, *where he observed the nature of this bird of night, and the Pelican.*

hundred fold even in this World, and in the world to come life everlasting.

As touching the letters, or Embassage rather of the *African* Bishops to *Paulinus*, it happened on this manner. *Alypius*, the Bishop of *Tagasta* in *Africk*, had at *Millain* (as I intimated before) taken speciall notice of *Paulinus*: And the rumour of his Conversion (as the actions of eminent and noble personages passe quickly into the most distant regions,) had filled with joy not onely the Churches of *Africk*, but the most remote corners of 10 Christianity, even the very wildernesse and the scattered Isles, which in those daies were more frequented by Christians, then populous Continents and splendid Cities. *Alypius* upon this (because he would not loose so fair an opportunity to ground his acquaintance,) dispatcheth a letter from *Tagasta* to *Paulinus*, to gratulate his conversion to the Faith; encouraging him withall *to hold fast his Crown*; and for a token, sent him five of Saint *Augustines* bookes against the *Manichæans*, which in that age (when the Invention of the *Presse* was not so much as thought of,) was a rich present. *Paulinus* was so taken with the reading of these Volumes, 20 that he conceived himself not onely engaged to *Alypius*, but to *Augustine* also. Whereupon he sent his servant from *Nola* with letters full of modestie and sweetnesse to them both, and with particular commendations to other eminent lights of the Church then shining in *Africk*. These letters received by *Augustine* and *Alypius*, and communicated by them to the other Bishops, and the *African* Clergy, were presently Coppied out by all, and nothing now was more desired by them, then a sight of this great Senatour, who was turned a *poor Priest, and a fool* (as Saint *Paul* saith) *for Christ his sake*, and *the off-scouring of the World*. But above all, 30 the Soules of holy *Augustine* and *Paulinus* (like *Jonathan* and *David*, or *Jacob* and *Joseph*) were *knit together*, and *the life of the one was bound up in the life of the other*. The perfect love and union of these two, can by none be more faithfully, or more elegantly described, then it is already by Saint *Augustine* himself. I shall therefore insert his own words, the words of that tongue of truth and Charity; *O bone vir, O bone frater! latebas animam meam; & ei dico ut toleret, quia adhuc lates oculos meos, & vix obtemperat, immo non obtemperat. Quomodo ergo non doleam quod nondum faciem tuam novi, hoc est,* 40 *domum animæ tuæ, quam sicut meam novi? legi enim literas tuas*

August. Epistol. 22. *ad Paulin.*

fluentes lac & mel, præferentes simplicitatem cordis, in quâ quæris dominum, sentiens de illo in bonitate, & afferens ei claritatem & honorem. Legerunt fratres & gaudent, infatigabiliter & ineffabiliter tam uberibus & tam excellentibus donis dei, bonis tuis. Quotquot eas legerunt, rapiunt; quia rapiuntur, cum legunt. Quàm suavis odor Christi, & quàm fragrat ex eis? dici non potest, illæ literæ cum te offerunt ut videaris, quantum nos excitent ut quæraris: nam et perspicabilem faciunt, & desiderabilem. Quantò enim præsentiam tuam nobis quodammodò exhibent, tantò absentiam nos ferre non sinunt. Amant te omnes in eis, & amari abs te cupiunt. Laudatur & 10 *benedicitur deus, cujus gratiâ tu talis es. Ibi excitatur Christus, ut ventos & Maria tibi placare tendenti ad stabilitatem suam dignetur. Ibi conjux excitatur, non dux ad mollitiem viro suo, sed ad fortitudinem redux in ossa viri sui: quam in tuam unitatem redactam, in spiritualibus tibi tantò firmioribus quantò castioribus nexibus copulatam, officijs vestræ sanctitati debitis in te, uno ore salutamus. Ibi cedri Libani ad terram depositæ, & in arcæ fabricam compagine charitatis erectæ, mundi hujus fluctus imputribilitèr secant. Ibi gloria ut acquiratur, contemnitur; & mundus, ut obtineatur, relinquitur. Ibi parvuli, sive etiam grandiusculi filij Babylonis eliduntur ad petram,* 20 *vitia scilicet confusionis, superbiæque secularis. Hæc atque hujusmodi suavissima & sacratissima spectacula literæ tuæ præbent legentibus; literæ illæ, literæ fidei non fictæ, literæ spei bonæ, literæ puræ charitatis. Quomodo nobis anhelant sitim tuam, & desiderium defectumque animæ tuæ in atria domini? Quid amoris sanctissimi spirant? Quantam opulentiam sinceri cordis excæstuant? Quas agunt gratias deo? Quas impetrant â deo? blandiores sunt, an ardentiores? luminosiores, an fæcundiores? Quid enim est, quòd ita nos mulcent, ita accendunt, ita compluunt; & ita serenæ sunt? Quid est, quæso te, aut quid tibi pro eis rependam, nisi quia totus sum tuus in eo, cujus* 30 *totus es tu? si parùm est, plus certê non habeo.* 'O good man, O good 'brother! you lay hidden from my Soul, and I spoke to my Spirit, 'that it should patiently bear it, because you are also hidden from 'my Eyes; but it scarse obeyes, yea it refuseth to obey. How then 'shall I not grieve, because I have not as yet knowne your face, 'the habitation of your Soul, which I am as well acquainted with 'as my owne? For I have read your letters flowing with milk and 'honey, manifesting the simplicity of your heart, in which you seek 'the Lord, thinking rightly of him, and bringing him glory and 'honor. Your brethren here have read them, and rejoyce with an 40 'unwearied and unspeakable Joy, for the bountifull and excellent 'gifts of God in you, which are your riches. As many as have read 'them, snatch them from me; because when they read them, they 'are ravished with them. How sweet an Odour of Christ, and how 'fragrant proceeds from them? It cannot be exprest how much 'those letters, while they offer you to be seen of us, excite us to seek 'for you: They make you both discerned and desired: For the more 'they represent you unto us, wee are the more impatient of your 'absence. All men love you in them, & desire to be beloved of you. 10 'God is blessed and praised by all, through whose grace you are 'such. There do we find that Christ is awaked by you, and vouch-'safeth to rebuke the winds and the Seas, that you may find them 'calme in your Course towards him. There is your dear wife stirred 'up, not to be your leader to softnesse and pleasures, but to 'Christian fortitude; becomming Masculine again, and restored 'into the bones of her Husband: whom we all with one voice salute 'and admire, being now united unto you, serving you in spiritual 'things, wherein you are coupled with mutuall embraces, which 'the more chast they be, are by so much the more firm. There do 20 'we see two Cedars of *Libanus* fell'd to the Earth, which joyned 'together by love, make up one Arke, that cuts through the Waves 'of this World without detriment or putrefaction. There glory, 'that it may be acquired, is contemned; and the World, that it may 'be obtained, is forsaken. There the Children of *Babylon*, whither 'litle ones, or of Maturer age; I mean the Evils of Confusion and 'secular pride, are dashed against the stones. Such sacred and 'delightfull spectacles do your letters present unto us: O those 'letters of yours! Those letters of an unfained faith, those letters 'of holy hope, those letters of pure Charity! How do they sigh and 30 'gaspe with your pious thirst, your holy longings, and the Ecstatical 'faintings of your Soul for the Courts of the Lord? What a most 'sacred love do they breath? with what treasures of a sincere heart 'do they abound? How thankfull to God? How earnest for more 'grace? How mild? How zealous? How full of light? How full of 'fruite? Whence is it that they do so please us, and so provoke us, 'so showre and raine upon us, and yet are so calm and so serene? 'What is this I beseech you? or what shall I returne unto you for 'these letters, unlesse I tell you, that I am wholly yours in him, 'whose you are altogether? If this be too little, in truth I have no 40 'more.

These were the first effects of *Paulinus* his letters; but shortly after, St. *Augustine* sent him others, nothing inferiour to this first, either in affection, or Piety. And the year following, being elected by *Valerius* to sit his Coadjutor in the Sea of *Hippo*, where he afterwards succeeded him; It was resolved by them all, namely by *Valerius*, *Augustine*, *Alypius*, *Severus*, and *Profuturus*, the *African* Bishops, that a messenger should be dispatched into *Campania* to present *Paulinus* with their several letters, and the sincere gratulations of their respective Clergy; which accordingly was performed. 10

In the beginning of this year, which was the three hundred ninety and fifth after *Christ*, *Theodosius Augustus* the first, a most pious Emperour, and a *Nursing Father* of the Church departed this life. The *Ethnick* writers hating his memory as virulently as his person, laboured with all manner of lyes and Libels to render him odious and detestable to posterity. Holy *Endelechius* awaked with these scandalous clamours, and the insolent aspersions cast upon so religious an Emperour, writes earnestly to *Paulinus*, and prevailes with him, to imploy those excellent abilities bestowed on him, in the defense of this faithfull Souldier of *Jesus Christ*, and 20 Champion of his Spouse. This task *Paulinus* performed, as appears by his owne words in his 9th Epistle to *Severus*, to whom hee sent a Coppy of his learned *Panegyrick*; however posterity have suffered in the losse of it. But we want not another witnesse: That learned Father, and happy translator of the booke of God in his thirteenth Epistle to *Paulinus*, gives us a very fair and full account of it. *Librum tuum quem pro Theodosio principe prudenter ornateque*, &c. 'Your booke (saith he) which elegantly and judiciously you com-'posed in the defense of the Emperor *Theodosius*, and sent to me 'by [a]*Vigilantius*, I have with much delight 30 'read over. What I admire in it, is your 'Method: For having excelled all other 'writers in the first parts, you excell your selfe in the last. Your 'stile is compact and neat, and with the perspicuity and purenesse 'of *Cicero*, and yet weighty and sententious; for that writing which 'hath nothing commendable in it, but words, is (as one saith) 'meer prating. The consequence besides is very great, and the 'coherence exact. What ever you infer, is either the confirmation 'of the antecedent, or the inchoation of the subsequent. Most 'happy *Theodosius*, to be vindicated by such a learned Oratour 40

[a] *He proved afterwards a most detestable Heretick.*

'of *Christ*! You have added to the glory of his Imperial robe, 'and made the utility of his just lawes sacred to posterity. But this rare peece, with many more mentioned by *Gennadius*, either through the envie of the Heathen, or the negligence of our own, are unfortunately lost; especially a *Volume of Epistles* written to his *Sister*, with some *controversial peeces* against the *Ethnick* Philosophers, mentioned also by Saint *Augustine* in his four and thirtieth Epistle; and a most learned *Treatise of true Repentance*, and *the glory of Martyrs*.

10 Much about this time, the name of *Paulinus* began to be famous in the *East*; and not onely there, but in all parts of the *Christian* World. It is almost incredible (especially in this age of Impieties and Abominations) how much the example of this one man prevailed over all. The Course he ran, drew another wealthy and noble *Roman* (I mean *Pammachius*) from the Senate to the Cell; and all the Fathers of that age, when they prest any to holy living, and a desertion of the World, brought in *Paulinus* for their great exemplar, and a star to lead them unto *Christ*. St. *Augustine* propounds him to *Romanianus* & *Licentius*, Saint *Hierome* to *Julian*, 20 and the Daughters of *Geruntius*; and Saint *Chrysostome* in his thirteenth homily upon *Genesis*, sets him downe for a pattern to the husbands, and *Therasia* to the wives. The reverend Bishop of *Hippo* did very earnestly sollicite him to come over into *Africk*, & he gives his reason for it in these words: *Non imprudenter ego vos rogo, & flagito, & postulo*, &c. 'Not unadvisedly doe I intreat 'and earnestly desire, and require you to come into *Africk*, where 'the Inhabitants labour more now with the thirst of seeing you, 'then with the famous thirstinesse of the Climate. God knowes, I 'ask it not for my private satisfaction, nor for those onely, who 30 'either by my mouth, or by the publick fame have heard of you; 'but for the rest, who either have not heard, or else having heard 'will not believe so great a change; but when they themselves shall 'see the truth, they will not onely believe, but love and imitate. 'It is for their sakes therefore, that I desire you to honour these 'parts with your bodily presence: Let the Eyes of our flocks also 'behold the glory of Christ in so eminent a Couple, the great 'exemplars to both Sexes, to tread pride under their feet, and not 'to despaire of attaining to perfection. And in his fifty ninth Epistle to *Paulinus*, when (according to the custome of those holy 40 times) hee had sent his Presbyter to him to be instructed, *he*

cannot (saith he) *profit more by my Doctrine*, *then he can by your life*. Saint *Hierome* useth the same Engine to bring down the high thoughts of *Julian*: 'Art thou (saith he) nobly descended? 'So were *Paulinus* and *Therasia*, and far nobler in Christ. Art 'thou rich and honourable? So were they: and from the height of 'honours and worldly riches became poor and inglorious, that 'they might gain Christ. Dearly did *Anastasius*, who succeeded *Siricius* in the Sea of *Rome*, affect this holy Bishop, as appears by his owne words in his sixteenth Epistle to *Delphinus* the Bishop of *Burdeaux*. 10

But amidst all these triumphs of the Church of God, for the conversion of so eminent a person, and the frequent gratulations of learned men, exprest by their letters or personall visits, there were none that raged with so much hatred and malice against him as his own kindred, and former acquaintance. *A Prophet hath no honour in his own Country*, *and those of his owne house will be his Enemies*. There are no such persecutors of the Church, as those that do it for selfe-ends, and their private advantage. Sweetly doth he complain of these bitter, unnatural dealings in his fifth Epistle to *Severus*. *Potiore mihi parente germanus es*, *quam illi quos caro* 20 *tantùm & sanguis mihi sociat*, &. 'You are my Brother now by a 'greater Father, then those who are tyed to me by flesh and blood 'onely. For where is now my great affinity by blood? Where are 'my old friends? where is my former acquaintance? I am become 'as a dream before them all, and as a stranger to my owne brothers, 'the Sons of my Mother. My kinsmen and my friends stand looking 'upon me afar off, and they passe by me like hasty floods, or the 'streames of a brook that will not be stay'd. They convey them-'selves away, and are ashamed of me, who displeased them by 'pleasing God. And in his first Epistle, I beseech you (saith he) If 30 'I shall have need (for now my servants, and those I made free-'men, are become my despisers,) that you would take care to send 'the old Wine, which I beleive I have still at *Narbon*, hither unto 'me, and to pay for the carriage: Do not fear, dear brother, to make 'the poor your debtor, *&c*. The Noble Spirit is the bravest bearer of indignities: and certainly extraction and a virtuous descent (let popular flatterers preach what they will to the contrary,) is attended with more Divinity, and a sweeter temper, then the indiscrete Issue of the multitude. There is an eminent difference betwixt flowers and weedes, though they spring from the same mould. The 40

Ape contending with the Lyonesse, told her, that she was a very fair creature, but very barren: For you (said the Ape) bring forth but one at a birth, and I bring six, or more; 'Tis true (replyed the Lionesse,) but thy six are six Apes, and my one is a Lyon. The greatest part of men, which we commonly terme the populacy, are a stiffe, uncivill generation, without any seed of honour or goodnesse, and sensible of nothing but private interest, & the base waies of acquiring it. What Virtue, or what humanity can be expected from a *Raymond Cabanes*, a *Massinello*, or some Son of a
10 Butcher? They have one barbarous shift, which Tigers and Beares would blush to commit: They will cut the throats of their most generous and Virtuous Benefactours, to comply with times, and advantage themselves; Yea, they will rejoyce to see them ruined, and like inhumane Salvages, insult over their innocent and helplesse posterity. I could compare those fawning Hypocrits, that waite not upon men, but upon their Fortunes, to that smiths bitch in the *Apologues* of *Locmannus* the *Persian*, which sleeping in the forge, could not be awaked with all the noise of the hammers, the Anvile, and the Bellowes: but if the smith would offer to stirre
20 his teeth to eat, shee would start up presently, and attend upon him with all officiousnesse. She would share with him in the fruits of his labours; but would not watch and look to the shop one minute while he laboured.

Paulinus had now first lost these false friends, but was loaded for it with the love and commendations of true ones; And I know not which offended him most, to be despised by the first, or commended by the last. He had (like Saint *Paul*,) great heavinesse, and continuall sorrow of heart, to see that his brethren and kinsmen according to the flesh, hated him because he loved Christ: And
30 on the other side, his humility would not suffer him to beare the *labour of love*, I meane the generall applause and sincere commendations conferred upon him by his Christian friends. *Severus* in one of his Epistles written to him (after hee had spent some lines in the commendation of his zeale and constancie,) contrary to the custome of that plaine age, subscribed himself, his Servant. To the first he replyed, that *his excessive love had drawn him to the sin of untruth*: And the last he desired him to desist from, for this reason; *Cave ergo ne posthac*, &c. 'Have a care hereafter (saith he) that
40 'you who are a Servant of Christ, called unto liberty, terme not

Te multa dilectio ad mendacii peccatum traxit.

'your self the servant of a sinner, and of one that is not worthy to 'be called your fellow-servant. The virtue of humility will not 'excuse the vice of flattery. Thus *Gregorie* the great, when Pope *Anastasius* had exceeded towards him in his laudatory elocutions, blasted them all with this humble reply; *Quod verò me os domini, quod lucernam*, &c. 'Your calling me the mouth of the Lord, a 'shining light, and a strong helper, is nothing else but an aug- 'mentation of my iniquity; for when I deserve to be punished for 'my sins, then do I instead of punishment receive praise. *Severus*, in another of his Epistles to *Paulinus*, earnestly intreated him to suffer his picture to be taken by a limner, which he had sent to him for that purpose, that he might have it to set up, together with the picture of Saint *Martin*, before the sacred font in a fair Church which *Severus* was then in building. This friendly motion *Paulinus* was very much offended with, and would by no means consent unto, teling *Severus*, *that too much love had made him mad*; And in his eighth Epistle, reasoning with him about this request, *What kind of picture* (saith he) *would you have from me, the picture of the earthly, or the Heavenly man? I know you love onely that incorruptible image, which the King of Heaven doth love in you. I am ashamed to picture what I am, and I dare not picture what I am not*. But *Severus* resolving to force it from him, would not be satisfied with any other returne; wherupon he sent it to him, with these following verses, the elegant expresse of his unfeined humility. The first coppy relates to the *pictures*, and the latter to the *Font*.

Abluitis quicunq; animas & membra lavacris,
Cernite propositas ad bona facta vias, &c.

You that to wash your flesh and Soules draw near,
Ponder these two examples set you here.
Great *Martin* shewes the holy life, and white;
Paulinus to repentance doth invite.
Martins pure, harmlesse life tooke Heaven by force,
Paulinus tooke it by teares and remorse.
Martin leads through victorious palms and flowers,
Paulinus leades you through the pooles and showres.
You that are sinners, on *Paulinus* look,
You that are Saints, great *Martin* is your book.
The first example bright and holy is,
The last, though sad and weeping, leads to blisse.

The verses relating to the *Font*, were these.

Hic reparandarum generator fons animarum
Vivum viventi lumine flumen agit, &c.

Here the great well-spring of wash'd Soules, with beams
Of living light quickens the lively streams;
The Dove descends, and stirs them with her wings,
So weds these waters to the upper springs,
They strait conceive: A new birth doth proceede
From the bright streams by an immortall seed.
10 O the rare love of God! sinners wash'd here,
Come forth pure Saints, all justified and clear.
So blest in death and life, man dyes to sins,
And lives to God; Sin dies, and life begins
To be reviv'd: Old *Adam* falls away,
And the new lives, born for eternal sway.

Nor did the manners of holy *Paulinus* differ from his mind: all his Garments, all the Utensils of his poor Cot, were so many emblems and memento's of humility. Grace is an Elixir of a contrary Nature to the Philosophers stone, it turn'd all the gold 20 and Silver vessells of this great Senatour into earthen dishes and wooden spoons. Righteousnesse and honesty are alwaies poor. In his first Epist. to *Severus*, he presents him with some of this innocent furniture; *Misimus testimonialem divitiarum scutellam buxeam*, &c. 'I have sent you (saith he) a platter made of a box-'tree, for a testimoniall of my riches; receive it as a pledge or 'earnest of Evangelicall poverty, and let it be an example to you, 'if as yet you will make use of any Silver platters. To this he addes, that he was very desirous to be supplyed with some more earthen dishes, which (saith he) *I do very much love*; and then subscribes 30 his reason, *quòd secundum Adam cognata nobis sint, & domini thesaurum in talibus vasis commissum habeamus*; because they are near kin to us by *Adam*, and because the treasure of the Lord is committed to our care in such vessells. Certainly poverty (as man is now to be considered) is his best, and his true estate. Riches, though they make themselves wings, yet do they not fly to Heaven. The home or house of gold, is the heart of the Earth, and mineralls are a fuel of hell-fire. Poverty was the Inauguration of the first man, who was made naked, and all his posterity are born so. *This onely have I found* (saith *Solomon*) *that God made man upright*, *but* *he hath sought out many inventions.* By Covetousnesse we loose our uprightnesse: Wee come here light and easie, but we load our selves afterwards with unnecessary burthens. *Perditio tua ex te*, these weights that we take up, sink us down: Our temporall misery as well as the Eternal is from our selves. The merriest creature that I can see, is the **Sparrow*. This makes me think, that hee is not troubled with forethoughts, which are the hands of covetousnesse. What man and beasts scatter and leave behind them, is his provision: his table is laid every where, and the first bush he meets with, is his bed. Our Saviour, who knew the nature and thoughts of all created things, was pleased to send us to school to the birds. They are alwaies full of Musical livelinesse, and a certain bright freedome, which descends not so low as men and beasts. Spirits, when they have businesse upon Earth, must assume bodies. Clarity and purification is a kind of poverty: it is a state that hath cast off dregs & burthens. Divine is that saying of *Gr. Pisides*.

* *Paulinus calls Christ (mistically) a sparrow:* Hic est ille passer, qui requirentibus se in viis hilaritèr ostendit; nunc in portis fit obvius, nunc in platis occurrit, nunc in muris vel turribus sublimis convocat ad se amatores suos, & invitat eos in altitudines habitationum suarum, ut impleat verbum suum, & exaltatus omnia ad se trahat. Quis dabit nobis pennas columbæ deargentatas, ut pennati pervolemus ad bravîum supernæ vocationis, sequentes istum passerem solitarium, qui est unicus dei filius, supervolitantem, qui in altis habitat, & humilia respicit?

Τὸ πτωχὸν ἦθος οὐρανόδρομον φύσει.

Poor habits are naturally heaven-seekers.

But *Paulinus*, though he was poor, yet was he charitable, and withall liberall. The widowes mite is more then the rich mens abundance. In the four hundred and tenth year after *Christ*, when the *Gothes* raged in *Italy*, and had sackt *Nola*, *Paulinus* (amongst many others,) was taken prisoner by them; *And thus* (saith Saint *Augustine*) *as I afterwards learnt from him, did he then pray in his heart.* Domine, ne excrucier propter aurum & argentum; ubi enim omnia mea sunt, tu scis. *O Lord suffer me not to be troubled with the losse of Gold & Silver, for thou knowest where all my riches are laid up.* His treasure was laid up in Heaven, where he commanded us to lay it, who foretold, that these calamities should come upon the World. And God (without doubt) had reguard unto his prayer, for the barbarous enemie leading all the rest into captivity, he onely was left behind. But amongst all these plunderings and outward afflictions, hee

Lib. I. de Civitate dei.

never failed in his daily almes to the poor, nor was the hand of his faithfull *Therasia* any way shortned. At last his store failing, and no more provision being left, then onely one loafe of bread; A poor man comming to the door for reliefe, *Paulinus* commands it should be given him. But *Therasia* (arguing with her selfe, that no begger could be poorer then *Paulinus* now was, and that it was as much charity to keepe it for him, as to give it to another,) conceal'd the loafe, and suffered the poor man to go without it. A day or two after, some men that were sent with relief to *Paulinus*, from his 10 friends, arrive at *Nola*, and tell him that they had been there much sooner, had not one of the ships, which was loaden with corn, been cast away almost in the Harbour; the rest that were fraught with Wine and other Victualls, being come safe to shore. Whereupon *Paulinus* turning towards *Therasia*, put her in mind of her over-much carefullnesse, with these words, *Understand now* Therasia, *that this great ship full laden with Corne, was cast away for that one loafe of bread which thou didst steale from the poore man.*

But passe we now to his *Episcopall* dignity. In his own Workes we have not one line that mentions this Ecclesiasticall honour, 20 nor any other passage of his life, that might but seem to conduce to his own glory. They breath nothing but humility, nothing but self-deniall and dedignation. Wee must be guided then through this part of his life by other Authors, and such faithfull records as are come unto us, from the hands of learned and publick persons; who either upon the generall interest and concernments of the Church, or their own private merits, and not by reflection were acquainted with him. The first that offers himself to us, is *Uranius*, his own Presbyter, who in that short narration which he wrote of his life, sets him forth to posterity in this following Character; 30 *Cum autem ad summum sacerdotij gradum*, &c. 'When he was 'honoured (saith he) with the highest degree in the Priesthood, 'he did not shew himself such a Bishop that desired to be feared, 'but one that endeavoured to be beloved. He was never so farre 'angry, as not in his anger to shew mercy. Nor could that man 'indeed be angry, for he regarded not calumnies, and he avoyded 'hatred. He never sate in Judgement, but mercy sate close by him. 'He was truly such a Bishop as laboured to get the love of all. For 'hee lived a Consolation to all, and their great example to make 'sure their Salvation. Nor is this my voyce onely: even the bar-40 'barous Nations who knew my Lord *Paulinus* by report onely, will 'testifie as much. And worthily was hee beloved of all, who was a 'friend to all. For who was there cast down, and he did not lift him 'up? who ever called to him for help, and was not piously and 'comfortably answered? For he was pious, tender hearted, humble 'and courteous, hating none, despising none. He gave to all, he 'cherished all: he encouraged the fearfull, pacified the violent, 'those with his words, these with his example; Some he comforted 'with his letters, and those that wanted, with his mony. He loved 'not any riches, nor any treasures, but those which Christ promised 'to his followers. Gold and Silver, and the other accommodations 10 'of life he approved of, if they were liberally given to the poor, not 'covetously hoorded up. Briefly, he had in him all goodnesse, for 'he loved Christ. Hee had Faith, Meeknesse, love towards his 'neighbours, a constant care of the poor, compassion upon the 'weak, and laboured for nothing in his life, but peace and charity. 'All his endeavours were to make men good, and to save their 'Soules. What place is there in the World, what solitude, what 'Seas which acknowledge not the good works of holy *Paulinus*? All 'men desired his acquaintance, and did extreamly long to have a 'sight of him. Who ever came to him without joy, or who went 20 'from him, but he desired to stay longer? those that could not see 'him in the body, desired to see him in his writings; for he was 'sweet and gentle in his Epistles, elegant and ravishing in his 'Poems. What more shall I say? The relations that may be given of 'him, would be scarse credible, but that his knowne integrity is 'above falshood.

Nola was at this time a very famous and splendid City, nothing inferiour to the best *Emporiums* of *Italie*, and had withall a very rich *Sea*; which questionlesse was a great occasion, that the piety of this blessed Bishop was so renowned, and so familiarly spoken 30 of in the most remote parts of the World. So the just and faithfull God exalteth those that humble themselves, and honours those that honour him. He had beene faithfull in those things that were his own, and was therefore intrusted with the treasures of the Church. *Prosper* in his second book, *de vitâ Contemplativâ*, and the ninth Chapter, tells us, how hee disposed of them; *Sanctus Paulinus* (*ut ipsi meliùs nostis*) *ingentia prædia quæ fuerunt sua*, *vendita pauperibus erogavit: sed cum posteà factus esset Episcopus*, *non contempsit Ecclesiæ facultates*, *sed fidelissime dispensavit*. 'Holy '*Paulinus* (saith he) as you best know, sold all those princely 40

'Possessions which were his own, and gave of them to the poor: 'but when he was afterwards consecrated Bishop, he neglected not 'the revenues of the Church, but was a most faithfull Steward and 'dispenser of them. So faithfull, that when he lay upon his death bed, hee had not one piece left to relieve himself, but was driven to lay out for some Cloathes which he had given to the poor, a small summe of mony, which God ordained to be sent to him for that very purpose a litle before the hour of his dissolution. So that living and dying, he kept to the Apostles rule, and *owed no man* 10 *any thing but love*: Hee was a great lover of learned and holy men, and confesseth in one of his Epistles to *Alypius*, that his affection to Saint *Ambrose*, was the first inducement which he felt to incline him to Christianity. His dearest and most intimate friends were Saint *Augustine*, Saint *Ambrose*, Saint *Hierome*, Saint *Martin* the Bishop of *Tours*, *Delphinus* the Bishop of *Burdeaux*, and *Amandus* his Successour; *Alypius* the Bishop of *Tagasta*, *Januarius* the Bishop of *Naples*, afterwards a Martyr, *Victricius* the *Rhotomagensis*, *Aper*, *Severus*, and *Nicetas* of *Dacia*. I may say of him as the Scripture saith of *Moses*, he was the meekest man upon the 20 face of the Earth. He was not onely obedient and serviceable to these Fathers, and pillars of the Church, but to his own *Presbyters* and *Domesticks*: he judged himself the most unworthy, and the most unable of all his brethren. *Victor* the Monk, sent from *Severus* to see him (according to the custome of those times) washed his feete. This was a ceremony, which in that age of holinesse could not be refused. But *Victor* by this did not onely wash his feet, but his face also; for he drew tears from him, because hee might not deny him the performance of that Evangelical service. *Servivit ergo mihi peccatori, & væ misero mihi quod passus sum; he served* 30 *me a sinner* (saith the holy Bishop) *and woe is to me because I suffered him*. But he staid not at tears, for as soone as *Victor* had done washing his feet, to requite his service, he fetched him clean water, and held the bason while he wash'd his hands. He was not like that insolent *Abbot* that did cast off his humility with his *Cowle*, and being asked by his brethren, *why he was then so proud, that was formerly such an humble Monk*, made answer; *that in his Monachisme, when he went so low, and stooping, he was searching for the keyes of the Abbey; but now having found them, he did hold up his head to ease himself.*

40 This true carriage of an Evangelist, made him both honourd

and beloved; the *Church* rejoyced, and glorified God for him, and the *Court* admired him. Holynesse is a light that cannot be hidden: It is a candle set upon a hill: stars never shine more glorious, then when they are neare black Clouds. In the year of our Lord, four hundred and nineteen (a grievous *Schism* then happening in the Church,) there was a convention of certain Bishops and Fathers at *Rome*, to quiet those groundlesse perturbations, and stop the breach. But *Honorius* the Emperour, judging by his skil in the temper of those Church-men, that no good would be done without the presence of *Paulinus*, who then lay sick at *Nola*, dispatched his Imperial letter to this holy Bishop, wherein he earnestly intreated him (if possible) to shake off his present indisposition, and to repaire in person to the Synod, lest that great blessing of peace, which he and the Church did earnestly hope and long for, might by his absence unfortunately miscarry. This royall record (because it is a monument of no lesse sincerity then concernment, and discovers unto us much of the face of those times) I shall *verbatim* insert.

Sancto & venerabili Patri, *Paulino*, Episcopo *Nolensi*

Tantùm fuit apud nos certa sententia, nihil ab his sacerdotibus, qui ad Synodum convenerant, posse definiri, cum beatitudo tua de corporis inæqualitate causata, itineris non potuit injuriam sustinere, ut propter absentiam sancti viri, non quidem obtentura: Interim tamen vitia gratulantur, cùm prava & vetus ambitio, & cum benedicto viro sanctæq; vitæ diù velit habere certamen, ut contra hæc Apostolicæ institutionis bona, de præsumptis per vim parietibus existimet confidendum. O verè digna causa quam non nisi coronæ tuæ beata vita designat! Dilatum itaq; Judicium nuntiamus, ut divina præcepta ex venerationis tuæ ore promantur, qui ea secutus implesti; nec potest alius eorum præceptorum lator existere, quam qui dignus Apostolicis disciplinis est approbatus. Specialiter itaq; domine sancte, meritò venerabilis pater, Justus dei famulus, divinum opus, contempto labore, tributum hoc nobis visitationis tuæ (si ita dicendum est) munus indulge, ut postpositis omnibus, quantùm temperantia his & tranquillitas suffragantur, Synodo profuturus, sine intermissione etiam desideriis nostris, & benedictioni quam cupimus, te præstare digneris.

To the holy and reverend Father PAULINUS, *Bishop of* Nola

'Such a firm opinion have we that nothing can be agreed and 'concluded upon by the Bishops met in this Synod, (your Holi-'nesse by reason of your bodily indisposition being not able to 'travel hither) that for your onely absence it is not like to con-'tinue: In the mean time offences triumph and rejoyce at it, and 'the old and wicked sinne of ambition, which of a long time desires 'to contend even with your holynesse and upright life, presumes 'now, and is confident that having forcibly taken the wall from us, 'it will carry you also against the wholsomnesse of Apostolicall 'institution. O! a cause truly worthy not to be determined, but by 'your holy life, which is your Crown! we therfore declare unto you, 'that we have suspended our judgement for the present, that we 'may have the truth of these Divine precepts pronounced by your 'reverend mouth, who have both followed them, and fullfilled 'them: For none can be a fit arbiter of those rules, but he that hath 'approved himself worthy and conformable to Apostolicall disci-'pline. Wherefore, holy Sir, worthily reverend Father, the faithfull 'Servant of God, and his Divine work, we intreat you particularly, 'that slighting the troubles of this Journey, you would favour us 'with this gift and tribute (if I may so speak) of your presence: and 'laying aside all other concernments (so far as your health and ease 'will permit,) be in your owne person at this Synod, and vouchsafe 'to lend your assistance to our desires, and that blessing which wee 'earnestly long for.

Wee see by this letter in what account hee was with the Emperour, and that his integrity and holyness were not dissimulations and popular Fables, but experimentall truths so known and so believed; hee was a true Christian, and no Impostour. It was not the Custome, but the nature (if I may so say) of those Primitive times to love holy and peacefull men. But some *great ones* in this later age, did nothing else but countenance *Schismaticks* and *seditious raylers*, *the despisers of dignities*, that covered their *abominable villanies* with a pretence of *transcendent holinesse*, and a certain *Sanctimonious excellencie* above the Sons of men. This *Vaile* (which then *cousend* weak eyes) is now fallen off their *faces*, and most of their patrons have by an unthought of Method received their rewards: The rest without doubt (though they shift themselves into a thousand shapes) shall not escape him, *whose anger is not yet turned away, but his hand is stretched out still.* But returne we to *Paulinus*: Whose Charity and tendernesse towards the poor, was both inimitable and incredible; This iron age wants faith as well as mercy: When he had given them all he had, to the last that begged he gave himself. *Gregorie* the great, in the third Book of his *Dialogues*, and the first Chapter, hath recorded this memorable passage. I shall cut it short, and in as few words, as conveniently may be, give you all that is material. When the *Vandals* had 10 miserably wasted *Campania*, and carried many of the inhabitants into *Africk*, blessed *Paulinus* gave all that he had both towards his own sustenance, and the reliefe of the poor, amongst the prisoners and Captives. The Enemy being departed, and his prey with him; a poor Widow (whose onely Son was (amongst the rest of the Natives) by a Son in law of the King of the *Vandals* carried into Bondage,) comes to petition *Paulinus* for so much Money as might serve to redeem him. *Paulinus* told her that he had nothing then left, either in money or other goods, but promised, if shee would accept of him, to go with her into *Africk*, and to be ex- 20 changed for her Son. The poore Widow taking this for a meere scoffe, turnes her back to be gone. *Paulinus* followes after, and with much adoe made her believe, that he meant it (as he did indeed) in earnest. Upon this, they travell'd both into *Africk*, and having opportunity to speake with the Kings Son in Law, the poor widow begged of him first, to have her son restor'd unto her *Gratis*: but the youthfull and haughty *Vandal* averse to all such requests, would hear her no farther; whereupon she presents him with *Paulinus*, and petitioned to have her Son set at liberty, and the other to serve in his stead. The Prince taken with the comely 30 and reverend countenance of *Paulinus*, asked him, what his occupation or trade was? *Paulinus* answered, that he never followed any trade, but that he had good skill in dressing of Herbes and Flowers. Upon this, the Prince delivered her Son to the Widow, who took him home with her, and sent *Paulinus* to work into his Gardens.

The Prince delighting much in Flowers and Sallets, would very frequently visit *Paulinus*, and took such delight in him, that he forsook all his Court-associates to enjoy the company of his new Gardiner. In one of these visits, *Paulinus* taking occasion to confer seriously with him, advised him to be very carefull of himselfe, 40 and to consider speedily of some means to secure and settle the Kingdome of the *Vandals*[a] in *Mauritania*; for (said he) the King your Father in law will shortly dye. The Prince something troubled with the suddain newes, without further delay acquaints the King with it; and tells him withall, that his Gardiner (whose prediction this was) excelled all other men both in wisedome and learning. Whereupon the King requested, that he might see him; you shall, replyed the Prince, for to morrow when you are at dinner, I will give order that hee shall come in person with the dishes of Sallate to the Table. This being agreed upon, and accordingly performed, the old Tyrant upon the first sight of *Paulinus* exceedingly trembled, and speaking to his Daughter, who sate next to him, to call to her husband, he told him, that the prediction of his Gardiner was very true; for *yesternight* (said he) *I saw in a dream a great tribunal with judges sitting thereon, and amongst them this Gardiner, by whose judgement a scourge which had been formerly put into my hands, was taken from me.* But learn of him what his profession is, and what dignity he had conferred upon him in his own Country, for I cannot believe him to be (as he pretends) an inferiour or ordinary person.

This was about the year of our L. 428. *about which time the Vandals after their excursions through* Polonia, Italy, Franconia, *and* Andalusia *had setled in* Africk, *where they continued quietly until the reigne of* Justinian, *but rebelling against him, they were together with their King* Gillimer *totally overthrown by the great Captaine* Belisarius *An. Christi* 533.

As soon as dinner was ended, the Prince stole from the *presence* into the Garden, and earnestly intreated *Paulinus* to tell him, who he was; I am (said he) your Gardiner, which you received in exchange for the Widowes Son. I know that, replyed the Prince, but I desire to know your profession in your own Country, and not the servitude you have put your self in with me for the present; To this *Paulinus* answered, that he was by profession a *Bishop, and a servant of Jesus Christ the Son of the living God.* At these words the Prince was mightily troubled, and requested him to depart againe into his own Country, assuring him, that before he departed, he would give him any thing that he should please demand. *Paulinus* replyed, that he would desire nothing, but to have those Captives which were carried out of *Campania*, set at liberty, and transported to their Native Country. To this the Prince consented, and for *Paulinus* his sake, furnished them with shipping and all other necessaries for their voyage, and sent them home joyfull in the Company of their blessed and beloved Bishop.

Some few daies after, the old Tyrant (as God had foretold by his holy Servant) departed out of this World *into his owne place*; And so that scourge which God had put into his hand for the punishment of a great part of the Christian World, was taken away, and the instrument cast into the fire. Wherefore whoever thou beest, that readest this book, and art a sufferer thy selfe, or doest see and grieve for the calamities of the Church, *the oppression of the poor, & the violent perverting of judgement & justice in a province, do not thou marvel at the matter*, nor vex thy self; *for he that is higher then the highest, regardeth it, and there be higher then* 10 *they. Envy not the glory of Sinners, for thou knowest not what will be their end;* but *submit thy self under the mighty hand of God*, expecting with patience the time of refreshing, and I do assure thee upon my Soul, thou shalt not be deceived.

Paulinus, with all his joyfull Captives, was now landed in *Campania*, where all the Inhabitants, as upon a solemne feast-day flocked together to welcome him, and to poure their joyes into his bosome; some received their Sonnes, some their brothers, and some their husbands: both the receivers and the received were beholding to *Paulinus*. They commended, honoured and admired 20 him: He exhorted, incouraged and confirmed them. Mutuall Consolations are a double banquet, they are the Churches *Eulogiæ*, which we both give and take. What the *Campanians* most admired in *Paulinus*, was that which the Scripture commends in *Moses*: *youthfullnesse in old age*. He was now as earnest, as hearty, and as active for the glory of God, as in his most vigorous years. *His spiritual force was not abated, nor the Eye of his Soul any way dimmed*. Hee did not coole towards his *setting*, but grew more large, more bright, and more fervent. Bearing trees, when their fruit is ripe, bend their boughes, and offer themselves to the gatherers 30 hands. He knew that his time of departure was at hand, and therefore *Moses*-like he made his *Doctrine to drop as the raine, and his speech distilled as the dew. Hee poured out his milk and his Wine, and made them drink abundantly*. To labour in the heat of the day, and to give over in the cool, is great indiscretion, the contention should be alwaies hottest towards the end of the race.

I am now come to my last *Paragraph*, which all this while I did reserve for his *Works of Piety*. And these indeede (if wee consider his unworldlinesse, and religious poverty) were very great and very sumptuous. He repaired and beautified the four old *Basilica's*, or 40

Churches, dedicated to the Martyr *Felix*, and built the *fifth*, which exceeded them all, both for beauty and largenesse. This he dedicated to our Lord and Saviour *Jesus Christ*. It was adorned with two stately Porches, the one opend towards the way of Publick resort, the other was a private *Postern*; and the path leading to it, was through a pleasant *green field* set with *fruit-trees* and other *shady wood*, fenced about with a very high and sumptuous wall; The entrance into this Court was through a fair Marble-Gate, in whose Front were cut these following verses.

10 *Cælestes intrate vias per amœna vireta*, &c.

Through pleasant green fields enter you the way
To blisse; and wel through shades and blossoms may
The walkes leade here, from whence directly lyes
The good mans path to sacred *Paradise*.

This Church was joyned to the other four, and an entrance made from the one into the other, by high and spatious *Arches*, supported with pillars of Marble. Through these pillars (whose height did almost reach to the roof,) as through a *traverse* was to be seene, by those that came from the old Church into the new, the picture
20 of the Crosse, limned in most lively and glorious Colours, and hung with Garlands of palms and flowers; above it shined a cleare and luminous skie, and on the Crosse, which was all Purple, sate perching a flock of white Doves; at the bottome of this *Paisage* were written these verses.

Ardua floriferæ Crux, &c.

The painfull Crosse with flowers and Palms is crown'd,
Which prove, it springs; though all in blood 'tis drown'd:
The Doves above it shew with one consent,
Heaven opens onely to the innocent.

30 In the Courts belonging to this Church, were very faire and spatious walks, paved with stone, and covered over head against the violence of weather. The outside was supported with Pillars, and the Inner was divided into neat and cleanly Cells, opening towards the Walks, where the people that came thither to celebrate the *Vigils* of *Felix*, reposed themselves. Round about these Courts were great *Cisterns*, and *Lavers* of severall kinds of Marble most curiously polished, whose diverse formes and colours were very delightfull, and much recreated the beholders. The Porches,

which were very large, and contained within them many private *Oratories*, or places of prayer, were all richly pictured with sacred Histories out of the *Pentateuch*, the book of *Joshuah*, *Judges* and *Ruth*; This Church is fully described in his twelfth Epistle to *Severus*, and his ninth *Natalis*, when *Nicetas* came out of *Dacia* to see him.

Ecce vidès quantus splendor velut æde renatâ
Rideat, insculptum camerâ crispante lacunar
In ligno mentitur ebur; tectoque supernè
Pendentes lychni spiris retinentur ahenis,
Et medio in vacuo laxis vaga lumina nutant 10
Funibus, undantes flammas levis aura fatigat, &c.

You see what splendour through the spatious Isle,
As if the Church were glorified, doth smile.
The Ivory-wrought beams seem to the sight
Ingraven, while the carv'd roofe looks curl'd and bright.
On brasse hoopes to the upmost vaults we tie
The hovering Lamps, which nod and tremble by
The yeelding Cords; fresh Oyle doth still repair
The waving flames, vex'd with the fleeting aire.

Having finished this Church, hee built another, not far from 20 *Nola*, in a litle Town called *Fundi*, where his possessions (which he afterwards sold and gave to the poor,) were situate; this also he dedicated to our Lord *Jesus*, whom he used to call the *Saint of Saints, and the Martyr of Martyrs.* In this Church in the great Isle leading to the Altar, he caused to be put up another peece of *Limning*, or sacred *Paisage*, which for beauty and excellencie exceeded all the former. We have it most lively described and explained in these following verses.

Sanctorum labor & merces sibi rite cohærent,
Ardua Crux, pretiumque crucis sublime, corona, &c. 30

The paines of Saints, and Saints rewards are twins,
The sad Crosse, and the Crowne which the Crosse wins.
Here *Christ* the Prince both of the Cross and Crown
Amongst fresh Groves and Lillies fully blown,
Stands, a white Lamb bearing the purple Crosse,
White shewes his purenesse, *Red* his bloods dear losse:
To ease his sorrowes the Chast *Turtle* sings,
And fans him swetting blood with her bright wings;
While from a shining Cloud the *Father* Eyes
His Sons sad conflict with his Enemies, 40

And on his blessed head lets gently down
Eternal glory made into a Crown.
About him stand two flocks of differing notes,
One of white sheepe, and one of speckled goates,
The first possesse his right hand, and the last
Stand on his left: The spotted Goates are cast
All into thick, deep shades, while from his right
The white sheepe passe into a whiter light.

But in all these sacred buildings, our most pious and humble
10 Bishop did not so much as dream of *Merit*. He thought (as blessed
Mr. *Herbert* did) that they were good works, if sprinkled with the
blood of *Christ*; otherwise hee thought them nothing. It will not
be amisse, nor perhaps needlesse, to produce his own words in
his own defense: *Nisi dominus ædificaverit domum, vano ædificantes
labore sudabimus. Oremus ergo dominum, ut dum nos illi ædificamus
domicilia quæ videntur, ille nobis intus ædificet illa quæ non videntur,
domum videlicet illam non manufactam.* 'Unlesse the Lord build the
'house, wee labour in vaine to build it. Let us therefore (saith he)
'pray to the Lord, that while wee outwardly build unto him these
20 'visible buildings, hee would build inwardly in us those which are
'invisible, that is to say, the house not made with hands. How can
a servant merit by making use of his masters goods? All we do,
and all we give are but his concessions and favours first given unto
us. *Cum suis & hìc & ibi rebus locupletamur*, in this World, and in
the World to come all our magnificence is but his munificence.
But *Paulinus* was not onely outwardly pious, but inwardly also.
He did so abound with private devotions, that all the time from
his Baptism to his buriall, may be truly called his *Prayer-time*. All
that he did think, all that he did speak, and all that he did write,
30 was pure devotion. Either publick or private prayers took up all
his time. Our Saviour tells us, that *Gods Elects cry day and*
Luk. 18. *night unto him*, and Saint *Paul* adviseth us *to pray without
ceasing, and in every thing to give thanks, for this* (saith he) *is the
will of God in Christ Iesus concerning you.* Holy *Paulinus* called
Saint *Paul* his Master, having made himselfe his Disciple, hee
would not neglect his commands: *If you continue in my word* (saith
our Saviour) *then are you my Disciples indeed.*

To this I shall adde his Conformity and obedience to the
Church, a blessing of no small consequence in all ages, especially in
40 this age of *Schismes* and *Heresies*. Hee highly honoured the memory

of the Saints of God, and was a most chearfull and devout observer of Sacred Festivals, or holy daies. His pious affection to these blessed seasons, together with the necessity and convenience of them, he hath most elegantly and learnedly demonstrated in his Poems.

——— hos per longa morantes
Tempora, dum tardi splendens rota vertitur anni
Sustineo intentis affecto pectore votis:
Quos cupio totis mihi prælucere diebus,
Vel quando veniunt ita compensare moras, ut
Æstivis possent spatiis producere lucem, 10
Aut illum pensare diem, qui sistere Jussis
Syderibus, longo lassavit lumine mundum,
Humanos duplicans dilatâ nocte labores.
Ergo velut cælum stellis, & floribus arva
Temporibusque annos dominus, sic ipse diebus
Tempora distinxit festis, ut pigra diurnis
Ingenia obsequiis, saltem discrimine facto,
Post intervallum reduci sollemnia voto
Sancta libenter agant, residesque per annua mentes
Festa parent domino, quia jugiter intemeratos 20
Justitiæ servare piget: delinquere suetis,
Parcere peccato labor est: decurritur omni
Valle, per ascensum non est evadere cursu.
Inde bonus dominus cunctos pietatis ut alis
Contegat, invalidis niti virtutis ad arcem
Congrua sanctorum dedit intervalla dierum,
Ut saltem officiis mediocribus ultima Christi
Vestimenta legant, & eos sacra fimbria sanet.
Primus enim gradus est cælo pertexere cunctos
Continuâ bonitate dies, & tempore toto 30
Pascha sacrum Christi Cultu celebrare pudico.
Quod si mista seges tribulis mihi germinat, & cor
Incultum stimulat terreni spina laboris,
Vel festis domino studeam me offere diebus,
Ut vel parte mei tangam confinia Vitæ,
Corpore ne toto trahar in Consortia mortis.

Englished thus

Those sacred daies by tedious time delai'd
While the slow years bright line about is laid,
I patiently expect, though much distrest 40
By busie longing, and a love-sicke brest:

I wish, they may outshine all other daies,
Or when they come, so recompence delaies
As to outlast the Summer-hours bright length,
Or that fam'd day, when stopt by Divine strength,
The Sun did tyre the World with his long light,
Doubling mens labours, and adjourning night.
As the bright Skye with stars, the fields with flowers,
The years with diff'ring seasons, months and houres
God hath distinguished and mark'd; so he
10 With sacred feasts did ease and beautifie
The working dayes: because that mixture may
Make men (loath to be holy ev'ry day,)
After long labours with a freer will
Adore their maker, and keepe mindfull still
Of holynesse, by keeping holy daies:
For otherwise they would dislike the wayes
Of piety as too severe. To cast
Old customes quite off, and from sinne to fast
Is a great work. To runne which way we will,
20 On plaines is easie, not so up a hill.
Hence 'tis our good God (who would all men bring
Under the Covert of his saving wing,)
Appointed at set times his solemne feasts,
That by mean services, men might at least
Take hold of Christ as by the hemme, and steal
Help from his lowest skirts their Soules to heal.
For the first step to Heaven, is to live well
All our life long, and each day to excel
In holynesse; but since that tares are found
30 In the best Corn, and thistles will Confound
And prick my heart with vaine cares, I will strive
To weed them out on feast-daies, and so thrive
By handfuls, 'till I may full life obtaine,
And not be swallow'd of Eternall paine.

Two places upon Earth were most renowned with the memory of our Saviour, *Bethlem* for his *birth*, and mount *Calvarie* for his *passion.* To extirpate all remembrance of his *Humanity* out of these places, *Hadrian* the persecutor caused the Idol of *Jupiter* to be set up, and worshiped in *Mount Calvarie*; and in *Bethlem* he 40 built a *Mosquie* for that *Egyptian* block *Adonis*, which the Idolatrous *Jewes* called *Thamuz.* Some men amongst us have done the like: Two *Seasons* in the year were consecrated by the *Church* to the memory of our *Saviour*: The *Feast* of his *Nativity* and *Circumcision*, and the *Feast* of his *Passion* and *Resurrection*. These two they have utterly taken away: endeavouring (in my opinion) to extinguish the *memory* of his *Incarnation* and *Passion*, and to race his blessed name out of those *bright columnes of light*, which the *Scripture* calls *daies*. They will not allow him two daies in the year, who made the dayes and the nights. But it is much to be feared, that he who hath appointed their daies here, will allow them for it long nights.

Holy *Paulinus* had now attained a good old age, the forerunners (as Master *Herbert* saith) were come, and the *Almond tree did flourish*: hee was all white with years, and worshiped (like *Jacob*) *leaning upon the top of his staffe*. His virtuous and deare *Therasia* had died (I believe) long before this time; God having ordained him to be hindmost, who was the stronger Vessell, and best able to bear her absence, and the unavoydable disconsolations of flesh and blood. And now (having for some time stood gazing after her,) he begins to follow, God visiting him with a strong paine in the side, which in a few daies did set him at liberty to overtake her, by breaking the prison.

Three daies before his dissolution, *Symmachus* and *Hyacinthinus*, two Bishops of his acquaintance came to visit him; whereupon hee spoke to *Uranius* his Presbyter, that hee should prepare to attend him in the administration of the Sacrament; for (said he) I desire to receive it in the company of my brethren, which are now come to see mee. This sacred Solemnity was no sooner ended, but suddenly hee began to ask, *where his brothers were?* One that stood by, supposing that he had asked for the two Bishops, answered, *Here they be*: I know that, replyed *Paulinus*, but I aske for my brothers **Januarius* and *Martinus*, *who were here with me just now*, *and promised to come to me again*. And having thus spoken, he looked up towards Heaven, and with a voyce as chearfull as his countenance, which seemed to shine and revive with joy, he sung out the one hundred and twentieth Psalme, *I lift up mine Eyes unto the hills from whence cometh my help. My help commeth from the Lord*, *who made Heaven and Earth*.

* *Januarius was Bishop of* Naples, *and a Martyr; and* Martinus *was the Bishop of* Tours *in* France.

This being done *Posthumianus*, another Presbyter that was then present, told *Paulinus*, *that there were forty shillings unpaid for the Cloathes which he had given to the poor*, *before he fell sick*. To this *Paulinus* replyed with a smile, that he remembred it very well:

and Son (said he) *take no thought for it*, *for beleive me*, *there is one that will not be wanting to pay the debt of the poor*. The words were no sooner out of his mouth, but presently there comes in from the parts of *Lucania* (now called *Basilicata*) a Presbyter sent from the holy Bishop *Exuperantius* to visit *Paulinus*; who brought him fifty shillings for a token from the Bishop. *Paulinus* receiving the money, blessed God, saying, *I thank thee O Lord*, *that hast not forsaken them that seek thee*. Of these fifty shillings he gave two with his owne hand to the Presbyter that brought them, and the
10 rest he delivered to *Posthumianus* to pay for the Cloathes which were given to the poor.

The Evening now drawing on, hee remained quiet and well at ease untill midnight: but the paine then increasing in his side, he was troubled with a great difficulty, and shortnesse of breathing, which held him till five in the morning. The day begining to break, he felt the usuall motions of holynesse awaking his Spirit, to which (though weak) he chearfully obeyed, and sitting up in his bed, celebrated *Mattins* himselfe. By this time all the *Deacons* and *Presbyters* of his diocesse were gathered together at the door, and
20 came (like the *Sons* of the *Prophets*) to see the translation of their aged Father. After some short exhortations to holynesse and Christian courage, he lifted up his hands and blessed them, mindfull (it seems) of our Saviours carriage at his ascension, whose peace he prayed might rest upon them.

Shortly after (the pain still encreasing and prevailing against him) hee became speechlesse, and so continued untill the Evening; when suddenly sitting up (as if hee had been awaked out of his sleep) he perceived it to be the time of the *Lucernarium*, or Evening-Office, and lifting up his hands towards Heaven, he repeated with
30 a low voyce, this verse out of the Psalmes, *Thy word is a Lantern unto my feet*, *and a light unto my paths*. About the fourth hour of the night, when all that were present sate diligently watching about him; his poor Cottage did suddenly shake with such a strong Earth-quake, that those who kneeled about his bed were something disordered with it, and fell all trembling to their prayers. The Guests of Eternal Glory were now entred under that narrow roof, where (after the abdication of his great worldly honours) he had lived so long in all holynesse and humility. For in that instant of time (saith *Uranius*) he was dissolved, the blessed Angels testify-
40 ing that they were present to conduct his happy and glorious Soul

into the joy of his Master. By the like signe did *Christ* signifie to his Church in *Hierusalem*, that he heard their prayers when they were persecuted by the mercilesse *Jews*. *Gregory* the great, in the place before cited, makes expresse mention of this Earthquake. And thus we see after what manner the righteous are taken away, though no man will lay it to his heart.

Three daies (saith *Uranius*) before *John* the Bishop of *Naples* departed out of this life, he affirmed that he saw *Paulinus* all clothed with Angelicall brightnesse, which shined like the stars, holding in his hand a kind of Heavenly foode in form like a honey-combe, 10 but white as the light, and speaking to him, *brother Iohn*, *what do you here? pray*, *that you may be dissolv'd*, *&* *come unto us*, *where we have enough of this provision which you see in my hand*. This pious Bishop did not long survive this vision, for the Sunday following, after he had ended his Sermon, and blessed the people (having the day before celebrated the Communion, and distributed to the poor,) he fell sicke and dyed in the Church. So that I may say of him, *Episcopos Concionantes*, *&* *Concionatores stantes mori docuit*: Hee taught Bishops to dye preaching, and preachers to die standing. 20

Blessed *Paulinus* departed out of this life in the year of our Lord four hundred and thirty one, in the seaven and seaventieth year of his age, upon the tenth of the kalends of *Iuly*, which according to our account is the two and twentieth day of *Iune*. His body was carried from *Nola* to *Rome*, and decently interred in the Church of St. *Bartholomew*, neare the Apostles own Tombe: where they both lye expecting the second comming of our Lord and Saviour *JESUS CHRIST*; which of his great mercy I earnestly beseech him to hasten, and to appeare himselfe the onely faithfull Judge, and most just Determiner of *Right* and *Wrong*, of *Truth* and 30 *Falshood*.

Gloria tibi mitissime Jesu!

St. *Paulinus* to his Wife *Therasia*

Come my true Consort in my Joyes and Care!
Let this uncertaine and still wasting share
Of our fraile life be giv'n to God. You see
How the swift dayes drive hence incessantlie,

And the fraile, drooping World (though still thought gay,)
In secret, slow consumption weares away.
All that we have, passe from us: and once past
Returne no more; like clouds, they seeme to last,
And so delude loose, greedy mindes. But where
Are now those trim deceits? to what darke sphere 10
Are all those false fires sunck, which once so shin'd
They captivated Soules, and rul'd mankind?
He that with fifty ploughes his lands did sow,
Will scarse be trusted for two Oxen now,
His rich, lowd Coach known to each crowded street
Is sold, and he quite tir'd walkes on his feet.
Merchants that (like the Sun) their voyage made
From East to West, and by whole-sale did trade,
Are now turn'd Sculler-men, or sadly swett
In a poore fishers boat with line and nett. 20
Kingdomes and Cities to a period tend,
Earth nothing hath, but what must have an end:
Mankind by plagues, distempers, dearth and warre,
Tortures and prisons dye both neare and farre;
Furie and hate rage in each living brest,
Princes with Princes, States with States contest;
An Vniversall discord mads each land,
Peace is quite lost, the last times are at hand;
But were these dayes from the last day secure,
So that the world might for more yeares endure, 30
Yet we (like hirelings) should our terme expect,
And on our day of death each day reflect.
For what (Therasia!) *doth it us availe*
That spatious streames shall flow and never faile,
That aged forrests live to tyre the Winds,
And flowers each spring returne and keepe their kinds?
Those still remaine: but all our Fathers dyed,
And we our selves but for few dayes abide.
This short time then was not giv'n us in vaine,
To whom tyme dyes, in which we dying gaine, 40
But that in time eternall life should be
Our care, and endlesse rest our industrie.
And yet, this Taske which the rebellious deeme
Too harsh, who god's mild lawes for chaines esteem

Suites with the meeke and harmelesse heart so right
That 'tis all ease, all comfort and delight.
'To love our God with all our strength and will;
'To covet nothing; to devise no ill
'Against our neighbours; to procure or doe
'Nothing to others, which we would not to 50
'Our very selves; not to revenge our wrong;
'To be content with little; not to long
'For wealth and greatnesse; to despise or jeare
'No man, and if we be despised, to bear;
'To feede the hungry; to hold fast our Crown;
'To take from others naught; to give our owne;
These are his precepts: and (alas!) in these
What is so hard, but faith can doe with ease?
He that the holy Prophets doth beleeve,
And on Gods words relies, words that still live 60
And cannot dye; that in his heart hath writ
His Saviour's death and tryumph, and doth yet
With constant care, admitting no neglect,
His second, dreadfull comming still expect:
To such a liver earthly things are dead,
With Heav'n alone, and hopes of heav'n hee's fed;
He is no Vassall unto worldly trash,
Nor that black knowledge, which pretends to wash,
But doth defile: A knowledge, by which Men
With studied care loose Paradise agen. 70
Commands and titles, the vaine worlds device,
With gold, the forward seed of sin and vice,
He never minds: his Ayme is farre more high,
And stoopes to nothing lower than the skie;
Nor griefe, nor pleasures breede him any pain,
He nothing feares to loose, would nothing gaine;
What ever hath not God, he doth detest:
He lives to Christ, is dead to all the rest.
This Holy one sent hither from above
A Virgin brought forth, shadow'd by the Dove; 80
His skin with stripes, with wicked hands his face,
And with foule spittle soyl'd and beaten was;
A Crown of thornes his blessed head did wound,
Nayles pierc'd his hands and feet, and he fast bound

Stuck to the painefull Crosse, where hang'd till dead
With a cold speare his hearts dear blood was shed.
All this for man, for bad, ungratefull Man
The true God suffer'd! not that sufferings can
Adde to his glory ought, who can receive
Accesse from nothing, whom none can bereave 90
Of his all-fullnesse: but the blest designe
Of his sad death was to save me from mine;
He dying bore my sins, and the third day
His early rising rais'd me from the clay.
To such great mercies what shall I preferre,
Or who from loving God shall me deterre?
Burne me alive, with curious, skilfull paine
Cut up and search each warme and breathing vaine:
When all is done, death brings a quick release,
And the poore mangled body sleepes in peace. 100
Hale me to prisons, shut me up in brasse:
My still free Soule from thence to God shall passe;
Banish or bind me, I can be no where
A stranger, nor alone; My God is there.
I feare not famine; how can he be sed
To sterve, who feedes upon the living bread?
And yet this courage springs not from my store,
Christ gave it me, who can give much, much more;
I of my selfe can nothing dare or doe,
He bids me fight, and makes me conquer too: 110
If (like great Abr'ham,) *I should have command*
To leave my fathers house and native Land,
I would with joy to unknown regions run,
Bearing the Banner of his blessed Son.
On worldly goods I will have no designe,
But use my owne, as if mine were not mine;
Wealth I'le not wonder at, nor greatnesse seeke,
But chuse (though laugh'd at,) to be poore & meeke.
In woe and wealth I'le keepe the same stay'd mind,
Griefe shall not breake me, nor joyes make me blind: 120
My dearest Jesus I'le still praise, and he
Shall with Songs of Deliverance compasse me.
Then come my faithfull Consort! joyne with me
In this good fight, and my true helper be;

Cheare me when sad; advise me when I stray;
Let us be each the others guide and stay;
Be your Lords Guardian*: give joynt ayde and due;*
Helpe him when falne; rise, when he helpeth you;
That so we may not onely one flesh be,
But in one Spirit, and one Will agree. 130

FINIS

Authoris (de se) Emblema

Tentâsti, fateor, sine vulnere sœpius, & me
Consultum voluit Vox, *sine voce, frequens;*
Ambivit placido divinior aura meatu,
Et frustrà sancto murmure prœmonuit.
Surdus eram, mutusq; Silex*: Tu,* (*quanta tuorum*
Cura tibi est!) *aliâ das renovare viâ,*
Permutas Curam; Jamq; *irritatus* Amorem
Posse negas, & vim, Vi, *superare paras,*
Accedis propior, molemq, & Saxea *rumpis*
Pectora, fitq; Caro, *quod fuit ante* Lapis. 10
En lacerum! Cœlosq; *tuos ardentia tandem*
Fragmenta, *& liquidas ex* Adamante *genas.*
Sic olim undantes Petras, Scopulosq; *vomentes*
Curâsti, O populi providus usq; *tui!*
Quam miranda tibi manus est! Moriendo, *revixi;*
Et fractas *jam sum* ditior *inter* opes.

Engraved title-page of *Silex Scintillans* (1650)

Silex Scintillans:
SACRED
POEMS
And private
EJACULATIONS.

The ſecond Edition, In two Books;
By *Henry Vaughan*, Siluriſt.

Job chap. 35. ver. 10, 11.

Where is God my Maker, who giveth Songs in the night?
Who teacheth us more then the beaſts of the earth, and maketh us wiſer then the fowls of heaven?

London, Printed for *Henry Crips*, and *Lodowick Lloyd*, next to the Caſtle in *Cornhil*, and in *Popes-head Alley*. 1655.

The Authors PREFACE To the following HYMNS

That this Kingdom hath abounded with those ingenious persons, which in the late notion are termed *Wits*, is too well known. Many of them having cast away all their fair portion of time, in no better imployments, then a deliberate search, or excogitation of *idle words*, and a most vain, insatiable desire to be reputed *Poets*; leaving behinde them no other Monuments of those excellent abilities conferred upon them, but such as they may (with a *Predecessor* of theirs) term *Parricides*, and a soul-killing Issue; for that is the Βραβεῖον, and Laureate *Crown*, which idle *Poems* will certainly bring to their unrelenting Authors. 10

And well it were for them, if those willingly-studied and wilfully-published vanities could defile no *spirits*, but their own; but the *case* is far worse. These *Vipers* survive their *Parents*, and for many ages after (like *Epidemic* diseases) infect whole Generations, corrupting always and unhallowing the best-gifted *Souls*, and the most capable *Vessels*: for whose sanctification and wellfare, the glorious *Son* of God laid down his *life*, and suffered the pretious *blood* of his blessed and innocent *heart* to be poured out. In the mean time it cannot be denyed, but these men are had in remembrance, though we cannot say with any comfort, *Their memorial* 20 *is blessed;* for, that I may speak no more then the truth (let their passionate *worshippers* say what they please) all the commendations that can be justly given them, will amount to no more, then what *Prudentius* the Christian-sacred *Poet* bestowed upon *Symmachus;*

Os dignum æterno tinctum quod fulgeat auro
Si mallet laudare deum: cui sordida monstra
Prætulit, & liquidam temeravit crimine vocem;
Haud aliter, quàm cum rastris qui tentat eburnis
Cænosum versare solum, &c.——

In English thus, 30

A wit most worthy in tryed Gold to shine,
Immortal Gold! had he sung the divine

Praise of his Maker: to whom he preferr'd
Obscene, vile fancies, and prophanely marr'd
A rich, rare stile with sinful, lewd contents;
No otherwise, then if with Instruments
Of polish'd Ivory, some drudge should stir
A dirty sink, *&c.*——

This *comparison* is nothing odious, and it is as *true*, as it is *apposite*; for a *good* wit in a *bad* subject, is (as *Solomon* said of the *fair* and *foolish woman*) *Like a jewel of gold in a swines snowt*,
10 Prov. 11. 22. Nay, the more acute the *Author is*, there is so much the more danger and death in the *work*. Where the *Sun* is busie upon a *dung-hill*, the *issue* is always some unclean *vermine*. Divers persons of eminent piety and learning (I meddle not with the seditious and *Schismatical*) have, long before my time, taken notice of this *malady*; for the complaint against *vitious verse*, even by peaceful and obedient *spirits*, is of some antiquity in this Kingdom. And yet, as if the evil consequence attending this inveterate *error*, were but a small thing, there is sprung very lately another prosperous *device* to assist it in the subversion of *souls*. Those that want
20 the *Genius* of *verse*, fall to *translating*; and the people are (every *term*) plentifully furnished with various *Foraign vanities*; so that the most lascivious compositions of *France* and *Italy* are here *naturalized* and made *English*: And this (as it is sadly observed) with so much favor and success, that nothing *takes* (as they rightly phrase it) like a *Romance*. And very frequently (if that *Character* be not an *Ivy-bush*) the *buyer* receives this lewd ware from *persons of honor*: who want not reason to forbear, much private misfortune having sprung from no other *seed* at first, then some infectious and dissolving *Legend*.

30 To continue (after years of discretion) in this *vanity*, is an inexcusable desertion of *pious sobriety*: and to persist so to the end, is a wilful despising of Gods *sacred exhortations*, by a constant, sensual volutation or wallowing in *impure thoughts* and *scurrilous conceits*, which both defile their Authors, and as many more, as they are communicated to. If *every idle word shall be accounted for*, and if *no corrupt communication should proceed out of our mouths*, how desperate (I beseech you) is their condition, who all their life time, and out of meer design, study *lascivious fictions*: then carefully record and publish them, that instead of
40 *grace* and *life*, they *may minister sin and death* unto their readers?

It was wisely considered, and piously said by one, *That he would read no idle books; both in regard of love to his own soul, and pity unto his that made them, for* (said he) *if I be corrupted by them, their Composer is immediatly a cause of my ill: and at the day of reckoning* (*though now dead*) *must give an account for it, because I am corrupted by his bad example, which he left behinde him: I will write none, lest I hurt them that come after me; I will read none, lest I augment his punishment that is gone before me. I will neither write, nor read, lest I prove a foe to my own soul: while I live, I sin too much; let me not continue longer in wickedness, then I do in life.* It is a sentence of sacred authority, that *he that is dead, is freed from sin*; because he cannot in that *state*, which is without the *body*, sin any more; but he that writes *idle books*, makes for himself another *body*, in which he always *lives*, and *sins* (after *death*) as *fast* and as *foul*, as ever he did in his *life*; which very consideration, deserves to be a sufficient *Antidote* against this evil disease.

And here, because I would prevent a just *censure* by my free *confession*, I must remember, that I my self have for many years together, languished of this very *sickness*; and it is no long time since I have recovered. But (blessed be God for it!) I have by his saving assistance supprest my *greatest follies*, and those which escaped from me, are (I think) as innoxious, as most of that *vein* use to be; besides, they are interlined with many virtuous, and some pious mixtures. What I speak of them, is truth; but let no man mistake it for an *extenuation* of faults, as if I intended an *Apology* for *them*, or my *self*, who am conscious of so much *guilt* in *both*, as can never be expiated without *special sorrows*, and that cleansing and pretious *effusion* of my Almighty Redeemer: and if the world will be so charitable, as to grant my request, I do here most humbly and earnestly beg that none would read them.

But an idle or sensual *subject* is not all the *poyson* in these Pamphlets. Certain Authors have been so irreverendly bold, as to dash *Scriptures*, and the *sacred Relatives* of *God* with their impious conceits; And (which I cannot speak without grief of heart) some of those desperate *adventurers* may (I think) be reckoned amongst the principal or most learned Writers of *English verse*.

Others of a later *date*, being corrupted (it may be) by that evil *Genius*, which came in with the publique distractions, have stuffed their books with *Oathes*, *horrid Execrations*, and a most gross and studied *filthiness*. But the *hurt* that ensues by the publication of *pieces* so notoriously ill, lies heavily upon the *Stationers* account, who ought in conscience to refuse them, when they are put into his hands. No *loss* is so doleful as that *gain*, that will endamage the soul; he that *prints* lewdness and impieties, is that mad man in the *Proverbs*, who *casteth firebrands*, *arrows and death*.

The suppression of this pleasing and prevailing *evil*, lies not altogether in the power of the *Magistrate*; for it will flie abroad in *Manuscripts*, when it fails of entertainment at the *press*. The true remedy lies wholly in their bosoms, who are the gifted persons, by a wise exchange of *vain* and *vitious subjects*, for *divine Themes* and *Celestial praise*. The *performance* is easie, and were it the most difficult in the world, the *reward* is so glorious, that it infinitely transcends it: for *they that turn many to righteousness*, *shall shine like the stars for ever and ever*: whence follows this undenyable *inference*, That the *corrupting of many*, being a contrary *work*, the *recompense* must be so too; and then I know nothing reserved for them, but *the blackness of darkness for ever*; from which (O God!) deliver all penitent and reformed *Spirits*!

The first, that with any effectual success attempted a *diversion* of this foul and overflowing *stream*, was the blessed man, Mr. *George Herbert*, whose holy *life* and *verse* gained many pious *Converts*, (of whom I am the least) and gave the first check to a most flourishing and admired *wit* of his time. After him followed diverse,—*Sed non passibus æquis;* they had more of *fashion*, then *force*: And the *reason* of their so vast *distance* from him, besides differing *spirits* and *qualifications* (for his *measure* was eminent) I suspect to be, because they aimed more at *verse*, then *perfection*; as may be easily gathered by their frequent *impressions*, and numerous *pages*: Hence sprang those wide, those weak, and lean *conceptions*, which in the most inclinable *Reader* will scarce give any nourishment or help to *devotion*; for not flowing from a true, practick piety, it was impossible they should effect those things abroad, which they never had acquaintance with at home; being onely the productions of a common spirit, and the obvious ebullitions of that light humor, which takes the pen in hand, out of no other consideration, then to be seen in print. It is true indeed, that to give up our thoughts to pious *Themes* and *Contemplations* (if it be done for pieties sake) is a great *step* towards *perfection*; because it will *refine*, and *dispose* to devotion and sanctity. And further, it will *procure* for us (so easily communicable is that *loving spirit*) some small *prelibation* of those heavenly *refreshments*, which descend but seldom, and then very sparingly, upon *men* of an ordinary or indifferent *holyness*; but he that desires to excel in this kinde of *Hagiography*, or holy writing, must strive (by all means) for *perfection* and true *holyness*, that a *door may be opened to him in heaven*, Rev. 4. 1. and then he will be able to write (with *Hierotheus* and holy *Herbert*) A *true Hymn*.

To effect this in some measure, I have begged leave to communicate this my poor *Talent* to the *Church*, under the *protection* and *conduct* of her *glorious Head*: who (if he will vouchsafe to own it, and *go along* with it) can make it as useful now in the *publick*, as it hath been to me in *private*. In the *perusal* of it, you will (peradventure) observe some *passages*, whose *history* or *reason* may seem something *remote*; but were they brought *nearer*, and plainly exposed to your view, (though that (perhaps) might quiet your *curiosity*) yet would it not conduce much to your greater *advantage*. And therefore I must desire you to accept of them in that *latitude*, which is already alowed them. By the last *Poems* in the book (were not that *mistake* here prevented) you would judge all to be *fatherless*, and the *Edition* posthume; for (indeed) *I was nigh unto death*, and am still at no great distance from it; which was the necessary reason for that solemn and accomplished *dress*, you will now finde this *impression* in.

But *the God of the spirits of all flesh*, hath granted me a further use of *mine*, then I did look for in the *body*; and when I expected, and had (by his assistance) prepared for a *message* of *death*, then did he *answer* me with *life*; I hope to his *glory*, and my great *advantage*: that I may flourish not with *leafe* onely, but with some *fruit* also; which *hope* and earnest *desire* of his poor *Creature*, I humbly beseech him to perfect and fulfil for his dear *Sons* sake, unto *whom*, with *him* and the most holy and loving *Spirit*, be ascribed by *Angels*, by *Men*, and by all his *Works*, All Glory, and Wisdom, and Dominion, in this the *temporal* and in the *Eternal* Being. *Amen*.

Newton by *Usk*, near
Sketh-rock, Septem. 30.
1654.

O Lord, the hope of Israel, all they that forsake thee shall be ashamed; and they that depart from thee, shall be written in the earth, because they have forsaken the Lord, the fountain of living waters.

Heal me, O Lord, and I shall be healed; save me, and I shall be saved, for thou art my health, and my great deliverer.

I said in the cutting off of my days, I shall go to the gates of the grave; I have deprived my self of the residue of my years.

I said, I shall not see the Lord, even the Lord in the Land of the
10 *living: I shall behold man no more with the Inhabitants of the world.*

O Lord! by thee doth man live, and from thee is the life of my spirit: therefore wilt thou recover me, and make me to live.

Thou hast in love to my soul delivered it from the pit of corruption; for thou hast cast all my sins behinde thy back.

For thy names sake hast thou put off thine anger; for thy praise hast thou refrained from me, that I should not be cut off.

For the grave cannot praise thee, death cannot celebrate thee: they that go down into the pit, cannot hope for thy truth.

The living, the living, he shall praise thee, as I do this day: the
20 *Father to the children shall make known thy truth.*

O Lord! thou hast been merciful, thou hast brought back my life from corruption: thou hast redeemed me from my sin.

They that follow after lying vanities, forsake their own mercy.

Therefore shall thy songs be with me, and my prayer unto the God of my life.

I will go unto the altar of my God, unto God, the joy of my youth; and in thy fear will I worship towards thy holy temple.

I will sacrifice unto thee with the voice of thanksgiving; I will pay that which I have vowed: salvation is of the Lord.

To my most merciful, my most loving, and dearly loved Redeemer, the ever blessed, the onely Holy and JUST ONE

JESVS CHRIST

The Son of the living GOD

And the sacred Virgin Mary

I

My God! thou that didst dye for me,
These thy deaths fruits I offer thee;
Death that to me was life and light,
But dark and deep pangs to thy sight.
Some drops of thy all-quickning blood
Fell on my heart; those made it bud
And put forth thus, though Lord, before
The ground was curst, and void of store.
Indeed I had some here to hire
Which long resisted thy desire, 10
That ston'd thy servants, and did move
To have the murthred for thy love;
But Lord, I have expell'd them, and so bent,
Beg, thou wouldst take thy Tenants Rent.

II

Dear Lord, 'tis finished! and now he
That copyed it, presents it thee.
'Twas thine first, and to thee returns,
From thee it shin'd, though here it burns;
If the Sun rise on rocks, is't right,
To call it their inherent light? 20
No, nor can I say, this is mine,
For, dearest Jesus, 'tis all thine.
As thy cloaths, (when thou with cloaths wert clad)
Both light from thee, and virtue had,
And now (as then within this place)
Thou to poor rags dost still give grace.

This is the earnest thy love sheds,
The *Candle* shining on some heads,
Till at thy charges they shall be,
Cloath'd all with immortality. 30

My dear Redeemer, the worlds light,
And life too, and my hearts delight!
For all thy mercies and thy truth
Shew'd to me in my sinful youth,
For my sad failings and my wilde
Murmurings at thee, when most milde:
For all my secret faults, and each
Frequent relapse and wilful breach,
For all designs meant against thee,
And ev'ry publish'd vanity 40
Which thou divinely hast forgiven,
While thy blood wash'd me white as heaven:
I nothing have to give to thee,
But this thy own gift, given to me;
Refuse it not! for now thy *Token*
Can tell thee where a heart is broken.

Revel. cap. 1. *ver.* 5, 6, 7

Unto him that loved us, and washed us from our sins in his own blood.

And hath made us Kings and Priests unto God and his Father; to him be glory and dominion, for ever and ever. Amen.

Behold, he cometh with clouds, and every eye shall see him, and they also which pierced him; and all kinreds of the earth shall wail because of him: even so. Amen.

¶

Vain Wits and eyes
Leave, and be wise:
Abuse not, shun not holy fire,
But with true tears wash off your mire.
Tears and these flames will soon grow kinde,
And mix an eye-salve for the blinde.
Tears cleanse and supple without fail,
And fire will purge your callous veyl.
Then comes the light! which when you spy,
And see your nakedness thereby, 10
Praise him, who dealt his gifts so free
In tears to you, in fire to me.

Silex Scintillans, &c.

Regeneration

A Ward, and still in bonds, one day
I stole abroad,
It was high-spring, and all the way
Primros'd, and hung with shade;
Yet, was it frost within,
And surly winds
Blasted my infant buds, and sinne
Like Clouds ecclips'd my mind.

2

Storm'd thus; I straight perceiv'd my spring
Meere stage, and show, 10
My walke a monstrous, mountain'd thing
Rough-cast with Rocks, and snow;
And as a Pilgrims Eye
Far from reliefe,
Measures the melancholy skye
Then drops, and rains for griefe,

3

So sigh'd I upwards still, at last
'Twixt steps, and falls
I reach'd the pinacle, where plac'd
I found a paire of scales, 20
I tooke them up and layd
In th'one late paines,
The other smoake, and pleasures weigh'd
But prov'd the heavier graines;

4

With that, some cryed, *Away*; straight I
Obey'd, and led
Full East, a faire, fresh field could spy
Some call'd it, *Jacobs Bed*;

A Virgin-soile, which no
Rude feet ere trod, 30
Where (since he stept there,) only go
Prophets, and friends of God.

5

Here, I repos'd; but scarse well set,
A grove descryed
Of stately height, whose branches met
And mixt on every side;
I entred, and once in
(Amaz'd to see't,)
Found all was chang'd, and a new spring
Did all my senses greet; 40

6

The unthrift Sunne shot vitall gold
A thousand peeces,
And heaven its azure did unfold
Checqur'd with snowie fleeces,
The aire was all in spice
And every bush
A garland wore; Thus fed my Eyes
But all the Eare lay hush.

7

Only a little Fountain lent
Some use for Eares, 50
And on the dumbe shades language spent
The Musick of her teares;
I drew her neere, and found
The Cisterne full
Of divers stones, some bright, and round
Others ill-shap'd, and dull.

8

The first (pray marke,) as quick as light
Danc'd through the floud,
But, th'last more heavy then the night
Nail'd to the Center stood; 60

I wonder'd much, but tyr'd
At last with thought,
My restless Eye that still desir'd
As strange an object brought;

9

It was a banke of flowers, where I descried
(Though 'twas mid-day,)
Some fast asleepe, others broad-eyed
And taking in the Ray,
Here musing long, I heard
A rushing wind 70
Which still increas'd, but whence it stirr'd
No where I could not find;

10

I turn'd me round, and to each shade
Dispatch'd an Eye,
To see, if any leafe had made
Least motion, or Reply,
But while I listning sought
My mind to ease
By knowing, where 'twas, or where not,
It whisper'd; *Where I please.* 80

Lord, then said I, *On me one breath,*
And let me dye before my death!

Cant. Cap. 5. ver. 17

Arise O North, and come thou South-wind, and blow upon my garden, that the spices thereof may flow out.

Death

A Dialogue

Soule. 'Tis a sad Land, that in one day
Hath dull'd thee thus, when death shall freeze
Thy bloud to Ice, and thou must stay
Tenant for Yeares, and Centuries,
How wilt thou brook't? ——

Body. I cannot tell,——
But if all sence wings not with thee,
And something still be left the dead,
I'le wish my Curtaines off to free
Me from so darke, and sad a bed; 10

A neast of nights, a gloomie sphere,
Where shadowes thicken, and the Cloud
Sits on the Suns brow all the yeare,
And nothing moves without a shrowd;

Soule. 'Tis so: But as thou sawest that night
Wee travell'd in, our first attempts
Were dull, and blind, but Custome straight
Our feares, and falls brought to contempt,

Then, when the gastly *twelve* was past
We breath'd still for a blushing *East*, 20
And bad the lazie Sunne make hast,
And on sure hopes, though long, did feast;

But when we saw the Clouds to crack
And in those Cranies light appear'd,
We thought the day then was not slack,
And pleas'd our selves with what wee feard;

Just so it is in death. But thou
Shalt in thy mothers bosome sleepe
Whilst I each minute grone to know
How neere Redemption creepes. 30

Then shall wee meet to mixe again, and met,
'Tis last good-night, our Sunne shall never set.

Job. Cap: 10. *ver.* 21. 22

Before I goe whence I shall not returne, even to the land of darknesse, and the shadow of death;

A Land of darknesse, as darkenesse it selfe, and of the shadow of death, without any order, and where the light is as darknesse.

Resurrection and Immortality:

Heb. cap. 10. *ve:* 20

By that new, and living way, which he hath prepared for us, through the veile, which is his flesh.

Body

1

Oft have I seen, when that renewing breath
That binds, and loosens death
Inspir'd a quickning power through the dead
Creatures a bed,
Some drowsie silk-worme creepe
From that long sleepe
And in weake, infant hummings chime, and knell
About her silent Cell
Untill at last full with the vitall Ray
She wing'd away, 10
And proud with life, and sence,
Heav'ns rich Expence,
Esteem'd (vaine things!) of two whole Elements
As meane, and span-extents.
Shall I then thinke such providence will be
Lesse friend to me?
Or that he can endure to be unjust
Who keeps his Covenant even with our dust.

Soule

2

Poore, querulous handfull! was't for this
I taught thee all that is? 20
Unbowel'd nature, shew'd thee her recruits,
And Change of suits
And how of death we make
A meere mistake,
For no thing can to *Nothing* fall, but still
Incorporates by skill,

And then returns, and from the wombe of things
Such treasure brings
As *Phenix*-like renew'th
Both life, and youth; 30
For a preserving spirit doth still passe
Untainted through this Masse,
Which doth resolve, produce, and ripen all
That to it fall;
Nor are those births which we
Thus suffering see
Destroy'd at all; But when times restles wave
Their substance doth deprave
And the more noble *Essence* finds his house
Sickly, and loose, 40
He, ever young, doth wing
Unto that spring,
And *source* of spirits, where he takes his lot
Till time no more shall rot
His passive Cottage; which (though laid aside,)
Like some spruce Bride,
Shall one day rise, and cloath'd with shining light
All pure, and bright
Re-marry to the soule, for 'tis most plaine
Thou only fal'st to be refin'd againe. 50

3

Then I that here saw darkly in a glasse
But mists, and shadows passe,
And, by their owne weake *Shine*, did search the springs
And Course of things
Shall with Inlightned Rayes
Peirce all their wayes;
And as thou saw'st, I in a thought could goe
To heav'n, or Earth below
To reade some *Starre*, or *Min'rall*, and in State
There often sate, 60
So shalt thou then with me
(Both wing'd, and free,)
Rove in that mighty, and eternall light
Where no rude shade, or night

Shall dare approach us; we shall there no more
Watch stars, or pore
Through melancholly clouds, and say
Would it were Day!
One everlasting *Saboth* there shall runne
Without *Succession*, and without a *Sunne*. 70

Dan: Cap: 12. ver: 13

But goe thou thy way untill the end be, for thou shalt rest, and stand up in thy lot, at the end of the dayes.

Day of Judgement

When through the North a fire shall rush
And rowle into the East,
And like a firie torrent brush
And sweepe up *South*, and *West*,

When all shall streame, and lighten round
And with surprizing flames
Both stars, and Elements confound
And quite blot out their names,

When thou shalt spend thy sacred store
Of thunders in that heate 10
And low as ere they lay before
Thy six-dayes-buildings beate,

When like a scrowle the heavens shal passe
And vanish cleane away,
And nought must stand of that vast space
Which held up night, and day,

When one lowd blast shall rend the deepe,
And from the wombe of earth
Summon up all that are asleepe
Unto a second birth, 20

When thou shalt make the Clouds thy seate,
And in the open aire
The Quick, and dead, both small and great
Must to thy barre repaire;

O then it wilbe all too late
To say, *What shall I doe?*
Repentance there is out of date
And so is *mercy* too;

Prepare, prepare me then, O God!
And let me now begin 30
To feele my loving fathers *Rod*
Killing the man of sinne!

Give me, O give me Crosses here,
Still more afflictions lend,
That pill, though bitter, is most deare
That brings health in the end;

Lord, God! I beg nor friends, nor wealth
But pray against them both;
Three things I'de have, my soules chief health!
And one of these seme loath, 40

A living *FAITH*, a *HEART* of flesh,
The *WORLD* an Enemie,
This last will keepe the first two fresh,
And bring me, where I'de be.

1 Pet. 4. 7

Now the end of all things is at hand, be you therefore sober, and watching in prayer.

Religion

My God, when I walke in those groves,
And leaves thy spirit doth still fan,
I see in each shade that there growes
An Angell talking with a man.

Under a *Juniper*, some house,
Or the coole *Mirtles* canopie,
Others beneath an *Oakes* greene boughs,
Or at some *fountaines* bubling Eye;

Here *Jacob* dreames, and wrestles; there
Elias by a Raven is fed, 10
Another time by th' Angell, where
He brings him water with his bread;

In *Abr'hams* Tent the winged guests
(O how familiar then was heaven!)
Eate, drinke, discourse, sit downe, and rest
Untill the Coole, and shady *Even*;

Nay thou thy selfe, my God, in *fire*,
Whirle-winds, and *Clouds*, and the *soft voice*
Speak'st there so much, that I admire
We have no Conf'rence in these daies; 20

Is the truce broke? or 'cause we have
A mediatour now with thee,
Doest thou therefore old Treaties wave
And by appeales from him decree?

Or is't so, as some green heads say
That now all miracles must cease?
Though thou hast promis'd they should stay
The tokens of the Church, and peace;

No, no; Religion is a Spring
That from some secret, golden Mine 30
Derives her birth, and thence doth bring
Cordials in every drop, and Wine;

But in her long, and hidden Course
Passing through the Earths darke veines,
Growes still from better unto worse,
And both her taste, and colour staines,

Then drilling on, learnes to encrease
False *Ecchoes*, and Confused sounds,
And unawares doth often seize
On veines of *Sulphur* under ground; 40

So poison'd, breaks forth in some Clime,
And at first sight doth many please,
But drunk, is puddle, or meere slime
And 'stead of Phisick, a disease;

Just such a tainted sink we have
Like that *Samaritans* dead *Well*,
Nor must we for the Kernell crave
Because most voices like the *shell*.

Heale then these waters, Lord; or bring thy flock,
Since these are troubled, to the springing rock, 50
Looke downe great Master of the feast; O shine,
And turn once more our *Water* into *Wine*!

Cant. cap. 4. ver. 12

My sister, my spouse is as a garden Inclosed, as a Spring shut up, and a fountain sealed up.

The Search

'Tis now cleare day: I see a Rose
Bud in the bright East, and disclose
The Pilgrim-Sunne; all night have I
Spent in a roving Extasie
To find my Saviour; I have been
As far as *Bethlem*, and have seen
His Inne, and Cradle; Being there
I met the *Wise-men*, askt them where
He might be found, or what starre can
Now point him out, grown up a Man? 10
To *Egypt* hence I fled, ran o're
All her parcht bosome to *Nile's* shore
Her yearly nurse; came back, enquir'd
Amongst the *Doctors*, and desir'd
To see the *Temple*, but was shown
A little dust, and for the Town
A heap of ashes, where some sed
A small bright sparkle was a bed,
Which would one day (beneath the pole,)
Awake, and then refine the whole. 20
Tyr'd here, I come to *Sychar*; thence
To *Jacobs wel*, bequeathed since
Unto his sonnes, (where often they
In those calme, golden Evenings lay
Watring their flocks, and having spent
Those white dayes, drove home to the Tent

Their *well-fleec'd* traine;) And here (O fate!)
I sit, where once my Saviour sate;
The angry Spring in bubbles swell'd
Which broke in sighes still, as they fill'd, 30
And whisper'd, *Jesus had been there*
But *Jacobs children would not heare.*
Loath hence to part, at last I rise
But with the fountain in my Eyes,
And here a fresh search is decreed
He must be found, where he did bleed;
I walke the garden, and there see
Idæa's of his Agonie,
And moving anguishments that set
His blest face in a bloudy sweat; 40
I climb'd the Hill, perus'd the Crosse
Hung with my gaine, and his great losse,
Never did tree beare fruit like this,
Balsam of Soules, the bodyes blisse;
But, O his grave! where I saw lent
(For he had none,) a Monument,
An undefil'd, and new-heaw'd one,
But there was not the *Corner-stone*;
Sure (then said I,) my Quest is vaine,
Hee'le not be found, where he was slaine, 50
So mild a Lamb can never be
'Midst so much bloud, and Crueltie;
I'le to the Wilderness, and can
Find beasts more mercifull then man,
He liv'd there safe, 'twas his retreat
From the fierce *Jew*, and *Herods* heat,
And forty dayes withstood the fell,
And high temptations of hell;
With Seraphins there talked he
His fathers flaming ministrie, 60
He heav'nd their *walks*, and with his eyes
Made those wild shades a Paradise,
Thus was the desert sanctified
To be the refuge of his bride;
I'le thither then; see, It is day,
The Sun's broke through to guide my way.

But as I urg'd thus, and writ down
What pleasures should my Journey crown,
What silent paths, what shades, and Cells,
Faire, virgin-flowers, and hallow'd *Wells* 70
I should rove in, and rest my head
Where my deare Lord did often tread,
Sugring all dangers with successe,
Me thought I heard one singing thus;

1

Leave, leave, thy gadding thoughts;
Who Pores
and spies
Still out of Doores
descries
Within them nought. 80

2

The skinne, and shell of things
Though faire,
are not
Thy wish, nor pray'r
but got
By meer Despair
of wings.

3

To rack old Elements,
or Dust
and say 90
Sure here he must
needs stay
Is not the way,
nor just.
Search well another world; who studies this,
Travels in Clouds, seeks *Manna*, where none is.

Acts Cap. 17. ver. 27, 28

That they should seek the Lord, if happily they might feel after him, and finde him, though he be not far off from every one of us, for in him we live, and move, and have our being.

Isaacs Marriage

Gen. cap. 24. ver. 63

And Isaac *went out to pray in the field at the Even-tide, and he lift up his eyes, and saw, and behold, the Camels were coming.*

Praying! and to be married? It was rare,
But now 'tis monstrous; and that pious care
Though of our selves, is so much out of date,
That to renew't were to degenerate.
But thou a Chosen sacrifice wert given,
And offer'd up so early unto heaven
Thy flames could not be out; Religion was
Ray'd into thee, like beams into a glasse,
Where, as thou grewst, it multipli'd and shin'd
The sacred Constellation of thy mind. 10
But being for a bride, prayer was such
A decryed course, sure it prevail'd not much.
Had'st ne'r an oath, nor Complement? thou wert
An odde dull sutor; Hadst thou but the art
Of these our dayes, thou couldst have coyn'd thee twenty
New sev'ral oathes, and Complements (too) plenty;
O sad, and wilde excesse! and happy those
White dayes, that durst no impious mirth expose!
When Conscience by lew'd use had not lost sense,
Nor bold-fac'd custome banish'd Innocence; 20
Thou hadst no pompous train, nor *Antick* crowd
Of young, gay swearers, with their needlesse, lowd
Retinue; All was here smooth as thy bride
And calm like her, or that mild Evening-tide;
Yet, hadst thou nobler guests: Angels did wind
And rove about thee, guardians of thy minde,
These fetch'd thee home thy bride, and all the way
Advis'd thy servant what to do, and say;
These taught him at the *well*, and thither brought
The Chast, and lovely object of thy thought; 30
But here was ne'r a Complement, not one
Spruce, supple cringe, or study'd look put on,
All was plain, modest truth: Nor did she come
In *rowles* and *Curles*, mincing and stately dumb,

But in a Virgins native blush and fears
Fresh as those roses, which the day-spring wears.
O sweet, divine simplicity! O grace
Beyond a Curled lock, or painted face!
A *Pitcher* too she had, nor thought it much
To carry that, which some would scorn to touch; 40
With which in mild, chast language she did wooe
To draw him drink, and for his Camels too.
  And now thou knewest her coming, It was time
To get thee wings on, and devoutly climbe
Unto thy God, for Marriage of all states
Makes most unhappy, or most fortunates;
This brought thee forth, where now thou didst undress
Thy soul, and with new pinions refresh
Her wearied wings, which so restor'd did flye
Above the stars, a track unknown, and high, 50
And in her piercing flight perfum'd the ayer
Scatt'ring the *Myrrhe*, and incense of thy pray'r.
So from **Lahai-roi's* Well some spicie cloud
Woo'd by the Sun swels up to be his shrowd,
And from his moist wombe weeps a fragrant showre,
Which, scatter'd in a thousand pearls, each flowre
And herb partakes, where having stood awhile
And something coold the parch'd, and thirstie Isle,
The thankful Earth unlocks her self, and blends,
A thousand odours, which (all mixt,) she sends
Up in one cloud, and so returns the skies
That dew they lent, a breathing sacrifice. 62
  Thus soar'd thy soul, who (though young,) didst inherit
Together with his bloud, thy fathers spirit,
Whose active zeal, and tried faith were to thee
Familiar ever since thy Infancie.
Others were tym'd, and train'd up to't but thou
Diddst thy swift yeers in piety out-grow,
Age made them rev'rend, and a snowie head,
But thou wert so, e're time his snow could shed; 70
Then, who would truly limne thee out, must paint
First, a *young Patriarch*, then a *marri'd Saint*.

* *A wel in the South Country where* Jacob *dwelt, between* Cadesh, & Bered; Heb. *the well of him that liveth, and seeth me.*

The Brittish Church

Ah! he is fled!
And while these here their *mists*, and *shadows* hatch,
My glorious head
Doth on those hills of Mirrhe, and Incense watch.
Haste, hast my dear,
The Souldiers here
Cast in their lots again,
That seamlesse coat
The Jews touch'd not,
These dare divide, and stain. 10

2

O get thee wings!
Or if as yet (until these clouds depart,
And the day springs,)
Thou think'st it good to tarry where thou art,
Write in thy bookes
My ravish'd looks
Slain flock, and pillag'd fleeces,
And hast thee so
As a young Roe
Upon the mounts of spices. 20

O Rosa Campi! O lilium Convallium! quomodò nunc facta es pabulum Aprorum!

The Lampe

'Tis dead night round about: Horrour doth creepe
And move on with the shades; stars nod, and sleepe,
And through the dark aire spin a firie thread
Such as doth gild the lazie glow-worms bed.
Yet, burn'st thou here, a full day; while I spend
My rest in Cares, and to the dark world lend
These flames, as thou dost thine to me; I watch
That houre, which must thy life, and mine dispatch;
But still thou doest out-goe me, I can see
Met in thy flames, all acts of piety; 10
Thy light, is *Charity*; Thy heat, is *Zeale*;
And thy aspiring, active fires reveale

Devotion still on wing; Then, thou dost weepe
Still as thou burn'st, and the warme droppings creepe
To measure out thy length, as if thou'dst know
What stock, and how much time were left thee now;
Nor dost thou spend one teare in vain, for still
As thou dissolv'st to them, and they distill,
They're stor'd up in the socket, where they lye,
When all is spent, thy last, and sure supply, 20
And such is true repentance, ev'ry breath
Wee spend in sighes, is treasure after death;
Only, one point escapes thee; That thy Oile
Is still out with thy flame, and so both faile;
But whensoe're I'm out, both shalbe in,
And where thou mad'st an end, there I'le begin.

Mark Cap. 13. ver. 35

Watch you therefore, for you know not when the master of the house commeth, at Even, or at mid-night, or at the Cock-crowing, or in the morning.

Mans fall, and Recovery

Farewell you Everlasting hills! I'm Cast
Here under Clouds, where stormes, and tempests blast
This sully'd flowre
Rob'd of your Calme, nor can I ever make
Transplanted thus, one leafe of his t'awake,
But ev'ry houre
He sleepes, and droops, and in this drowsie state
Leaves me a slave to passions, and my fate;
Besides I've lost
A traine of lights, which in those Sun-shine dayes 10
Were my sure guides, and only with me stayes
(Unto my cost,)
One sullen beame, whose charge is to dispense
More punishment, than knowledge to my sense;
Two thousand yeares
I sojourn'd thus; at last *Jeshuruns* king
Those famous tables did from *Sinai* bring;
These swell'd my feares,
Guilts, trespasses, and all this Inward Awe,
For sinne tooke strength, and vigour from the Law. 20

Yet have I found
A plenteous way, (thanks to that holy one!)
To cancell all that e're was writ in stone,
His saving wound
Wept bloud, that broke this Adamant, and gave
To sinners Confidence, life to the grave;
This makes me span
My fathers journeys, and in one faire step
O're all their pilgrimage, and labours leap,
For God (made man,) 30
Reduc'd th'Extent of works of faith; so made
Of their *Red Sea*, a *Spring*; I wash, they wade.

Rom. Cap. 18. ver. 19

As by the offence of one, the fault came on all men to condemnation; So by the Righteousness of one, the benefit abounded towards all men to the Justification of life.

The Showre

'Twas so, I saw thy birth: That drowsie Lake
From her faint bosome breath'd thee, the disease
Of her sick waters, and Infectious Ease.
But, now at Even
Too grosse for heaven,
Thou fall'st in teares, and weep'st for thy mistake.

2

Ah! it is so with me; oft have I prest
Heaven with a lazie breath, but fruitles this
Peirc'd not; Love only can with quick accesse
Unlock the way, 10
When all else stray
The smoke, and Exhalations of the brest.

3

Yet, if as thou doest melt, and with thy traine
Of drops make soft the Earth, my eyes could weep
O're my hard heart, that's bound up, and asleep,
Perhaps at last
(Some such showres past,)
My God would give a Sun-shine after raine.

Distraction

O knit me, that am crumbled dust! the heape
Is all dispers'd, and cheape;
Give for a handfull, but a thought
And it is bought;
Hadst thou
Made me a starre, a pearle, or a rain-bow,
The beames I then had shot
My light had lessend not,
But now
I find my selfe the lesse, the more I grow; 10
The world
Is full of voices; Man is call'd, and hurl'd
By each, he answers all,
Knows ev'ry note, and call,
Hence, still
Fresh dotage tempts, or old usurps his will.
Yet, hadst thou clipt my wings, when Coffin'd in
This quicken'd masse of sinne,
And saved that light, which freely thou
Didst then bestow, 20
I feare
I should have spurn'd, and said thou didst forbeare;
Or that thy store was lesse,
But now since thou didst blesse
So much,
I grieve, my God! that thou hast made me such.
I grieve?
O, yes! thou know'st I doe; Come, and releive
And tame, and keepe downe with thy light
Dust that would rise, and dimme my sight, 30
Lest left alone too long
Amidst the noise, and throng,
Oppressed I
Striving to save the whole, by parcells dye.

The Pursuite

Lord! what a busie, restles thing
        Hast thou made man?
Each day, and houre he is on wing,
        Rests not a span;
Then having lost the Sunne, and light
        By clouds surpriz'd
He keepes a Commerce in the night
        With aire disguis'd;
Hadst thou given to this active dust
        A state untir'd, 10
The lost Sonne had not left the huske
        Nor home desir'd;
That was thy secret, and it is
        Thy mercy too,
For when all failes to bring to blisse,
        Then, this must doe.
Ah! Lord! and what a Purchase will that be
To take us sick, that sound would not take thee?

Mount of Olives

Sweete, sacred hill! on whose fair brow
My Saviour sate, shall I allow
    Language to love
And Idolize some shade, or grove,
Neglecting thee? such ill-plac'd wit,
Conceit, or call it what you please
        Is the braines fit,
        And meere disease;

2

Cotswold, and *Coopers* both have met
With learned swaines, and Eccho yet 10
    Their pipes, and wit;
But thou sleep'st in a deepe neglect
Untouch'd by any; And what need
The sheep bleat thee a silly Lay
        That heard'st both reed
        And sheepward play?

3

Yet, if Poets mind thee well
They shall find thou art their hill,
        And fountaine too,
Their Lord with thee had most to doe; 20
He wept once, walkt whole nights on thee,
And from thence (his suff'rings ended,)
                Unto glorie
                Was attended;

4

Being there, this spacious ball
Is but his narrow footstoole all,
        And what we thinke
Unsearchable, now with one winke
He doth comprise; But in this aire
When he did stay to beare our Ill 30
                And sinne, this Hill
                Was then his Chaire.

The Incarnation, and Passion

Lord! when thou didst thy selfe undresse
Laying by thy robes of glory,
To make us more, thou wouldst be lesse,
And becam'st a wofull story.

To put on Clouds instead of light,
And cloath the morning-starre with dust,
Was a translation of such height
As, but in thee, was ne'r exprest;

Brave wormes, and Earth! that thus could have
A God Enclos'd within your Cell, 10
Your maker pent up in a grave,
Life lockt in death, heav'n in a shell;

Ah, my deare Lord! what couldst thou spye
In this impure, rebellious clay,
That made thee thus resolve to dye
For those that kill thee every day?

O what strange wonders could thee move
To slight thy precious bloud, and breath!
Sure it was *Love*, my Lord; for *Love*
Is only stronger far than death. 20

The Call

Come my heart! come my head
In sighes, and teares!
'Tis now, since you have laine thus dead
Some twenty years;
Awake, awake,
Some pitty take
Upon your selves——
Who never wake to grone, nor weepe,
Shall be sentenc'd for their sleepe.

2

Doe but see your sad estate, 10
How many sands
Have left us, while we careles sate
With folded hands;
What stock of nights,
Of dayes, and yeares
In silent flights
Stole by our eares,
How ill have we our selves bestow'd
Whose suns are all set in a Cloud?

3

Yet, come, and let's peruse them all; 20
And as we passe,
What sins on every minute fall
Score on the glasse;
Then weigh, and rate
Their heavy State
Untill
The glasse with teares you fill;
That done, we shalbe safe, and good,
Those beasts were cleane, that chew'd the Cud.

¶

Thou that know'st for whom I mourne,
    And why these teares appeare,
That keep'st account, till he returne
    Of all his dust left here;
As easily thou mightst prevent
    As now produce these teares,
And adde unto that day he went
    A faire supply of yeares.
But 'twas my sinne that forc'd thy hand
    To cull this *Prim-rose* out, 10
That by thy early choice forewarn'd
    My soule might looke about.
O what a vanity is man!
    How like the Eyes quick winke
His Cottage failes; whose narrow span
    Begins even at the brink!
Nine months thy hands are fashioning us,
    And many yeares (alas!)
E're we can lisp, or ought discusse
    Concerning thee, must passe; 20
Yet have I knowne thy slightest things
    A *feather*, or a *shell*,
A *stick*, or *Rod* which some Chance brings
    The best of us excell,
Yea, I have knowne these shreds out last
    A faire-compacted frame
And for one *Twenty* we have past
    Almost outlive our name.
Thus hast thou plac'd in mans outside
    Death to the Common Eye, 30
That heaven within him might abide,
    And close eternitie;
Hence, youth, and folly (mans first shame,)
    Are put unto the slaughter,
And serious thoughts begin to tame
    The wise-mans-madnes *Laughter*;
Dull, wretched wormes! that would not keepe
    Within our first faire bed,

But out of *Paradise* must creepe
For ev'ry foote to tread; 40
Yet, had our Pilgrimage bin free,
And smooth without a thorne,
Pleasures had foil'd Eternitie,
And *tares* had choakt the *Corne*.
Thus by the Crosse Salvation runnes,
Affliction is a mother,
Whose painfull throws yield many sons,
Each fairer than the other;
A silent teare can peirce thy throne,
When lowd Joyes want a wing, 50
And sweeter aires streame from a grone,
Than any arted string;
Thus, Lord, I see my gaine is great,
My losse but little to it,
Yet something more I must intreate
And only thou canst doe it.
O let me (like him,) know my End!
And be as glad to find it,
And whatsoe'r thou shalt Commend,
Still let thy Servant mind it! 60
Then make my soule white as his owne,
My faith as pure, and steddy,
And deck me, Lord, with the same Crowne
Thou hast crownd him already!

Vanity of Spirit

Quite spent with thoughts I left my Cell, and lay
Where a shrill spring tun'd to the early day.
I beg'd here long, and gron'd to know
Who gave the Clouds so brave a bow,
Who bent the spheres, and circled in
Corruption with this glorious Ring,
What is his name, and how I might
Descry some part of his great light.
I summon'd nature: peirc'd through all her store,
Broke up some seales, which none had touch'd before, 10

Her wombe, her bosome, and her head
Where all her secrets lay a bed
I rifled quite, and having past
Through all the Creatures, came at last
To search my selfe, where I did find
Traces, and sounds of a strange kind.
Here of this mighty spring, I found some drills,
With Ecchoes beaten from th' eternall hills;
Weake beames, and fires flash'd to my sight,
Like a young East, or Moone-shine night, 20
Which shew'd me in a nook cast by
A peece of much antiquity,
With Hyerogliphicks quite dismembred,
And broken letters scarce remembred.
I tooke them up, and (much Joy'd,) went about
T' unite those peeces, hoping to find out
The mystery; but this neer done,
That little light I had was gone:
It griev'd me much. At last, said I,
Since in these veyls my Ecclips'd Eye 30
May not approach thee, (*for at night*
Who can have commerce with the light?)
I'le disapparell, *and to buy*
But one half glaunce, *most gladly dye*.

The Retreate

Happy those early dayes! when I
Shin'd in my Angell-infancy.
Before I understood this place
Appointed for my second race,
Or taught my soul to fancy ought
But a white, Celestiall thought,
When yet I had not walkt above
A mile, or two, from my first love,
And looking back (at that short space,)
Could see a glimpse of his bright-face; 10
When on some *gilded Cloud*, or *flowre*
My gazing soul would dwell an houre,

And in those weaker glories spy
Some shadows of eternity;
Before I taught my tongue to wound
My Conscience with a sinfull sound,
Or had the black art to dispence
A sev'rall sinne to ev'ry sence,
But felt through all this fleshly dresse
Bright *shootes* of everlastingnesse. 20
  O how I long to travell back
And tread again that ancient track!
That I might once more reach that plaine,
Where first I left my glorious traine,
From whence th' Inlightned spirit sees
That shady City of Palme trees;
But (ah!) my soul with too much stay
Is drunk, and staggers in the way.
Some men a forward motion love,
But I by backward steps would move, 30
And when this dust falls to the urn
In that state I came return.

¶

Come, come, what doe I here?
    Since he is gone
Each day is grown a dozen year,
    And each houre, one;
    Come, come!
  Cut off the sum,
  By these soil'd teares!
  (Which only thou
  Know'st to be true,)
  Dayes are my feares. 10

2

Ther's not a wind can stir,
    Or beam passe by,
But strait I think (though far,)
    Thy hand is nigh;

Come, come!
Strike these lips dumb:
This restles breath
That soiles thy name,
Will ne'r be tame
Untill in death. 20

3

Perhaps some think a tombe
No house of store,
But a dark, and seal'd up wombe,
Which ne'r breeds more.
Come, come!
Such thoughts benum;
But I would be
With him I weep
A bed, and sleep
To wake in thee. 30

¶ Midnight

When to my Eyes
(Whilst deep sleep others catches,)
Thine hoast of spyes
The starres shine in their watches,
I doe survey
Each busie Ray,
And how they work, and wind,
And wish each beame
My soul doth streame,
With the like ardour shin'd; 10
What Emanations,
Quick vibrations
And bright stirs are there?
What thin Ejections,
Cold Affections,
And slow motions here?

2

Thy heav'ns (some say,)
Are a firie-liquid light,
Which mingling aye
Streames, and flames thus to the sight. 20
Come then, my god!
Shine on this bloud,
And water in one beame,
And thou shalt see
Kindled by thee
Both liquors burne, and streame.
O what bright quicknes,
Active brightnes,
And celestiall flowes
Will follow after 30
On that water,
Which thy spirit blowes!

Math. Cap. 3. ver. xi

I indeed baptize you with water unto repentance, but he that commeth after me, is mightier than I, whose shooes I am not worthy to beare, he shall baptize you with the holy Ghost, and with fire.

¶ Content

Peace, peace! I know 'twas brave,
But this corse fleece
I shelter in, is slave
To no such peece.
When I am gone,
I shall no ward-robes leave
To friend, or sonne
But what their own homes weave,

2

Such, though not proud, nor full,
May make them weep, 10
And mourn to see the wooll
Outlast the sheep;

Poore, Pious weare!
Hadst thou bin rich, or fine
Perhaps that teare
Had mourn'd thy losse, not mine.

3

Why then these curl'd, puff'd points,
Or a laced story?
Death sets all out of Joint
And scornes their glory; 20
Some Love a *Rose*
In hand, some in the skin;
But crosse to those,
I would have mine *within*.

¶

Joy of my life! while left me here,
And still my Love!
How in thy absence thou dost steere
Me from above!
A life well lead
This truth commends,
With quick, or dead
It never ends.

2

Stars are of mighty use: The night
Is dark, and long; 10
The Rode foul, and where one goes right,
Six may go wrong.
One twinkling ray
Shot o'r some cloud,
May clear much way
And guide a croud.

3

Gods Saints are shining lights: who stays
Here long must passe
O're dark hills, swift streames, and steep ways
As smooth as glasse; 20

But these all night
Like Candles, shed
Their beams, and light
Us into Bed.

4

They are (indeed,) our Pillar-fires
Seen as we go,
They are that Cities shining spires
We travell too;
A swordlike gleame
Kept man for sin 30
First *Out*; This beame
Will guide him *In*.

The Storm

I see the use: and know my bloud
Is not a Sea,
But a shallow, bounded floud
Though red as he;
Yet have I flows, as strong as his,
And boyling stremes that rave
With the same curling force, and hisse,
As doth the mountain'd wave.

2

But when his waters billow thus,
Dark storms, and wind 10
Incite them to that fierce discusse,
Else not Inclin'd,
Thus the Enlarg'd, inraged air
Uncalmes these to a floud,
But still the weather that's most fair
Breeds tempests in my bloud;

3

Lord, then round me with weeping Clouds,
And let my mind
In quick blasts sigh beneath those shrouds
A spirit-wind, 20

So shall that storme purge this *Recluse*
Which sinfull ease made foul,
And *wind*, and *water* to thy use
Both *wash*, and *wing* my soul.

The Morning-watch

O Joyes! Infinite sweetnes! with what flowres,
And shoots of glory, my soul breakes, and buds!
All the long houres
Of night, and Rest
Through the still shrouds
Of sleep, and Clouds,
This Dew fell on my Breast;
O how it *Blouds*,
And *Spirits* all my Earth! heark! In what Rings,
And *Hymning Circulations* the quick world 10
Awakes, and sings;
The rising winds,
And falling springs,
Birds, beasts, all things
Adore him in their kinds.
Thus all is hurl'd
In sacred *Hymnes*, and *Order*, The great *Chime*
And *Symphony* of nature. Prayer is
The world in tune,
A spirit-voyce, 20
And vocall joyes
Whose *Eccho is* heav'ns blisse.
O let me climbe
When I lye down! The Pious soul by night
Is like a clouded starre, whose beames though sed
To shed their light
Under some Cloud
Yet are above,
And shine, and move
Beyond that mistie shrowd. 30
So in my Bed
That Curtain'd grave, though sleep, like ashes, hide
My lamp, and life, both shall in thee abide.

The Evening-watch

A Dialogue

Farewell! I goe to sleep; but when *Body*
The day-star springs, I'le wake agen.

Goe, sleep in peace; and when thou lyest *Soul*
Unnumber'd in thy dust, when all this frame
Is but one dramme, and what thou now descriest
In sev'rall parts shall want a name,
Then may his peace be with thee, and each dust
Writ in his book, who ne'r betray'd mans trust!

Amen! but hark, e'r we two stray, *Body*
How many hours do'st think 'till day? 10

Ah! go; th'art weak, and sleepie. Heav'n *Soul*
Is a plain watch, and without figures winds
All ages up; who drew this Circle even
He fils it; Dayes, and hours are *Blinds*.
Yet, this take with thee; The last gasp of time
Is thy first breath, and mans *eternall Prime*.

¶

Silence, and stealth of dayes! 'tis now
Since thou art gone,
Twelve hundred houres, and not a brow
But Clouds hang on.
As he that in some Caves thick damp
Lockt from the light,
Fixeth a solitary lamp,
To brave the night
And walking from his Sun, when past
That glim'ring Ray 10
Cuts through the heavy mists in haste
Back to his day,
So o'r fled minutes I retreat
Unto that hour

Which shew'd thee last, but did defeat
Thy light, and pow'r,
I search, and rack my soul to see
Those beams again,
But nothing but the snuff to me
Appeareth plain; 20
That dark, and dead sleeps in its known,
And common urn,
But those fled to their Makers throne,
There shine, and burn;
O could I track them! but souls must
Track one the other,
And now the spirit, not the dust
Must be thy brother.
Yet I have one *Pearle* by whose light
All things I see, 30
And in the heart of Earth, and night
Find Heaven, and thee.

Church-Service

Blest be the God of Harmony, and Love!
The God above!
And holy dove!
Whose Interceding, spirituall grones
Make restless mones
For dust, and stones,
For dust in every part,
But a hard, stonie heart.

2

O how in this thy Quire of Souls I stand
(Propt by thy hand) 10
A heap of sand!
Which busie thoughts (like winds) would scatter quite
And put to flight,
But for thy might;
Thy hand alone doth tame
Those blasts, and knit my frame,

3

So that both stones, and dust, and all of me
Joyntly agree
To cry to thee,
And in this Musick by thy Martyrs bloud 20
Seal'd, and made good
Present, O God!
The Eccho of these stones
——My sighes, and grones.

Buriall

O thou! the first fruits of the dead
And their dark bed,
When I am cast into that deep
And senseless sleep
The wages of my sinne,
O then,
Thou great Preserver of all men!
Watch o're that loose
And empty house,
Which I sometimes liv'd in. 10

2

It is (in truth!) a ruin'd peece
Not worth thy Eyes,
And scarce a room but wind, and rain
Beat through, and stain
The seats, and Cells within;
Yet thou
Led by thy Love wouldst stoop thus low,
And in this Cott
All filth, and spott,
Didst with thy servant Inne. 20

3

And nothing can, I hourely see,
Drive thee from me,
Thou art the same, faithfull, and just
In life, or Dust;

Though then (thus crumm'd) I stray
In blasts,
Or Exhalations, and wasts
Beyond all Eyes
Yet thy love spies
That Change, and knows thy Clay. 30

4

The world's thy boxe: how then (there tost,)
Can I be lost?
But the delay is all; Tyme now
Is old, and slow,
His wings are dull, and sickly;
Yet he
Thy servant is, and waits on thee,
Cutt then the summe,
Lord haste, Lord come,
O come Lord *Jesus* quickly! 40

Rom. Cap. 8. ver. 23

And not only they, but our selves also, which have the first fruits of the spirit, even wee our selves grone within our selves, waiting for the adoption, to wit, *the redemption of our body.*

Chearfulness

Lord, with what courage, and delight
I doe each thing
When thy least breath sustaines my wing!
I shine, and move
Like those above,
And (with much gladnesse
Quitting sadnesse,)
Make me faire dayes of every night.

2

Affliction thus, meere pleasure is,
And hap what will, 10
If thou be in't, 'tis welcome still;

But since thy rayes
In Sunnie dayes
Thou dost thus lend
And freely spend,
Ah! what shall I return for this?

3

O that I were all Soul! that thou
Wouldst make each part
Of this poor, sinfull frame pure heart!
Then would I drown 20
My single one,
And to thy praise
A Consort raise
Of *Hallelujahs* here below.

¶

Sure, there's a tye of Bodyes! and as they
Dissolve (with it,) to Clay,
Love languisheth, and memory doth rust
O'r-cast with that cold dust;
For things thus *Center'd*, without *Beames*, or *Action*
Nor give, nor take *Contaction*,
And man is such a Marygold, these fled,
That shuts, and hangs the head.

2

Absents within the Line Conspire, and *Sense*
Things distant doth unite, 10
Herbs sleep unto the *East*, and some fowles thence
Watch the Returns of light;
But hearts are not so kind: false, short delights
Tell us the world is brave,
And wrap us in Imaginary flights
Wide of a faithfull grave;
Thus *Lazarus* was carried out of town;
For 'tis our foes chief art
By distance all good objects first to drown,
And then besiege the heart. 20

But I will be my own *Deaths-head*; and though
The flatt'rer say, *I live*,
Because Incertainties we cannot know
Be sure, not to believe.

Peace

My Soul, there is a Countrie
Far beyond the stars,
Where stands a winged Centrie
All skilfull in the wars,
There above noise, and danger
Sweet peace sits crown'd with smiles,
And one born in a Manger
Commands the Beauteous files,
He is thy gracious friend,
And (O my Soul awake!) 10
Did in pure love descend
To die here for thy sake,
If thou canst get but thither,
There growes the flowre of peace,
The Rose that cannot wither,
Thy fortresse, and thy ease;
Leave then thy foolish ranges;
For none can thee secure,
But one, who never changes,
Thy God, thy life, thy Cure. 20

The Passion

O my chief good!
My dear, dear God!
When thy blest bloud
Did Issue forth forc'd by the Rod,
What pain didst thou
Feel in each blow!
How didst thou weep,
And thy self steep

In thy own precious, saving teares!
What cruell smart 10
Did teare thy heart!
How didst thou grone it
In the spirit,
O thou, whom my soul Loves, and feares!

2

Most blessed Vine!
Whose juice so good
I feel as Wine,
But thy faire branches felt as bloud,
How wert thou prest
To be my feast! 20
In what deep anguish
Didst thou languish,
What springs of Sweat, and bloud did drown thee!
How in one path
Did the full wrath
Of thy great Father
Crowd, and gather,
Doubling thy griefs, when none would own thee!

3

How did the weight
Of all our sinnes, 30
And death unite
To wrench, and Rack thy blessed limbes!
How pale, and bloudie
Lookt thy Body!
How bruis'd, and broke
With every stroke!
How meek, and patient was thy spirit!
How didst thou cry,
And grone on high
Father forgive, 40
And let them live,
I dye to make my foes inherit!

4

O blessed Lamb!
That took'st my sinne,
That took'st my shame
How shall thy dust thy praises sing!
I would I were
One hearty tear!
One constant spring!
Then would I bring 50
Thee two small mites, and be at strife
Which should most vie,
My heart, or eye,
Teaching my years
In smiles, and tears
To weep, to sing, thy *Death*, my *Life*.

Rom. Cap. 8. ver. 19

Etenim res Creatæ exerto Capite observantes expectant revelationem Filiorum Dei.

And do they so? have they a Sense
Of ought but Influence?
Can they their heads lift, and expect,
And grone too? why th'Elect
Can do no more: my volumes sed
They were all dull, and dead,
They judg'd them senslesse, and their state
Wholly Inanimate.
Go, go; Seal up thy looks,
And burn thy books. 10

2

I would I were a stone, or tree,
Or flowre by pedigree,
Or some poor high-way herb, or Spring
To flow, or bird to sing!
Then should I (tyed to one sure state,)
All day expect my date;

But I am sadly loose, and stray
A giddy blast each way;
O let me not thus range!
Thou canst not change. 20

3

Sometimes I sit with thee, and tarry
An hour, or so, then vary.
Thy other Creatures in this Scene
Thee only aym, and mean;
Some rise to seek thee, and with heads
Erect peep from their beds;
Others, whose birth is in the tomb,
And cannot quit the womb,
Sigh there, and grone for thee,
Their liberty. 30

4

O let not me do lesse! shall they
Watch, while I sleep, or play?
Shall I thy mercies still abuse
With fancies, friends, or newes?
O brook it not! thy bloud is mine,
And my soul should be thine;
O brook it not! why wilt thou stop
After whole showres one drop?
Sure, thou wilt joy to see
Thy sheep with thee. 40

The Relapse

My God, how gracious art thou! I had slipt
Almost to hell,
And on the verge of that dark, dreadful pit
Did hear them yell,
But O thy love! thy rich, almighty love
That sav'd my soul,
And checkt their furie, when I saw them move,
And heard them howl;

O my sole Comfort, take no more these wayes,
This hideous path, 10
And I wil mend my own without delayes,
Cease thou thy wrath!
I have deserv'd a thick, Egyptian damp,
Dark as my deeds,
Should *mist* within me, and put out that lamp
Thy spirit feeds;
A darting Conscience full of stabs, and fears;
No shade but *Yewgh*,
Sullen, and sad Ecclipses, Cloudie spheres,
These are my due. 20
But he that with his bloud, (a price too deere,)
My scores did pay,
Bid me, by vertue from him, chalenge here
The brightest day;
Sweet, downie thoughts; soft *Lilly*-shades; Calm streams;
Joyes full, and true;
Fresh, spicie mornings; and eternal beams
These are his due.

The Resolve

I have consider'd it; and find
A longer stay
Is but excus'd neglect. To mind
One path, and stray
Into another, or to none,
Cannot be love;
When shal that traveller come home,
That will not move?
If thou wouldst thither, linger not,
Catch at the place, 10
Tell youth, and beauty they must rot,
They'r but a *Case*;
Loose, parcell'd hearts wil freeze: The Sun
With scatter'd locks
Scarce warms, but by contraction
Can heat rocks;

Call in thy *Powers*; run, and reach
Home with the light,
Be there, before the shadows stretch,
And *Span* up night; 20
Follow the *Cry* no more: there is
An ancient way
All strewed with flowres, and happiness
And fresh as *May*;
There turn, and turn no more; Let wits,
Smile at fair eies,
Or lips; But who there weeping sits,
Hath got the *Prize*.

The Match

Dear friend! whose holy, ever-living lines
Have done much good
To many, and have checkt my blood,
My fierce, wild blood that still heaves, and inclines,
But is still tam'd
By those bright fires which thee inflam'd;
Here I joyn hands, and thrust my stubborn heart
Into thy *Deed*,
There from no *Duties* to be freed,
And if hereafter *youth*, or *folly* thwart 10
And claim their share,
Here I renounce the pois'nous ware.

ii

Accept, dread Lord, the poor Oblation,
It is but poore,
Yet through thy Mercies may be more.
O thou! that canst not wish my souls damnation,
Afford me life,
And save me from all inward strife!
Two *Lifes* I hold from thee, my gracious Lord,
Both cost thee deer, 20
For one, I am thy Tenant here;
The other, the true life, in the next world
And endless is,
O let me still mind *that* in *this*!

To thee therefore my *Thoughts*, *Words*, *Actions*
I do resign,
Thy will in all be done, not mine.
Settle my *house*, and shut out all distractions
That may unknit
My heart, and thee planted in it; 30
Lord *Jesu*! thou didst bow thy blessed head
Upon a tree,
O do as much, now unto me!
O hear, and heal thy servant! Lord, strike dead
All lusts in me,
Who onely wish life to serve thee?
Suffer no more this dust to overflow
And drown my eies,
But seal, or pin them to thy skies.
And let this *grain* which here in tears I sow 40
Though *dead*, and *sick*,
Through thy *Increase* grow *new*, and *quick*.

Rules *and* Lessons

When first thy Eies unveil, give thy Soul leave
To do the like; our Bodies but forerun
The spirits duty; True hearts spread, and heave
Unto their God, as flow'rs do to the Sun.
Give him thy first thoughts then; so shalt thou keep
Him company all day, and in him sleep.

Yet, never sleep the Sun up; Prayer shou'd
Dawn with the day; There are set, awful hours
'Twixt heaven, and us; The *Manna* was not good
After Sun-rising, far-day sullies flowres. 10
Rise to prevent the Sun; sleep doth sins glut,
And heav'ns gate opens, when this world's is shut.

Walk with thy fellow-creatures: note the *hush*
And *whispers* amongst them. There's not a *Spring*,
Or *Leafe* but hath his *Morning-hymn*; Each *Bush*
And *Oak* doth know *I AM*; canst thou not sing?
O leave thy Cares, and follies! go this way
And thou art sure to prosper all the day.

Serve God before the world; let him not go
Until thou hast a blessing, then resigne 20
The whole unto him; and remember who
Prevail'd by *wrestling* ere the *Sun* did *shine*.
Poure *Oyle* upon the *stones*, weep for thy sin,
Then journey on, and have an eie to heav'n.

Mornings are *Mysteries*; the first worlds *Youth*,
Mans *Resurrection*, and the futures *Bud*
Shrowd in their births: The Crown of life, light, truth
Is stil'd their *starre*, the *stone*, and *hidden food*.
Three *blessings* wait upon them, two of which
Should move; They make us *holy*, *happy*, rich. 30

When the world's up, and ev'ry swarm abroad,
Keep thou thy temper, mix not with each Clay;
Dispatch necessities, life hath a load
Which must be carri'd on, and safely may.
Yet keep those cares without thee, let the heart
Be Gods alone, and choose the better part.

Through all thy *Actions*, *Counsels*, and *Discourse*,
Let *Mildness*, and *Religion* guide thee out,
If truth be thine, what needs a brutish force?
But what's not *good*, and *just* ne'r go about. 40
Wrong not thy Conscience for a rotten stick,
That gain is dreadful, which makes spirits sick.

To God, thy Countrie, and thy friend be true,
If *Priest*, and *People* change, keep thou thy ground.
Who sels Religion, is a *Judas Jew*,
And, oathes once broke, the soul cannot be sound.
The perjurer's a devil let loose: what can
Tie up his hands, that dares mock God, and man?

Seek not the same steps with the *Crowd*; stick thou
To thy sure trot; a Constant, humble mind 50
Is both his own Joy, and his Makers too;
Let folly dust it on, or lag behind.
A sweet *self-privacy* in a right soul
Out-runs the Earth, and lines the utmost pole.

To all that seek thee, bear an open heart;
Make not thy breast a *Labyrinth*, or *Trap*;
If tryals come, this wil make good thy part,
For honesty is safe, come what can hap;
    It is the good mans *feast*; The prince of flowres 59
    Which thrives in *storms*, and smels best after *showres*.

Seal not thy Eyes up from the poor, but give
Proportion to their *Merits*, and thy *Purse*;
Thou mai'st in Rags a mighty Prince relieve
Who, when thy sins call for't, can fence a Curse.
    Thou shalt not lose one *mite*. Though waters stray,
    The Bread we cast returns in fraughts one day.

Spend not an hour so, as to weep another,
For tears are not thine own; If thou giv'st words
Dash not thy *friend*, nor *Heav'n*; O smother
A vip'rous thought; some *Syllables* are *Swords*. 70
    Unbitted tongues are in their penance double,
    They shame their *owners*, and the *hearers* trouble.

Injure not modest bloud, whose *spirits* rise
In judgement against *Lewdness*; that's base wit
That voyds but *filth*, and *stench*. Hast thou no prize
But *sickness*, or *Infection*? stifle it.
    Who makes his jests of sins, must be at least
    If not a very *devill*, worse than a *Beast*.

Yet, fly no friend, if he be such indeed,
But meet to quench his *Longings*, and thy *Thirst*; 80
Allow your Joyes *Religion*; That done, speed
And bring the same man back, thou wert at first.
    Who so returns not, cannot pray aright,
    But shuts his door, and leaves God out all night.

To highten thy *Devotions*, and keep low
All mutinous thoughts, what busines e'r thou hast
Observe God in his works; here *fountains* flow,
Birds sing, *Beasts* feed, *Fish* leap, and th'*Earth* stands fast;
    Above are restles *motions*, running *Lights*,
    Vast Circling *Azure*, giddy *Clouds*, days, nights. 90

When *Seasons* change, then lay before thine Eys
His wondrous *Method*; mark the various *Scenes*
In heav'n; *Hail*, *Thunder*, *Rain-bows*, *Snow*, and *Ice*,
Calmes, *Tempests*, *Light*, and *darknes* by his means;
    Thou canst not misse his Praise; Each *tree*, *herb*, *flowre*
    Are shadows of his *wisedome*, and his Pow'r.

To *meales* when thou doest come, give him the praise
Whose *Arm* supply'd thee; Take what may suffice,
And then be thankful; O admire his ways
Who fils the worlds unempty'd granaries! 100
    A thankles feeder is a *Theif*, his feast
    A very *Robbery*, and himself no *guest*.

High-noon thus past, thy time decays; provide
Thee other thoughts; Away with friends, and mirth;
The Sun now stoops, and hasts his beams to hide
Under the dark, and melancholy Earth.
    All but preludes thy End. Thou art the man
    Whose *Rise*, *hight*, and *Descent* is but a span.

Yet, set as he doth, and 'tis well. Have all
Thy Beams home with thee: trim thy *Lamp*, buy *Oyl*, 110
And then set forth; who is thus drest, The *Fall*
Furthers his glory, and gives death the foyl.
    Man is a *Summers day*; whose *youth*, and *fire*
    Cool to a glorious *Evening*, and Expire.

When night comes, list thy deeds; make plain the way
'Twixt Heaven, and thee; block it not with delays,
But perfect all before thou sleep'st; Then say
Ther's one Sun more strung on my Bead of days.
    What's good score up for Joy; The bad wel scann'd
    Wash off with tears, and get thy *Masters* hand. 120

Thy Accounts thus made, spend in the grave one houre
Before thy time; Be not a stranger there
Where thou may'st sleep whole ages; Lifes poor flowr
Lasts not a night sometimes. Bad spirits fear
    This Conversation; But the good man lyes
    Intombed many days before he dyes.

Being laid, and drest for sleep, Close not thy Eys
Up with thy Curtains; Give thy soul the wing
In some good thoughts; So when the day shall rise
And thou *unrak'st* thy *fire*, those *sparks* will bring 130
  New *flames*; Besides where these lodge vain *heats* mourn
  And die; That *Bush* where God is, shall not burn.

When thy *Nap's* over, stir thy fire, unrake
In that *dead age*; one beam i'th' dark outvies
Two in the day; Then from the *Damps*, and *Ake*
Of night shut up thy *leaves*, be Chast; God prys
  Through thickest nights; Though then the Sun be far
  Do thou the works of *Day*, and rise a *Star*.

Briefly, *Doe as thou would'st be done unto*,
Love God, *and Love thy Neighbour ; Watch*, *and Pray*. 140
These are the *Words*, and *Works* of life; This do,
And live; who doth not thus, hath lost *Heav'ns way*.
  O lose it not! look up, wilt Change those *Lights*
  For *Chains* of *Darknes*, and *Eternal Nights*?

Corruption

Sure, It was so. Man in those early days
    Was not all stone, and Earth,
He shin'd a little, and by those weak Rays
    Had some glimpse of his birth.
He saw Heaven o'r his head, and knew from whence
    He came (condemned,) hither,
And, as first Love draws strongest, so from hence
    His mind sure progress'd thither.
Things here were strange unto him: Swet, and till
    All was a thorn, or weed, 10
Nor did those last, but (like himself,) dyed still
    As soon as they did *Seed*,
They seem'd to quarrel with him; for that Act
    That fel him, foyl'd them all,
He drew the Curse upon the world, and Crackt
    The whole frame with his fall.
This made him long for *home*, as loath to stay
    With murmurers, and foes;

He sigh'd for *Eden*, and would often say
Ah! what bright days were those? 20
Nor was Heav'n cold unto him; for each day
The vally, or the Mountain
Afforded visits, and still *Paradise* lay
In some green shade, or fountain.
Angels lay *Leiger* here; Each Bush, and Cel,
Each Oke, and high-way knew them,
Walk but the fields, or sit down at some *wel*,
And he was sure to view them.
Almighty *Love*! where art thou now? mad man
Sits down, and freezeth on, 30
He raves, and swears to stir nor fire, nor fan,
But bids the thread be spun.
I see, thy Curtains are Close-drawn; Thy bow
Looks dim too in the Cloud,
Sin triumphs still, and man is sunk below
The Center, and his shrowd;
All's in deep sleep, and night; Thick darknes lyes
And hatcheth o'r thy people;
But hark! what trumpets that? what Angel cries
Arise! Thrust in thy sickle. 40

H. Scriptures

Welcome dear book, souls Joy, and food! The feast
Of Spirits, Heav'n extracted lyes in thee;
Thou art lifes Charter, The Doves spotless neast
Where souls are hatch'd unto Eternitie.

In thee the hidden stone, the *Manna* lies,
Thou art the great *Elixir*, rare, and Choice;
The Key that opens to all Mysteries,
The *Word* in Characters, God in the *Voice*.

O that I had deep Cut in my hard heart
Each line in thee! Then would I plead in groans 10
Of my Lords penning, and by sweetest Art
Return upon himself the *Law*, and *Stones*.
Read here, my faults are thine. This Book, and I
Will tell thee so; *Sweet Saviour thou didst dye!*

Unprofitablenes

How rich, O Lord! how fresh thy visits are!
'Twas but Just now my bleak leaves hopeles hung
    Sullyed with dust and mud;
Each snarling blast shot through me, and did share
Their Youth, and beauty, Cold showres nipt, and
      wrung
    Their spiciness, and bloud;
But since thou didst in one sweet glance survey
Their sad decays, I flourish, and once more
    Breath all perfumes, and spice; 10
I smell a dew like *Myrrh*, and all the day
Wear in my bosome a full Sun; such store
    Hath one beame from thy Eys.
But, ah, my God! what fruit hast thou of this?
What one poor leaf did ever I yet fall
    To wait upon thy wreath?
Thus thou all day a thankless weed doest dress,
And when th' hast done, a stench, or fog is all
    The odour I bequeath.

CHRISTS Nativity

Awake, glad heart! get up, and Sing,
It is the Birth-day of thy King,
    Awake! awake!
    The Sun doth shake
Light from his locks, and all the way
Breathing Perfumes, doth spice the day.

2

Awak, awak! heark, how th' *wood* rings,
Winds whisper, and the busie *springs*
    A Consort make;
    Awake, awake! 10
Man is their high-priest, and should rise
To offer up the sacrifice.

3

I would I were some *Bird*, or Star,
Flutt'ring in woods, or lifted far
    Above this *Inne*
    And Rode of sin!
Then either Star, or *Bird*, should be
Shining, or singing still to thee.

4

I would I had in my best part
Fit Roomes for thee! or that my heart   20
    Were so clean as
    Thy manger was!
But I am all filth, and obscene,
Yet, if thou wilt, thou canst make clean.

5

Sweet *Jesu*! will then; Let no more
This Leper haunt, and soyl thy door,
    Cure him, Ease him
    O release him!
And let once more by mystick birth
The Lord of life be borne in Earth.   30

II

How kind is heav'n to man! If here
    One sinner doth amend
Strait there is Joy, and ev'ry sphere
    In musick doth Contend;
And shall we then no voices lift?
    Are mercy, and salvation
Not worth our thanks? Is life a gift
    Of no more acceptation?
Shal he that did come down from thence,
    And here for us was slain,   10
Shal he be now cast off? no sense
    Of all his woes remain?
Can neither Love, nor suff'rings bind?
    Are we all stone, and Earth?

Neither his bloudy passions mind,
Nor one day blesse his birth?
Alas, my God! Thy birth now here
Must not be numbred in the year.

The Check

Peace, peace! I blush to hear thee; when thou art
A dusty story
A speechlesse heap, and in the midst my heart
In the same livery drest
Lyes tame as all the rest;
When six years thence digg'd up, some youthfull Eie
Seeks there for Symmetry
But finding none, shal leave thee to the wind,
Or the next foot to Crush,
Scatt'ring thy kind 10
And humble dust, tell then dear flesh
Where is thy glory?

2

As he that in the midst of day Expects
The hideous night,
Sleeps not, but shaking off sloth, and neglects,
Works with the Sun, and sets
Paying the day its debts;
That (for Repose, and darknes bound,) he might
Rest from the fears i'th' night;
So should we too. All things teach us to die 20
And point us out the way
While we passe by
And mind it not; play not away
Thy glimpse of light.

3

View thy fore-runners: Creatures giv'n to be
Thy youths Companions,
Take their leave, and die; Birds, beasts, each tree
All that have growth, or breath
Have one large language, *Death*.

O then play not! but strive to him, who Can 30
Make these sad shades pure Sun,
Turning their mists to beams, their damps to day,
Whose pow'r doth so excell
As to make Clay
A spirit, and true glory dwell
In dust, and stones.

4

Heark, how he doth Invite thee! with what voice
Of Love, and sorrow
He begs, and Calls; *O that in these thy days*
Thou knew'st but thy own good! 40
Shall not the Crys of bloud,
Of Gods own bloud awake thee? He bids beware
Of drunknes, surfeits, Care,
But thou sleep'st on; wher's now thy protestation,
Thy Lines, thy Love? Away,
Redeem the day,
The day that gives no observation,
Perhaps to morrow.

Disorder *and* frailty

When first thou didst even from the grave
And womb of darknes becken out
My brutish soul, and to thy slave
Becam'st thy self, both guide, and Scout;
Even from that hour
Thou gotst my heart; And though here tost
By winds, and bit with frost
I pine, and shrink
Breaking the link
'Twixt thee, and me; And oftimes creep 10
Into th' old silence, and dead sleep,
Quitting thy way
All the long day,
Yet, sure, my God! I love thee most.
Alas, thy love!

2

I threaten heaven, and from my Cell
Of Clay, and frailty break, and bud
Touch'd by thy fire, and breath; Thy bloud
Too, is my Dew, and springing wel.
But while I grow 20
And stretch to thee, ayming at all
Thy stars, and spangled hall,
Each fly doth tast,
Poyson, and blast
My yielding leaves; sometimes a showr
Beats them quite off, and in an hour
Not one poor shoot
But the bare root
Hid under ground survives the fall.
Alas, frail weed! 30

3

Thus like some sleeping Exhalation
(Which wak'd by heat, and beams, makes up
Unto that Comforter, the Sun,
And soars, and shines; But e'r we sup
And walk two steps
Cool'd by the damps of night, descends,
And, whence it sprung, there ends,)
Doth my weak fire
Pine, and retire,
And (after all my hight of flames,) 40
In sickly Expirations tames
Leaving me dead
On my first bed
Untill thy Sun again ascends.
Poor, falling Star!

4

O, is! but give wings to my fire,
And hatch my soul, untill it fly
Up where thou art, amongst thy tire
Of Stars, above Infirmity;

Let not perverse, 50
And foolish thoughts adde to my Bil
Of forward sins, and Kil
That seed, which thou
In me didst sow,
But dresse, and water with thy grace
Together with the seed, the place;
And for his sake
Who died to stake
His life for mine, tune to thy will
My heart, my verse. 60

Hosea Cap. 6. ver. 4

O Ephraim what shall I do unto thee? O Judah how shall I intreat thee? for thy goodness is as a morning Cloud, and as the early Dew it goeth away.

Idle Verse

Go, go, queint folies, sugred sin,
Shadow no more my door;
I will no longer Cobwebs spin,
I'm too much on the score.

For since amidst my youth, and night,
My great preserver smiles,
Wee'l make a Match, my only light,
And Joyn against their wiles;

Blind, desp'rate *fits*, that study how
To dresse, and trim our shame, 10
That gild rank poyson, and allow
Vice in a fairer name;

The *Purles* of youthfull bloud, and bowles,
Lust in the Robes of Love,
The idle talk of feav'rish souls
Sick with a scarf, or glove;

Let it suffice my warmer days
Simper'd, and shin'd on you,
Twist not my Cypresse with your Bays,
Or Roses with my Yewgh; 20

Go, go, seek out some greener thing,
It snows, and freezeth here;
Let Nightingales attend the spring,
Winter is all my year.

Son-dayes

Bright shadows of true Rest! some shoots of blisse,
Heaven once a week;
The next worlds gladnes prepossest in this;
A day to seek

Eternity in time; the steps by which
We Climb above all ages; Lamps that light
Man through his heap of dark days; and the rich,
And full redemption of the whole weeks flight.

2

The Pulleys unto headlong man; times bower;
The narrow way; 10
Transplanted Paradise; Gods walking houre;
The Cool o'th' day;

The Creatures *Jubile*; Gods parle with dust;
Heaven here; Man on those hills of Myrrh, and flowres;
Angels descending; the Returns of Trust;
A Gleam of glory, after six-days-showres.

3

The Churches love-feasts; Times Prerogative,
And Interest
Deducted from the whole; The Combs, and hive,
And home of rest. 20

The milky way Chalkt out with Suns; a Clue
That guides through erring hours; and in full story
A taste of Heav'n on earth; the pledge, and Cue
Of a full feast; And the Out Courts of glory.

Repentance

Lord, since thou didst in this vile Clay
   That sacred Ray
Thy spirit plant, quickning the whole
With that one grains Infused wealth,
My forward flesh creept on, and subtly stole
Both growth, and power; Checking the health
And heat of thine: That little gate
And narrow way, by which to thee
The Passage is, He term'd a grate
And Entrance to Captivitie; 10
Thy laws but nets, where some small birds
(And those but seldome too) were caught,
Thy Promises but empty words
Which none but Children heard, or taught.
This I believed: And though a friend
Came oft from far, and whisper'd, *No*;
Yet that not sorting to my end
I wholy listen'd to my foe.
Wherefore, pierc'd through with grief, my sad
Seduced soul sighs up to thee, 20
To thee who with true light art Clad
And seest all things just as they be.
Look from thy throne upon this Rowl
Of heavy sins, my high transgressions,
Which I Confesse withall my soul,
My God, Accept of my Confession.
   It was last day
(Touch'd with the guilt of my own way)
I sate alone, and taking up
   The bitter Cup, 30
Through all thy fair, and various store
Sought out what might outvie my score.
  The blades of grasse, thy Creatures feeding,
  The trees, their leafs; the flowres, their seeding;
  The Dust, of which I am a part,
  The Stones much softer than my heart,
  The drops of rain, the sighs of wind,
  The Stars to which I am stark blind,

The Dew thy herbs drink up by night,
The beams they warm them at i'th' light, 40
All that have signature or life,
I summon'd to decide this strife,
And lest I should lack for Arrears,
A spring ran by, I told her tears,
But when these came unto the scale,
My sins alone outweigh'd them all.
O my dear God! my life, my love!
Most blessed lamb! and mildest dove!
Forgive your penitent Offender,
And no more his sins remember, 50
Scatter these shades of death, and give
Light to my soul, that it may live;
Cut me not off for my transgressions,
Wilful rebellions, and suppressions,
But give them in those streams a part
Whose spring is in my Saviours heart.
Lord, I confesse the heynous score,
And pray, I may do so no more,
Though then all sinners I exceed
O think on this; *Thy Son did bleed;* 60
O call to mind his wounds, his woes,
His Agony, and bloudy throws;
Then look on all that thou hast made,
And mark how they do fail, and fade,
The heavens themselves, though fair and bright
Are dark, and unclean in thy sight,
How then, with thee, Can man be holy
Who doest thine Angels charge with folly?
O what am I, that I should breed
Figs on a thorne, flowres on a weed! 70
I am the gourd of sin, and sorrow
Growing o'r night, and gone to morrow,
In all this *Round* of life and death
Nothing's more vile than is my breath,
Profanenes on my tongue doth rest,
Defects, and darknes in my brest,
Pollutions all my body wed,
And even my soul to thee is dead,

Only in him, on whom I feast,
Both soul, and body are well drest, 80
His pure perfection quits all score,
And fills the Boxes of his poor;
He is the Center of long life, and light,
I am but finite, He is Infinite.
O let thy *Justice* then in him Confine,
And through his merits, make thy mercy mine!

The Burial Of an Infant

Blest Infant Bud, whose Blossome-life
Did only look about, and fal,
Wearyed out in a harmles strife
Of tears, and milk, the food of all;

Sweetly didst thou expire: Thy soul
Flew home unstain'd by his new kin,
For ere thou knew'st how to be foul,
Death *wean'd* thee from the world, and sin.

Softly rest all thy Virgin-Crums!
Lapt in the sweets of thy young breath, 10
Expecting till thy Saviour Comes
To *dresse* them, and *unswadle* death.

Faith

Bright, and blest beame! whose strong projection
Equall to all,
Reacheth as well things of dejection
As th' high, and tall;
How hath my God by raying thee
Inlarg'd his spouse,
And of a private familie
Made open house?
All may be now Co-heirs; no noise
Of *Bond*, or *Free* 10
Can Interdict us from those Joys
That wait on thee,

The Law, and Ceremonies made
    A glorious night,
Where Stars, and Clouds, both light, and shade
    Had equal right;
But, as in nature, when the day
    Breaks, night adjourns,
Stars shut up shop, mists pack away,
    And the Moon mourns; 20
So when the Sun of righteousness
    Did once appear,
That Scene was chang'd, and a new dresse
    Left for us here;
Veiles became useles, Altars fel,
    Fires smoking die;
And all that sacred pomp, and shel
    Of things did flie;
Then did he shine forth, whose sad fall,
    And bitter fights 30
Were figur'd in those mystical,
    And Cloudie Rites;
And as i'th' natural Sun, these three,
    Light, *motion*, *heat*,
So are now *Faith*, *Hope*, *Charity*
    Through him Compleat;
Faith spans up blisse; what sin, and death
    Put us quite from,
Lest we should run for't out of breath,
    Faith brings us home; 40
So that I need no more, but say
    I do believe,
And my most loving Lord straitway
    Doth answer, *Live*.

The Dawning

Ah! what time wilt thou come? when shall that crie
    The *Bridegroome's Comming*! fil the sky?
    Shall it in the Evening run
    When our words and works are done?

Or wil thy all-surprizing light
    Break at midnight?
When either sleep, or some dark pleasure
Possesseth mad man without measure;
Or shal these early, fragrant hours
    Unlock thy bowres? 10
And with their blush of light descry
Thy locks crown'd with eternitie;
Indeed, it is the only time
That with thy glory doth best chime,
All now are stirring, ev'ry field
    Ful hymns doth yield,
The whole Creation shakes off night,
And for thy shadow looks the light,
Stars now vanish without number,
Sleepie Planets set, and slumber, 20
The pursie Clouds disband, and scatter,
All expect some sudden matter,
Not one beam triumphs, but from far
    That morning-star;

O at what time soever thou
(Unknown to us,) the heavens wilt bow,
And, with thy Angels in the *Van*,
Descend to Judge poor careless man,
Grant, I may not like puddle lie
In a Corrupt securitie, 30
Where, if a traveller water crave,
He finds it dead, and in a grave;
But as this restless, vocall *Spring*
All day, and night doth run, and sing,
And though here born, yet is acquainted
Elsewhere, and flowing keeps untainted;
So let me all my busie age
In thy free services ingage,
And though (while here) of force I must
Have Commerce somtimes with poor dust, 40
And in my flesh, though vile, and low,
As this doth in her Channel, flow,
Yet let my Course, my aym, my Love,
And chief acquaintance be above;

So when that day, and hour shal come
In which thy self wil be the Sun,
Thou'lt find me drest and on my way,
Watching the Break of thy great day.

Admission

How shril are silent tears? when sin got head
And all my Bowels turn'd
To brasse, and iron; when my stock lay dead,
And all my powers mourn'd;
Then did these drops (for Marble sweats,
And Rocks have tears,)
As rain here at our windows beats,
Chide in thine Ears;

2

No quiet couldst thou have: nor didst thou wink,
And let thy Begger lie, 10
But e'r my eies could overflow their brink
Didst to each drop reply;
Bowels of Love! at what low rate,
And slight a price
Dost thou relieve us at thy gate,
And stil our Cries?

3

Wee are thy Infants, and suck thee; If thou
But hide, or turn thy face,
Because where thou art, yet, we cannot go,
We send tears to the place, 20
These find thee out, and though our sins
Drove thee away,
Yet with thy love that absence wins
Us double pay.

4

O give me then a thankful heart! a heart
After thy own, not mine;
So after thine, that all, and ev'ry part
Of mine, may wait on thine;

O hear! yet not my tears alone,
Hear now a floud, 30
A floud that drowns both tears, and grones,
My Saviours bloud.

Praise

King of Comforts! King of life!
Thou hast cheer'd me,
And when fears, and doubts were rife,
Thou hast cleer'd me!

Not a nook in all my Breast
But thou fill'st it,
Not a thought, that breaks my rest,
But thou kill'st it;

Wherefore with my utmost strength
I wil praise thee, 10
And as thou giv'st line, and length,
I wil raise thee;

Day, and night, not once a day
I will blesse thee,
And my soul in new array
I will dresse thee;

Not one minute in the year
But I'l mind thee,
As my seal, and bracelet here
I wil bind thee; 20

In thy word, as if in heaven
I wil rest me,
And thy promise 'til made even
There shall feast me.

Then, thy sayings all my life
They shal please me,
And thy bloudy wounds, and strife
They wil ease me;

With thy grones my daily breath
  I will measure, 30
And my life hid in thy death
  I will treasure.

  Though then thou art
  Past thought of heart
All perfect fulness,
  And canst no whit
  Accesse admit
From dust and dulness;

  Yet to thy name
  (As not the same 40
With thy bright Essence,)
  Our foul, Clay hands
  At thy Commands
Bring praise, and Incense;

  If then, dread Lord,
  When to thy board
Thy wretch comes begging,
  He hath a flowre
  Or (to his pow'r,)
Some such poor Off'ring; 50

  When thou hast made
  Thy begger glad,
And fill'd his bosome,
  Let him (though poor,)
  Strow at thy door
That one poor Blossome.

Dressing

O thou that lovest a pure, and whitend soul!
That feedst among the Lillies, 'till the day
Break, and the shadows flee; touch with one Coal
My frozen heart; and with thy secret key

Open my desolate rooms; my gloomie Brest
With thy cleer fire refine, burning to dust
These dark Confusions, that within me nest,
And soyl thy Temple with a sinful rust.

Thou holy, harmless, undefil'd high-priest!
The perfect, ful oblation for all sin, 10
Whose glorious conquest nothing can resist,
But even in babes doest triumph still and win;

Give to thy wretched one
Thy mysticall *Communion*,
That, absent, he may see,
Live, die, and rise with thee;
Let him so follow here, that in the end
He may take thee, as thou doest him intend.

Give him thy private seal,
Earnest, and sign; Thy gifts so deal 20
That these forerunners here
May make the future cleer;
Whatever thou dost bid, let faith make good,
Bread for thy body, and Wine for thy blood.

Give him (with pitty) love,
Two flowres that grew with thee above;
Love that shal not admit
Anger for one short fit,
And pitty of such a divine extent
That may thy members, more than mine, resent. 30

Give me, my God! thy grace,
The beams, and brightnes of thy face,
That never like a beast
I take thy sacred feast,
Or the dread mysteries of thy blest bloud
Use, with like Custome, as my Kitchin food.

Some sit to thee, and eat
Thy body as their Common meat,
O let not me do so!
Poor dust should ly still low, 40
Then kneel my soul, and body; kneel, and bow;
If *Saints*, and *Angels* fal down, much more thou.

Easter-day

Thou, whose sad heart, and weeping head lyes low,
Whose Cloudy brest cold damps invade,
Who never feel'st the Sun, nor smooth'st thy brow,
But sitt'st oppressed in the shade,
Awake, awake,
And in his Resurrection partake,
Who on this day (that thou might'st rise as he,)
Rose up, and cancell'd two deaths due to thee.

Awake, awake; and, like the Sun, disperse
All mists that would usurp this day; 10
Where are thy Palmes, thy branches, and thy verse?
Hosanna! heark; why doest thou stay?
Arise, arise,
And with his healing bloud anoint thine Eys,
Thy inward Eys; his bloud will cure thy mind,
Whose spittle only could restore the blind.

Easter Hymn

Death, and darkness get you packing,
Nothing now to man is lacking,
All your triumphs now are ended,
And what *Adam* marr'd, is mended;
Graves are beds now for the weary,
Death a nap, to wake more merry;
Youth now, full of pious duty,
Seeks in thee for perfect beauty,
The weak, and aged tir'd, with length
Of daies, from thee look for new strength, 10
And Infants with thy pangs Contest
As pleasant, as if with the brest;
Then, unto him, who thus hath thrown
Even to Contempt thy kingdome down,
And by his blood did us advance
Unto his own Inheritance,
To him be glory, power, praise,
From this, unto the last of daies.

The Holy Communion

Welcome sweet, and sacred feast; welcome life!
Dead I was, and deep in trouble;
But grace, and blessings came with thee so rife,
That they have quicken'd even drie stubble;
Thus soules their bodies animate,
And thus, at first, when things were rude,
Dark, void, and Crude
They, by thy Word, their beauty had, and date;
All were by thee,
And stil must be, 10
Nothing that is, or lives,
But hath his Quicknings, and reprieves
As thy hand opes, or shuts;
Healings, and Cuts,
Darkness, and day-light, life, and death
Are but meer leaves turn'd by thy breath.
Spirits without thee die,
And blackness sits
On the divinest wits,
As on the Sun Ecclipses lie. 20
But that great darkness at thy death
When the veyl broke with thy last breath,
Did make us see
The way to thee;
And now by these sure, sacred ties,
After thy blood
(Our sov'rain good,)
Had clear'd our eies,
And given us sight;
Thou dost unto thy self betroth 30
Our souls, and bodies both
In everlasting light.

Was't not enough that thou hadst payd the price
And given us eies
When we had none, but thou must also take
Us by the hand
And keep us still awake,

When we would sleep,
Or from thee creep,
Who without thee cannot stand? 40

Was't not enough to lose thy breath
And blood by an accursed death,
But thou must also leave
To us that did bereave
Thee of them both, these seals the means
That should both cleanse
And keep us so,
Who wrought thy wo?
O rose of *Sharon*! O the Lilly
Of the valley! 50
How art thou now, thy flock to keep,
Become both *food*, and *Shepheard* to thy sheep.

Psalm 121

Up to those bright, and gladsome hils
Whence flowes my weal, and mirth,
I look, and sigh for him, who fils
(Unseen,) both heaven, and earth.

He is alone my help, and hope,
That I shall not be moved,
His watchful Eye is ever ope,
And guardeth his beloved;

The glorious God is my sole stay,
He is my Sun, and shade, 10
The cold by night, the heat by day,
Neither shall me invade.

He keeps me from the spite of foes,
Doth all their plots controul,
And is a shield (not reckoning those,)
Unto my very soul.

Whether abroad, amidst the Crowd,
Or els within my door,
He is my Pillar, and my Cloud,
Now, and for evermore. 20

Affliction

Peace, peace; It is not so. Thou doest miscall
Thy Physick; Pils that change
Thy sick Accessions into setled health,
This is the great *Elixir* that turns gall
To wine, and sweetness; Poverty to wealth,
And brings man home, when he doth range.
Did not he, who ordain'd the day,
Ordain night too?
And in the greater world display
What in the lesser he would do? 10
All flesh is Clay, thou know'st; and but that God
Doth use his rod,
And by a fruitfull Change of frosts, and showres
Cherish, and bind thy *pow'rs*,
Thou wouldst to weeds, and thistles quite dis-
perse,
And be more wild than is thy verse;
Sickness is wholsome, and Crosses are but curbs
To check the mule, unruly man,
They are heavens husbandry, the famous fan 20
Purging the floor which Chaff disturbs.
Were all the year one constant Sun-shine, wee
Should have no flowres,
All would be drought, and leanness; not a tree
Would make us bowres;
Beauty consists in colours; and that's best
Which is not fixt, but flies, and flowes;
The settled *Red* is dull, and *whites* that rest
Something of sickness would disclose.
Vicissitude plaies all the game, 30
Nothing that stirrs,
Or hath a name,
But waits upon this wheel,
Kingdomes too have their Physick, and for steel,
Exchange their peace, and furrs.
Thus doth God *Key* disorder'd man
(Which none else can,)

Tuning his brest to rise, or fall;
And by a sacred, needfull art
Like strings, stretch ev'ry part 40
Making the whole most Musicall.

The Tempest

How is man parcell'd out? how ev'ry hour
Shews him himself, or somthing he should see?
This late, long heat may his Instruction be,
And tempests have more in them than a showr.

When nature on her bosome saw
Her Infants die,
And all her flowres wither'd to straw,
Her brests grown dry;
She made the Earth their nurse, & tomb,
Sigh to the sky, 10
'Til to those sighes fetch'd from her womb
Rain did reply,
So in the midst of all her fears
And faint requests
Her Earnest sighes procur'd her tears
And fill'd her brests.

O that man could do so! that he would hear
The world read to him! all the vast expence
In the Creation shed, and slav'd to sence
Makes up but lectures for his eie, and ear. 20

Sure, mighty love foreseeing the discent
Of this poor Creature, by a gracious art
Hid in these low things snares to gain his heart,
And layd surprizes in each Element.

All things here shew him heaven; *Waters* that fall
Chide, and fly up; *Mists* of corruptest fome
Quit their first beds & mount; trees, herbs, flowres, all
Strive upwards stil, and point him the way home.

How do they cast off grossness? only *Earth*,
  And *Man* (like *Issachar*) in lodes delight, 30
  Water's refin'd to *Motion*, Aire to *Light*,
Fire to all *three, but man hath no such mirth.

* *Light, Motion, heat.*

Plants in the *root* with Earth do most Comply,
  Their *Leafs* with water, and humiditie,
  The *Flowres* to air draw neer, and subtiltie,
And *seeds* a kinred fire have with the sky.

All have their *keyes*, and set *ascents*; but man
  Though he knows these, and hath more of his own,
  Sleeps at the ladders foot; alas! what can
These new discoveries do, except they drown? 40

Thus groveling in the shade, and darkness, he
  Sinks to a dead oblivion; and though all
  He sees, (like *Pyramids*,) shoot from this ball
And less'ning still grow up invisibly,

Yet hugs he stil his durt; The *stuffe* he wears
  And painted trimming takes down both his eies,
  Heaven hath less beauty than the dust he spies,
And money better musick than the *Spheres*.

Life's but a blast, he knows it; what? shal straw,
  And bul-rush-fetters temper his short hour? 50
  Must he nor sip, nor sing? grows ne'r a flowr
To crown his temples? shal dreams be his law?

O foolish man! how hast thou lost thy sight?
  How is it that the Sun to thee alone
  Is grown thick darkness, and thy bread, a stone?
Hath flesh no softness now? mid-day no light?

Lord! thou didst put a soul here; If I must
  Be broke again, for flints will give no fire
  Without a steel, O let thy power cleer
Thy gift once more, and grind this flint to dust! 60

Retirement

Who on yon throne of Azure sits,
Keeping close house
Above the morning-starre,
Whose meaner showes,
And outward utensils these glories are
That shine and share
Part of his mansion; He one day
When I went quite astray
Out of meer love
By his mild Dove 10
Did shew me home, and put me in the way.

2

Let it suffice at length thy fits
And lusts (said he,)
Have had their wish, and way;
Presse not to be
Still thy own foe, and mine; for to this day
I did delay,
And would not see, but chose to wink,
Nay, at the very brink
And edge of all 20
When thou wouldst fall
My *love-twist* held thee up, my *unseen link*.

3

I know thee well; for I have fram'd
And hate thee not,
Thy spirit too is mine;
I know thy lot,
Extent, and end, for my hands drew the line
Assigned thine;
If then thou would'st unto my seat,
'Tis not th'applause, and feat 30
Of dust, and clay
Leads to that way,
But from those follies a resolv'd Retreat.

4

Now here below where yet untam'd
Thou doest thus rove
I have a house as well
As there above,
In it my *Name*, and *honour* both do dwell
And shall untill
I make all new; there nothing gay 40
In perfumes, or Array,
Dust lies with dust
And hath but just
The same Respect, and room, with ev'ry clay.

5

A faithful school where thou maist see
In Heraldrie
Of stones, and speechless Earth
Thy true descent;
Where dead men preach, who can turn feasts, and mirth
To funerals, and *Lent*. 50
There dust that out of doors might fill
Thy eies, and blind thee still,
Is fast asleep;
Up then, and keep
Within those doors, (my doors) dost hear? *I will.*

Love, and Discipline

Since in a land not barren stil
(Because thou dost thy grace distil,)
My lott is faln, Blest be thy will!

And since these biting frosts but kil
Some tares in me which choke, or spil
That seed thou sow'st, Blest be thy skil!

Blest be thy Dew, and blest thy frost,
And happy I to be so crost,
And cur'd by Crosses at thy cost.

The Dew doth Cheer what is distrest, 10
The frosts ill weeds nip, and molest,
In both thou work'st unto the best.

Thus while thy sev'ral mercies plot,
And work on me now cold, now hot,
The work goes on, and slacketh not,

For as thy hand the weather steers,
So thrive I best, 'twixt joyes, and tears,
And all the year have some grean Ears.

The Pilgrimage

As travellours when the twilight's come,
And in the sky the stars appear,
The past daies accidents do summe
With, *Thus wee saw there*, *and thus here.*

Then *Jacob*-like lodge in a place
(A place, and no more, is set down,)
Where till the day restore the race
They rest and dream homes of their own.

So for this night I linger here,
And full of tossings too and fro, 10
Expect stil when thou wilt appear
That I may get me up, and go.

I long, and grone, and grieve for thee,
For thee my words, my tears do gush,
O that I were but where I see!
Is all the note within my Bush.

As Birds rob'd of their native wood,
Although their Diet may be fine,
Yet neither sing, nor like their food,
But with the thought of home do pine; 20

So do I mourn, and hang my head,
And though thou dost me fullnes give,
Yet look I for far better bread
Because by this man cannot live.

O feed me then! and since I may
Have yet more days, more nights to Count,
So strengthen me, Lord, all the way,
That I may travel to thy Mount.

Heb. Cap. xi. ver. 13

And they Confessed, that they were strangers, and Pilgrims on the earth.

The Law, and the Gospel

Lord, when thou didst on *Sinai* pitch
And shine from *Paran*, when a firie Law
Pronounc'd with thunder, and thy threats did thaw
Thy Peoples hearts, when all thy weeds were rich
And Inaccessible for light,
Terrour, and might,
How did poor flesh (which after thou didst weare,)
Then faint, and fear!
Thy Chosen flock, like leafs in a high wind,
Whisper'd obedience, and their heads Inclin'd. 10

2

But now since we to *Sion* came,
And through thy bloud thy glory see,
With filial Confidence we touch ev'n thee;
And where the other mount all clad in flame,
And threatning Clouds would not so much
As 'bide the touch,
We Climb up this, and have too all the way
Thy hand our stay,
Nay, thou tak'st ours, and (which ful Comfort brings)
Thy Dove too bears us on her sacred wings. 20

3

Yet since man is a very brute
And after all thy Acts of grace doth kick,
Slighting that health thou gav'st, when he was sick,
Be not displeas'd, If I, who have a sute

To thee each houre, beg at thy door
For this one more;
O plant in me thy *Gospel*, and thy *Law*,
Both *Faith*, and *Awe*;
So twist them in my heart, that ever there
I may as wel as *Love*, find too thy *fear*! 30

4

Let me not spil, but drink thy bloud,
Not break thy fence, and by a black Excess
Force down a Just Curse, when thy hands would bless;
Let me not scatter, and despise my food,
Or nail those blessed limbs again
Which bore my pain;
So Shall thy mercies flow: for while I fear,
I know, thou'lt bear,
But should thy mild Injunction nothing move me,
I would both think, and Judge I did not love thee. 40

John Cap. 14. ver. 15
If ye love me, keep my Commandements.

The World

I saw Eternity the other night
Like a great *Ring* of pure and endless light,
All calm, as it was bright,
And round beneath it, Time in hours, days, years
Driv'n by the spheres
Like a vast shadow mov'd, In which the world
And all her train were hurl'd;
The doting Lover in his queintest strain
Did their Complain,
Neer him, his Lute, his fancy, and his flights, 10
Wits sour delights,
With gloves, and knots the silly snares of pleasure
Yet his dear Treasure
All scatter'd lay, while he his eys did pour
Upon a flowr.

2

The darksome States-man hung with weights and woe
Like a thick midnight-fog mov'd there so slow
He did nor stay, nor go;
Condemning thoughts (like sad Ecclipses) scowl
Upon his soul, 20
And Clouds of crying witnesses without
Pursued him with one shout.
Yet dig'd the Mole, and lest his ways be found
Workt under ground,
Where he did Clutch his prey, but one did see
That policie,
Churches and altars fed him, Perjuries
Were gnats and flies,
It rain'd about him bloud and tears, but he
Drank them as free. 30

3

The fearfull miser on a heap of rust
Sate pining all his life there, did scarce trust
His own hands with the dust,
Yet would not place one peece above, but lives
In feare of theeves.
Thousands there were as frantick as himself
And hug'd each one his pelf,
The down-right Epicure plac'd heav'n in sense
And scornd pretence
While others slipt into a wide Excesse 40
Said little lesse;
The weaker sort slight, triviall wares Inslave
Who think them brave,
And poor, despised truth sate Counting by
Their victory.

4

Yet some, who all this while did weep and sing,
And sing, and weep, soar'd up into the *Ring*,
But most would use no wing.
O fools (said I,) thus to prefer dark night
Before true light, 50

To live in grots, and caves, and hate the day
Because it shews the way,
The way which from this dead and dark abode
Leads up to God,
A way where you might tread the Sun, and be
More bright than he.
But as I did their madnes so discusse
One whisper'd thus,
This Ring the Bride-groome did for none provide
But for his bride. 60

John Cap. 2. ver. 16, 17

All that is in the world, the lust of the flesh, the lust of the Eys, and the pride of life, is not of the father, but is of the world.

And the world passeth away, and the lusts thereof, but he that doth the will of God abideth for ever.

The Mutinie

Weary of this same Clay, and straw, I laid
Me down to breath, and casting in my heart
The after-burthens, and griefs yet to come,
The heavy sum
So shook my brest, that (sick and sore dismai'd)
My thoughts, like water which some stone doth start
Did quit their troubled Channel, and retire
Unto the banks, where, storming at those bounds,
They murmur'd sore; But I, who felt them boyl
And knew their Coyl, 10
Turning to him, who made poor sand to tire
And tame proud waves, If yet these barren grounds
And thirstie brick must be (said I)
My taske, and Destinie,

2

Let me so strive and struggle with thy foes
(Not thine alone, but mine too,) that when all
Their Arts and force are built unto the height
That Babel-weight
May prove thy glory, and their shame; so Close
And knit me to thee, That though in this vale 20

Of sin, and death I sojourn, yet one Eie
May look to thee, To thee the finisher
And Author of my faith; so shew me home
That all this fome
And frothie noise which up and down doth flie
May find no lodging in mine Eie, or Eare,
O seal them up! that these may flie
Like other tempests by.

3

Not but I know thou hast a shorter Cut
To bring me home, than through a wildernes, 30
A Sea, or Sands and Serpents; Yet since thou
(As thy words show)
Though in this desart I were wholy shut,
Canst light and lead me there with such redress
That no decay shal touch me; O be pleas'd
To fix my steps, and whatsoever path
Thy sacred and eternal wil decreed
For thy bruis'd reed
O give it ful obedience, that so seiz'd
Of all I have, I may nor move thy wrath 40
Nor grieve thy *Dove*, but soft and mild
Both live and die thy Child.

Revel. Cap. 2. ver. 17

To him that overcometh wil I give to eate of the hidden Manna, *and I wil give him a white stone, and in the stone a new name written, which no man knoweth, saving he that receiveth it.*

The Constellation

Fair, order'd lights (whose motion without noise
Resembles those true Joys
Whose spring is on that hil where you do grow
And we here tast sometimes below,)

With what exact obedience do you move
Now beneath, and now above,
And in your vast progressions overlook
The darkest night, and closest nook!

Some nights I see you in the gladsome East,
    Some others neer the West, 10
And when I cannot see, yet do you shine
    And beat about your endles line.

Silence, and light, and watchfulnes with you
    Attend and wind the Clue,
No sleep, nor sloth assailes you, but poor man
    Still either sleeps, or slips his span.

He grops beneath here, and with restless Care
    First makes, then hugs a snare,
Adores dead dust, sets heart on Corne and grass
    But seldom doth make heav'n his glass. 20

Musick and mirth (if there be musick here)
    Take up, and tune his year,
These things are Kin to him, and must be had,
    Who kneels, or sighs a life is mad.

Perhaps some nights hee'l watch with you, and peep
    When it were best to sleep,
Dares know Effects, and Judge them long before,
    When th' herb he treads knows much, much more.

But seeks he your *Obedience*, *Order*, *Light*,
    Your calm and wel-train'd flight, 30
Where, though the glory differ in each star,
    Yet is there peace still, and no war?

Since plac'd by him who calls you by your names
    And fixt there all your flames,
Without Command you never acted ought
    And then you in your Courses fought.

But here Commission'd by a black self-wil
    The sons the father kil,
The Children Chase the mother, and would heal
    The wounds they give, by crying, zeale. 40

Then Cast her bloud, and tears upon thy book
    Where they for fashion look,
And like that Lamb which had the Dragons voice
    Seem mild, but are known by their noise.

Thus by our lusts disorder'd into wars
Our guides prove wandring stars,
Which for these mists, and black days were reserv'd,
What time we from our first love swerv'd.

Yet O for his sake who sits now by thee
All crown'd with victory, 50
So guide us through this Darknes, that we may
Be more and more in love with day;

Settle, and fix our hearts, that we may move
In order, peace, and love,
And taught obedience by thy whole Creation,
Become an humble, holy nation.

Give to thy spouse her perfect, and pure dress,
Beauty and *holiness*,
And so repair these Rents, that men may see
And say, *Where God is, all agree.* 60

The Shepheards

Sweet, harmles livers! (on whose holy leisure
Waits Innocence and pleasure,)
Whose leaders to those pastures, and cleer springs,
Were *Patriarchs*, Saints, and Kings,
How happend it that in the dead of night
You only saw true light,
While *Palestine* was fast a sleep, and lay
Without one thought of Day?
Was it because those first and blessed swains
Were pilgrims on those plains 10
When they receiv'd the promise, for which now
'Twas there first shown to you?
'Tis true, he loves that Dust whereon they go
That serve him here below,
And therefore might for memory of those
His love there first disclose;
But wretched *Salem* once his love, must now
No voice, nor vision know,

Her stately Piles with all their height and pride
    Now languished and died, 20
And *Bethlems* humble Cotts above them stept
    While all her Seers slept;
Her Cedar, firr, hew'd stones and gold were all
    Polluted through their fall,
And those once sacred mansions were now
    Meer emptiness and show,
This made the Angel call at reeds and thatch,
    Yet where the shepheards watch,
And Gods own lodging (though he could not lack,)
    To be a common *Rack*; 30
No costly pride, no soft-cloath'd luxurie
    In those thin Cels could lie,
Each stirring wind and storm blew through their Cots
    Which never harbour'd plots,
Only Content, and love, and humble joys
    Lived there without all noise,
Perhaps some harmless Cares for the next day
    Did in their bosomes play,
As where to lead their sheep, what silent nook,
    What springs or shades to look, 40
But that was all; And now with gladsome care
    They for the town prepare,
They leave their flock, and in a busie talk
    All towards *Bethlem* walk
To see their souls great shepheard, who was come
    To bring all straglers home,
Where now they find him out, and taught before
    That Lamb of God adore,
That Lamb whose daies great Kings and Prophets wish'd
    And long'd to see, but miss'd. 50
The first light they beheld was bright and gay
    And turn'd their night to day,
But to this later light they saw in him,
    Their day was dark, and dim.

Misery

Lord, bind me up, and let me lye
A Pris'ner to my libertie,
If such a state at all can be
As an Impris'ment serving thee;
The wind, though gather'd in thy fist,
Yet doth it blow stil where it list,
And yet shouldst thou let go thy hold
Those gusts might quarrel and grow bold.
  As waters here, headlong and loose
The lower grounds stil chase, and choose, 10
Where spreading all the way they seek
And search out ev'ry hole, and Creek;
So my spilt thoughts winding from thee
Take the down-rode to vanitie,
Where they all stray and strive, which shal
Find out the first and steepest fal;
I cheer their flow, giving supply
To what's already grown too high,
And having thus perform'd that part
Feed on those vomits of my heart. 20
I break the fence my own hands made
Then lay that trespasse in the shade,
Some fig-leafs stil I do devise
As if thou hadst nor ears, nor Eyes.
Excesse of friends, of words, and wine
Take up my day, while thou dost shine
All unregarded, and thy book
Hath not so much as one poor look.
If thou steal in amidst the mirth
And kindly tel me, *I am Earth*, 30
I shut thee out, and let that slip,
Such Musick spoils good fellowship.
Thus wretched I, and most unkind,
Exclude my dear God from my mind,
Exclude him thence, who of that Cel
Would make a Court, should he there dwel.
He goes, he yields; And troubled sore
His holy spirit grieves therefore,

The mighty God, th' eternal King
Doth grieve for Dust, and Dust doth sing. 40
But I go on, haste to Devest
My self of reason, till opprest
And buried in my surfeits I
Prove my own shame and miserie.
Next day I call and cry for thee
Who shouldst not then come neer to me,
But now it is thy servants pleasure
Thou must (and dost) give him his measure.
Thou dost, thou com'st, and in a showr
Of healing sweets thy self dost powr 50
Into my wounds, and now thy grace
(I know it wel,) fils all the place;
I sit with thee by this new light,
And for that hour th'art my delight,
No man can more the world despise
Or thy great mercies better prize.
I School my Eys, and strictly dwel
Within the Circle of my Cel,
That Calm and silence are my Joys
Which to thy peace are but meer noise. 60
At length I feel my head to ake,
My fingers Itch, and burn to take
Some new Imployment, I begin
To swel and fome and fret within.
'*The Age*, *the present times are not*
'*To snudge in*, *and embrace a Cot*,
'*Action and bloud now get the game*,
'*Disdein treads on the peaceful name*,
'*Who sits at home too bears a loade*
'*Greater than those that gad abroad*. 70
Thus do I make thy gifts giv'n me
The only quarrellers with thee,
I'd loose those knots thy hands did tie,
Then would go travel, fight or die.
Thousands of wild and waste Infusions
Like waves beat on my resolutions,
As flames about their fuel run
And work, and wind til all be done,

So my fierce soul bustles about
And never rests til all be out. 80
Thus wilded by a peevish heart
Which in thy musick bears no part
I storm at thee, calling my peace
A Lethargy, and meer disease,
Nay, those bright beams shot from thy eys
To calm me in these mutinies
I stile meer tempers, which take place
At some set times, but are thy grace.
  Such is mans life, and such is mine
The worst of men, and yet stil thine, 90
Stil thine thou know'st, and if not so
Then give me over to my foe.
Yet since as easie 'tis for thee
To make man good, as bid him be,
And with one glaunce (could he that gain,)
To look him out of all his pain,
O send me from thy holy hil
So much of strength, as may fulfil
All thy delight (what e'r they be)
And sacred Institutes in me; 100
Open my rockie heart, and fil
It with obedience to thy wil,
Then seal it up, that as none see,
So none may enter there but thee.
  O hear my God! hear him, whose bloud
Speaks more and better for my good!
O let my Crie come to thy throne!
My crie not pour'd with tears alone,
(For tears alone are often foul)
But with the bloud of all my soul, 110
With spirit-sighs, and earnest grones,
Faithful and most repenting mones,
With these I crie, and crying pine
Till thou both mend and make me thine.

The Sap

Come sapless Blossom, creep not stil on Earth
    Forgetting thy first birth;
'Tis not from dust, or if so, why dost thou
    Thus cal and thirst for dew?
It tends not thither, if it doth, why then
    This growth and stretch for heav'n?
Thy root sucks but diseases, worms there seat
    And claim it for their meat.
Who plac'd thee here, did something then Infuse
    Which now can tel thee news. 10
There is beyond the Stars an hil of myrrh
    From which some drops fal here,
On it the Prince of *Salem* sits, who deals
    To thee thy secret meals,
There is thy Country, and he is the way
    And hath withal the key.
Yet liv'd he here sometimes, and bore for thee
    A world of miserie,
For thee, who in the first mans loyns didst fal
    From that hil to this vale, 20
And had not he so done, it is most true
    Two deaths had bin thy due;
But going hence, and knowing wel what woes
    Might his friends discompose,
To shew what strange love he had to our good
    He gave his sacred bloud
By wil our sap, and Cordial; now in this
    Lies such a heav'n of bliss,
That, who but truly tasts it, no decay
    Can touch him any way, 30
Such secret life, and vertue in it lies
    It wil exalt and rise
And actuate such spirits as are shed
    Or ready to be dead,
And bring new too. Get then this sap, and get
    Good store of it, but let
The vessel where you put it be for sure
    To all your pow'r most pure;

There is at all times (though shut up) in you
  A powerful, rare dew, 40
Which only grief and love extract; with this
  Be sure, and never miss,
To wash your vessel wel: Then humbly take
  This balm for souls that ake,
And one who drank it thus, assures that you
  Shal find a Joy so true,
Such perfect Ease, and such a lively sense
  Of grace against all sins,
That you'l Confess the Comfort such, as even
  Brings to, and comes from Heaven. 50

Mount of Olives

When first I saw true beauty, and thy Joys
Active as light, and calm without all noise
Shin'd on my soul, I felt through all my powr's
Such a rich air of sweets, as Evening showrs
Fand by a gentle gale Convey and breath
On some parch'd bank, crown'd with a flowrie
  wreath;
Odors, and Myrrh, and balm in one rich floud
O'r-ran my heart, and spirited my bloud,
My thoughts did swim in Comforts, and mine eie 10
Confest, *The world did only paint and lie.*
And where before I did no safe Course steer
But wander'd under tempests all the year,
Went bleak and bare in body as in mind,
And was blow'n through by ev'ry storm and wind,
I am so warm'd now by this glance on me,
That, midst all storms I feel a Ray of thee;
So have I known some beauteous *Paisage* rise
In suddain flowres and arbours to my Eies,
And in the depth and dead of winter bring 20
To my Cold thoughts a lively sense of spring.
  Thus fed by thee, who dost all beings nourish,
My wither'd leafs again look green and flourish,

I shine and shelter underneath thy wing
Where sick with love I strive thy name to sing,
Thy glorious name! which grant I may so do
That these may be thy *Praise*, and my *Joy* too.

Man

Weighing the stedfastness and state
Of some mean things which here below reside,
Where birds like watchful Clocks the noiseless date
And Intercourse of times divide,
Where Bees at night get home and hive, and flowrs
Early, aswel as late,
Rise with the Sun, and set in the same bowrs;

2

I would (said I) my God would give
The staidness of these things to man! for these
To his divine appointments ever cleave, 10
And no new business breaks their peace;
The birds nor sow, nor reap, yet sup and dine,
The flowres without clothes live,
Yet *Solomon* was never drest so fine.

3

Man hath stil either toyes, or Care,
He hath no root, nor to one place is ty'd,
But ever restless and Irregular
About this Earth doth run and ride,
He knows he hath a home, but scarce knows where,
He sayes it is so far 20
That he hath quite forgot how to go there.

4

He knocks at all doors, strays and roams,
Nay hath not so much wit as some stones have
Which in the darkest nights point to their homes,
By some hid sense their Maker gave;
Man is the shuttle, to whose winding quest
And passage through these looms
God order'd motion, but ordain'd no rest.

¶

I walkt the other day (to spend my hour)
Into a field
Where I sometimes had seen the soil to yield
A gallant flowre,
But Winter now had ruffled all the bowre
And curious store
I knew there heretofore.

2

Yet I whose search lov'd not to peep and peer
I'th' face of things
Thought with my self, there might be other springs 10
Besides this here
Which, like cold friends, sees us but once a year,
And so the flowre
Might have some other bowre.

3

Then taking up what I could neerest spie
I digg'd about
That place where I had seen him to grow out,
And by and by
I saw the warm Recluse alone to lie
Where fresh and green 20
He lived of us unseen.

4

Many a question Intricate and rare
Did I there strow,
But all I could extort was, that he now
Did there repair
Such losses as befel him in this air
And would e'r long
Come forth most fair and young.

5

This past, I threw the Clothes quite o'r his head,
And stung with fear 30
Of my own frailty dropt down many a tear
Upon his bed,

Then sighing whisper'd, *Happy are the dead!*
What peace doth now
Rock him asleep below?

6

And yet, how few believe such doctrine springs
From a poor root
Which all the Winter sleeps here under foot
And hath no wings
To raise it to the truth and light of things, 40
But is stil trod
By ev'ry wandring clod.

7

O thou! whose spirit did at first inflame
And warm the dead,
And by a sacred Incubation fed
With life this frame
Which once had neither being, forme, nor name,
Grant I may so
Thy steps track here below,

8

That in these Masques and shadows I may see 50
Thy sacred way,
And by those hid ascents climb to that day
Which breaks from thee
Who art in all things, though invisibly;
Shew me thy peace,
Thy mercy, love, and ease,

9

And from this Care, where dreams and sorrows raign
Lead me above
Where Light, Joy, Leisure, and true Comforts move
Without all pain, 60
There, hid in thee, shew me his life again
At whose dumbe urn
Thus all the year I mourn.

Begging

King of Mercy, King of Love,
In whom I live, in whom I move,
Perfect what thou hast begun,
Let no night put out this Sun;
Grant I may, my chief desire!
Long for thee, to thee aspire,
Let my youth, my bloom of dayes
Be my Comfort, and thy praise,
That hereafter, when I look
O'r the sullyed, sinful book, 10
I may find thy hand therein
Wiping out my shame, and sin.
O it is thy only Art
To reduce a stubborn heart,
And since thine is victorie,
Strong holds should belong to thee;
Lord then take it, leave it not
Unto my dispose or lot,
But since I would not have it mine,
O my God, let it be thine! 20

Jude ver. 24, 25

Now unto him that is able to keep us from falling, and to present us faultless before the presence of his glory with exceeding joy,

To the only wise God, our Saviour, be glory, and majesty, Dominion and power, now and ever, Amen.

FINIS

Silex Scintillans, &c.

Ascension-day

Lord Jesus! with what sweetness and delights,
Sure, holy hopes, high joys and quickning flights
Dost thou feed thine! O thou! the hand that lifts
To him, who gives all good and perfect gifts.
Thy glorious, bright Ascension (though remov'd
So many Ages from me) is so prov'd
And by thy Spirit seal'd to me, that I
Feel me a sharer in thy victory.
I soar and rise
Up to the skies, 10
Leaving the world their day,
And in my flight,
For the true light
Go seeking all the way;
I greet thy Sepulchre, salute thy Grave,
That blest inclosure, where the Angels gave
The first glad tidings of thy early light,
And resurrection from the earth and night.
I see that morning in thy *Converts tears,
Fresh as the dew, which but this dawning wears? 20
I smell her spices, and her ointment yields,
As rich a scent as the now Primros'd-fields:
The Day-star smiles, and light with the deceast,
Now shines in all the Chambers of the East.
What stirs, what posting intercourse and mirth
Of Saints and Angels glorifie the earth?
What sighs, what whispers, busie stops and stays;
Private and holy talk fill all the ways?
They pass as at the last great day, and run
In their white robes to seek the risen Sun; 30
I see them, hear them, mark their haste, and move
Amongst them, with them, wing'd with faith and love.

* *St. Mary Magdalene.*

Thy forty days more secret commerce here,
After thy death and Funeral, so clear
And indisputable, shews to my sight
As the Sun doth, which to those days gave light.
I walk the fields of *Bethani* which shine
All now as fresh as *Eden*, and as fine.
Such was the bright world, on the first seventh day,
Before man brought forth sin, and sin decay; 40
When like a Virgin clad in *Flowers* and *green*
The pure earth sat, and the fair woods had seen
No frost, but flourish'd in that youthful vest,
With which their great Creator had them drest:
When Heav'n above them shin'd like molten glass,
While all the Planets did unclouded pass;
And Springs, like dissolv'd Pearls their Streams did pour
Ne'r marr'd with floods, nor anger'd with a showre.
With these fair thoughts I move in this fair place,
And the last steps of my milde Master trace; 50
I see him leading out his chosen Train,
All sad with tears, which like warm Summer-rain
In silent drops steal from their holy eyes,
Fix'd lately on the Cross, now on the skies.
And now (eternal Jesus!) thou dost heave
Thy blessed hands to bless, these thou dost leave;
The cloud doth now receive thee, and their sight
Having lost thee, behold two men in white!
Two and no more: *what two attest, is true*,
Was thine own answer to the stubborn Jew. 60
Come then thou faithful witness! come dear Lord
Upon the Clouds again to judge this world!

Ascension-Hymn

Dust and clay
Mans antient wear!
Here you must stay,
But I elsewhere;
Souls sojourn here, but may not rest;
Who will ascend, must be undrest.

And yet some
That know to die
Before death come,
Walk to the skie 10
Even in this life; but all such can
Leave behinde them the old Man.

If a star
Should leave the Sphære,
She must first mar
Her flaming wear,
And after fall, for in her dress
Of glory, she cannot transgress.

Man of old
Within the line 20
Of *Eden* could
Like the Sun shine
All naked, innocent and bright,
And intimate with Heav'n, as light;

But since he
That brightness soil'd,
His garments be
All dark and spoil'd,
And here are left as nothing worth,
Till the Refiners fire breaks forth. 30

Then comes he!
Whose mighty light
Made his cloathes be
Like Heav'n, all bright;
The Fuller, whose pure blood did flow
To make stain'd man more white then snow.

Hee alone
And none else can
Bring bone to bone
And rebuild man, 40
And by his all subduing might
Make clay ascend more quick then light.

¶

They are all gone into the world of light!
And I alone sit lingring here;
Their very memory is fair and bright,
And my sad thoughts doth clear.

It glows and glitters in my cloudy brest
Like stars upon some gloomy grove,
Or those faint beams in which this hill is drest,
After the Sun's remove.

I see them walking in an Air of glory,
Whose light doth trample on my days: 10
My days, which are at best but dull and hoary,
Meer glimering and decays.

O holy hope! and high humility,
High as the Heavens above!
These are your walks, and you have shew'd them me
To kindle my cold love,

Dear, beauteous death! the Jewel of the Just,
Shining nowhere, but in the dark;
What mysteries do lie beyond thy dust;
Could man outlook that mark! 20

He that hath found some fledg'd birds nest, may know
At first sight, if the bird be flown;
But what fair Well, or Grove he sings in now,
That is to him unknown.

And yet, as Angels in some brighter dreams
Call to the soul, when man doth sleep:
So some strange thoughts transcend our wonted theams,
And into glory peep.

If a star were confin'd into a Tomb
Her captive flames must needs burn there; 30
But when the hand that lockt her up, gives room,
She'l shine through all the sphære.

O Father of eternal life, and all
    Created glories under thee!
Resume thy spirit from this world of thrall
    Into true liberty.

Either disperse these mists, which blot and fill
    My perspective (still) as they pass,
Or else remove me hence unto that hill,
    Where I shall need no glass. 40

White Sunday

Wellcome white day! a thousand Suns,
Though seen at once, were black to thee;
For after their light, darkness comes,
But thine shines to eternity.

Those flames which on the Apostles rush'd
At this great feast, and in a tyre
Of cloven Tongues their heads all brush'd,
And crown'd them with Prophetic fire:

Can these new lights be like to those,
These lights of Serpents like the Dove? 10
Thou hadst no *gall*, ev'n for thy foes,
And thy two wings were *Grief* and *Love*.

Though then some boast that fire each day,
And on Christs coat pin all their shreds;
Not sparing openly to say,
His candle shines upon their heads:

Yet while some rays of that great light
Shine here below within thy Book,
They never shall so blinde my sight
But I will know which way to look. 20

For though thou doest that great light lock,
And by this lesser commerce keep:
Yet by these glances of the flock
I can discern Wolves from the Sheep.

Not, but that I have wishes too,
And pray, *These last may be as first,*
Or better; but thou long ago
Hast said, *These last should be the worst.*

Besides, thy method with thy own,
Thy own dear people pens our times, 30
Our stories are in theirs set down
And penalties spread to our Crimes.

Again, if worst and worst implies
A State, that no redress admits,
Then from thy Cross unto these days
The *rule* without *Exception* fits.

And yet, as in nights gloomy page
One silent star may interline:
So in this last and lewdest age,
Thy antient love on some may shine. 40

For, though we hourly breath decays,
And our best *note* and highest *ease*
Is but meer changing of the *keys*,
And a *Consumption* that doth please;

Yet thou the great eternal Rock
Whose height above all ages shines,
Art still the same, and canst unlock
Thy waters to a soul that pines.

Since then thou art the same this day
And ever, as thou wert of old, 50
And nothing doth thy love allay
But our hearts dead and sinful cold:

As thou long since wert pleas'd to buy
Our drown'd estate, taking the Curse
Upon thy self, so to destroy
The knots we tyed upon thy purse,

So let thy grace now make the way
Even for thy love; for by that means
We, who are nothing but foul clay,
Shal be fine gold, which thou didst cleanse. 60

O come! refine us with thy fire!
Refine us! we are at a loss.
Let not thy stars for *Balaams* hire
Dissolve into the common dross!

The Proffer

Be still black Parasites,
Flutter no more;
Were it still winter, as it was before,
You'd make no flights;
But now the dew and Sun have warm'd my bowres,
You flie and flock to suck the flowers.

But you would honey make:
These buds will wither,
And what you now extract, in harder weather
Will serve to take; 10
Wise husbands will (you say) there wants prevent,
Who do not so, too late repent.

O poys'nous, subtile fowls!
The flyes of hell
That buz in every ear, and blow on souls
Until they smell
And rot, descend not here, nor think to stay,
I've read, who 'twas, drove you away.

Think you these longing eyes,
Though sick and spent, 20
And almost famish'd, ever will consent
To leave those skies,
That glass of souls and spirits, where well drest
They shine in white (like stars) and rest.

Shall my short hour, my inch,
My one poor sand,
And crum of life, now ready to disband
Revolt and flinch,
And having born the burthen all the day,
Now cast at night my Crown away? 30

No, No; I am not he,
Go seek elsewhere.
I skill not your fine tinsel, and false hair,
Your Sorcery
And smooth seducements: I'le not stuff my story
With your Commonwealth and glory.

There are, that will sow tares
And scatter death
Amongst the quick, selling their souls and breath
For any wares; 40
But when thy Master comes, they'l finde and see
There's a reward for them and thee.

Then keep the antient way!
Spit out their phlegm
And fill thy brest with home; think on thy dream:
A calm, bright day!
A Land of flowers and spices! the word given,
If these be fair, O what is Heaven!

Cock-crowing

Father of lights! what Sunnie seed,
What glance of day hast thou confin'd
Into this bird? To all the breed
This busie Ray thou hast assign'd;
Their magnetisme works all night,
And dreams of Paradise and light.

Their eyes watch for the morning hue,
Their little grain expelling night
So shines and sings, as if it knew
The path unto the house of light. 10
It seems their candle, howe'r done,
Was tinn'd and lighted at the sunne.

If such a tincture, such a touch,
So firm a longing can impowre
Shall thy own image think it much
To watch for thy appearing hour?
If a meer blast so fill the sail,
Shall not the breath of God prevail?

O thou immortall light and heat!
Whose hand so shines through all this frame, 20
That by the beauty of the seat,
We plainly see, who made the same.
Seeing thy seed abides in me,
Dwell thou in it, and I in thee.

To sleep without thee, is to die;
Yea, 'tis a death partakes of hell:
For where thou dost not close the eye
It never opens, I can tell.
In such a dark, Ægyptian border,
The shades of death dwell and disorder. 30

If joyes, and hopes, and earnest throws,
And hearts, whose Pulse beats still for light
Are given to birds; who, but thee, knows
A love-sick souls exalted flight?
Can souls be track'd by any eye
But his, who gave them wings to flie?

Onely this Veyle which thou hast broke,
And must be broken yet in me,
This veyle, I say, is all the cloke
And cloud which shadows thee from me. 40
This veyle thy full-ey'd love denies,
And onely gleams and fractions spies.

O take it off! make no delay,
But brush me with thy light, that I
May shine unto a perfect day,
And warme me at thy glorious Eye!
O take it off! or till it flee,
Though with no Lilie, stay with me!

The Starre

What ever 'tis, whose beauty here below
Attracts thee thus & makes thee stream & flow,
And wind and curle, and wink and smile,
Shifting thy gate and guile:

Though thy close commerce nought at all imbarrs
My present search, for Eagles eye not starrs,
And still the lesser by the best
And highest good is blest:

Yet, seeing all things that subsist and be,
Have their Commissions from Divinitie, 10
And teach us duty, I will see
What man may learn from thee.

First, I am sure, the Subject so respected
Is well disposed, for bodies once infected,
Deprav'd or dead, can have with thee
No hold, nor sympathie.

Next, there's in it a restless, pure desire
And longing for thy bright and vitall fire,
Desire that never will be quench'd,
Nor can be writh'd, nor wrench'd. 20

These are the Magnets which so strongly move
And work all night upon thy light and love,
As beauteous shapes, we know not why,
Command and guide the eye.

For where desire, celestiall, pure desire
Hath taken root, and grows, and doth not tire,
There God a Commerce states, and sheds
His Secret on their heads.

This is the Heart he craves; and who so will
But give it him, and grudge not; he shall feel 30
That God is true, as herbs unseen
Put on their youth and green.

The Palm-tree

Deare friend sit down, and bear awhile this shade
As I have yours long since; This Plant, you see
So prest and bow'd, before sin did degrade
Both you and it, had equall liberty

With other trees: but now shut from the breath
And air of *Eden*, like a male-content
It thrives no where. This makes these weights (like death
And sin) hang at him; for the more he's bent

The more he grows. Celestial natures still
Aspire for home; This *Solomon* of old 10
By flowers and carvings and mysterious skill
Of Wings, and Cherubims, and Palms foretold.

This is the life which hid above with Christ
In God, doth always (hidden) multiply,
And spring, and grow, a tree ne'r to be pric'd,
A Tree, whose fruit is immortality.

Here Spirits that have run their race and fought
And won the fight, and have not fear'd the frowns
Nor lov'd the smiles of greatness, but have wrought
Their masters will, meet to receive their Crowns. 20

Here is the patience of the Saints: this Tree
Is water'd by their tears, as flowers are fed
With dew by night; but One you cannot see
Sits here and numbers all the tears they shed.

Here is their faith too, which if you will keep
When we two part, I will a journey make
To pluck a Garland hence, while you do sleep
And weave it for your head against you wake.

Joy

Be dumb course measures, jar no more; to me
There is no discord, but your harmony.
False, jugling sounds; a grone well drest, where care
Moves in disguise, and sighs afflict the air:
Sorrows in white; griefs tun'd; a sugerd Dosis
Of Wormwood, and a Deaths-head crown'd with Roses.
He weighs not your forc'd accents, who can have
A lesson plaid him by a winde or wave.

Such numbers tell their days, whose spirits be
Lull'd by those Charmers to a Lethargy. 10
But as for thee, whose faults long since require
More eyes then stars; whose breath could it aspire
To equal winds: would prove too short: Thou hast
Another mirth, a mirth though overcast
With clouds and rain, yet full as calm and fine
As those *clear heights* which above tempests shine.
Therefore while the various showers
Kill and cure the tender flowers,
While the winds refresh the year
Now with clouds, now making clear, 20
Be sure under pains of death
To ply both thine eyes and breath.
As leafs in Bowers
Whisper their hours,
And Hermit-wells
Drop in their Cells:
So in sighs and unseen tears
Pass thy solitary years,
And going hence, leave written on some Tree,
Sighs make joy sure, *and shaking fastens thee*. 30

The Favour

O thy bright looks! thy glance of love
Shown, & but shown me from above!
Rare looks! that can dispense such joy
As without wooing wins the coy.
And makes him mourn, and pine and dye
Like a starv'd Eaglet, for thine eye.
Some kinde herbs here, though low & far,
Watch for, and know their loving star.
O let no star compare with thee!
Nor any herb out-duty me! 10
So shall my nights and mornings be
Thy time to shine, and mine to see.

The Garland

Thou, who dost flow and flourish here below,
To whom a falling star and nine dayes glory,
Or some frail beauty makes the bravest shew,
Hark, and make use of this ensuing story.

When first my youthfull, sinfull age
  Grew master of my wayes,
Appointing errour for my Page,
  And darknesse for my dayes;
I flung away, and with full crie
  Of wild affections, rid 10
In post for pleasures, bent to trie
  All gamesters that would bid.
I played with fire, did counsell spurn,
  Made life my common stake;
But never thought that fire would burn,
  Or that a soul could ake.
Glorious deceptions, gilded mists,
  False joyes, phantastick flights,
Peeces of sackcloth with silk-lists,
  These were my prime delights. 20
I sought choice bowres, haunted the spring,
  Cull'd flowres and made me posies:
Gave my fond humours their full wing,
  And crown'd my head with Roses.
But at the height of this Careire
  I met with a dead man,
Who noting well my vain Abear,
  Thus unto me began:
Desist fond fool, be not undone,
  What thou hast cut to day 30
Will fade at night, and with this Sun
  Quite vanish and decay.

Flowres gather'd in this world, die here; if thou
Wouldst have a wreath that fades not, let them grow,
And grow for thee; who spares them here, shall find
A Garland, where comes neither rain, nor wind.

Love-sick

Iesus, my life! how shall I truly love thee?
O that thy Spirit would so strongly move me,
That thou wert pleas'd to shed thy grace so farr
As to make man all pure love, flesh a star!
A star that would ne'r set, but ever rise,
So rise and run, as to out-run these skies,
These narrow skies (narrow to me) that barre,
So barre me in, that I am still at warre,
At constant warre with them. O come and rend,
Or bow the heavens! Lord bow them and descend, 10
And at thy presence make these mountains flow,
These mountains of cold Ice in me! Thou art
Refining fire, O then refine my heart,
My foul, foul heart! Thou art immortall heat,
Heat motion gives; Then warm it, till it beat,
So beat for thee, till thou in mercy hear,
So hear that thou must open: open to
A sinfull wretch, A wretch that caus'd thy woe,
Thy woe, who caus'd his weal; so far his weal
That thou forgott'st thine own, for thou didst seal 20
Mine with thy blood, thy blood which makes thee mine,
Mine ever, ever; And me ever thine.

Trinity-Sunday

O holy, blessed, glorious three,
Eternall witnesses that be
In heaven, One God in trinitie!

As here on earth (when men with-stood,)
The Spirit, Water, and the Blood,
Made my Lords Incarnation good:

So let the *Anty-types* in me
Elected, bought and seal'd for free,
Be own'd, sav'd, *Sainted* by you three!

Psalme 104

Up, O my soul, and blesse the Lord. O God,
My God, how great, how very great art thou!
Honour and majesty have their abode
With thee, and crown thy brow.

Thou cloath'st thy self with light, as with a robe,
And the high, glorious heav'ns thy mighty hand
Doth spread like curtains round about this globe
Of Air, and Sea, and Land.

The beams of thy bright Chambers thou dost lay
In the deep waters, which no eye can find; 10
The clouds thy chariots are, and thy path-way
The wings of the swift wind.

In thy celestiall, gladsome messages
Dispatch'd to holy souls, sick with desire
And love of thee, each willing Angel is
Thy minister in fire.

Thy arm unmoveable for ever laid
And founded the firm earth; then with the deep
As with a vail thou hidst it, thy floods plaid
Above the mountains steep. 20

At thy rebuke they fled, at the known voice
Of their Lords thunder they retir'd apace:
Some up the mountains past by secret ways,
Some downwards to their place.

For thou to them a bound hast set, a bound
Which (though but sand) keeps in and curbs whole seas:
There all their fury, fome and hideous sound
Must languish and decrease.

And as thy care bounds these, so thy rich love
Doth broach the earth, and lesser brooks lets forth, 30
Which run from hills to valleys, and improve
Their pleasure and their worth.

These to the beasts of every field give drink;
 There the wilde asses swallow the cool spring:
And birds amongst the branches on their brink
 Their dwellings have and sing.

Thou from thy upper Springs above, from those
 Chambers of rain, where Heav'ns large bottles lie,
Doest water the parch'd hills, whose breaches close
 Heal'd by the showers from high. 40

Grass for the cattel, and herbs for mans use
 Thou mak'st to grow; these (blest by thee) the earth
Brings forth, with wine, oyl, bread: All which infuse
 To mans heart strength and mirth.

Thou giv'st the trees their greenness, ev'n to those
 Cedars in *Lebanon*, in whose thick boughs
The birds their nests build; though the Stork doth choose
 The fir-trees for her house.

To the wilde goats the high hills serve for folds,
 The rocks give Conies a retyring place: 50
Above them the cool Moon her known course holds,
 And the Sun runs his race.

Thou makest darkness, and then comes the night;
 In whose thick shades and silence each wilde beast
Creeps forth, and pinch'd for food, with scent and sight
 Hunts in an eager quest.

The Lyons whelps impatient of delay
 Roar in the covert of the woods, and seek
Their meat from thee, who doest appoint the prey
 And feed'st them all the week. 60

This past, the Sun shines on the earth, and they
 Retire into their dens; Man goes abroad
Unto his work, and at the close of day
 Returns home with his load.

O Lord my God, how many and how rare
 Are thy great works! In wisdom hast thou made
Them all, and this the earth, and every blade
 Of grass, we tread, declare.

So doth the deep and wide sea, wherein are
Innumerable, creeping things both small 70
And great: there ships go, and the shipmens fear
The comely spacious Whale.

These all upon thee wait, that thou maist feed
Them in due season: what thou giv'st, they take;
Thy bounteous open hand helps them at need,
And plenteous meals they make.

When thou doest hide thy face (thy face which keeps
All things in being) they consume and mourn:
When thou with-draw'st their breath, their vigour sleeps,
And they to dust return. 80

Thou send'st thy spirit forth, and they revive,
The frozen earths dead face thou dost renew.
Thus thou thy glory through the world dost drive,
And to thy works art true.

Thine eyes behold the earth, and the whole stage
Is mov'd and trembles, the hills melt & smoke
With thy least touch: lightnings and winds that rage
At thy rebuke are broke.

Therefore as long as thou wilt give me breath
I will in songs to thy great name imploy 90
That gift of thine, and to my day of death
Thou shalt be all my joy.

Ile *spice* my thoughts with thee, and from thy word
Gather true comforts; but the wicked liver
Shall be consum'd. O my soul, bless thy Lord!
Yea, blesse thou him for ever!

The Bird

Hither thou com'st: the busie wind all night
Blew through thy lodging, where thy own warm wing
Thy pillow was. Many a sullen storm
(For which course man seems much the fitter born,)
Rain'd on thy bed
And harmless head.

And now as fresh and chearful as the light
Thy little heart in early hymns doth sing
Unto that *Providence*, whose unseen arm
Curb'd them, and cloath'd thee well and warm. 10
All things that be, praise him; and had
Their lesson taught them, when first made.

So hills and valleys into singing break,
And though poor stones have neither speech nor tongue,
While active winds and streams both run and speak,
Yet stones are deep in admiration.
Thus Praise and Prayer here beneath the Sun
Make lesser mornings, when the great are done.

For each inclosed Spirit is a star
Inlightning his own little sphære, 20
Whose light, though fetcht and borrowed from far,
Both mornings makes, and evenings there.

But as these Birds of light make a land glad,
Chirping their solemn Matins on each tree:
So in the shades of night some dark fowls be,
Whose heavy notes make all that hear them, sad.

The Turtle then in Palm-trees mourns,
While Owls and Satyrs howl;
The pleasant Land to brimstone turns
And all her streams grow foul. 30

Brightness and mirth, and love and faith, all flye,
Till the Day-spring breaks forth again from high.

The Timber

Sure thou didst flourish once! and many Springs,
Many bright mornings, much dew, many showers
Past ore thy head: many light *Hearts* and *Wings*
Which now are dead, lodg'd in thy living bowers.

And still a new succession sings and flies;
Fresh Groves grow up, and their green branches shoot
Towards the old and still enduring skies,
While the low *Violet* thrives at their root.

But thou beneath the sad and heavy *Line*
Of death, dost waste all senseless, cold and dark; 10
Where not so much as dreams of light may shine,
Nor any thought of greenness, leaf or bark.

And yet (as if some deep hate and dissent,
Bred in thy growth betwixt high winds and thee,
Were still alive) thou dost great storms resent
Before they come, and know'st how near they be.

Else all at rest thou lyest, and the fierce breath
Of tempests can no more disturb thy ease;
But this thy strange resentment after death
Means onely those, who broke (in life) thy peace. 20

So murthered man, when lovely life is done,
And his blood freez'd, keeps in the Center still
Some secret sense, which makes the dead blood run
At his approach, that did the body kill.

And is there any murth'rer worse then sin?
Or any storms more foul then a lewd life?
Or what *Resentient* can work more within,
Then true remorse, when with past sins at strife?

He that hath left lifes vain joys and vain care,
And truly hates to be detain'd on earth, 30
Hath got an house where many mansions are,
And keeps his soul unto eternal mirth.

But though thus dead unto the world, and ceas'd
From sin, he walks a narrow, private way;
Yet grief and old wounds make him sore displeas'd,
And all his life a rainy, weeping day.

For though he should forsake the world, and live
As meer a stranger, as men long since dead;
Yet joy it self will make a right soul grieve
To think, he should be so long vainly lead. 40

But as shades set off light, so tears and grief
(Though of themselves but a sad blubber'd story)
By shewing the sin great, shew the relief
Far greater, and so speak my Saviors glory.

If my way lies through deserts and wilde woods;
Where all the Land with scorching heat is curst;
Better, the pools should flow with rain and floods
To fill my bottle, then I die with thirst.

Blest showers they are, and streams sent from above
Begetting *Virgins* where they use to flow; 50
And trees of life no other waters love,
These upper springs and none else make them grow.

But these chaste fountains flow not till we dye;
Some drops may fall before, but a clear spring
And ever running, till we leave to fling
Dirt in her way, will keep above the skie.

Rom. Cap. 6. ver. 7

He that is dead, is freed from sin.

The Jews

When the fair year
Of your deliverer comes,
And that long frost which now benums
Your hearts shall thaw; when Angels here
Shall yet to man appear,
And familiarly confer
Beneath the Oke and Juniper:
When the bright *Dove*
Which now these many, many Springs
Hath kept above, 10
Shall with spread wings
Descend, and living waters flow
To make drie dust, and dead trees grow;

O then that I
Might live, and see the Olive bear
Her proper branches! which now lie
Scattered each where,
And without root and sap decay
Cast by the husband-man away.

And sure it is not far! 20
For as your fast and foul decays
Forerunning the bright morning-star,
Did sadly note his healing rayes
Would shine elsewhere, since you were blind,
And would be cross, when God was kinde:
So by all signs
Our fulness too is now come in,
And the same Sun which here declines
And sets, will few hours hence begin
To rise on you again, and look 30
Towards old *Mamre* and *Eshcols* brook.
For surely he
Who lov'd the world so, as to give
His onely Son to make it free,
Whose spirit too doth mourn and grieve
To see man lost, will for old love
From your dark hearts this veil remove.

Faith sojourn'd first on earth in you,
You were the dear and chosen stock:
The Arm of God, glorious and true, 40
Was first reveal'd to be your rock.

You were the *eldest* childe, and when
Your stony hearts despised love,
The *youngest*, ev'n the Gentiles then
Were chear'd, your jealousie to move.

Thus, Righteous Father! doest thou deal
With Brutish men; Thy gifts go round
By turns, and timely, and so heal
The lost Son by the newly found.

Begging

O, do not go! thou know'st, I'le dye!
My *Spring* and *Fall* are in thy book!
Or, if thou goest, do not deny
To lend me, though from far, one look!

My sins long since have made thee strange,
A very stranger unto me;
No morning-meetings since this change,
Nor evening-walks have I with thee.

Why is my God thus slow and cold,
When I am most, most sick and sad? 10
Well fare those blessed days of old
When thou didst hear the *weeping Lad*!

O do not thou do as I did,
Do not despise a Love-sick heart!
What though some clouds defiance bid
Thy Sun must shine in every part.

Though I have spoil'd, O spoil not thou!
Hate not thine own dear gift and token!
Poor birds sing best, and prettiest show,
When their nest is faln and broken. 20

Dear Lord! restore thy ancient peace,
Thy quikning friendship, mans bright wealth!
And if thou wilt not give me ease
From sicknesse, give my spirit health!

Palm-Sunday

Come, drop your branches, strow the way
Plants of the day!
Whom sufferings make most green and gay.

The King of grief, the man of sorrow
Weeping still, like the wet morrow,
Your shades and freshness comes to borrow.

Put on, put on your best array;
Let the joy'd rode make holy-day,
And flowers that into fields do stray,
Or secret groves, keep the high-way. 10

Trees, flowers & herbs; birds, beasts & stones,
That since man fell, expect with groans
To see the lamb, which all at once,
Lift up your heads and leave your moans!
    For here comes he
    Whose death will be
Mans life, and your full liberty.

Hark! how the children shril and high
    Hosanna cry,
Their joys provoke the distant skie, 20
Where thrones and Seraphins reply,
And their own Angels shine and sing
    In a bright ring:
    Such yong, sweet mirth
    Makes heaven and earth
Joyn in a joyful Symphony,

The harmless, yong and happy Ass,
Seen long before *this came to pass,
Is in these joys an high partaker
Ordain'd, and made to bear his Maker. 30

Dear feast of Palms, of Flowers and Dew!
Whose fruitful dawn sheds hopes and lights;
Thy bright solemnities did shew,
The third glad day through two sad nights.

I'le get me up before the Sun,
I'le cut me boughs off many a tree,
And all alone full early run
To gather flowers to wellcome thee.

Then like the *Palm*, though wrong, I'le bear,
I will be still a childe, still meek 40
As the poor Ass, which the proud jear,
And onely my dear *Jesus* seek.

If I lose all, and must endure
The proverb'd griefs of holy *Job*,
I care not, so I may secure
But one *green Branch* and a *white robe*.

* *Zechariah*, *chap*. 9. *ver*. 9.

Jesus weeping

S. Luke 19. *ver.* 41

Blessed, unhappy City? dearly lov'd
But still unkinde! art this day nothing mov'd!
    Art senseless still? O can'st thou sleep
    When God himself for thee doth weep!
    Stiff-necked *Jews*! your fathers breed
    That serv'd the calf, not *Abr'ams* seed,
    Had not the Babes *Hosanna* cryed,
    The stones had spoke, what you denyed.

Dear *Jesus* weep on! pour this latter
Soul-quickning rain, this living water   10
    On their dead hearts; but (O my fears!)
    They will drink blood, that despise tears.
    My dear, bright Lord! my Morning-star!
    Shed this live-dew on fields which far
    From hence long for it! shed it there,
    Where the starv'd earth groans for one tear!

This land, though with thy hearts blest extract fed,
Will nothing yield but thorns to wound thy head.

The Daughter of *Herodias*

St. Matth. chap. 14. *ver.* 6. *&c.*

Vain, sinful Art! who first did fit
Thy lewd loath'd *Motions* unto *sounds*,
And made grave *Musique* like wilde *wit*
Erre in loose airs beyond her bounds?

What fires hath he heap'd on his head?
Since to his sins (as needs it must,)
His *Art* adds still (though he be dead,)
New fresh accounts of blood and lust.

Leave then *yong Sorceress; the *Ice*
Will those coy spirits cast asleep, 10
Which teach thee now to please *his eyes
Who doth thy lothsome mother keep.

But thou hast pleas'd so well, he swears,
And gratifies thy sin with vows:
His shameless lust in publick wears,
And to thy soft arts strongly bows.

Skilful Inchantress and true bred!
Who out of evil can bring forth good?
Thy mothers nets in thee were spred,
She tempts to *Incest*, thou to *blood.* 20

* *Her name was* Salome *; in passing over a frozen river, the ice broke under her, and chopt off her head.*
* Herod Antipas.

Jesus weeping

St. John chap. 11. *ver.* 35

My dear, Almighty Lord! why dost thou weep?
Why dost thou groan and groan again,
And with such deep,
Repeated sighs thy kinde heart pain,
Since the same sacred breath which thus
Doth Mourn for us,
Can make mans dead and scatter'd bones
Unite, and raise up all that dyed, at once?

O holy groans! Groans of the Dove!
O healing tears! the tears of love! 10
Dew of the dead! which makes dust move
And spring, how is't that you so sadly grieve,
Who can relieve?

Should not thy sighs refrain thy store
Of tears, and not provoke to more?
Since two afflictions may not raign
In one at one time, as some feign.

Those blasts, which o'r our heads here stray,
If showers then fall, will showers allay,
As those poor Pilgrims oft have tryed, 20
Who in this windy world abide.

Dear Lord! thou art all grief and love,
But which thou art most, none can prove.
Thou griev'st, man should himself undo,
And lov'st him, though he works thy wo.

'Twas not that vast, almighty measure
Which is requir'd to make up life,
(Though purchas'd with thy hearts dear treasure,)
Did breed this strife
Of grief and pity in thy brest, 30
The throne where peace and power rest:
But 'twas thy love that (without leave,)
Made thine eyes melt, and thy heart heave;
For though death cannot so undo
What thou hast done, (but though man too
Should help to spoil) thou canst restore
All better far then 'twas before;
Yet, thou so full of pity art
(Pity which overflows thy heart!)
That, though the Cure of all mans harm 40
Is nothing to thy glorious arm,
Yet canst not thou that free Cure do,
But thou must sorrow for him too.

Then farewel joys! for while I live,
My business here shall be to grieve:
A grief that shall outshine all joys
For mirth and life, yet without noise.
A grief, whose silent dew shall breed
Lilies and Myrrhe, where the curs'd seed
Did sometimes rule. A grief so bright 50
'Twill make the Land of darkness light;
And while too many sadly roam,
Shall send me (*Swan-like*) singing home.

Psal. 73. ver. 25

Whom have I in heaven but thee? and there is none upon earth, that I desire besides thee.

Providence

Sacred and secret hand!
By whose assisting, swift command
The Angel shewd that holy Well,
Which freed poor *Hagar* from her fears,
And turn'd to smiles the begging tears
Of yong, distressed *Ishmael.*

How in a mystick Cloud
(Which doth thy strange sure mercies shroud)
Doest thou convey man food and money
Unseen by him, till they arrive 10
Just at his mouth, that thankless hive
Which kills thy Bees, and eats thy honey!

If I thy servant be
(Whose service makes ev'n captives free,)
A fish shall all my tribute pay,
The swift-wing'd Raven shall bring me meat,
And I, like Flowers shall still go neat,
As if I knew no moneth but *May.*

I will not fear what man,
With all his plots and power can; 20
Bags that wax old may plundered be,
But none can sequester or let
A state that with the Sun doth set
And comes next morning fresh as he.

Poor birds this doctrine sing,
And herbs which on dry hills do spring
Or in the howling wilderness
Do know thy dewy morning-hours,
And watch all night for mists or showers,
Then drink and praise thy bounteousness 30

May he for ever dye
Who trusts not thee! but wretchedly
Hunts gold and wealth, and will not lend
Thy service, nor his soul one day:
May his Crown, like his hopes, be clay,
And what he saves, may his foes spend!

If all my portion here,
The measure given by thee each year
Were by my causless enemies
Usurp'd; it never should me grieve 40
Who know, how well thou canst relieve,
Whose hands are open as thine eyes.

Great King of love and truth!
Who would'st not hate my froward youth,
And wilt not leave me, when grown old;
Gladly will I, like *Pontick* sheep,
Unto their wormwood-diet keep
Since thou hast made thy Arm my fold.

The Knot

Bright Queen of Heaven! Gods Virgin Spouse
The glad worlds blessed maid!
Whose beauty tyed life to thy house,
And brought us saving ayd.

Thou art the true Loves-knot; by thee
God is made our Allie,
And mans inferior Essence he
With his did dignifie.

For Coalescent by that Band
We are his body grown, 10
Nourished with favors from his hand
Whom for our head we own.

And such a Knot, what arm dares loose,
What life, what death can sever?
Which us in him, and him in us
United keeps for ever.

The Ornament

The lucky world shewd me one day
Her gorgeous Mart and glittering store,
Where with proud haste the rich made way
To buy, the poor came to adore.

Serious they seem'd and bought up all
The latest Modes of pride and lust,
Although the first must surely fall,
And the last is most loathsome dust.

But while each gay, alluring wear
With idle hearts and busie looks 10
They viewd, (for idleness hath there
Laid up all her Archives and books.)

Quite through their proud and pompous file
Blushing, and in meek weeds array'd
With native looks, which knew no guile,
Came the sheep-keeping *Syrian* Maid.

Whom strait the shining Row all fac'd
Forc'd by her artless looks and dress,
While one cryed out, We are disgrac'd
For she is bravest, you confess. 20

St. Mary Magdalen

Dear, beauteous Saint! more white then day,
When in his naked, pure array;
Fresher then morning-flowers which shew
As thou in tears dost, best in dew.
How art thou chang'd! how lively-fair,
Pleasing and innocent an air,
Not tutor'd by thy glass, but free,
Native and pure shines now in thee!
But since thy beauty doth still keep
Bloomy and fresh, why dost thou weep? 10
This dusky state of sighs and tears
Durst not look on those smiling years,
When *Magdal*-castle was thy seat,
Where all was sumptuous, rare and neat.
Why lies this *Hair* despised now
Which once thy care and art did show?
Who then did dress the much lov'd toy,
In *Spires*, *Globes*, angry *Curls* and coy,
Which with skill'd negligence seem'd shed
About thy curious, wilde, yong head? 20

Why is this rich, this *Pistic* Nard
Spilt, and the box quite broke and marr'd?
What pretty sullenness did hast
Thy easie hands to do this waste?
Why art thou humbled thus, and low
As earth, thy lovely head dost bow?
Dear *Soul*! thou knew'st, flowers here on earth
At their Lords foot-stool have their birth;
Therefore thy wither'd self in haste
Beneath his blest feet thou didst cast, 30
That at the root of this green tree
Thy great decays restor'd might be.
Thy curious vanities and rare
Odorous ointments kept with care,
And dearly bought, (when thou didst see
They could not cure, nor comfort thee,)
Like a wise, early Penitent
Thou sadly didst to him present,
Whose interceding, meek and calm
Blood, is the worlds all-healing *Balm*. 40
This, this Divine Restorative
Call'd forth thy tears, which ran in live
And hasty drops, as if they had
(Their Lord so near) sense to be glad.
Learn, *Ladies*, here the faithful cure
Makes beauty lasting, fresh and pure;
Learn *Marys* art of tears, and then
Say, *You have got the day from men.*
Cheap, mighty Art! her Art of love,
Who lov'd much and much more could move; 50
Her Art! whose memory must last
Till truth through all the world be past,
Till his abus'd, despised flame
Return to Heaven, from whence it came,
And send a fire down, that shall bring
Destruction on his ruddy wing.

Her Art! whose pensive, weeping eyes,
Were once sins loose and tempting spies,
But now are fixed stars, whose light
Helps such dark straglers to their sight. 60

Self-boasting *Pharisee*! how blinde
A Judge wert thou, and how unkinde?
It was impossible, that thou
Who wert all false, should'st true grief know;
Is't just to judge her faithful tears
By that foul rheum thy false eye wears?

This Woman (say'st thou) *is a sinner:*
And sate there none such at thy dinner?
Go Leper, go; wash till thy flesh
Comes like a childes, spotless and fresh; 70
He is still leprous, that still paints:
Who Saint themselves, they are no *Saints*.

The Rain-bow

Still yong and fine! but what is still in view
We slight as old and soil'd, though fresh and new.
How bright wert thou, when *Shems* admiring eye
Thy burnisht, flaming *Arch* did first descry!
When *Terah*, *Nahor*, *Haran*, *Abram*, *Lot*,
The youthful worlds gray fathers in one knot,
Did with intentive looks watch every hour
For thy new light, and trembled at each shower!
When thou dost shine darkness looks white and fair,
Storms turn to Musick, clouds to smiles and air: 10
Rain gently spends his honey-drops, and pours
Balm on the cleft earth, milk on grass and flowers.
Bright pledge of peace and Sun-shine! the sure tye
Of thy Lords hand, the *object of his eye.
When I behold thee, though my light be dim,
Distant and low, I can in thine see him,
Who looks upon thee from his glorious throne
And mindes the Covenant 'twixt *All* and *One*.
O foul, deceitful men! my God doth keep
His promise still, but we break ours and sleep. 20
After the *Fall*, the first sin was in *Blood*,
And *Drunkenness* quickly did succeed the flood;
But since *Christ* dyed, (as if we did devise
To lose him too, as well as *Paradise*,)

* *Gen. chap.* 9. *ver.* 16.

These two grand sins we joyn and act together,
Though blood & drunkeness make but foul, foul weather.
Water (though both Heavens windows and the deep,
Full forty days o'r the drown'd world did weep,)
Could not reform us, and blood (in despight)
Yea Gods own blood we tread upon and slight. 30
So those bad daughters, which God sav'd from fire,
While *Sodom* yet did smoke, lay with their sire.

Then peaceful, signal bow, but in a cloud
Still lodged, where all thy unseen arrows shrowd,
I will on thee, as on a Comet look,
A Comet, the sad worlds ill-boding book;
Thy light as luctual and stain'd with woes
I'le judge, where penal flames sit mixt and close.
For though some think, thou shin'st but to restrain
Bold storms, and simply dost attend on rain, 40
Yet I know well, and so our sins require,
Thou dost but Court cold rain, till *Rain* turns *Fire*.

The Seed growing secretly

S. Mark 4. 26

If this worlds friends might see but once
What some poor man may often feel,
Glory, and gold, and Crowns and Thrones
They would soon quit and learn to kneel.

My dew, my dew! my early love,
My souls bright food, thy absence kills!
Hover not long, eternal Dove!
Life without thee is loose and spills.

Somthing I had, which long ago
Did learn to suck, and sip, and taste, 10
But now grown sickly, sad and slow,
Doth fret and wrangle, pine and waste.

O spred thy sacred wings and shake
One living drop! one drop life keeps!
If pious griefs Heavens joys awake,
O fill his bottle! thy childe weeps!

Slowly and sadly doth he grow,
And soon as left, shrinks back to ill;
O feed that life, which makes him blow
And spred and open to thy will! 20

For thy eternal, living wells
None stain'd or wither'd shall come near:
A fresh, immortal *green* there dwells,
And spotless *white* is all the wear.

Dear, secret *Greenness*! nurst below
Tempests and windes, and winter-nights,
Vex not, that but one sees thee grow,
That *One* made all these lesser lights.

If those bright joys he singly sheds
On thee, were all met in one Crown, 30
Both Sun and Stars would hide their heads;
And Moons, though full, would get them down.

Let glory be their bait, whose mindes
Are all too high for a low Cell:
Though Hawks can prey through storms and winds,
The poor Bee in her hive must dwel.

Glory, the Crouds cheap tinsel still
To what most takes them, is a drudge;
And they too oft take good for ill,
And thriving vice for vertue judge. 40

What needs a Conscience calm and bright
Within it self an outward test?
Who breaks his glass to take more light,
Makes way for storms into his rest.

Then bless thy secret growth, nor catch
At noise, but thrive unseen and dumb;
Keep clean, bear fruit, earn life and watch
Till the white winged Reapers come!

¶

As time one day by me did pass
    Through a large dusky glasse
    He held, I chanc'd to look
    And spyed his curious book
Of past days, where sad Heav'n did shed
A mourning light upon the dead.

Many disordered lives I saw
    And foul records which thaw
    My kinde eyes still, but in
    A fair, white page of thin 10
And ev'n, smooth lines, like the Suns rays,
Thy name was writ, and all thy days.

O bright and happy Kalendar!
    Where youth shines like a star
    All pearl'd with tears, and may
    Teach age, *The Holy way*;
Where through thick pangs, high agonies
Faith into life breaks, and death dies.

As some meek *night-piece* which day quails,
    To candle-light unveils: 20
    So by one beamy line
    From thy bright lamp did shine,
In the same page thy humble grave
Set with green herbs, glad hopes and brave.

Here slept my thoughts dear mark! which dust
    Seem'd to devour, like rust;
    But dust (I did observe)
    By hiding doth preserve,
As we for long and sure recruits,
Candy with sugar our choice fruits. 30

O calm and sacred bed where lies
    In deaths dark mysteries
    A beauty far more bright
    Then the noons cloudless light
For whose dry dust green branches bud
And robes are bleach'd in the *Lambs* blood.

Sleep happy ashes! (blessed sleep!)
While haplesse I still weep;
Weep that I have out-liv'd
My life, and unreliev'd 40
Must (soul-lesse shadow!) so live on,
Though life be dead, and my joys gone.

¶

Fair and yong light! my guide to holy
Grief and soul-curing melancholy;
Whom living here I did still shun
As sullen night-ravens do the Sun,
And lead by my own foolish fire
Wandred through darkness, dens and mire.
How am I now in love with all
That I term'd then meer bonds and thrall,
And to thy name, which still I keep,
Like the surviving turtle, weep! 10
O bitter curs'd delights of men!
Our souls diseases first, and then
Our bodies; poysons that intreat
With fatal sweetness, till we eat;
How artfully do you destroy,
That kill with smiles and seeming joy?
If all the subtilties of vice
Stood bare before unpractic'd eyes,
And every act she doth commence
Had writ down its sad consequence, 20
Yet would not men grant, their ill fate
Lodged in those false looks, till too late.
O holy, happy, healthy heaven,
Where all is pure, where all is even,
Plain, harmless, faithful, fair and bright,
But what Earth breaths against thy light!
How blest had men been, had their *Sire*
Liv'd still in league with thy chaste fire,
Nor made life through her long descents,
A slave to lustful Elements! 30

I did once read in an old book
Soil'd with many a weeping look,
That the seeds of foul sorrows be
The finest things that are, to see.
So that fam'd fruit which made all dye
Seem'd fair unto the womans eye.
If these supplanters in the shade
Of Paradise, could make man fade,
How in this world should they deter
This world, their fellow-murtherer! 40
And why then grieve we to be sent
Home by our first fair punishment,
Without addition to our woes
And lingring wounds from weaker foes?
Since that doth quickly freedom win,
For he that's dead, is freed from sin.

O that I were winged and free
And quite undrest just now with thee,
Where freed souls dwel by living fountains
On everlasting, spicy mountains! 50
Alas! my God! take home thy sheep;
This world but laughs at those that weep.

The Stone

Josh. chap. 24. ver. 27

I have it now:
But where to act, that none shall know,
Where I shall have no cause to fear
An eye or ear,
What man will show?
If nights, and shades, and secret rooms,
Silent as tombs,
Will nor conceal nor assent to
My dark designs, what shall I do?
Man I can bribe, and woman will 10
Consent to any gainful ill,
But these dumb creatures are so true,
No gold nor gifts can them subdue.

Hedges have ears, said the old *sooth*,
And ev'ry bush is somethings booth;
This cautious fools mistake, and fear
Nothing but man, when ambush'd there.

But I (Alas!)
Was shown one day in a strange glass
That busie commerce kept between 20
God and his Creatures, though unseen.

They hear, see, speak,
And into loud discoveries break,
As loud as blood. Not that God needs
Intelligence, whose spirit feeds
All things with life, before whose eyes,
Hell and all hearts stark naked lyes.
But *he that judgeth as he hears,
He that accuseth none, so steers
His righteous course, that though he knows 30
All that man doth, conceals or shows,
Yet will not he by his own light
(Though both all-seeing and all right,)
Condemn men; but will try them by
A process, which ev'n mans own eye
Must needs acknowledge to be just.
Hence sand and dust
Are shak'd for witnesses, and stones
Which some think dead, shall all at once
With one attesting voice detect 40
Those secret sins we least suspect.
For know, wilde men, that when you erre
Each thing turns Scribe and Register,
And in obedience to his Lord,
Doth your most private sins record.

The *Law* delivered to the *Jews*,
Who promis'd much, but did refuse
Performance, will for that same deed
Against them by a *stone* proceed;
Whose substance, though 'tis hard enough, 50
Will prove their hearts more stiff and tuff.

* *John chap*. 5. *ver*. 30. 45.

But now, since God on himself took
What all mankinde could never brook,
If any (for he all invites)
His easie yoke rejects or slights,
The *Gospel* then (for 'tis his word
And not himself *shall judge the world)
Will by loose *Dust* that man arraign,
As one then dust more vile and vain.

* *St. John, chap.* 12. *ver.* 47, 48.

The dwelling-place

S. John, chap. 1. *ver.* 38, 39

What happy, secret fountain,
Fair shade, or mountain,
Whose undiscover'd virgin glory
Boasts it this day, though not in story,
Was then thy dwelling? did some cloud
Fix'd to a Tent, descend and shrowd
My distrest Lord? or did a star
Becken'd by thee, though high and far,
In sparkling smiles haste gladly down
To lodge light, and increase her own? 10
My dear, dear God! I do not know
What lodgd thee then, nor where, nor how;
But I am sure, thou dost now come
Oft to a narrow, homely room,
Where thou too hast but the least part,
My God, I mean *my sinful heart.*

The Men of War

S. Luke, chap. 23. *ver.* 11

If any have an ear
Saith holy **John, then let him hear.*
He that into Captivity
Leads others, shall a Captive be.

* *Revel. chap.* 13. *ver.* 10.

Who with the sword doth others kill,
A sword shall his blood likewise spill.
Here is the patience of the Saints,
And the true faith, which never faints.
Were not thy word (dear Lord!) my light,
How would I run to endless night, 10
And persecuting thee and thine,
Enact for *Saints* my self and mine.
But now enlighten'd thus by thee,
I dare not think such villany;
Nor for a temporal self-end
Successful wickedness commend.
For in this bright, instructing verse
Thy Saints are not the Conquerers;
But patient, meek, and overcome
Like thee, when set at naught and dumb. 20
Armies thou hast in Heaven, which fight,
And follow thee all cloath'd in white,
But here on earth (though thou hast need)
Thou wouldst no legions, but wouldst bleed.
The sword wherewith thou dost command
Is in thy mouth, not in thy hand,
And all thy Saints do overcome
By thy blood, and their Martyrdom.
But seeing Soldiers long ago
Did spit on thee, and smote thee too; 30
Crown'd thee with thorns, and bow'd the knee,
But in contempt, as still we see,
I'le marvel not at ought they do,
Because they us'd my Savior so;
Since of my *Lord* they had their will,
The servant must not take it ill.

Dear *Jesus* give me patience here,
And faith to see my Crown as near
And almost reach'd, because 'tis sure
If I hold fast and slight the *Lure*. 40
Give me humility and peace,
Contented thoughts, innoxious ease,
A sweet, revengeless, quiet minde,
And to my greatest haters kinde.

Give me, my God! a heart as milde
And plain, as when I was a childe;
That when *thy Throne is set*, and all
These *Conquerors* before it fall,
I may be found (preserv'd by thee)
Amongst that chosen company, 50
Who by no blood (here) overcame
But the blood of the *blessed Lamb*.

The Ass

St. Matt. 21

Thou! who didst place me in this busie street
Of flesh and blood, where two ways meet:
The *One* of goodness, peace and life,
The *other* of death, sin and strife;
Where frail visibles rule the minde,
And present things finde men most kinde:
Where obscure cares the *mean* defeat,
And splendid vice destroys the *great*;
As thou didst set no law for me,
But that of perfect liberty, 10
Which neither tyres, nor doth corrode,
But is a *Pillow*, not a *Load*:
So give me grace ever to rest,
And build on it, because the best;
Teach both mine eyes and feet to move
Within those bounds set by thy love;
Grant I may soft and lowly be,
And minde those things I cannot see;
Tye me to faith, though above reason,
Who question power, they speak treason: 20
Let me thy Ass be onely wise
To carry, not search mysteries;
Who carries thee, is by thee lead,
Who argues, follows his own head.
To check bad motions, keep me still
Amongst the dead, where thriving ill

Without his brags and conquests lies,
And truth (opprest here) gets the prize.
At all times, whatsoe'r I do,
Let me not fail to question, who 30
Shares in the *act*, and puts me to't?
And if not thou, let not me do't.
Above all, make me love the poor,
Those burthens to the rich mans door,
Let me admire those, and be kinde
To low estates, and a low minde.
If the world offers to me ought,
That by thy book must not be sought,
Or though it should be lawful, may
Prove not expedient for thy way; 40
To shun that peril, let thy grace
Prevail with me to shun the place.
Let me be wise to please thee still,
And let men call me what they will.
When thus thy milde, instructing hand
Findes thy poor *foal* at thy command,
When he from wilde is become wise,
And slights that most, which men most prize;
When all things here to thistles turn
Pricking his lips, till he doth mourn 50
And hang the head, sighing for those
Pastures of life, where the Lamb goes:
O then, just then! break or untye
These bonds, this sad captivity,
This leaden state, which men miscal
Being and life, but is dead thrall.
And when (O God!) the Ass is free,
In a state known to none but thee;
O let him by his *Lord* be led,
To living springs, and there be fed 60
Where light, joy, health and perfect peace
Shut out all pain and each disease;
Where death and frailty are forgotten,
And bones rejoyce, which once were broken!

The hidden Treasure

S. Matt. 13. 44

*What can the man do that succeeds the *King?*
Even what was done before, and no new thing.
Who shews me but one grain of sincere light?
False stars and fire-drakes, the deceits of night
Set forth to fool and foil thee, do not boast;
Such Coal-flames shew but Kitchin-rooms at most.
And those I saw search'd through; yea those and all
That these three thousand years time did let fall
To blinde the eyes of lookers-back, and I
Now all is done, finde all is vanity. 10
Those secret searches, which afflict the wise,
Paths that are hidden from the *Vulturs* eyes
I saw at distance, and where grows that fruit
Which others onely grope for and dispute.
The worlds lov'd wisdom (for the worlds friends think
There is none else) did not the dreadful brink
And precipice it leads to, bid me flie
None could with more advantage use, then I.
Mans favorite sins, those tainting appetites
Which nature breeds, and some fine clay invites, 20
With all their soft, kinde arts and easie strains
Which strongly operate, though without pains,
Did not a greater beauty rule mine eyes,
None would more dote on, nor so soon entice.
But since these sweets are sowre, and poyson'd here
Where the impure seeds flourish all the year,
And private Tapers will but help to stray
Ev'n those, who *by them* would finde out the day,
I'le seal my eyes up, and to thy commands
Submit my wilde heart, and restrain my hands; 30
I will do nothing, nothing know, nor see
But what thou bidst, and shew'st, and teachest me.
Look what thou gav'st; all that I do restore
But for one thing, though purchas'd once before.

* *Ecclesiastes, chap.* 2. 12.

Childe-hood

I cannot reach it; and my striving eye
Dazles at it, as at eternity.
Were now that Chronicle alive,
Those white designs which children drive,
And the thoughts of each harmless hour,
With their content too in my pow'r,
Quickly would I make my path even,
And by meer playing go to Heaven.

Why should men love
A Wolf, more then a Lamb or Dove? 10
Or choose hell-fire and brimstone streams
Before bright stars, and Gods own beams?
Who kisseth thorns, will hurt his face,
But flowers do both refresh and grace,
And sweetly living (*fie on men!*)
Are when dead, medicinal then.
If seeing much should make staid eyes,
And long experience should make wise;
Since all that age doth teach, is ill,
Why should I not love childe-hood still? 20
Why if I see a rock or shelf,
Shall I from thence cast down my self,
Or by complying with the world,
From the same precipice be hurl'd?
Those observations are but foul
Which make me wise to lose my soul.

And yet the *Practice* worldlings call
Business and weighty action all,
Checking the poor childe for his play,
But gravely cast themselves away. 30

Dear, harmless age! the short, swift span,
Where weeping virtue parts with man;
Where love without lust dwells, and bends
What way we please, without self-ends.

An age of mysteries! which he
Must live twice, that would Gods face see;
Which *Angels* guard, and with it play,
Angels! which foul men drive away.

How do I study now, and scan
Thee, more then ere I studyed man, 40
And onely see through a long night
Thy edges, and thy bordering light!
O for thy Center and mid-day!
For sure that is the *narrow way*.

The Night

John 2. 3

Through that pure *Virgin-shrine*,
That sacred vail drawn o'r thy glorious noon
That men might look and live as Glo-worms shine,
And face the Moon:
Wise *Nicodemus* saw such light
As made him know his God by night.

Most blest believer he!
Who in that land of darkness and blinde eyes
Thy long expected healing wings could see,
When thou didst rise, 10
And what can never more be done,
Did at mid-night speak with the Sun!

O who will tell me, where
He found thee at that dead and silent hour!
What hallow'd solitary ground did bear
So rare a flower,
Within whose sacred leafs did lie
The fulness of the Deity.

No mercy-seat of gold,
No dead and dusty *Cherub*, nor carv'd stone, 20
But his own living works did my Lord hold
And lodge alone;
Where *trees* and *herbs* did watch and peep
And wonder, while the *Jews* did sleep.

Dear night! this worlds defeat;
The stop to busie fools; cares check and curb;
The day of Spirits; my souls calm retreat
Which none disturb!
Christs *progress, and his prayer time;
The hours to which high Heaven doth chime. 30

Gods silent, searching flight:
When my Lords head is fill'd with dew, and all
His locks are wet with the clear drops of night;
His still, soft call;
His knocking time; The souls dumb watch,
When Spirits their fair kinred catch.

Were all my loud, evil days
Calm and unhaunted as is thy dark Tent,
Whose peace but by some *Angels* wing or voice
Is seldom rent; 40
Then I in Heaven all the long year
Would keep, and never wander here.

But living where the Sun
Doth all things wake, and where all mix and tyre
Themselves and others, I consent and run
To ev'ry myre,
And by this worlds ill-guiding light,
Erre more then I can do by night.

There is in God (some say)
A deep, but dazling darkness; As men here 50
Say it is late and dusky, because they
See not all clear;
O for that night! where I in him
Might live invisible and dim.

* *Mark*, *chap*. 1. 35. *S. Luke*, *chap*. 21. 37.

Abels blood

Sad, purple well! whose bubling eye
Did first against a Murth'rer cry;
Whose streams still vocal, still complain
Of bloody *Cain*,

And now at evening are as red
As in the morning when first shed.
If single thou
(Though single voices are but low,)
Could'st such a shrill and long cry rear
As speaks still in thy makers ear, 10
What thunders shall those men arraign
Who cannot count those they have slain,
Who bath not in a shallow flood,
But in a deep, wide sea of blood?
A sea, whose lowd waves cannot sleep,
But *Deep* still calleth upon *deep*:
Whose urgent *sound* like unto that
Of many waters, beateth at
The everlasting doors above,
Where souls behinde the altar move, 20
And with one strong, incessant cry
Inquire *How long?* of the most high.
Almighty Judge!
At whose just laws no just men grudge;
Whose blessed, sweet commands do pour
Comforts and joys, and hopes each hour
On those that keep them; O accept
Of his vow'd heart, whom thou hast kept
From bloody men! and grant, I may
That sworn memorial duly pay 30
To thy bright arm, which was my light
And leader through thick death and night!
I, may that flood,
That proudly spilt and despis'd blood,
Speechless and calm, as Infants sleep!
Or if it watch, forgive and weep
For those that spilt it! May no cries
From the low earth to high Heaven rise,
But what (like his, whose blood peace brings)
Shall (when they rise) *speak better things*, 40
Then *Abels* doth! may *Abel* be
Still single heard, while these agree
With his milde blood in voice and will,
Who pray'd for those that did him kill!

Righteousness

Fair, solitary path! Whose blessed shades
The old, white Prophets planted first and drest:
Leaving for us (whose goodness quickly fades,)
A shelter all the way, and bowers to rest.

Who is the man that walks in thee? who loves
Heav'ns secret solitude, those fair abodes
Where turtles build, and carelesse sparrows move
Without to morrows evils and future loads?

Who hath the upright heart, the single eye,
The clean, pure hand, which never medled pitch? 10
Who sees *Invisibles*, and doth comply
With hidden treasures that make truly rich?

He that doth seek and love
The things above,
Whose spirit ever poor, is meek and low;
Who simple still and wise,
Still homewards flies,
Quick to advance, and to retreat most slow.

Whose acts, words and pretence
Have all one sense, 20
One aim and end; who walks not by his sight:
Whose eyes are both put out,
And goes about
Guided by faith, not by exterior light.

Who spills no blood, nor spreds
Thorns in the beds
Of the distrest, hasting their overthrow;
Making the time they had
Bitter and sad
Like *Chronic* pains, which surely kill, though slow. 30

Who knows earth nothing hath
Worth love or wrath,
But in his *hope* and *Rock* is ever glad.
Who seeks and follows peace,
When with the ease
And health of conscience it is to be had.

Who bears his cross with joy
And doth imploy
His heart and tongue in prayers for his foes;
Who lends, not to be paid, 40
And gives full aid
Without that bribe which Usurers impose.

Who never looks on man
Fearful and wan,
But firmly trusts in God; the great mans measure
Though high and haughty must
Be ta'en in dust,
But the good man is Gods peculiar treasure.

Who doth thus, and doth not
These good deeds blot 50
With bad, or with neglect; and heaps not wrath
By secret filth, nor feeds
Some snake, or weeds,
Cheating himself; That man walks in this path.

Anguish

My God and King! to thee
I bow my knee,
I bow my troubled soul, and greet
With my foul heart thy holy feet.
Cast it, or tread it! It shall do
Even what thou wilt, and praise thee too.

My God, could I weep blood,
Gladly I would;
Or if thou wilt give me that Art,
Which through the eyes pours out the hart, 10
I will exhaust it all, and make
My self all tears, a weeping lake.

O! 'tis an easie thing
To write and sing;

But to write true, unfeigned verse
Is very hard! O God, disperse
These weights, and give my spirit leave
To act as well as to conceive!

O my God, hear my cry;
Or let me dye!—— 20

Tears

O when my God, my glory brings
His white and holy train,
Unto those clear and living *Springs*,
Where comes no *stain*!

Where all is *light*, and *flowers*, and *fruit*,
And *joy*, and *rest*,
Make me amongst them ('tis my suit!)
The last one, and the least.

And when they all are fed, and have
Drunk of thy living stream, 10
Bid thy poor Ass (with tears I crave!)
Drink after them.

Thy love claims highest thanks, my sin
The lowest pitch:
But if he pays, who *loves much*, then
Thou hast made beggers rich.

Jacobs Pillow, and Pillar

I see the Temple in thy Pillar rear'd,
And that dread glory, which thy children fear'd,
In milde, clear visions, without a frown,
Unto thy solitary self is shown.
'Tis number makes a Schism: throngs are rude,
And God himself dyed by the multitude.

This made him put on clouds, and fire and smoke,
Hence he in thunder to thy Off-spring spoke;
The small, still voice, at some low Cottage knocks,
But a strong wind must break thy lofty rocks. 10

The first true worship of the worlds great King
From private and selected hearts did spring,
But he most willing to save all mankinde,
Inlarg'd that light, and to the bad was kinde.
Hence Catholick or Universal came
A most fair notion, but a very name.
For this rich Pearl, like some more common stone,
When once made publique, is esteem'd by none.
Man slights his Maker, when familiar grown,
And sets up laws, to pull his honor down. 20
This God foresaw: And when slain by the crowd
(Under that stately and mysterious cloud
Which his death scatter'd) he foretold the place,
And form to serve him in, should be true grace
And the meek heart, not in a Mount, nor at
Jerusalem, with blood of beasts, and fat.
A heart is that dread place, that awful Cell,
That secret Ark, where the milde Dove doth dwell
When the proud waters rage: when Heathens rule
By Gods permission, and man turns a Mule. 30
This litle *Goshen*, in the midst of night,
And Satans seat, in all her Coasts hath light,
Yea *Bethel* shall have Tithes (saith *Israels* stone)
And vows and visions, though her foes crye, None.
Thus is the solemn temple sunk agen
Into a Pillar, and conceal'd from men.
And glory be to his eternal Name!
Who is contented, that this holy flame
Shall lodge in such a narrow pit, till he
With his strong arm turns our captivity. 40

But blessed *Jacob*, though thy sad distress
Was just the same with ours, and nothing less;
For thou a brother, and blood-thirsty too
Didst flye, *whose children wrought thy childrens wo:

* *Obadiah chap.* 1. 11. *Amos chap.* 1. 11.

Yet thou in all thy solitude and grief,
On stones didst sleep and found'st but cold relief;
Thou from the Day-star a long way didst stand
And all that distance was Law and command.
But we a healing Sun by day and night,
Have our sure Guardian, and our leading light; 50
What thou didst hope for and believe, we finde
And feel a friend most ready, sure and kinde.
Thy pillow was but type and shade at best,
But we the substance have, and on him rest.

The Agreement

I wrote it down. But one that saw
And envyed that Record, did since
Such a mist over my minde draw,
It quite forgot that purpos'd glimpse.
I read it sadly oft, but still
Simply believ'd, 'twas not my Quill;

At length, my lifes kinde Angel came,
And with his bright and busie wing
Scatt'ring that cloud, shewd me the flame
Which strait, like Morning-stars did sing, 10
And shine, and point me to a place,
Which all the year sees the Suns face.

O beamy book! O my mid-day
Exterminating fears and night!
The mount, whose white Ascendents may
Be in conjunction with true light!
My thoughts, when towards thee they move,
Glitter and kindle with thy love.

Thou art the oyl and the wine-house:
Thine are the present healing leaves, 20
Blown from the tree of life to us
By his breath whom my dead heart heaves.
Each page of thine hath true life in't,
And Gods bright minde exprest in print.

Most modern books are blots on thee,
Their doctrine chaff and windy fits:
Darken'd along, as their scribes be,
With those foul storms, when they were writ;
While the mans zeal lays out and blends
Onely self-worship and self-ends. 30

Thou art the faithful, pearly rock,
The Hive of beamy, living lights,
Ever the same, whose diffus'd stock
Entire still, wears out blackest nights.
Thy lines are rays, the true Sun sheds;
Thy leaves are healing wings he spreads.

For until thou didst comfort me,
I had not one poor word to say:
Thick busie clouds did multiply,
And said, I was no childe of day; 40
They said, my own hands did remove
That candle given me from above.

O God! I know and do confess
My sins are great and still prevail,
Most heynous sins and numberless!
But thy *Compassions* cannot fail.
If thy sure mercies can be broken,
Then all is true, my foes have spoken.

But while time runs, and after it
Eternity, which never ends, 50
Quite through them both, still infinite
Thy Covenant by *Christ* extends;
No sins of frailty, nor of youth
Can foil his merits, and thy truth.

And this I hourly finde, for thou
Dost still renew, and purge and heal:
Thy care and love, which joyntly flow
New Cordials, new *Cathartics* deal.
But were I once cast off by thee
I know (my God!) this would not be. 60

Wherefore with tears (tears by thee sent)
I beg, my faith may never fail!
And when in death my speech is spent,
O let that silence then prevail!
    O chase in that *cold calm* my foes,
    And hear my hearts last private throws!

So thou, who didst the work begin
(For *I till** *drawn came not to thee*)
Wilt finish it, and by no sin
Will thy free mercies hindred be. 70
    For which, O God, I onely can
    Bless thee, and blame unthankful man.

* *St. John*, *chap*. 6. *ver*. 44. 65.

The day of Judgement

O day of life, of light, of love!
The onely day dealt from above!
A day so fresh, so bright, so brave
Twill shew us each forgotten grave,
And make the dead, like flowers, arise
Youthful and fair to see new skies.
All other days, compar'd to thee,
Are but lights weak minority,
They are but veils, and Cypers drawn
Like Clouds, before thy glorious dawn. 10
O come, arise, shine, do not stay
        Dearly lov'd day!
The fields are long since white, and I
With earnest groans for freedom cry,
My fellow-creatures too say, *Come!*
And stones, though speechless, are not dumb.
When shall we hear that glorious voice
        Of life and joys?
That voice, which to each secret bed
        Of my Lords dead, 20
Shall bring true day, and make dust see,
The way to immortality.

When shall those first white Pilgrims rise,
Whose holy, happy Histories
(Because they sleep so long) some men
Count but the blots of a vain pen?
Dear Lord! make haste,
Sin every day commits more waste,
And thy old enemy, which knows
His time is short, more raging grows. 30
Nor moan I onely (though profuse)
Thy Creatures bondage and abuse;
But what is highest sin and shame,
The vile despight done to thy name;
The forgeries, which impious wit
And power force on Holy Writ,
With all detestable designs
That may dishonor those pure lines.
O God! though mercy be in thee
The greatest attribute we see, 40
And the most needful for our sins;
Yet, when thy mercy nothing wins
But meer disdain, let not man say
Thy arm doth sleep; but write this day
Thy judging one: Descend, descend!
Make all things new! and without end!

Psalm 65

Sions true, glorious God! on thee
Praise waits in all humility.
All flesh shall unto thee repair,
To thee, O thou that hearest prayer!
But sinful words and works still spread
And over-run my heart and head;
Transgressions make me foul each day,
O purge them, purge them all away!
Happy is he! whom thou wilt choose
To serve thee in thy blessed house! 10
Who in thy holy Temple dwells,
And fill'd with joy, thy goodness tells!

King of Salvation! by strange things
And terrible, Thy Justice brings
Man to his duty. Thou alone
Art the worlds hope, and but thee, none.
Sailers that flote on flowing seas
Stand firm by thee, and have sure peace.
Thou still'st the loud waves, when most wild
And mak'st the raging people mild. 20
Thy arm did first the mountains lay
And girds their rocky heads this day.
The most remote, who know not thee,
At thy great works astonish'd be.

The *outgoings* of the *Even* and *Dawn*,
In *Antiphones* sing to thy Name.
Thou visit'st the low earth, and then
Water'st it for the sons of men,
Thy upper river, which abounds
With fertil streams, makes rich all grounds, 30
And by thy mercies still supplied
The sower doth his bread provide.
Thou water'st every ridge of land
And settlest with thy secret hand
The furrows of it; then thy warm
And opening showers (restrain'd from harm)
Soften the mould, while all unseen
The blade grows up alive and green.
The year is with thy goodness crown'd,
And all thy paths drop fatness round, 40
They drop upon the wilderness,
For thou dost even the desarts bless,
And hills full of springing pride,
Wear fresh adornments on each side.
The fruitful flocks fill every Dale,
And purling Corn doth cloath the Vale;
They shout for joy, and joyntly sing,
Glory to the eternal King!

The Throne

Revel. chap. 20. *ver.* 11

When with these eyes clos'd now by thee,
But then restor'd,
The great and white throne I shall see
Of my dread Lord:
And lowly kneeling (for the most
Stiff then must kneel)
Shall look on him, at whose high cost
(Unseen) such joys I feel.

What ever arguments, or skill
Wise heads shall use, 10
Tears onely and my blushes still
I will produce.
And should those speechless beggers fail,
Which oft have won;
Then taught by thee, I will prevail,
And say, *Thy will be done!*

Death

Though since thy first sad entrance by
Just *Abels* blood,
'Tis now six thousand years well nigh,
And still thy sov'rainty holds good:
Yet by none art thou understood.

We talk and name thee with much ease
As a tryed thing,
And every one can slight his lease
As if it ended in a Spring,
Which shades & bowers doth rent-free bring. 10

To thy dark land these heedless go:
But there was *One*,
Who search'd it quite through to and fro,
And then returning, like the Sun,
Discover'd all, that there is done.

And since his death, we throughly see
All thy dark way;
Thy shades but thin and narrow be,
Which his first looks will quickly fray:
Mists make but triumphs for the day. 20

As harmless violets, which give
Their virtues here
For salves and syrups, while they live,
Do after calmly disappear,
And neither grieve, repine, nor fear:

So dye his servants; and as sure
Shall they revive.
Then let not dust your eyes obscure,
But lift them up, where still alive,
Though fled from you, their spirits hive. 30

The Feast

O come away,
Make no delay,
Come while my heart is clean & steddy!
While Faith and Grace
Adorn the place,
Making dust and ashes ready.

No bliss here lent
Is permanent,
Such triumphs poor flesh cannot merit;
Short sips and sights 10
Endear delights,
Who seeks for more, he would inherit.

Come then true bread,
Quickning the dead,
Whose eater shall not, cannot dye,
Come, antedate
On me that state
Which brings poor dust the victory.

I victory
Which from thine eye 20
    Breaks as the day doth from the east,
When the spilt dew,
Like tears doth shew
    The sad world wept to be releast.

Spring up, O wine,
And springing shine
    With some glad message from his heart,
Who did, when slain,
These means ordain
    For me to have in him a part. 30

Such a sure part
In his blest heart,
    The well, where living waters spring,
That with it fed
Poor dust though dead
    Shall rise again, and live and sing.

O drink and bread
Which strikes death dead,
    The food of mans immortal being!
Under veyls here 40
Thou art my chear,
    Present and sure without my seeing.

How dost thou flye
And search and pry
    Through all my parts, and like a quick
And knowing lamp
Hunt out each damp,
    Whose shadow makes me sad or sick?

O what high joys
The Turtles voice 50
    And songs I hear! O quickning showers
Of my Lords blood
You make rocks bud
    And crown dry hils with wells & flowers!

For this true ease
This healing peace,
  For this taste of living glory,
My soul and all,
Kneel down and fall
  And sing his sad victorious story. 60

O thorny crown
More soft then down!
  O painful Cross, my bed of rest!
O spear, the key
Opening the way!
  O thy worst state, my onely best!

Oh! all thy griefs
Are my reliefs,
  And all my sins, thy sorrows were!
And what can I, 70
To this reply;
  What (O God!) but a silent tear?

Some toil and sow,
That wealth may flow,
  And dress this earth for next years meat:
But let me heed,
Why thou didst bleed,
  And what in the next world to eat.

Revel. chap. 19. ver. 9

Blessed are they, which are called unto the marriage Supper of the Lamb!

The Obsequies

Since dying for me, thou didst crave no more
    Then common pay,
  Some few true tears, and those shed for
    My own ill way;
  With a cheap, plain remembrance still
    Of thy sad death,
  Because forgetfulness would kill
    Even lifes own breath:

I were most foolish and unkinde
In my own sense, 10
Should I not ever bear in minde
If not thy mighty love, my own defense.
Therefore, those loose delights and lusts, which here
Men call good chear,
I will close girt and tyed
For mourning sack-cloth wear, all mortified.

Not but that mourners too, can have
Rich weeds and shrouds;
For some wore *White* ev'n in thy grave,
And Joy, like light, shines oft in clouds: 20
But thou, who didst mans whole life earn,
Doest so invite, and woo me still,
That to be merry I want skill,
And time to learn.
Besides, those Kerchiefs sometimes shed
To make me brave,
I cannot finde, but where thy head
Was once laid for me in thy grave.
Thy grave! To which my thoughts shal move
Like Bees in storms unto their Hive, 30
That from the murd'ring worlds false love
Thy death may keep my soul alive.

The Water-fall

With what deep murmurs through times silent stealth
Doth thy transparent, cool and watry wealth
Here flowing fall,
And chide, and call,
As if his liquid, loose Retinue staid
Lingring, and were of this steep place afraid,
The common pass
Where, clear as glass,
All must descend
Not to an end: 10
But quickned by this deep and rocky grave,
Rise to a longer course more bright and brave.

Dear stream! dear bank, where often I
Have sate, and pleas'd my pensive eye,
Why, since each drop of thy quick store
Runs thither, whence it flow'd before,
Should poor souls fear a shade or night,
Who came (sure) from a sea of light?
Or since those drops are all sent back
So sure to thee, that none doth lack, 20
Why should frail flesh doubt any more
That what God takes, hee'l not restore?
O useful Element and clear!
My sacred wash and cleanser here,
My first consigner unto those
Fountains of life, where the Lamb goes?
What sublime truths, and wholesome themes,
Lodge in thy mystical, deep streams!
Such as dull man can never finde
Unless that Spirit lead his minde, 30
Which first upon thy face did move,
And hatch'd all with his quickning love.
As this loud brooks incessant fall
In streaming rings restagnates all,
Which reach by course the bank, and then
Are no more seen, just so pass men.
O my invisible estate,
My glorious liberty, still late!
Thou art the Channel my soul seeks,
Not this with Cataracts and Creeks. 40

Quickness

False life! a foil and no more, when
Wilt thou be gone?
Thou foul deception of all men
That would not have the true come on.

Thou art a Moon-like toil; a blinde
Self-posing state;
A dark contest of waves and winde;
A meer tempestuous debate.

Life is a fix'd, discerning light,
A knowing Joy; 10
No chance, or fit: but ever bright,
And calm and full, yet doth not cloy.

'Tis such a blissful thing, that still
Doth vivifie,
And shine and smile, and hath the skill
To please without Eternity.

Thou art a toylsom Mole, or less
A moving mist
But life is, what none can express,
A quickness, which my God hath kist. 20

The Wreath

Since I in storms us'd most to be
And seldom yielded flowers,
How shall I get a wreath for thee
From those rude, barren hours?

The softer dressings of the Spring,
Or Summers later store
I will not for thy temples bring,
Which *Thorns*, not *Roses* wore.

But a twin'd wreath of *grief* and *praise*,
Praise soil'd with tears, and tears again 10
Shining with joy, like dewy days,
This day I bring for all thy pain,
Thy causless pain! and sad as death;
Which sadness breeds in the most vain,
(O not in vain!) now beg thy breath;
Thy quickning breath, which gladly bears
Through saddest clouds to that glad place,
Where cloudless Quires sing without tears,
Sing thy just praise, and see thy face.

The Queer

O tell me whence that joy doth spring
Whose diet is divine and fair,
Which wears heaven, like a bridal ring,
And tramples on doubts and despair?

Whose Eastern traffique deals in bright
And boundless Empyrean themes,
Mountains of spice, Day-stars and light,
Green trees of life, and living streams?

Tell me, O tell who did thee bring
And here, without my knowledge, plac'd, 10
Till thou didst grow and get a wing,
A wing with eyes, and eyes that taste?

Sure, *holyness* the *Magnet* is,
And *Love* the *Lure*, that woos thee down;
Which makes the high transcendent bliss
Of knowing thee, so rarely known.

The Book

Eternal God! maker of all
That have liv'd here, since the mans fall;
The Rock of ages! in whose shade
They live unseen, when here they fade.

Thou knew'st this *papyr*, when it was
Meer *seed*, and after that but *grass*;
Before 'twas *drest* or *spun*, and when
Made *linen*, who did *wear* it then:
What were their lifes, their thoughts & deeds
Whither good *corn*, or fruitless *weeds*. 10

Thou knew'st this *Tree*, when a green *shade*
Cover'd it, since a *Cover* made,
And where it flourish'd, grew and spread,
As if it never should be dead.

Thou knew'st this harmless *beast*, when he
Did live and feed by thy decree
On each green thing; then slept (well fed)
Cloath'd with this *skin*, which now lies spred
A *Covering* o're this aged book,
Which makes me wisely weep and look 20
On my own dust; meer dust it is,
But not so dry and clean as this.
Thou knew'st and saw'st them all and though
Now scatter'd thus, dost know them so.

O knowing, glorious spirit! when
Thou shalt restore trees, beasts and men,
When thou shalt make all new again,
Destroying onely death and pain,
Give him amongst thy works a place,
Who in them lov'd and sought thy face! 30

To the Holy Bible

O book! lifes guide! how shall we part,
And thou so long seiz'd of my heart!
Take this last kiss, and let me weep
True thanks to thee, before I sleep.
Thou wert the first put in my hand,
When yet I could not understand,
And daily didst my yong eyes lead
To letters, till I learnt to read.
But as rash youths, when once grown strong
Flye from their Nurses to the throng, 10
Where they new Consorts choose, & stick
To those, till either hurt or sick:
So with that first light gain'd from thee
Ran I in chase of vanity,
Cryed dross for gold, and never thought
My first cheap Book had all I sought.
Long reign'd this vogue; and thou cast by
With meek, dumb looks didst woo mine eye,
And oft left open would'st convey
A sudden and most searching ray 20

Into my soul, with whose quick touch
Refining still, I strugled much.
By this milde art of love at length
Thou overcam'st my sinful strength,
And having brought me home, didst there
Shew me that pearl I sought elsewhere.
Gladness, and peace, and hope, and love,
The secret favors of the Dove,
Her quickning kindness, smiles and kisses,
Exalted pleasures, crowning blisses, 30
Fruition, union, glory, life
Thou didst lead to, and still all strife.
Living, thou wert my souls sure ease,
And dying mak'st me go in peace:
Thy next *Effects* no tongue can tell;
Farewel O book of God! farewel!

S. Luke chap. 2. *ver.* 14

Glory be to God in the highest, and on
Earth peace, good will towards men.

L'Envoy

O the new worlds new, quickning Sun!
Ever the same, and never done!
The seers of whose sacred light
Shall all be drest in shining white,
And made conformable to his
Immortal shape, who wrought their bliss,
Arise, arise!
And like old cloaths fold up these skies,
This long worn veyl: then shine and spread
Thy own bright self over each head, 10
And through thy creatures pierce and pass
Till all becomes thy cloudless glass,
Transparent as the purest day
And without blemish or decay,
Fixt by thy spirit to a state
For evermore immaculate.

A state fit for the sight of thy
Immediate, pure and unveil'd eye,
A state agreeing with thy minde,
A state thy birth, and death design'd: 20
A state for which thy creatures all
Travel and groan, and look and call.
O seeing thou hast paid our score,
Why should the curse reign any more?
But since thy number is as yet
Unfinish'd, we shall gladly sit
Till all be ready, that the train
May fully fit thy glorious reign.
Onely, let not our haters brag,
Thy seamless coat is grown a rag, 30
Or that thy truth was not here known,
Because we forc'd thy judgements down.
Dry up their arms, who vex thy spouse,
And take the glory of thy house
To deck their own; then give thy saints
That faithful zeal, which neither faints
Nor wildly burns, but meekly still
Dares own the truth, and shew the ill.
Frustrate those cancerous, close arts
Which cause solution in all parts, 40
And strike them dumb, who for meer words
Wound thy beloved, more then swords.
Dear Lord, do this! and then let grace
Descend, and hallow all the place.
Incline each hard heart to do good,
And cement us with thy sons blood,
That like true sheep, all in one fold
We may be fed, and one minde hold.
Give watchful spirits to our guides!
For sin (like water) hourly glides 50
By each mans door, and quickly will
Turn in, if not obstructed still.
Therefore write in their hearts thy law,
And let these long, sharp judgements aw
Their very thoughts, that by their clear
And holy lives, mercy may here

Sit regent yet, and blessings flow
As fast, as persecutions now.
So shall we know in war and peace
Thy service to be our sole ease, 60
With prostrate souls adoring thee,
Who turn'd our sad captivity!

S. Clemens apud Basil:

Ζῇ ὁ Θεὸς, καὶ ὁ κύριος Ιησοῦς Χριστὸς, καὶ τὸ πνεῦμα τὸ ἅγιον.

FINIS

An Alphabetical
TABLE
Containing the several Titles of all the Hymns or Sacred Poems in these two Books

FINIS

Thalia Rediviva:

THE

Paſs-Times and *Diverſions*

OF A

COUNTREY-MUSE,

In Choice

POEMS

On ſeveral Occaſions.

WITH

Some Learned *Remains* of the Eminent

Eugenius Philalethes.

Never made Publick till now.

——Nec erubuit ſylvas habitare Thalia. *Virgil.*

Licenſed, *Roger L'Eſtrange.*

London, Printed for *Robert Pawlet* at the Bible in *Chancery-lane,* near *Fleetſtreet,* 1678.

TO THE

Most Honourable and truly Noble HENRY Lord Marquis and Earl of *WORCESTER*, &c.

My Lord,

Though *Dedications* are now become a kind of Tyranny over the Peace and Repose of great Men; yet I have confidence I shall so manage the present Address as to entertain your Lordship without much disturbance; and because my purposes are govern'd by deep Respect and Veneration, I hope to find your Lordship more facile and accessible. And I am already absolv'd from a great part of that fulsome and designing guilt, being sufficiently remov'd from the causes of it: for I consider, my Lord! that you are already so well
10 known to the World in your several Characters, and advantages of Honour; it was yours by traduction, and the adjunct of your Nativity, you were swaddl'd and rock'd in't, bred up and grew in't to your now wonderful height and eminence: that for me under pretence of the inscription to give you the heraldry of your family, or to carry your person through the fam'd Topicks of Mind Body, or Estate, were all one as to perswade the World that Fire and Light were very bright Bodies, or that the Luminaries themselves had Glory. In point of Protection I beg to fall in with the common wont, and to be satisfied by the reasonableness of the thing, and
20 abundant worthy precedents; and although I should have secret prophecy and assurance that the ensuing Verse would live eternally, yet would I, as I now do, humbly crave it might be fortifi'd with your Patronage; for so the Sextile Aspects and Influences are watch'd for, and applied to the actions of Life, thereby to make the Scheme and good Auguries of the Birth pass into Fate, and a success infallible.

My Lord! By a happy obliging Intercession, and your own consequent Indulgence, I have now recourse to your Lordship; hopeing, I shall not much displease by putting these Twin Poets
30 into your Hands. The Minion and Vertical Planet of the Roman

Lustre and Bravery was never better pleased, than when he had a whole Constellation about him: not his finishing Five several Wars to the promoting of his own Interest, nor particularly the prodigious success at *Actium*, where he held in chase the Wealth, Beauty and Prowess of the East; not the Triumphs and absolute Dominions which followed, all this gave him not half that serene Pride and Satisfaction of Spirit as when he retir'd himself to umpire the different Excellencies of his insipid Friends, and to distribute Lawrels among his Poetick Heroes: If now upon the Authority of this, and several such Examples I had the Ability and 10 Opportunity of drawing the Value and strange Worth of a Poet, and withall of applying some of the Lineaments to the following pieces; I should then do my self a real Service, and attone in a great measure for the present insolence. But best of all will it serve my Defence and Interest to appeal to your Lordships own conceptions and image of *Genuine* Verse; with which so just, so regular Original, if these Copies shall hold proportion and resemblance, then am I advanced very far in your Lordships pardon: the rest will entirely be supplied me by your Lordships Goodness, and my own awful Zeal of being, 20

My Lord!

Your Lordships most
obedient, most humbly
devoted Servant
J. W.

To the Reader

The Nation of Poets *above all Writers has ever challeng'd perpetuity of Name, or as they please by their Charter of Liberty to call it*, Immortality. *Nor has the World much disputed their claim, either easily resigning a Patrimony in it self not very substantial; or, it may be, out of despair to controule the authority of Inspiration and Oracle. Howsoever the price as now quarrell'd for among the* Poets *themselves is no such rich bargain: 'tis only a vanishing interest in the Lees and Dreggs of Time, in the Rear of those Fathers and Worthies in the Art, who if they know anything of the heats and fury of their Successors must extreamly pity them.* 10

I am to assure, that the Author has no portion of that aiery happiness to lose by any injury or unkindness which may be done to his Verse: his Reputation is better built in the sentiment of several judicious Persons, who know him very well able to give himself a lasting Monument, by undertaking any Argument of note in the whole Circle of Learning.

But even these his Diversions have been valuable with the matchless Orinda, *and since they deserv'd her esteem and commendations; who so thinks them not worth the publishing, will put himself in the opposite Scale, where his own arrogance will blow him up.* 20

I. W.

To Mr. Henry Vaughan *the Silurist: upon these and his former* Poems

Had I ador'd the Multitude, and thence
Got an Antipathy to wit and sence,
And hugg'd that Fate, in hope the World would
grant
'Twas *good Affection* to be Ignorant:
Yet the least Ray of thy bright fancy seen
I had converted, or excuseless been.
For each Birth of thy Muse to after-times
Shall expiate for all this Ages Crimes.
First shines thy *Amoret*, twice crown'd by thee: 10
Once by thy Love, next by thy Poetrie,
Where thou the best of Unions dost dispense
Truth cloath'd in Wit, and Love in Innocence.
So that the muddie Lover may learn here,
No Fountains can be sweet, that are not clear.
There *Juvenal*, by thee reviv'd declares
How flat man's Joys are, and how mean his Cares;
And wisely doth upbraid the World, that they
Should such a value for their ruine pay.
But when thy sacred Muse diverts her Quill 20
The Landskip to design of *Sions* Hill,
As nothing else was worthy her, or thee:
So we admire almost t' Idolatrie.
What savage Breast would not be rap'd to find
Such Jewels in such Cabinets enshrin'd?
Thou fill'd with joys (too great to see or count:)
Descend'st from thence, like *Moses* from the Mount,
And with a candid, yet unquestion'd awe
Restor'st the Golden Age, when Verse was Law.
Instructing us, thou so secur'st thy Fame, 30
That nothing can disturb it, but my name.
Nay I have hopes, that standing so near thine
'Twill loose its dross, and by degrees refine.
Live! till the disabused World consent
All Truths of Use, of Strength or Ornament

Are with such Harmony by thee display'd
As the whole World was first by number made;
And from the charming rigour thy Muse brings
Learn, there's no pleasure but in serious things!

Orinda

Upon the Ingenious Poems *of his Learned Friend, Mr.* Henry Vaughan *the Silurist*

Fairly design'd! to charm our *Civil* Rage
With *Verse*, and plant *Bayes* in an *Iron* Age.
But hath steel'd *Mars* so ductible a Soul,
That *Love* and *Poesie* may it controule?
Yes: brave *Tyrtæus*, as we read of old,
The *Grecian* Armies, as he pleas'd cou'd *mold*;
They march'd to his high *Numbers*, and did fight
With that *instinct* and *rage*, which he did write.
When he fell *lower*, they would strait *retreat*,
Grow soft and calm: and temper their bold heat. 10
Such *Magick* is in *Vertue*! See hear a young
Tyrtæus too, whose sweet persuasive Song
Can lead our *Spirits* any way, and move
To all *Adventures*: either *War* or *Love*.

Then veil the bright *Etesia*, that choice *She*,
Lest *Mars*, (*Timander's* Friend) his Rival be.
So fair a *Nymph*, drest by a *Muse* so neat,
Might warm the *North*, and thaw the frozen *Gete*.

Tho. Powel, D.D.

To the ingenious Author of Thalia Rediviva

Ode I

Where Reverend Bards of old have sate
And sung the pleasant enterludes of Fate,
Thou takest the hereditary shade
Which Natures homely Art had made,

And thence thou giv'st thy Muse her swing, and she
Advances to the Galaxie;
There with the sparkling *Cowley* she above
Does hand in hand in graceful Measures move.
We groveling Mortals gaze below,
And long in vain to know 10
Her wondrous paths, her wondrous flight
In vaine; alas! we grope,
In vain we use our earthly Telescope,
We'r blinded by an intermedial night:
Thine *Eagle-Muse* can only face
The fiery Coursers in their race,
While with unequal paces we do try
To bear her train aloft, and keep her company.

II

The loud harmonious *Mantuan*
Once charm'd the world, and here's the *Uscan* Swan 20
In his declining years does chime,
And challenges the last remains of Time.
Ages run on, and soon give o're,
They have their Graves as well as we,
Time swallows all that's past and more,
Yet time is swallow'd in eternity:
This is the only profits Poets see.
There thy triumphant Muse shall ride in state
And lead in Chains devouring Fate;
Claudian's bright Phœnix she shall bring 30
Thee an immortal offering;
Nor shall my humble tributary Muse
Her homage and attendance too refuse,
She thrusts her self among the Crowd
And joyning in th' applause she strives to clap aloud.

III

Tell me no more that Nature is severe
Thou great Philosopher!
Lo she has laid her vast Exchequer here.
Tell me no more that she has sent
So much already she is spent; 40

Here is a vast *America* behind
Which none but the great Silurist could find.
Nature her last edition was the best,
As big, as rich as all the rest
So will we here admit
Another world of Wit.
No rude or savage fancy here shall stay
The travailing Reader in his way,
But every coast is clear: go where he will
Vertu's the road *Thalia* leads him still: 50
Long may she live, and wreath thy sacred head
For this her happy resurrection from the dead.

N. W. Jes. Coll. *Oxon.*

To my worthy Friend, Mr. Henry Vaughan *the Silurist*

See what thou wert! by what Platonick round
Art thou in thy first youth and Glories found!
Or from thy Muse does this Retrieve accrue,
Do's she which once inspir'd thee, now renew!
Bringing thee back those Golden years which time
Smooth'd to thy Lays, and polisht with thy Rhyme.
Nor is't to thee alone she do's convey
Such happy change, but bountiful as day
On whatsoever Reader she do's shine
She makes him like thee, and for ever thine. 10

And first thy manual op'ning gives to see
Ecclipse and suff'rings burnish Majesty,
Where thou so artfully the draught hast made
That we best read the lustre in the shade,
And find our Sov'raign greater in that shroud:
So Lightning dazzles from its night and cloud;
So the *first Light himself* has for his Throne
Blackness, and Darkness his Pavilion.
Who can refuse thee company, or stay,
By thy next charming summons forc'd away, 20

If that be force which we can so resent
That only in its joys 'tis violent:
Upward thy *Eagle* bears us e're aware
Till above Storms and all tempestuous Air
We radiant Worlds with their bright people meet,
Leaving this little *All* beneath our feet.
But now the pleasure is too great to tell,
Nor have we other bus'ness than to dwell
As on the hallow'd Mount th' Apostles meant
To build and fix their glorious banishment. 30
Yet we must know and find thy skilful Vein
Shall gently bear us to our homes again;
By which descent thy former flight's impli'd
To be thy extasie and not thy pride.
And here how well do's the wise *Muse* demeane
Her self, and fit her song to ev'ry Scene!
Riot of Courts, the bloody wreaths of War,
Cheats of the Mart, and clamours of the Bar,
Nay, life it self thou dost so well express
Its hollow Joyes, and real Emptiness, 40
That *Dorian* Minstrel never did excite,
Or raise for dying so much appetite.

Nor does thy other softer Magick move
Us less thy fam'd *Etesia* to love;
Where such a *Character* thou giv'st that shame
Nor envy dare approach the Vestal Dame:
So at bright Prime *Idea's* none repine,
They safely in th' *Eternal Poet* shine.

Gladly th' *Assyrian Phœnix* now resumes
From thee this last reprizal of his Plumes; 50
He seems another more miraculous thing
Brighter of Crest, and stronger of his Wing;
Proof against Fate in spicy Urns to come,
Immortal past all risque of Martyrdome.

Nor be concern'd, nor fancy thou art rude
T' adventure from thy Cambrian solitude,
Best from those lofty Cliffs thy *Muse* does spring
Upwards, and boldly spreads her Cherub-wing.

So when the *Sage* of *Memphis* would converse
With boding Skies, and th' Azure Universe, 60
He climbs his starry Pyramid, and thence
Freely sucks clean prophetique influence,
And all Serene, and rap't and gay he pries
Through the Æthereal volum's Mysteries,
Loth to come down, or ever to know more
The *Nile's* luxurious, but dull foggy shore.

I. W. A.M. Oxon.

Choice POEMS on several occasions

To his Learned Friend and Loyal Fellow-Prisoner, Thomas Powel *of* Cant. *Doctor of Divinity*

If sever'd Friends by *Sympathy* can joyn,
And absent *Kings* be honour'd in their *coin*;
May they do both, who are so curb'd! but we
Whom no such *Abstracts* torture, that can see
And pay each other a full self-return,
May laugh, though all such *Metaphysics* burn.
'Tis a kind Soul in *Magnets*, that attones
Such two hard things as *Iron* are and *Stones*,
And in their dumb *compliance* we learn more
Of Love, than ever Books could speak before. 10
For though *attraction* hath got all the name,
As if that *power* but from one side came,
Which both unites; yet, where there is no *sence*,
There is no *Passion*, nor *Intelligence*:
And so by consequence we cannot state
A Commerce, unless both we animate.
For senseless things, though ne'r so call'd upon,
Are deaf, and feel no Invitation;
But such as at the last day shall be shed
By the great Lord of Life into the Dead. 20
'Tis then no *Heresie* to end the strife
With such rare Doctrine as gives *Iron* life.
For were it otherwise (which cannot be,
And do thou judge my bold Philosophie:)
Then it would follow that if I were dead,
Thy love, as now in life, would in that Bed
Of Earth and darkness warm me, and dispense,
Effectual informing Influence.
Since then 'tis clear, that Friendship is nought else
But a Joint, kind propension: and excess 30

In none, but such whose equal easie hearts
Comply and meet both in their *whole* and *parts*:
And when they cannot meet, do not forget
To mingle Souls, but secretly reflect
And some third place their Center make, where they
Silently mix, and make an unseen stay:
Let me not say (though *Poets* may be bold,)
Thou art more hard than *Steel*, than *Stones* more cold,
But as the *Mary-gold* in Feasts of Dew
And early Sun-beams, though but thin and few 40
Unfolds its self, then from the Earths cold breast
Heaves gently, and salutes the hopeful *East*:
So from thy quiet *Cell*, the retir'd Throne
Of thy fair thoughts, which silently bemoan
Our sad distractions, come: and richly drest
With reverend mirth and manners, check the rest
Of loose, loath'd men! why should I longer be
Rack't 'twixt two Ev'ls? *I see and cannot see.*

Thalia Rediviva

The King Disguis'd

Written about the same time that Mr. John Cleveland *wrote his*

A King and no King! Is he gone from us,
And stoln alive into his Coffin thus?
This was to ravish Death, and so prevent
The Rebells treason and their punishment.
He would not have them damn'd, and therefore he
Himself deposed his own Majesty.
Wolves did pursue him, and to fly the Ill
He wanders (Royal Saint!) in sheep-skin still.
Poor, obscure shelter! if that shelter be
Obscure, which harbours so much Majesty. 10
Hence prophane Eyes! the mysterie's so deep,
Like *Esdras* books, the vulgar must not see't.
  Thou flying Roll, written with tears and woe,
Not for thy Royal self, but for thy Foe:
Thy grief is prophecy, and doth portend,
Like sad *Ezekiel's* sighs, the Rebells end.
Thy robes forc'd off, like *Samuel's* when rent,
Do figure out anothers Punishment.
Nor grieve thou hast put off thy self a while,
To serve as Prophet to this sinful Isle; 20
These are our days of *Purim*, which oppress
The Church, and force thee to the Wilderness.
But all these Clouds cannot thy light confine,
The Sun in storms and after them, will shine.
Thy day of life cannot be yet compleat,
'Tis early sure; thy shadow is so great.
  But I am vex'd, that we at all can guess
This change, and trust great *Charles* to such a dress.
When he was first obscur'd with this coarse thing,
He grac'd *Plebeians*, but prophan'd the King. 30
Like some fair Church, which Zeal to Charcoals burn'd,
Or his own Court now to an Ale-house turn'd.

But full as well may we blame Night, and chide
His wisdom, who doth light with darkness hide:
Or deny Curtains to thy Royal Bed,
As take this sacred cov'ring from thy Head.
Secrets of State are points we must not know;
This vizard is thy privy Councel now,
Thou Royal Riddle, and in every thing
The true white Prince, our Hieroglyphic King! 40
Ride safely in his shade, who gives thee Light:
And can with blindness thy pursuers smite.
O may they wander all from thee as farr
As they from peace are, and thy self from Warr!
And wheresoe're thou do'st design to be
With thy (now spotted) spottles Majestie,
Be sure to look no Sanctuary there,
Nor hope for safety in a temple, where
Buyers and Sellers trade: O strengthen not
With too much trust the Treason of a Scot! 50

The Eagle

'Tis madness sure; And I am in the *Fitt*,
To dare an *Eagle* with my *unfledg'd* witt.
For what did ever *Rome* or *Athens* sing
In all their *Lines*, as loftie as his wing?
He that an Eagles *Powers* would rehearse
Should with his plumes first feather all his Verse.
I know not, when into thee I would prie,
Which to admire, thy *Wing* first: or thine *Eye*;
Or whether Nature at thy birth design'd
More of her *Fire* for thee, or of her *Wind*. 10
When thou in the clear *Heights* and upmost *Air*
Do'st face the Sun, and his dispersed Hair,
Ev'n from that distance thou the *Sea* do'st spie
And sporting in its deep, wide Lap the *Frie*.
Not the least *Minoe* there, but thou can'st see;
Whole Seas are narrow spectacles to thee.
Nor is this Element of water here
Below, of all thy miracles the sphere.

If Poets ought may add unto thy store,
Thou hast in Heav'n of wonders many more. 20
For when just *Jove* to Earth his thunder bends
And from that bright, eternal Fortress sends
His louder vollies: strait this Bird doth fly
To *Ætna*, where his Magazine doth lye:
And in his active Talons brings him more
Of ammunition, and recruits his store.
Nor is't a low, or easie *Lift*. He soares
'Bove *Wind* and *Fire*; gets to the *Moon*, and pores
With scorn upon her duller face; for she
Gives him but shadows and obscurity. 30
Here much displeas'd, that any thing like night
Should meet him in his proud and loftie flight,
That such dull *Tinctures* should advance so farr,
And rival in the glories of a star:
Resolv'd he is a nobler Course to try
And measures out his voyage with his Eye.
Then with such furie he begins his flight,
As if his *Wings* contended with his sight.
Leaving the Moon, whose humble light doth trade
With *Spotts*, and deals most in the *dark* and *shade*: 40
To the day's Royal *Planet* he doth pass
With daring Eyes, and makes the Sun his glass.
Here doth he plume and dress himself, the Beams
Rushing upon him, like so many Streams;
While with direct looks he doth entertain
The thronging flames, and shoots them back again.
And thus from star to star he doth repaire
And wantons in that pure and peaceful air.
Sometimes he frights the starrie *Swan*, and now
Orion's fearful *Hare* and then the Crow. 50
Then with the *Orbe* it self he moves, to see
Which is more swift th' *Intelligence* or *He*.
Thus with his wings his body he hath brought
Where man can travell only in a thought.

I will not seek, rare bird, what *Spirit* 'tis
That mounts thee thus; I'le be content with this;
To think, that Nature made thee to express
Our souls bold *Heights* in a material dress.

To Mr. M. L. *upon his reduction of the* Psalms *into Method*

SIR,

You have oblig'd the *Patriarch*. And tis known
He is your Debtor now, though for his own.
What he wrote, is a *Medley*. We can see
Confusion trespass on his Piety.
Misfortunes did not only Strike at him;
They charged further, and oppress'd his pen.
For he wrote as his *Crosses* came, and went
By no safe *Rule*, but by his *Punishment*.
His *quill* mov'd by the *Rod*; his witts and he 10
Did know no *Method*, but their *Misery*.
You brought his *Psalms* now into *Tune*. Nay, all
His measures thus are more than musical.
Your *Method* and his *Aires* are justly sweet,
And (what's *Church-musick* right) like *Anthems* meet.
You did so much in this, that I believe
He gave the *Matter*, you the *form* did give.
And yet I wish you were not understood,
For now '*tis a misfortune to be good*!
Why then, you'l say, all I would have, is this; 20
None must be good, because the time's amiss.
For since wise Nature did ordain the *Night*,
I would not have the *Sun* to give us Light.
Whereas this doth not take the *Use* away:
But urgeth the *Necessity* of day.
Proceed to make your pious work as free,
Stop not your seasonable charity.
Good works despis'd, or censur'd by bad times,
Should be sent out to aggravate their Crimes.
They should first *Share* and then *Reject* our store: 30
Abuse our *Good*, to make their *Guilt* the more.
'Tis *Warr* strikes at our *Sins*, but it must be
A *Persecution* wounds our *Pietie*.

To the pious memorie of C. W. Esquire *who finished his Course here, and made his Entrance into Immortality upon the* 13 *of* September, *in the year of* Redemption 1653

Now, that the publick Sorrow doth subside,
And those slight tears which *Custom* Springs, are dried;
While all the rich & *out-side-Mourners* pass
Home from thy *Dust* to empty their own *Glass*:
I (who the throng affect not, nor their state:)
Steal to thy grave undress'd, to meditate
On our sad loss, accompanied by none,
An obscure mourner that would weep alone.
So when the world's great Luminary setts,
Some scarce known Star into the *Zenith* gets, 10
Twinkles and curls a weak but willing spark:
As Gloworms here do glitter in the dark.
Yet, since the dimmest flame that kindles there,
An humble love unto the light doth bear,
And true devotion from an Hermits Cell
Will Heav'ns kind King as soon reach and as well
As that which from rich Shrines and Altars flyes
Lead by ascending Incense to the Skies:
'Tis no malicious rudeness, if the might
Of love makes dark things wait upon the bright, 20
And from my sad retirements calls me forth
The Just Recorder of thy death and worth.
Long did'st thou live (if length be measured by
The tedious Reign of our Calamity:)
And Counter to all storms and changes still
Kept'st the same temper, and the self same will.
Though trials came as duly as the day,
And in such mists, that none could see his way:
Yet thee I found still virtuous, and saw
The Sun give Clouds: and *Charles* give both the Law. 30
When private Interest did all hearts bend
And wild dissents the public peace did rend:
Thou neither won, nor worn wer't still thy self;
Not aw'd by force, nor basely brib'd with pelf.

What the insuperable stream of times
Did dash thee with, those *Suff'rings* were, not *Crimes*.
So the bright *Sun* Ecclipses bears; and we
Because then passive, blame him not, should he
For inforc'd shades, and the *Moon's* ruder veile
Much nearer us, than him; be Judg'd to fail? 40
Who traduce thee, so erre. As poisons by
Correction are made Antidotes, so thy
Just Soul did turn ev'n hurtful things to Good;
Us'd bad Laws so, they drew not Tears, nor Blood.
Heav'n was thy Aime, and thy great rare Design
Was not to Lord it here, but there to shine.
Earth nothing had, could tempt thee. All that e're
Thou pray'dst for here, was *Peace*; and *Glory* there.
For though thy Course in times long progress fell
On a sad age, when Warr and open'd Hell 50
Licens'd all Artes and Sects, and made it free
To thrive by fraud and blood and blasphemy:
Yet thou thy just Inheritance did'st by
No sacrilege, nor pillage multiply;
No rapine swell'd thy state: no bribes, nor fees
Our new oppressors best Annuities.
Such clean, pure hands had'st thou! And for thy heart
Man's secret region and his noblest part;
Since I was privy to't, and had the Key
Of that faire Room, where thy bright Spirit lay: 60
I must affirm, it did as much surpass
Most I have known, as the clear Sky doth glass.
Constant and kind, and plain and meek and Mild
It was, and with no new Conceits defil'd.
Busie, but sacred thoughts (like *Bees*) did still
Within it stirr, and strive unto that Hill,
Where redeem'd Spirits evermore alive
After their Work is done, ascend and *Hive*.
No outward tumults reach'd this inward place,
'Twas holy ground: where peace, and love and grace 70
Kept house: where the immortal restles life
In a most dutiful and pious strife
Like a fix'd *watch*, mov'd all in order, still;
The *Will* serv'd God, and ev'ry *Sense* the Will!

In this safe state death mett thee. Death which is
But a kind Usher of the good to bliss.
Therefore to Weep because thy Course is run,
Or droop like Flow'rs, which lately lost the *Sun*:
I cannot yield, since faith will not permitt,
A *Tenure* got by *Conquest* to the *Pitt*. 80
For the great Victour fought for us, and Hee
Counts ev'ry dust, that is lay'd up of thee.
Besides, Death now grows decrepit and hath
Spent the most part both of its time and wrath.
That thick, black night which mankind fear'd, is torn
By *Troops* of Stars, and the bright day's *Forlorn*.
The next glad news (most glad unto the Just!)
Will be the Trumpet's summons from the dust.
Then Ile not grieve; nay more, I'le not allow
My Soul should think thee absent from me now. 90
Some bid their Dead *good night!* but I will say
Good morrow to dear Charles! for it is day.

In Zodiacum Marcelli Palingenii

It is perform'd! and thy great *Name* doth run
Through ev'ry *Sign* an everlasting *Sun*.
Not Planet-like, but *fix'd*; and we can see
Thy *Genius* stand still in his *Apogie*.
For how canst thou an *Aux* eternal miss,
Where ev'ry *House* thine *Exaltation* is?
Here's no *Ecclyptic* threatens thee with night,
Although the wiser few take in thy light.
They are not at that glorious *pitch*, to be
In a *Conjunction* with *Divinitie*. 10
Could we partake some oblique *Ray* of thine,
Salute thee in a *Sextile*, or a *Trine*,
It were enough; but thou art flown so high,
The *Telescope* is turn'd a Common Eye.
Had the grave *Chaldee* liv'd thy Book to see,
He had known no *Astrologie*, but thee;
Nay more, (for I believ't,) thou shouldst have been
Tutor to all his Planets, and to him.

Thus whosoever reads thee, his charm'd sense
Proves captive to thy *Zodiac's* influence. 20
Were it not foul to erre so, I should look
Here for the *Rabbins* universal Book:
And say, their fancies did but dream of thee,
When first they doted on that mystery.
Each line's a *via lactea*, where we may
See thy fair steps, and tread that happy way
Thy *Genius* lead thee in. Still I will be
Lodg'd in some *Sign*, some *Face* and some *Degree*
Of thy bright *Zodiac*, Thus I'le teach my *Sense*
To move by that, and thee th' *Intelligence*. 30

To Lysimachus, *the Author being with him in* London

Saw not, *Lysimachus*, last day, when wee
Took the pure Air in its simplicity,
And our own too: how the trim'd *Gallants* went
Cringing, & past each step some Complement?
What strange, phantastic *Diagrams* they drew
With Legs and Arms; the like we never knew
In *Euclid*, *Archimed*: nor all of those
Whose learned lines are neither Verse nor Prose?
What store of *Lace* was there? how did the *Gold*
Run in rich *Traces*, but withall made bold 10
To measure the proud *things*, and so deride
The *Fops* with that, which was part of their pride?
How did they point at us, and boldly call,
As if we had been Vassals to them all,
Their poor *Men-mules* sent thither by hard fate
To yoke our selves for their *Sedans* and State?
Of all ambitions, this was not the least,
Whose drift translated man into a beast.
What blind discourse the *Heroes* did afford?
This *Lady* was their Friend, and such a *Lord*. 20
How much of *Blood* was in it? one could tell
He came from *Bevis* and his *Arundel*;

Morglay was yet with him, and he could do
More feats with it, than his old Grandsire too.
  Wonders my Friend at this? what is't to thee,
Who canst produce a nobler Pedigree,
And in meer truth affirm thy Soul of kin
To some bright *Star*, or to a *Cherubin*?
When these in their profuse *moods* spend the night
With the same sins, they drive away the light, 30
Thy learned *thrift* puts her to use; while she
Reveals her firy Volume unto thee;
And looking on the separated skies
And their clear Lamps with careful thoughts & eyes
Thou break'st through Natures upmost rooms & bars
To Heav'n, and there conversest with the Stars.
  Well fare such harmless, happy *nights* that be
Obscur'd with nothing but their *privacie*:
And missing but the false world's *glories*, do
Miss all those *vices*, which attend them too! 40
Fret not to hear their ill-got, ill-giv'n praise;
Thy darkest nights outshine their brightest dayes.

On Sir Thomas Bodley's *Library; the Author being then in* Oxford

Boast not proud *Golgotha*: that thou can'st show
The ruines of mankind, and let us know
How fraile a thing is flesh! though we see there
But empty Skulls, the *Rabbins* still live here.
They are not dead, but full of *Blood* again,
I mean the *Sense*, and ev'ry *Line* a *Vein*.
Triumph not o're their Dust; whoever looks
In here, shall find their *Brains* all in their Books.
  Nor is't old *Palestine* alone survives,
Athens lives here, more than in *Plutarch's* lives. 10
The stones which sometimes danc'd unto the strain
Of *Orpheus*, here do lodge his muse again.
And you the *Roman* Spirits, learning has
Made your lives longer, than your Empire was.

Cæsar had perish'd from the World of men,
Had not his *Sword* been rescu'd by his *pen*.
Rare *Seneca*! how lasting is thy breath?
Though *Nero* did, thou could'st not bleed to Death.
How dull the expert Tyrant was, to look
For that in thee, which lived in thy Book? 20
Afflictions turn our *Blood* to *Ink*, and we
Commence when *Writing*, our *Eternity*.
Lucilius here I can behold, and see
His *Counsels* and his *Life* proceed from thee.
But what care I to whom thy *Letters* be?
I change the *Name*, and thou do'st write to me;
And in this Age, as sad almost as thine,
Thy stately *Consolations* are mine.
Poor Earth! what though thy viler dust enrouls
The frail Inclosures of these mighty Souls? 30
Their graves are all upon Record; not one
But is as bright, and open as the Sun.
And though some part of them obscurely fell
And perish'd in an unknown, private Cell:
Yet in their books they found a glorious way
To live unto the Resurrection-day.
Most noble *Bodley*! we are bound to thee
For no small part of our *Eternity*.
Thy treasure was not spent on *Horse* and *Hound*,
Nor that new Mode, which doth old *States* confound. 40
Thy legacies another way did go:
Nor were they left to those would spend them so.
Thy safe, discreet Expence on us did flow;
Walsam is in the mid'st of *Oxford* now.
Th' hast made us all thine *Heirs*: whatever we
Hereafter write, 'tis thy *Posterity*.
This is thy *Monument*! here thou shalt stand
Till the times fail in their last grain of Sand.
And wheresoe're thy silent *Reliques* keep,
This *Tomb* will never let thine honour sleep. 50
Still we shall think upon thee; all our fame
Meets here to speak one *Letter* of thy name.
Thou can'st not dye! here thou art more than safe
Where every *Book* is thy large *Epitaph*.

The importunate Fortune, written to Doctor Powel *of* Cantre

For shame desist, why should'st thou seek my fall?
It cannot make thee more Monarchical.
Leave off; thy Empire is already built;
To ruine me were to inlarge thy guilt,
Not thy Prerogative. I am not he
Must be the measure to thy victory.
The Fates hatch more for thee; 'twere a disgrace
If in thy Annals I should make a Clause.
The future Ages will disclose such men,
Shall be the glory, and the end of them. 10
Nor do I flatter. So long as there be
Descents in Nature, or Posterity,
There must be Fortunes; whether they be good,
As swimming in thy Tide and plenteous Flood,
Or stuck fast in the shallow Ebb, when we
Miss to deserve thy gorgeous charity.
Thus, Fortune, the great World thy period is;
Nature and you are *Parallels* in this.
But thou wilt urge me still. Away, be gone;
I am resolv'd, I will not be undone. 20
I scorn thy trash and thee: nay more, I do
Despise my self, because thy Subject too.
Name me Heir to thy malice, and I'le be;
Thy hate's the best Inheritance for me.
I care not for your wondrous *Hat* and *Purse*:
Make me a *Fortunatus* with thy Curse.
How careful of my self then should I be,
Were I neglected by the world and thee?
Why do'st thou tempt me with thy dirty Ore,
And with thy Riches make my Soul so poor? 30
My Fancy's pris'ner to thy Gold and thee,
Thy favours rob me of my liberty.
I'le to my Speculations. Is't best
To be confin'd to some dark narrow chest
And Idolize thy Stamps, when I may be
Lord of all Nature, and not slave to thee?

The world's my Palace. I'le contemplate there,
And make my progress into ev'ry Sphere.
The Chambers of the *Air* are mine; those three
Well furnish'd *Stories* my possession be. 40
I hold them all *in Capite*, and stand
Propt by my Fancy there. I scorn your Land,
It lies so far below me. Here I see
How all the Sacred Stars do circle me.
Thou to the *Great* giv'st rich Food, and I do
Want no Content; I feed on *Manna* too.
They have their *Tapers*; I gaze without fear
On flying *Lamps*, and flaming *Comets* here.
Their wanton flesh in *Silks* and *Purple* Shrouds,
And Fancy wraps me in a *Robe* of *Clouds*. 50
There some delicious beauty they may woo,
And I have *Nature* for my Mistris too.
But these are mean; the *Archtype* I can see,
And humbly touch the *hem* of Majestie.
The power of my Soul is such, I can
Expire, and so *analyse* all that's man.
First my dull Clay I give unto the *Earth*,
Our common Mother, which gives all their birth.
My growing Faculties I send as soon
Whence first I took them, to the humid *Moon*. 60
All Subtilties and every cunning Art
To witty *Mercury* I do impart.
Those fond Affections which made me a slave
To handsome Faces, *Venus* thou shalt have.
And saucy Pride (if there was ought in me,)
Sol, I return it to thy Royalty.
My daring Rashness and Presumptions be
To *Mars* himself an equal Legacy.
My ill-plac'd Avarice (sure 'tis but small;)
Jove, to thy Flames I do bequeath it all. 70
And my false *Magic*, which I did believe,
And mystic Lyes to *Saturn* I do give.
My dark Imaginations rest you there,
This is your grave and Superstitious Sphære.
Get up my disintangled Soul, thy fire
Is now refin'd & nothing left to tire,

Or clog thy wings. Now my auspicious flight
Hath brought me to the *Empyrean* light.
I am a sep'rate *Essence*, and can see
The *Emanations* of the Deitie, 80
And how they pass the *Seraphims*, and run
Through ev'ry *Throne* and *Domination*.
So rushing through the Guard, the Sacred streams
Flow to the neighbour Stars, and in their beams
(A glorious Cataract!) descend to Earth
And give Impressions unto ev'ry birth.
With Angels now and Spirits I do dwell.
And here it is my Nature to do well,
Thus, though my Body you confined see,
My boundless thoughts have their *Ubiquitie*. 90
And shall I then forsake the *Stars* and *Signs*
To dote upon thy dark and cursed *Mines*?
Unhappy, sad exchange! what, must I buy
Guiana with the loss of all the skie?
Intelligences shall I leave, and be
Familiar only with mortalitie?
Must I know nought, but thy Exchequer? shall
My purse and fancy be Symmetrical?
Are there no Objects left but one? must we
In gaining that, lose our Varietie? 100
Fortune, this is the reason I refuse
Thy Wealth; it puts my Books all out of use.
'Tis poverty that makes me wise; my mind
Is big with speculation, when I find
My purse as *Randolph's* was, and I confess
There is no Blessing to an Emptiness!
The *Species* of all things to me resort
And dwell then in my breast, as in their port.
Then leave to Court me with thy hated store,
Thou giv'st me that, to rob my Soul of more. 110

To I. Morgan *of* White-Hall Esq; *upon his sudden Journey and succeeding Marriage*

So from our cold, rude World, which all things tires
To his warm *Indies* the bright sun retires.
Where in those provinces of Gold and spice
Perfumes his progress: *pleasures* fill his Eyes.
Which so refresh'd in their return convey
Fire into *Rubies*, into *Chrystalls* day;
And prove, that *Light* in kinder Climates can
Work more on senseless *Stones*, than here on *man*.
  But you, like one ordain'd to shine, take in
Both *Light* and *Heat*: can *Love* and *Wisdom* spin   10
Into one thred, and with that firmly tye
The same bright Blessings on posterity;
Which so intail'd, like *Jewels* of the Crown,
Shall with your *Name* descend still to your own.
  When I am dead, and malice or neglect
The worst they can upon my dust reflect,
(For *Poets* yet have left no names, but such
As men have *envied*, or *despis'd* too much;)
You above both (and what *state* more excells
Since a just Fame like *Health*, nor *wants*, nor *swells*?)   20
To after ages shall remain Entire,
And shine still spottles, like your planets Fire.
No single lustre neither; the access
Of your fair *Love* will yours adorn and bless;
Till from that bright *Conjunction*, men may view
A *Constellation* circling her and you:
  So two sweet *Rose-buds* from their *Virgin-beds*
First peep and blush, then kiss and couple heads;
Till yearly blessings so increase their store
Those two can number two and twenty more,   30
And the fair *Bank* (by heav'ns free bounty Crown'd)
With choice of *Sweets* and *Beauties* doth abound;
Till time, which *Familys* like *Flowers* far spreads;
Gives them for *Garlands* to the best of heads.
Then late posterity (if chance, or some
Weak *Eccho*, almost quite expir'd and dumb

Shall tell them, who the *Poet* was, and how
He liv'd and lov'd thee too; which thou do'st know)
Strait to my grave will *Flowers* and *spices* bring
With *Lights* and *Hymns*, and for an *Offering* 40
There vow this truth; That *Love* (which in old times
Was censur'd *blind*, and will contract worse Crimes
If hearts mend not;) did for thy sake in me
Find both his *Eyes*, and all foretell and see.

FIDA: *Or the Country-beauty: to* Lysimachus

Now I have seen her; And by *Cupid*
The young *Medusa* made me stupid!
A face, that hath no Lovers slain,
Wants forces, and is near disdain.
For every *Fop* will freely peep
At Majesty that is asleep.
But she (fair Tyrant!) hates to be
Gaz'd on with such impunity.
Whose prudent Rigor bravely bears
And scorns the trick of whining tears: 10
Or sighs, those false All-arms of grief,
Which kill not, but afford relief.
Nor is it thy hard fate to be
Alone in this Calamity,
Since I who came but to be gone,
Am plagu'd for meerly looking on.
Mark from her forhead to her foot
What charming *Sweets* are there to do't.
A *Head* adorn'd with all those glories
That *Witt* hath shadow'd in quaint stories: 20
Or *pencill* with rich colours drew
In imitation of the true.
Her *Hair* lay'd out in curious *Setts*
And *Twists*, doth shew like silken *Nets*,
Where (since he play'd at *Hitt* or *Miss*:)
The God of *Love* her pris'ner is,

And fluttering with his skittish Wings
Puts all her locks in Curls and Rings.
  Like twinkling Stars her *Eyes* invite
All gazers to so sweet a light, 30
But then two *arched Clouds* of brown
Stand o're, and guard them with a frown.
  Beneath these rayes of her bright Eyes
Beautie's rich *Bed* of *blushes* lyes.
Blushes, which lightning-like come on,
Yet stay not to be gaz'd upon;
But leave the *Lilies* of her Skin
As fair as ever, and run in:
Like swift *Salutes* (which dull *paint* scorn,)
Twixt a *white* noon, and *Crimson* Morne. 40
  What *Corall* can her *Lips* resemble?
For hers are warm, swell, melt and tremble:
And if you dare contend for *Red*,
This is *alive*, the other *dead*.
  Her equal *Teeth* (above, below:)
All of a *Cise*, and *Smoothness* grow.
Where under close restraint and awe
(Which is the Maiden, Tyrant law:)
Like a cag'd, sullen *Linnet*, dwells
Her *Tongue*, the *Key* to potent spells. 50
  Her *Skin*, like heav'n when calm and bright,
Shews a rich *azure* under *white*,
With *touch* more soft than heart supposes,
And *Breath* as sweet as new blown *Roses*.
  Betwixt this *Head-land* and the *Main*,
Which is a rich and flowry *Plain*:
Lyes her fair *Neck*, so fine and slender
That (gently) how you please, 'twill bend her.
  This leads you to her *Heart*, which ta'ne
Pants under *Sheets* of whitest *Lawn*, 60
And at the first seems much distrest,
But nobly treated, lyes at rest.
  Here like two *Balls* of new fall'n snow,
Her *Breasts*, Loves native *pillows* grow;
And out of each a *Rose-bud* Peeps
Which *Infant* beauty sucking, sleeps.

Say now my *Stoic*, that mak'st soure faces
At all the *Beauties* and the *Graces*,
That criest *unclean!* though known thy self
To ev'ry coorse, and dirty shelfe: 70
Could'st thou but see a *piece* like this,
A piece so full of *Sweets* and *bliss*:
In *shape* so rare, in *Soul* so rich,
Would'st thou not swear she is a witch?

Fida forsaken

Fool that I was! to believe blood
While swoll'n with greatness, then most good;
And the false thing, forgetful man:
To trust more than our true God, *Pan*,
Such swellings to a dropsie tend,
And meanest things such great ones bend.

Then live deceived! and *Fida* by
That life destroy fidelity.
For living wrongs will make some wise,
While death chokes lowdest Injuries: 10
And skreens the *faulty*, making Blinds
To hide the most unworthy minds.

And yet do what thou can'st to hide
A bad trees fruit will be descri'd
For that foul guilt which first took place
In his dark heart, now damns his face:
And makes those Eyes, where life should dwell,
Look like the pits of Death and Hell.

Bloud, whose rich *purple* shews and seals
Their faith in *Moors*, in him reveals 20
A blackness at the heart, and is
Turn'd *Inke*, to write his faithlesness.
Only his lips with bloud look *red*,
As if asham'd of what they sed.

Then, since he wears in a dark skin
The shadows of his hell within,

Expose him no more to the light,
But thine own *Epitaph* thus write.
Here burst, and dead and unregarded
Lyes Fida's *heart! O well rewarded!* 30

To the Editor of the matchless Orinda

Long since great witts have left the Stage
Unto the *Drollers* of the age,
And noble numbers with good sense
Are like good works, grown an offence.
While much of verse (worse than old story,)
Speaks but *Jack-Pudding*, or *John-Dory*.
Such trash-admirers made us poor,
And *Pyes* turn'd *Poets* out of door.
For the nice Spirit of rich verse
Which scorns absurd and low commerce, 10
Although a flame from heav'n, if shed
On *Rooks* or *Daws*: warms no such head.
Or else the Poet, like bad priest,
Is seldom good, but when opprest:
And wit, as well as piety
Doth thrive best in adversity;
For since the thunder left our air
Their *Laurels* look not half so fair.
However 'tis 'twere worse than rude
Not to profess our gratitude 20
And debts to thee, who at so low
An Ebbe do'st make us thus to flow:
And when we did a Famine fear,
Hast blest us with a fruitful year.
So while the world his absence mourns
The glorious Sun at last returns,
And with his kind and vital looks
Warms the cold Earth and frozen brooks:
Puts drowsie nature into play
And rids impediments away, 30
Till Flow'rs and Fruits and spices through
Her pregnant lap get up and grow.

But if among those sweet things, we
A miracle like that could see
Which nature brought but once to pass:
A *Muse*, such as *Orinda* was,
Phœbus himself won by these charms
Would give her up into thy arms;
And recondemn'd to kiss his *Tree*,
Yield the young *Goddess* unto thee. 40

Upon sudden news of the much lamented death of Judge Trevers

Learning and *Law* your *Day* is done,
And your *work* too; you may be gone!
Trever, that lov'd you, hence is fled:
And *Right*, which long lay *Sick*, is *dead*.
Trever! whose rare and envied *part*
Was both a wise and winning heart,
Whose sweet civilitys could move
Tartars and *Goths* to noblest love.
  Bold *Vice* and *blindness* now dare act,
And (like the *gray groat*,) pass, though crack't; 10
While those sage lips lye dumb and cold,
Whose words are well-weigh'd and tried gold.
O how much to descreet desires
Differs pure *Light* from foolish *fires*!
But nasty *Dregs* out last the *Wine*,
And after Sun-set *Gloworms* shine.

To Etesia (*for* Timander,) *the first Sight*

What smiling *Star* in that fair Night,
Which gave you *Birth* gave me this *Sight*,
And with a kind *Aspect* tho keen
Made me the *Subject*: you the *Queen*?
That sparkling *Planet* is got now
Into your Eyes, and shines below;

Where nearer force, and more acute
It doth dispence, without dispute,
For I who yesterday did know
Loves fire no more, than doth cool Snow 10
With one bright look am since undone;
Yet must adore and seek my Sun.
  Before I walk'd free as the wind,
And if but stay'd (like it,) unkind.
I could like daring Eagles gaze
And not be blinded by a face;
For what I saw, till I saw thee,
Was only not deformity.
Such shapes appear (compar'd with thine,)
In *Arras*, or a tavern-sign, 20
And do but mind me to explore
A fairer piece, that is in store.
So some hang *Ivy* to their Wine,
To signify, there is a *Vine*.
  Those princely Flow'rs (by no storms vex'd,)
Which smile one day, and droop the next:
The gallant *Tulip* and the *Rose*,
Emblems which some use to disclose
Bodyed *Idea's*: their weak grace
Is meer imposture to thy face. 30
For nature in all things, but thee,
Did practise only *Sophistry*;
Or else she made them to express
How she could vary in her dress:
But thou wert form'd, that we might see
Perfection, not Variety.
  Have you observ'd how the Day-star
Sparkles and smiles and shines from far:
Then to the gazer doth convey
A silent, but a piercing Ray? 40
So wounds my love, but that her Eys
Are in *Effects*, the better Skys.
A brisk bright *Agent* from them Streams
Arm'd with no arrows, but their beams,
And with such stillness smites our hearts,
No noise betrays him, nor his darts.

He working on my easie Soul
Did soon persuade, and then controul;
And now he flyes (and I conspire)
Through all my blood with wings of fire, 50
And when I would (which will be never)
With cold despair allay the fever:
The spiteful thing *Etesia* names,
And that new-fuells all my flames.

The Character, to Etesia

Go catch the *Phœnix*, and then bring
A *quill* drawn for me from his wing.
Give me a Maiden-beautie's *Bloud*,
A pure, rich *Crimson*, without mudd:
In whose sweet *Blushes* that may live,
Which a dull verse can never give.
Now for an untouch'd, spottles *white*,
For blackest things on paper write;
Etesia at thine own Expence
Give me the *Robes* of innocence. 10
Could we but see a *Spring* to run
Pure *Milk*, as sometimes Springs have done,
And in the *Snow-white* streams it sheds
Carnations wash their *bloudy* heads.
While ev'ry *Eddy* that came down
Did (as thou do'st,) both *smile* and *frown*.
Such objects and so fresh would be
But dull Resemblances of thee.
Thou art the dark worlds Morning-star,
Seen only, and seen but from far; 20
Where like Astronomers we gaze
Upon the glories of thy face,
But no acquaintance more can have,
Though all our lives we watch and Crave.
Thou art a world thy self alone,
Yea three great worlds refin'd to one.
Which shews all those, and in thine Eyes
The shining *East*, and *Paradise*.

Thy Soul (a *Spark* of the first *Fire*,)
Is like the *Sun*, the worlds desire; 30
And with a nobler influence
Works upon all, that claim to sense;
But in *Summers* hath no *fever*,
And in frosts is chearful ever.
As *Flowr's*, besides their curious *dress*
Rich *odours* have, and *Sweetnesses*.
Which tacitely infuse desire
And ev'n oblige us to admire:
Such and so full of innocence
Are all the *Charms*, thou do'st dispence; 40
And like fair *Nature*, without *Arts*
At once they seize, and please our hearts.
O thou art such, that I could be
A lover to Idolatry!
I could, and should from heav'n stray,
But that thy life shews mine the way,
And leave a while the *Diety*,
To serve his *Image* here in thee.

To Etesia *looking from her Casement at the full* Moon

See you that beauteous *Queen*, which no age tames?
Her Train is *Azure*, set with *golden* flames.
My brighter *fair*, fix on the *East* your Eyes,
And view that bed of Clouds, whence she doth rise.
Above all others in that one short hour
Which most concern'd me, she had greatest pow'r.
This made my *Fortunes* humorous as wind,
But fix'd *Affections* to my constant mind.
She fed me with the *tears* of *Starrs*, and thence
I suck'd in *Sorrows* with their *Influence*. 10
To some in *smiles*, and store of *light* she broke:
To me in sad *Eclipses* still she spoke.
She bent me with the motion of her *Sphere*,
And made me feel, what first I did but fear.

But when I came to Age, and had o'regrown
Her Rules, and saw my freedom was my own,
I did reply unto the Laws of Fate,
And made my Reason, my great Advocate:
I labour'd to inherit my just right;
But then (O hear *Etesia*!) lest I might 20
Redeem my self, my unkind Starry Mother
Took my poor Heart, and gave it to another.

To Etesia *parted from him, and looking back*

O Subtile Love! thy Peace is War;
It wounds and kills without a scar:
It works unknown to any sense,
Like the Decrees of Providence,
And with strange silence shoots me through;
The *Fire* of Love doth fall like *Snow*.
Hath she no *Quiver*, but my Heart?
Must all her Arrows hit that part?
Beauties like Heav'n, their Gifts should deal
Not to destroy us, but to heal. 10
Strange *Art* of Love! that can make sound,
And yet exasperates the wound;
That *look* she lent to ease my heart,
Hath pierc't it, and improv'd the smart.

In Etesiam lachrymantem

O dulcis luctus, risuque potentior omni!
Quem decorant lachrymis Sydera tanta suis.
Quam tacitæ spirant auræ! vultusque nitentes
Contristant veneres, collachrymantque suæ!
Ornat gutta genas, oculisque simillima gemma:
Et tepido vivas irrigat imbre rosas.
Dicite Chaldæi*! quæ me fortuna fatigat,*
Cum formosa dies & sine nube perit?

To Etesia *going beyond Sea*

Go, if you must! but stay—and know
And mind before you go, my vow.
  To ev'ry thing, but *Heav'n* and *you*,
With all my Heart, I bid Adieu!
Now to those happy *Shades* I'le go
Where first I saw my beauteous Foe.
I'le seek each silent *path*, where we
Did walk, and where you sate with me
I'le sit again, and never rest
Till I can find some *flow'r* you prest. 10
That near my dying Heart I'le keep,
And when it wants *Dew*, I will weep:
Sadly I will repeat past Joyes,
And Words, which you did sometimes voice:
I'le listen to the *Woods*, and hear
The *Eccho* answer for you there.
But famish'd with long absence I
Like *Infants* left, at last shall cry,
And Tears (as they do *Milk*) will sup
Until you come, and take me up. 20

Etesia *absent*

Love, the Worlds Life! what a sad death
Thy absence is? to lose our breath
At once and dye, is but to live
Inlarg'd, without the scant reprieve
Of *Pulse* and *Air*: whose dull *returns*
And narrow *Circles* the Soul mourns.
  But to be dead alive, and still
To wish, but never have our will:
To be possess'd, and yet to miss;
To wed a true but absent bliss: 10
Are lingring tortures, and their smart
Dissects and racks and grinds the Heart!
As Soul and Body in that state
Which unto us seems separate,

Cannot be said to live, until
Reunion; which dayes fulfill
And slow-pac'd seasons: So in vain
Through hours and minutes (Times long *train*,)
I look for thee, and from thy sight,
As from my Soul, for life and light. 20
For till thine Eyes shine so on me,
Mine are fast-clos'd and will not see.

Translations

Some *Odes* of the Excellent and Knowing *Severinus*, Englished

Metrum 12. *Lib.* 3

Happy is he, that with fix'd Eyes
The Fountain of all goodness spies!
Happy is he, that can break through
Those Bonds, which tie him here below!
  The *Thracian* Poet long ago
Kind *Orpheus*, full of tears and wo
Did for his lov'd *Euridice*
In such sad Numbers mourn, that he
Made the *Trees* run in to his mone,
And *Streams* stand still to hear him grone. 10
The *Does* came fearless in one throng
With *Lyons* to his mournful Song,
And charm'd by the harmonious sound
The *Hare* stay'd by the quiet *Hound*.
  But when *Love* heightned by *despair*
And deep *reflections* on his *Fair*
Had swell'd his Heart, and made it rise
And run in Tears out at his Eyes:
And those sweet *Aires*, which did appease
Wild Beasts, could give their Lord no ease; 20
Then vex'd, that so much grief and Love
Mov'd not at all the gods above,

With desperate thoughts and bold intent,
Towards the *Shades* below he went;
For thither his fair Love was fled,
And he must have her from the dead.
There in such *Lines*, as did well suit
With sad *Aires* and a Lovers *Lute*,
And in the richest Language drest
That could be thought on, or exprest, 30
Did he complain, whatever *Grief*,
Or *Art*, or *Love* (which is the chief,
And all innobles,) could lay out;
In well-tun'd woes he dealt about.
And humbly bowing to the *Prince*
Of Ghosts, begg'd some Intelligence
Of his *Euridice*, and where
His beauteous *Saint* resided there.
Then to his *Lutes* instructed grones
He sigh'd out new melodious mones; 40
And in a melting charming *strain*
Begg'd his dear *Love* to life again.
The *Music* flowing through the shade
And darkness, did with ease invade
The silent and attentive Ghosts;
And *Cerberus*, which guards those coasts
With his lowd barkings, overcome
By the sweet *Notes*, was now struck dumb.
The *Furies*, us'd to rave and howl
And prosecute each guilty Soul, 50
Had lost their rage, and in a deep
Transport did most profusely weep.
Ixion's wheel stopt, and the curst
Tantalus almost kill'd with thirst,
Though the *Streams* now did make no haste,
But waited for him, none would taste.
That *Vultur*, which fed still upon
Tityus his liver, now was gone
To feed on *Air*, and would not stay
Though almost famish'd, with her prey. 60
Won with these wonders, their fierce Prince
At last cry'd out, *We yield! and since*

Thy merits claim no less, take hence
Thy Consort for thy Recompence.
But, Orpheus, *to this law we bind*
Our grant, *you must not look behind*,
Nor of your fair Love have one Sight,
Till out of our Dominions quite.
Alas! what laws can Lovers awe?
Love is it self the greatest Law! 70
Or who can such hard bondage brook
To be in Love, and not to Look?
Poor *Orpheus* almost in the light
Lost his dear Love for one short sight;
And by those Eyes, which Love did guide,
What he most lov'd unkindly dyed!
This tale of *Orpheus* and his *Love*
Was meant for you, who ever move
Upwards, and tend into that light,
Which is not seen by mortal sight. 80
For if, while you strive to ascend,
You droop, and towards Earth once bend
Your seduc'd Eyes, down you will fall
Ev'n while you look, and forfeit all.

Metrum 2. Lib. 3

What fix'd *Affections*, and lov'd *Laws*
(Which are the hid, magnetic *Cause*;)
Wise *Nature* governs with, and by
What fast, inviolable *tye*
The whole Creation to her ends
For ever provident she bends:
All this I purpose to rehearse
In the sweet *Airs* of solemn Verse.
Although the *Lybian Lyons* should
Be bound with chains of purest Gold, 10
And duely fed, were taught to know
Their keepers voice, and fear his blow:
Yet, if they chance to taste of bloud,
Their rage which slept, stirr'd by that food
In furious roarings will awake,
And fiercely for their freedom make.

No chains, nor bars their fury brooks,
But with inrag'd and bloody looks
They will break through, and dull'd with fear
Their keeper all to pieces tear. 20
  The *Bird*, which on the *Woods* tall boughs
Sings sweetly, if you Cage or house,
And out of kindest care should think
To give her honey with her drink,
And get her store of pleasant meat,
Ev'n such as she delights to Eat:
Yet, if from her close prison she
The *shady-groves* doth chance to see,
Straitway she loaths her pleasant food
And with sad looks longs for the *Wood*. 30
The wood, the wood alone she loves!
And towards it she looks and moves:
And in sweet *notes* (though distant from,)
Sings to her first and happy home!
  That *Plant*, which of it self doth grow
Upwards, if forc'd, will downwards bow;
But give it freedom, and it will
Get up, and grow erectly still.
  The *Sun*, which by his prone descent
Seems westward in the Evening bent, 40
Doth nightly by an unseen way
Haste to the *East*, and bring up day.
  Thus all things long for their first State,
And gladly to't return, though late.
Nor is there here to any thing
A *Course* allow'd, but in a *Ring*;
Which, where it first *began*, must *end*:
And to that *Point* directly tend.

Metrum 6. Lib. 4

Who would unclouded see the Laws
Of the supreme, eternal *Cause*,
Let him with careful thoughts and eyes
Observe the high and spatious Skyes.
There in one league of Love the *Stars*
Keep their old peace, and shew our wars.

The *Sun*, though flaming still and hot,
The cold, pale *Moon* annoyeth not.
Arcturus with his *Sons* (though they
See other stars go a far way, 10
And out of sight,) yet still are found
Near the *North-pole*, their noted bound.
Bright *Hesper* (at set times) delights
To usher in the dusky nights:
And in the *East* again attends
To warn us, when the day ascends,
So alternate *Love* supplys
Eternal Courses still, and vies
Mutual kindness; that no Jars
Nor discord can disturb the Stars. 20

The same sweet *Concord* here below
Makes the fierce *Elements* to flow
And *Circle* without quarrel still,
Though temper'd diversly; thus will
The *Hot* assist the *Cold*: the *Dry*
Is a friend to *Humidity*.
And by the *Law* of *kindness* they
The like relief to them repay.
The *fire*, which active is and bright,
Tends upward, and from thence gives light. 30
The *Earth* allows it all that space
And makes choice of the lower place;
For things of weight hast to the Center
A fall to them is no adventure.

From these kind *turns* and *Circulation*
Seasons proceed and *Generation*.
This makes the *Spring* to yield us flow'rs,
And melts the Clouds to gentle show'rs.
The *Summer* thus matures all seeds
And ripens both the Corn and weeds. 40
This brings on *Autumn*, which recruits
Our old, spent store with new fresh fruits.
And the cold *Winters* blustring Season
Hath snow and storms for the same reason.
This *temper* and wise *mixture* breed
And bring forth ev'ry living *seed*.

And when their *strength* and *substance* spend
(For while they *live*, they drive and tend
Still to a *change*,) it takes them hence
And shifts their *dress*; and to our sense 50
Their *Course* is over, as their *birth*:
And hid from us, they turn to Earth.
  But all this while the *Prince* of life
Sits without *loss*, or *change*, or *strife*:
Holding the *Rains*, by which all move;
(And those his *wisdom*, *power*, *Love*
And *Justice* are;) And still what he
The *first life* bids, that needs must be,
And live on for a time; that done
He calls it back, meerly to shun 60
The mischief, which his *creature* might
Run into by a further flight.
For if this dear and tender sense
Of his preventing providence
Did not restrain and call things back:
Both heav'n and earth would go to wrack.
And from their great *preserver* part,
As *blood* let out forsakes the *Heart*
And perisheth; but what returns
With fresh and Brighter spirits burns. 70
  This is the *Cause* why ev'ry living
Creature affects an *endless being*.
A *grain* of this bright *love* each thing
Had giv'n at first by their great King;
And still they creep (drawn on by this:)
And look back towards their *first bliss*.
For otherwise, it is most sure,
Nothing that liveth could *endure*:
Unless it's Love turn'd retrograde
Sought that *first life*, which all things made. 80

Metrum 3. Lib. 4

If old tradition hath not fail'd,
Ulysses, when from *Troy* he sail'd,
Was by a tempest forc'd to land
Where beauteous *Circe* did command.

Circe, the daughter of the Sun,
Which had with *Charms* and *Herbs* undone
Many poor strangers, and could then
Turn into Beasts, the bravest Men.
Such *Magic* in her potions lay
That whosoever past that way 10
And drank, his shape was quickly lost;
Some into *Swine* she turn'd, but most
To *Lyons* arm'd with teeth and claws;
Others like *Wolves*, with open Jaws
Did howl; But some (more savage) took
The *Tiger's* dreadful shape and look.
But wise *Ulysses* by the *Aid*
Of *Hermes*, had to him convey'd
A *Flow'r*, whose virtue did suppress
The force of charms, and their success. 20
While his *Mates* drank so deep, that they
Were turn'd to *Swine*, which fed all day
On *Mast*, and humane food had left;
Of shape and voice at once bereft.
Only the *Mind* (above all charms,)
Unchang'd, did mourn those monstrous harms.
O worthless *herbs*, and weaker *Arts*
To change their *Limbs*, but not their *Hearts*!
Mans *life and vigor* keep within,
Lodg'd in the *Center*, not the *Skin*. 30
Those piercing charms and poysons, which
His *inward parts* taint and bewitch,
More fatal are, than such, which can
Outwardly only spoile the man.
Those change his *shape* and make it foul;
But these deform and kill his soul.

Metrum 6. Lib. 3

All *sorts* of men, that live on Earth,
Have one *beginning* and one *birth*.
For all things there is one *Father*,
Who *lays out* all, and all doth *gather*.
He the warm Sun with rays adorns,
And fils with brightness the Moon's horns.

The azur'd heav'ns with stars he burnish'd
And the round world with creatures furnish'd.
But *Men* (made to inherit all,)
His *own Sons* he was pleas'd to call, 10
And that they might be so indeed,
He gave them *Souls* of divine seed.
A noble *Offspring* surely then
Without distinction, are all men.
O why so vainly do some boast
Their *Birth* and *Blood*, and a great *Hoste*
Of Ancestors, whose *Coats* and *Crests*
Are some rav'nous *Birds* or *Beasts*!
If *Extraction* they look for
And *God*, the great *Progenitor*: 20
No man, though of the meanest state
Is *base*, or can *degenerate*;
Unless to *Vice* and *lewdness* bent
He leaves and *taints* his true *descent*.

The old man of Verona *out of* Claudian

Fælix, qui propriis ævum transegit in arvis,
Una domus puerum &c.

Most happy man! who in his own sweet *fields*
Spent all his time, to whom one *Cottage* yields
In *age* and *youth* a lodging: who grown *old*
Walks with his *staff* on the same *soil* and *mold*
Where he did creep an *infant*, and can tell
Many fair years spent in one quiet *Cell*!
No *toils* of fate made him from home far known,
Nor forreign *waters* drank, driv'n from his own.
No loss by *Sea*, no wild *lands* wastful war
Vex'd him; not the brib'd *Coil* of *gowns* at bar. 10
Exempt from *cares*, in *Cities* never seen
The fresh *field-air* he loves, and rural *green*.
The years set *turns* by *fruits*, not *Consuls* knows;
Autumn by apples: *May* by blossom'd boughs.
Within one hedg his *Sun* doth set and rise,
The world's wide day his short Demeasnes comprise.

Where he observes some known, concrescent *twig*
Now grown an *Oak*, and old, like him, and big.
Verona he doth for the *Indies* take,
And as the *red Sea* counts *Benacus* lake. 20
Yet are his *limbs* and *strength* untir'd, and he
A lusty *Grandsire* three *descents* doth see.
Travel and sail who will, search sea, or shore;
This man hath *liv'd*, and that hath *wander'd* more.

The Sphere of Archimedes *out of* Claudian

Jupiter *in parvo cum cerneret æthera vitro*
Risit, & ad superos &c.

When *Jove* a heav'n of small glass did behold,
He smil'd, and to the Gods these words he told.
Comes then the power of mans *Art* to this?
In a fraile *Orbe* my work new acted is.
The *poles* decrees, the *fate* of things: *God's* laws
Down by his *Art* old *Archimedes* draws.
Spirits inclos'd the sev'ral *Stars* attend,
And orderly the *living work* they bend.
A feigned *Zodiac* measures out the year,
Ev'ry new *month* a false *Moon* doth appear. 10
And now bold *industry* is proud, it can
Wheel round its *world*, and rule the *Stars* by man.
Why at *Salmoneus* thunder do I stand?
Nature is rivall'd by a *single hand*.

The Phœnix *out of* Claudian

Oceani summo circumfluus æquore lucus
Trans Indos, Eurumque viret &c,

A grove there grows round with the *Sea* confin'd
Beyond the *Indies*, and the *Eastern* wind.
Which, as the *Sun* breaks forth in his first beam,
Salutes his *steeds*, and hears him whip his *team*.
When with his dewy *Coach* the *Eastern* Bay
Crackles, whence blusheth the approaching day;

And blasted with his burnish'd *wheels*, the night
In a pale dress doth vanish from the light.
  This the blest *Phœnix* Empire is, here he
Alone exempted from mortality, 10
Enjoys a land, where no diseases raign;
And ne'r afflicted, like our world, with pain.
A *Bird* most equal to the Gods, which vies
For length of life and durance, with the skyes;
And with renewed limbs tires ev'ry age,
His appetite he never doth asswage
With common food. Nor doth he use to drink
When thirsty, on some *River's* muddy brink.
A purer, vital *heat* shot from the Sun
Doth nourish him, and *airy sweets* that come 20
From *Tethis* lap, he tasteth at his need;
On such *abstracted Diet* doth he feed.
  A secret *Light* there streams from both his Eyes
A firy *hue* about his *cheeks* doth rise.
His *Crest* grows up into a glorious *Star*
Giv'n t' adorn his head, and shines so far,
That piercing through the bosom of the night
It rends the darkness with a gladsome light.
His thighs like *Tyrian* scarlet, and his wings
(More swift than *Winds* are,) have skie-colour'd *rings* 30
Flowry and rich: and round about inroll'd
Their utmost *borders* glister all with gold.
Hee's not conceiv'd, nor springs he from the Earth,
But is himself the *Parent*, and the *birth*.
None him begets; his fruitful death reprieves
Old age, and by his funerals he lives.
For when the tedious *Summer*'s gone about
A thousand times: so many *Winters* out,
So many *Springs*: and *May* doth still restore
Those leaves, which *Autumn* had blown off before; 40
Then prest with years his vigour doth decline
Foil'd with the number; as a stately *Pine*
Tir'd out with storms, bends from the top & height
Of *Caucasus*, and falls with its own weight:
Whose part is torn with dayly *blasts*, with *Rain*
Part is consum'd, and part with *Age* again.

So now his Eyes grown dusky, fail to see
Far off, and drops of colder rheums there be
Fall'n slow and dreggy from them; such in sight
The cloudy *Moon* is, having spent her light. 50
And now his *wings*, which used to contend
With *Tempests*, scarce from the low Earth ascend.
He knows his time is out! and doth provide
New principles of life; herbs he brings dried
From the hot hills, and with rich spices frames
A *Pile* shall burn, and *Hatch* him with its flames.
On this the *weakling* sits; salutes the Sun
With pleasant noise, and prays and begs for some
Of his own fire, that quickly may restore
The youth and vigour, which he had before. 60
Whom soon as *Phœbus* spyes, stopping his rayns,
He makes a stand and thus allayes his pains.
O thou that buriest old age in thy grave,
And art by seeming funerals to have
A new return of life! whose custom 'tis
To rise by ruin, and by death to miss
Ev'n death it self: a new beginning take,
And that thy wither'd body now forsake!
Better thy self by this thy change! This sed,
He shakes his *locks*, and from his golden *head* 70
Shoots one bright *beam*, which smites with vital fire
The willing bird; to burn is his desire,
That he may live again: he's proud in death,
And goes in haste to gain a better breath.
The spicie heap fir'd with cœlestial rays
Doth burn the aged *Phœnix*, when strait stays
The Chariot of th' amazed *Moon*; the *pole*
Resists the wheeling, swift *Orbs*, and the whole
Fabric of *Nature* at a stand remains,
Till the old bird a new, young being gains. 80
All stop and charge the faithful flames, that they
Suffer not nature's glory to decay.
By this time, *life* which in the ashes lurks
Hath fram'd the *Heart*, and taught new *bloud* new *works*;
The whole *heap* stirs, and ev'ry *part* assumes
Due vigour; th' *Embers* too are turn'd to *plumes*.

The parent in the Issue now revives,
But young and brisk; the bounds of both these lives
With very little space between the same,
Were parted only by the middle flame. 90
To *Nilus* straight he goes to consecrate
His parents ghoste; his mind is to translate
His dust to *Egypt*. Now he hastes away
Into a distant land, and doth convey
The ashes in a turf. Birds do attend
His Journey without number, and defend
His pious flight like to a guard; the sky
Is clouded with the Army, as they fly.
Nor is there one of all those thousands dares
Affront his leader: they with solomn cares 100
Attend the progress of their youthful king;
Not the rude hawk, nor th' Eagle that doth bring
Arms up to *Jove*, fight now; lest they displease;
The miracle enacts a common peace.
So doth the *Parthian* lead from *Tigris* side
His barbarous troops, full of a lavish pride
In pearls and habit, he adorns his head
With royal tires: his steed with gold is lead.
His robes, for which the scarlet fish is sought,
With rare *Assyrian* needle work are wrought. 110
And proudly reigning o're his rascal bands,
He raves and triumphs in his large Commands.
A City of *Egypt* famous in all lands
For rites, adores the *Sun*, his temple stands
There on a hundred pillars by account
Dig'd from the quarries of the *Theban* mount.
Here, as the Custom did require (they say,)
His happy parents dust down he doth lay;
Then to the Image of his *Lord* he bends
And to the flames his burden strait commends. 120
Unto the *Altars* thus he destinates
His own Remains: the light doth gild the gates;
Perfumes divine the *Censers* up do send:
While th' *Indian* odour doth it self extend
To the *Pelusian* fens, and filleth all
The men it meets with the sweet storm. A gale

To which compar'd, *Nectar* it self is vile:
Fills the seav'n channels of the misty *Nile*.
  O happy bird! sole heir to thy own dust!
Death, to whose force all other Creatures must 130
Submit, saves thee. Thy ashes make thee rise;
'Tis not thy nature, but thy age that dies.
Thou hast seen All! and to the times that run
Thou art as great a witness, as the Sun.
Thou saw'st the *deluge*, when the sea outvied
The land, and drown'd the mountains with the tide.
What year the stragling *Phaeton* did fire
The world, thou know'st. And no plagues can conspire
Against thy life; alone thou do'st arise
Above mortality; the Destinies 140
Spin not thy days out with their fatal Clue;
They have no Law, to which thy life is due.

Pious thoughts and Ejaculations

To his Books

Bright books! the *perspectives* to our weak sights:
The clear *projections* of discerning lights.
Burning and shining *Thoughts*; man's posthume *day*:
The *track* of fled souls, and their *Milkie-way*.
The dead *alive* and *busie*, the still *voice*
Of inlarg'd Spirits, kind heav'ns white *Decoys*.
Who lives with you, lives like those knowing *flow'rs*,
Which in commerce with *light*, spend all their hours:
Which shut to *Clouds*, and *shadows* nicely shun;
But with glad haste unveil to *kiss* the Sun. 10
Beneath you all is dark and a dead night;
Which whoso lives in, wants both health and sight.
  By sucking you, the wise (like *Bees*) do grow
Healing and rich, though this they do most slow:
Because most choicely, for as great a store
Have we of *Books*, as Bees of *herbs*, or more.

And the great task to *try*, then know the good:
To discern *weeds*, and Judge of wholsome *Food*,
Is a rare, scant performance; for *Man* dyes
Oft e're 'tis done, while the *bee* feeds and flyes. 20
But you were all choice *Flow'rs*, all set and drest
By old, sage *florists*, who well knew the best.
And I amidst you all am turn'd a *weed*!
Not wanting knowledge, but for want of heed.
Then thank thy self *wild fool*, that would'st not be
Content to know——what was to much for thee!

Looking back

Fair, shining *Mountains* of my pilgrimage,
And flow'ry *Vales*, whose flow'rs were stars:
The *days* and *nights* of my first, happy age;
An age without distast and warrs:
When I by thoughts ascend your *Sunny heads*,
And mind those sacred, *midnight* Lights:
By which I walk'd, when curtain'd Rooms and Beds
Confin'd, or seal'd up others sights:
O then how bright
And quick a light 10
Doth brush my heart and scatter night;
Chasing that shade
Which my sins made,
While I so *spring*, as if I could not *fade*!

How brave a prospect is a bright *Back-side*!
Where flow'rs and palms refresh the Eye:
And days well spent like the glad *East* abide,
Whose morning-glories cannot dye!

The Shower

Waters above! eternal Springs!
The dew, that silvers the *Doves* wings!
O welcom, welcom to the sad:
Give dry dust drink; drink that makes glad!

Many fair *Ev'nings*, many *Flowr's*
Sweeten'd with rich and gentle showers
Have I enjoy'd, and down have run
Many a fine and shining *Sun*;
But never till this happy hour
Was blest with such an *Evening-shower*! 10

Discipline

Fair prince of life, lights living well!
Who hast the keys of death and hell!
If the mole man despise thy day,
Put chains of darkness in his way.
Teach him how deep, how various are
The Councels of thy love and care.
When Acts of grace and a long peace
Breed but rebellion and displease;
Then give him his own way and will,
Where lawless he may run until 10
His own choice hurts him, and the sting
Of his foul sins full sorrows bring.
If Heav'n and Angels, hopes and mirth
Please not the *mole* so much as Earth:
Give him his *Mine* to dig, or dwell;
And one sad *Scheme* of hideous hell.

The Ecclipse

Whither, O whither did'st thou fly
When I did grieve thine holy Eye?
When thou did'st mourn to see me lost,
And all thy Care and Councels crost.
O do not grieve where e'er thou art!
Thy grief is an undoing smart.
Which doth not only pain, but break
My heart, and makes me blush to speak.
Thy anger I could kiss, and will:
But (O!) thy grief, thy grief doth kill. 10

Affliction

O come, and welcom! Come, refine;
For *Moors* if wash'd by thee, will shine.
Man *blossoms* at thy touch; and he
When thou draw'st blood, is thy *Rose-tree*.
Crosses make strait his *crooked* ways,
And *Clouds* but cool his *dog-star* days.
Diseases too, when by thee blest,
Are both *restoratives* and *rest*.
  Flow'rs that in *Sun-shines* riot still,
Dye scorch'd and sapless; though *storms* kill. 10
The fall is fair ev'n to desire,
Where in their *sweetness* all expire.
O come, pour on! what *calms* can be
So fair as *storms*, that appease thee?

Retirement

Fresh *fields* and *woods*! the Earth's fair *face*,
God's *foot-stool*, and mans *dwelling-place*.
I ask not why the first *Believer*
Did love to be a Country liver?
Who to secure pious content
Did pitch by *groves* and *wells* his tent;
Where he might view the boundless *skie*,
And all those glorious *lights* on high:
With flying *meteors*, *mists* and *show'rs*,
Subjected *hills*, *trees*, *meads* and *Flow'rs*: 10
And ev'ry minute bless the King
And wise Creatour of each thing.
  I ask not why he did remove
To happy *Mamre*'s holy grove,
Leaving the *Citie*'s of the plain
To *Lot* and his successless train?
All various Lusts in *Cities* still
Are found; they are the *Thrones* of Ill.
The dismal *Sinks*, where blood is spill'd,
Cages with much uncleanness fill'd. 20

But *rural shades* are the sweet fense
Of piety and innocence.
They are the *Meek*'s calm region, where
Angels descend, and rule the sphere:
Where heav'n lyes *Leiguer*, and the *Dove*
Duely as *Dew*, comes from above.
If *Eden* be on Earth at all,
'Tis that, which we the *Country* call.

The Revival

Unfold, unfold! take in his light,
Who makes thy Cares more short than night.
The Joys, which with his *Day-star* rise,
He deals to all, but drowsy Eyes:
And what the men of this world miss,
Some *drops* and *dews* of future bliss.
Hark! how his *winds* have chang'd their *note*,
And with warm *whispers* call thee out.
The *frosts* are past, the *storms* are gone:
And backward *life* at last comes on. 10
The lofty *groves* in express Joyes
Reply unto the *Turtles* voice,
And here in *dust* and *dirt*, O here
The *Lilies* of his love appear!

The Day-spring

Early, while yet the *dark* was gay,
And *gilt* with stars, more trim than day:
Heav'ns *Lily*, and the Earth's chast *Rose*: } *S. Mark*
The green, immortal BRANCH arose; } *c.* I. *v.* 35
And in a solitary place
Bow'd to his father his bless'd face.
If this calm season pleas'd my *Prince*,
Whose *fullness* no need could evince,
Why should not I poor, silly sheep
His *hours*, as well as *practice* keep? 10

Not that his hand is tyed to these,
From whom *time* holds his transient *Lease:*
But *mornings*, new Creations are,
When men all night sav'd by his Care,
Are still reviv'd; and well he may
Expect them grateful with the day.
So for that first *drawght* of his hand,
Which finish'd heav'n and sea and land,
The *Sons* of God their thanks did bring, — Job. *c.* 38. *v.* 7
And all the *Morning-stars* did sing. 20
Besides, as his part heretofore
The *firstlings* were of all, that bore:
So now each day from all he saves,
Their Soul's *first thoughts* and fruits he craves.
This makes him daily shed and shower
His graces at this early hour;
Which both his Care and Kindness show,
Chearing the good: quickning the slow.
As holy friends mourn at delay,
And think each minute an hour's stay: 30
So his divine and loving *Dove*
With longing throws doth heave and move,
And soare about us, while we sleep:
Sometimes quite through that *lock* doth *peep*,
And shine; but always without fail
Before the slow Sun can unveile,
In new *Compassions* breaks like light,
And *Morning-looks*, which scatter night.
And wilt thou let thy *creature* be
When *thou* hast watch'd, asleep to thee? 40
Why to unwellcome, loath'd surprises
Do'st leave him, having left his vices?
Since these, if suffer'd, may again
Lead back the *living*, to the *slain*.
O change this *Scourge*! or, if as yet
None less will my transgressions fit:
Dissolve, dissolve! death cannot do
What I would not submit unto.

The Recovery

Fair *Vessell* of our daily light, whose proud
And previous *glories* gild that blushing Cloud:
Whose lively *fires* in swift projections glance
From hill to hill, and by refracted chance
Burnish some neighbour-*rock*, or tree, and then
Fly off in coy and winged *flams* agen:
If thou this day
Hold on thy way,
Know, I have got a greater *light* than thine;
A light, whose *shade* and *back-parts* make thee shine. 10
Then get thee down: then get thee down;
I have a *Sun* now of my own.

II

Those nicer livers, who without thy Rays
Stirr not abroad, those may thy lustre praise:
And wanting light (*light*, which no *wants* doth know!)
To thee (weak *shiner*!) like blind *Persians* bow;
But where that *Sun*, which tramples on thy head,
From his own bright, eternal *Eye* doth shed
One living *Ray*,
There thy dead day 20
Is needless, and man to a *light* made free,
Which shews what thou can'st neither shew, nor see.
Then get thee down, Then get thee down;
I have a *Sun* now of my own.

The Nativity

Written in the year 1656

Peace? and to all the world? sure, one
And he the prince of peace, hath none.
He travels to be born, and then
Is born to travel more agen.
Poor *Galile*! thou can'st not be
The place for his Nativity.
His restless mother's call'd away,
And not deliver'd, till she pay.

A *Tax*? 'tis so still! we can see
The Church thrive in her misery; 10
And like her head at *Bethlem*, rise
When she opprest with troubles, lyes.
Rise? should all fall, we cannot be
In more extremities than he.
Great *Type* of passions! come what will,
Thy grief exceeds all *copies* still.
Thou cam'st from heav'n to earth, that we
Might go from Earth to Heav'n with thee.
And though thou found'st no welcom here,
Thou did'st provide us *mansions* there. 20
A *stable* was thy *Court*, and when
Men turn'd to *beasts*; Beasts would be *Men*.
They were thy *Courtiers*, others none;
And their poor *Manger* was thy *Throne*.
No swadling *silks* thy Limbs did fold,
Though thou could'st turn thy Rays to gold.
No *Rockers* waited on thy birth,
No *Cradles* stirr'd: nor songs of mirth;
But her chast *Lap* and sacred *Brest*
Which lodg'd thee first, did give thee *rest*. 30
But stay: what light is that doth stream,
And drop here in a gilded beam?
It is thy Star runs *page*, and brings
Thy tributary *Eastern* Kings.
Lord! grant some *Light* to us, that we
May with them find the way to thee.
Behold what mists eclipse the day:
How dark it is! shed down one *Ray*
To guide us out of this sad night,
And say once more, *Let there be Light*. 40

The true Christmas

So stick up *Ivie* and the *Bays*,
And then restore the *heathen* ways.
Green will remind you of the spring,
Though this great day denies the thing.

And mortifies the Earth and all
But your wild *Revels*, and loose *Hall*.
Could you wear *Flow'rs*, and *Roses* strow
Blushing upon your breasts *warm Snow*,
That very *dress* your lightness will
Rebuke, and wither at the Ill. 10
The brightness of this day we owe
Not unto *Music*, *Masque* nor *Showe*:
Nor gallant *furniture*, nor *Plate*;
But to the *Manger's* mean Estate.
His *life* while here, as well as *birth*,
Was but a check to *pomp* and *mirth*;
And all mans *greatness* you may see
Condemn'd by his *humility*.
Then leave your open *house* and *noise*,
To welcom him with *holy Joys*, 20
And the poor *Shepherd's* watchfulness:
Whom *light* and *hymns* from Heav'n did bless.
What you *abound* with, cast abroad
To those that *want*, and ease your loade.
Who empties thus, will bring more in;
But riot is both *loss* and *Sin*.
Dress finely what comes not in sight,
And then you keep your *Christmas* right.

The Request

O thou! who did'st deny to me
This world's ador'd felicity,
And ev'ry big, imperious lust,
Which fools admire in sinful Dust;
With those fine, subtile *twists*, that tye
Their *bundles* of foul gallantry:
Keep still my weak Eyes from the *shine*
Of those gay things, which are not thine,
And shut my Ears against the noise
Of wicked, though applauded *Joys*. 10
For thou in any land hast store
Of shades and Coverts for thy poor,

Where from the busie dust and heat,
As well as storms, they may retreat.
A Rock, or Bush are douny beds,
When thou art there crowning their heads
With secret blessings: or a *Tire*
Made of the *Comforter's* live-fire.
And when thy goodness in the *dress*
Of anger, will not seem to bless: 20
Yet do'st thou give them that rich *Rain*,
Which as it drops, clears all again.
  O what kind *Visits* daily pass
'Twixt thy great self and such poor *grass*,
With what sweet looks doth thy love shine
On those low *Violets* of thine!
While the tall *Tulip* is accurst,
And *Crowns Imperial* dye with thirst.
O give me still those secret meals,
Those rare *Repasts*, which thy love deals! 30
Give me that Joy, which none can grieve,
And which in all griefs doth relieve.
This is the portion thy Child begs,
Not that of rust, and rags and dregs.

Jordanis

Quid celebras auratam undam, Et combusta pyropis
  Flumina, vel Medio quæ serit æthra salo?
Æternùm refluis si pernoctaret in undis
  Phœbus, *&* *incertam sydera suda* Tethyn
Si colerent, tantæ gemmæ! nil cærula librem:
  Sorderet rubro in littore dives Eos.
Pactoli *mea lympha macras ditabit arenas,*
  Atq; Universum gutta minuta Tagum.
O charum caput! O cincinnos unda beatos
  Libata! O domini balnea Sancta mei! 10
Quod fortunatum voluit spectare Canalem,
  Hoc erat in laudes area parva tuas.
Jordanis *in medio perfusus flumine lavit,*
  Divinoq; tuas ore beavit aquas.

Ah! Solyma *infœlix rivis obsessa prophanis!*
Amisit Genium porta Bethesda *suum.*
Hic Orientis *aquæ currunt, & apostata* Pharpar,
Atq; Abana *immundo turbidus amne fluit.*
Ethnica te totam cum fædavere fluenta,
Mansit Christicolâ Jordanis *unus aqua.* 20

Servilii Fatum, *sive* Vindicta divina

Et sic in cythara, *sic in* dulcedine *vitæ*
Et facti & luctus *regnat* amarities.
Quàm subitò in fastum *extensos atq;* effera *vultus*
Ultrici *oppressit* vilis *arena sinu!*
Si violæ, spiransque crocus: si lilium ἄεινον
Non nisi Justorum nascitur è cinere:
Spinarum, tribuliq; atq; infœlicis avenæ
Quantus in hoc tumulo & qualis acervus erit?
Dii superi! damnosa piis sub sydera longum
Mansuris stabilem conciliate fidem! 10
Sic olim in cœlum post nimbos clariùs ibunt,
Supremo occidui tot velut astra die.
Quippe ruunt horæ, qualisq; in Corpore vixit,
Talis it in tenebras bis moriturus homo.

De Salmone

Ad virum optimum, & sibi familiariùs notum: D. *Thomam Poellum* Cantrevensem: S. S. Theologiæ Doctorem.

Accipe prærapido Salmonem in gurgite captum,
Ex imo in summas cum penetrâsset aquas.
Mentitæ culicis quem forma elusit inanis:
Picta coloratis plumea musca notis.
Dum captat, capitur; vorat inscius, ipse vorandus;
Fitq; cibi raptor grata rapina mali.
Alma quies! miseræ merces ditissima vitæ,
Quàm tutò in tacitis hic latuisset aquis!
Qui dum spumosi fremitus & murmura rivi
Quæritat, hamato fit cita præda cibo. 10
Quam grave magnarum specimen dant ludicra rerum?
Gurges est mundus: Salmo, homo: pluma, dolus.

The World

Can any tell me what it is? can you,
That wind your thoughts into a *Clue*
To guide out others, while your selves stay in,
And hug the Sin?
I, who so long have in it liv'd,
That if I might,
In truth I would not be repriev'd:
Have neither sight,
Nor sense that knows
These *Ebbs* and *Flows*. 10
But since of all, all may be said,
And *likelines* doth but upbraid,
And mock the *Truth*, which still is lost
In fine *Conceits*, like streams in a sharp frost:
I will not strive, nor the *Rule* break
Which doth give Loosers leave to speak.
Then false and foul World, and unknown
Ev'n to thy own:
Here I renounce thee, and resign
Whatever thou can'st say, is thine. 20
Thou art not *Truth*; for he that tries
Shall find thee all deceit and lyes.
Thou art not *friendship*; for in thee
'Tis but the *bait* of policy.
Which, like a *Viper* lodg'd in *Flow'rs*,
Its venom through that sweetness pours.
And when not so, then always 'tis
A fadeing *paint*; the short-liv'd bliss
Of *air* and *Humour*: out and in
Like *Colours* in a *Dolphin*'s skin. 30
But must not live beyond *one day*,
Or *Convenience*; then away.
Thou art not *Riches*; for that *Trash*
Which one age hoords, the next doth wash
And so severely sweep away;
That few remember, where it lay.
So rapid *streams* the wealthy *land*
About them, have at their command:

And shifting *channels* here restore,
There break down, what they bank'd before. 40
Thou art not *Honour*; for those gay
Feathers will wear, and drop away;
And princes to some upstart *line*
Give new ones, that are full as fine.
Thou art not *pleasure*; for thy *Rose*
Upon a *thorn* doth still repose;
Which if not cropt, will quickly shed;
But soon as cropt, grows dull and dead.
  Thou art the *sand*, which fills one *glass*,
And then doth to another pass; 50
And could I put thee to a stay,
Thou art but *dust*! then go thy way,
And leave me *clean* and bright, though *poor*;
Who stops thee, doth but *dawb* his floor,
And *Swallow*-like, when he hath done,
To *unknown dwellings* must be gone!
  Welcom pure thoughts and peaceful hours
Inrich'd with *Sunshine* and with *show'rs*;
Welcom fair hopes and holy Cares,
The not to be repented *shares* 60
Of time and business: the sure *rode*
Unto my last and lov'd *Abode*!
O supreme *Bliss*!
The Circle, Center and Abyss
Of blessings, never let me miss
Nor leave that *Path*, which leads to thee:
Who art alone all things to me!
I hear, I see all the long day
The noise and pomp of the *broad way*;
I note their Course and proud approaches: 70
Their silks, perfumes and glittering Coaches.
But in the *narrow way* to thee
I observe only poverty,
And despis'd things: and all along
The ragged, mean and humble throng
Are still on foot, and as they go,
They sigh and say; *Their Lord went so*!

Give me my *staff* then, as it stood
When green and growing in the Wood.
(Those *stones*, which for the *Altar* serv'd, 80
Might not be smooth'd, nor finely carv'd:)
With this *poor stick* I'le pass the *Foord*
As *Jacob* did; and thy dear *word*,
As thou hast dress'd it: not as *Witt*
And *deprav'd tastes* have poyson'd it:
Shall in the passage be my meat,
And none else will thy Servant eat.
Thus, thus and in no other sort
Will I set forth, though laugh'd at for't;
And leaving the wise *World* their way, 90
Go through; though Judg'd to go astray.

The Bee

From fruitful *beds* and flowry *borders*
Parcell'd to wastful Ranks and Orders,
Where *state* grasps more than plain *Truth* needs
And wholesome *Herbs* are starv'd by *Weeds*:
To the wild Woods I will be gone,
And the course Meals of great *Saint John*.
When truth and piety are mist
Both in the Rulers and the Priest;
When pity is not cold, but dead,
And the rich eat the Poor like bread; 10
While factious heads with open Coile
And force first make, then share the spoile:
To *Horeb* then *Elias* goes,
And in the *Desart* grows the *Rose*.
Hail Christal Fountains and fresh shades,
Where no proud look invades.
No busie worldling hunts away
The sad Retirer all the day:
Haile happy harmless solitude,
Our Sanctuary from the rude 20
And scornful world: the calm recess
Of faith, and hope and holiness!

Here something still like *Eden* looks,
Hony in Woods, *Julips* in Brooks:
And *Flow'rs*, whose rich, unrifled *Sweets*
With a chast kiss the cool dew greets.
When the toyls of the Day are done
And the tir'd world sets with the Sun,
Here *flying* winds and *flowing* Wells
Are the wise, watchful Hermits *Bells*; 30
Their buisie *murmurs* all the night
To *praise* or *prayer* do invite,
And with an awful sound arrest
And piously employ his breast.
When in the *East* the Dawn doth blush,
Here cool, fresh *Spirits* the air brush;
Herbs (strait) get up, *Flow'rs* peep and spread:
Trees whisper praise, and bow the head.
Birds from the shades of night releast
Look round about, then quit the neast, 40
And with united gladness sing
The glory of the morning's King.
The *Hermit* hears, and with meek voice
Offers his own up, and their Joys:
Then prays, that all the world may be
Blest with as sweet an unity.
If sudden storms the day invade,
They flock about him to the shade:
Where wisely they expect the end,
Giving the tempest time to spend; 50
And hard by shelters on some bough
Hilarion's servant, the sage *Crow*.
O purer years of light, and grace!
The *diff'rence* is great, as the *space*
'Twixt you and us: who blindly run
After *false-fires*, and leave the *Sun*.
Is not fair *Nature* of her self
Much richer than dull *paint*, or *pelf*?
And are not *streams* at the *Spring-head*
More sweet than in carv'd *Stone*, or *Lead*? 60
But *fancy* and some *Artist's* tools
Frame a Religion for fools.

The *truth*, which once was plainly taught,
With *thorns* and *briars* now is fraught.
Some part is with bold *Fables* spotted,
Some by strange *Comments* wildly blotted:
And *discord* (old Corruption's Crest,)
With *blood* and *blame* hath stain'd the rest.
So *Snow*, which in its first descents
A whiteness, like pure heav'n presents, 70
When touch'd by *Man* is quickly soil'd
And after trodden down, and spoil'd.
O lead me, where I may be free
In *truth* and *Spirit* to serve thee!
Where undisturb'd I may converse
With thy great self, and there rehearse
Thy gifts with thanks, and from thy store
Who art all blessings, beg much more!
Give me the Wisdom of the *Bee*,
And her unwearied Industry: 80
That from the *wild Gourds* of these days
I may extract Health and thy praise;
Who can'st turn darkness into light,
And in my weakness shew thy might!
Suffer me not in any want
To seek refreshment from a *Plant*,
Thou did'st not *set*! since all must be
Pluck'd up, whose *growth* is not from thee.
'Tis not the *garden* and the *Bowrs*,
Nor *fense* and *forms* that give to flow'rs 90
Their *wholsomness*: but thy *good will*,
Which *truth* and *pureness* purchase still.
Then since corrupt man hath driv'n hence
Thy kind and saving *Influence*,
And *Balm* is no more to be had
In all the Coasts of *Gilead*:
Go with me to the *shade* and *cell*,
Where thy best *Servants* once did dwell.
There let me know thy *Will*, and see
Exil'd *Religion* own'd by thee. 100
For thou can'st turn dark *Grots* to *Halls*,
And make *Hills* blossome like the *vales*:

Decking their untill'd *heads* with flow'rs
And fresh delights for all sad hours:
Till from them, like a laden *Bee*,
I may fly home, and *hive* with thee.

To Christian Religion

Farewel thou true and tried Refection
Of the still poor and meek *Election*!
Farewel Souls *Joy*, the quickning *health*
Of Spirits, and their secret *wealth*!
Farewel my *Morning-star*, the bright
And dawning *looks* of the true Light!
O blessed *shiner*! tell me whither
Thou will be gone, when night comes hither?
A *Seer*, that observ'd thee in
Thy Course, and watch'd the growth of Sin, 10
Hath giv'n his Judgment and foretold,
That *West-ward* hence thy *Course* will hold:
And when the day with us is done,
There fix, and shine a glorious Sun.
O hated *shades* and *darkness*! when
You have got here the Sway agen,
And like unwholsome *fogs* withstood
The light, and blasted all that's good:
Who shall the happy *shepherds* be
To watch the next *Nativity* 20
Of Truth and brightness, and make way
For the returning, rising day?
O! what year will bring back our bliss,
Or who shall live, when God doth this?
Thou *Rock* of Ages, and the *Rest*
Of all, that for thee are opprest!
Send down the *Spirit* of thy truth,
That Spirit, which the tender *Youth*
And first *growths* of thy *Spouse* did spread
Through all the world, from one small *head*! 30
Then, if *to blood we must resist*
Let thy mild *Dove*, and our high *Priest*

Help us, when man proves false, or frowns,
To bear the *Cross*, and save our *Crowns*:
O! honour those, that honour thee!
Make *Babes* to still the Enemy:
And teach an *Infant* of few days
To perfect by his death, thy praise!
Let none defile what thou did'st *wed*,
Nor tear the *garland* from her head: 40
But chast and chearful let her dye,
And pretious in the *Bridegrooms* Eye!
So to thy glory, and her praise
These last shall be her brightest dayes.

Revel. Chap. last, vers. 17
The Spirit and the Bride say, Come

DAPHNIS

An Elegiac *Eclogue*

The Interlocutors, *Damon*, *Menalcas*

Da. What clouds, *Menalcas*, do oppress thy brow?
Flow'rs in a Sunshine never look so low.
Is *Nisa* still cold Flint? or have thy Lambs
Met with the Fox by straying from their Dams?

Men. Ah! *Damon*, no; my Lambs are safe, & she
Is kind, and much more white than they can be.
But what doth life, when most serene, afford
Without a worm, which gnaws her fairest gourd?
Our days of gladness are but short reliefs,
Giv'n to reserve us for enduring griefs. 10
So smiling Calms close Tempests breed, wch break
Like spoilers out, and kill our flocks, when weak.
I heard last *May* (and *May* is still high Spring,)
The pleasant *Philomel* her Vespers sing.
The green wood glitter'd with the golden Sun
And all the West like Silver shin'd; not one
Black cloud, no rags, nor spots did stain
The Welkins beauty: nothing frown'd like rain;

But e're night came, that Scene of fine sights turn'd
To fierce dark showrs; the Air with lightnings burn'd; 20
The woods sweet Syren rudely thus opprest,
Gave to the Storm her weak and weary Breast.
I saw her next day on her last cold bed;
And *Daphnis* so, just so is *Daphnis* dead!

Da. So Violets, so doth the Primrose fall,
At once the Springs pride and its funeral.
Such easy sweets get off still in their prime,
And stay not here, to wear the soil of Time.
While courser Flow'rs (which none would miss, if past;)
To scorching Summers, and cold Autumns last. 30

Men. Souls need not time, the early forward things
Are always fledg'd, and gladly use their Wings,
Or else great parts, when injur'd quit the Crowd,
To shine above still, not behind the Cloud.
And is't not just to leave those to the night,
That madly hate, and persecute the light?
Who doubly dark, all *Negroes* do exceed,
And inwardly are true black Moores indeed.

Da. The punishment still manifests the Sin,
As outward signs shew the disease within. 40
While worth opprest mounts to a nobler height,
And Palm-like bravely overtops the weight.
So where swift *Isca* from our lofty hills
With lowd farewels descends, and foming fills
A wider Channel, like some great port-vein,
With large rich streams to feed the humble plain:
I saw an Oak, whose stately height and shade
Projected far, a goodly shelter made,
And from the top with thick diffused Boughs
In distant rounds grew, like a Wood-nymphs house. 50
Here many Garlands won at Roundel-lays
Old shepheards hung up in those happy days,
With knots and girdles, the dear spoils and dress
Of such bright maids, as did true lovers bless.
And many times had old *Amphion* made
His beauteous Flock acquainted with this shade;

A Flock, whose fleeces were as smooth and white
As those, the wellkin shews in Moonshine night.
Here, when the careless world did sleep, have I
In dark records and numbers noblie high 60
The visions of our black, but brightest Bard
From old *Amphion*'s mouth full often heard;
With all those plagues poor shepheards since have known,
And Ridles more, which future times must own.
While on his pipe young *Hylas* plaid, and made
Musick as solemn as the song and shade.
But the curs'd owner from the trembling top
To the firm brink, did all those branches lop,
And in one hour what many years had bred,
The pride and beauty of the plain lay dead. 70
The undone Swains in sad songs mourn'd their loss,
While storms & cold winds did improve the Cross.
But Nature, which (like vertue) scorns to yield
Brought new recruits and succours to the Field;
For by next Spring the check'd Sap wak'd from sleep
And upwards still to feel the Sun did creep,
Till at those wounds, the hated Hewer made,
There sprang a thicker and a fresher shade.

Men. So thrives afflicted Truth! and so the light,
When put out, gains a value from the Night. 80
How glad are we, when but one twinkling Star
Peeps betwixt clouds, more black than is our Tar?
And Providence was kind, that order'd this
To the brave Suff'rer should be solid bliss;
Nor is it so till this short life be done,
But goes hence with him, and is still his Sun.

Da. Come Shepherds then, and with your greenest Bays
Refresh his dust, who lov'd your learned Lays.
Bring here the florid glories of the Spring,
And as you strew them pious *Anthems* sing, 90
Which to your children and the years to come
May speak of *Daphnis*, and be never dumb.
While prostrate I drop on his quiet Urn
My Tears, not gifts; and like the poor, that mourn

With green, but humble Turfs; write o're his Hearse
For false, foul Prose-men this fair Truth in Verse.

'Here *Daphnis* sleeps! & while the great watch goes
'Of loud and restless Time, takes his repose.
'Fame is but noise, all Learning but a thought:
'Which one admires, another sets at nought. 100
'Nature mocks both, and Wit still keeps adoe;
'But Death brings knowledge and assurance too.

Men. Cast in your Garlands, strew on all the flow'rs
Which *May* with smiles, or *April* feeds with show'rs.
Let this days Rites as stedfast as the Sun
Keep pace with Time, and through all Ages run,
The publick character and famous Test
Of our long sorrows and his lasting rest;
And when we make procession on the plains,
Or yearly keep the Holyday of Swains, 110
Let *Daphnis* still be the recorded name
And solemn honour of our feasts and fame.
For though the *Isis* and the prouder *Thames*
Can shew his reliques lodg'd hard by their streams,
And must for ever to the honour'd name
Of Noble *Murrey* chiefly owe that fame:
Yet, here his Stars first saw him, and when fate
Beckon'd him hence, it knew no other date.
Nor will these vocal Woods and Valleys fail,
Nor *Isca*'s lowder Streams this to bewail, 120
But while Swains hope and Seasons change, will glide
With moving murmurs, because *Daphnis* di'd.

Da. A fatal sadness, such as still foregoes,
Then runs along with publick plagues and woes,
Lies heavy on us, and the very light
Turn'd Mourner too, hath the dull looks of Night.
Our vales like those of Death, a darkness shew
More sad than Cypress, or the gloomy Yew,
And on our hills, where health with height complied,
Thick drowsie Mists hang round and there reside. 130
Not one short parcel of the tedious year
In its old dress and beauty doth appear;

Flowr's hate the Spring, and with a sullen bend
Thrust down their Heads, which to the Root still tend,
And though the Sun like a cold Lover, peeps
A little at them, still the Days-eye sleeps.
But when the Crab and Lion with acute
And active Fires their sluggish heat recruit,
Our grass straight russets, and each scorching day
Drinks up our Brooks as fast as dew in May. 140
Till the sad Heardsman with his Cattel faints,
And empty Channels ring with loud Complaints.

Men. Heaven's just displeasure & our unjust ways
Change Natures course, bring plagues dearth and decays.
This turns our lands to Dust, the skies to Brass,
Makes old kind blessings into curses pass.
And when we learn unknown and forraign Crimes,
Brings in the vengeance due unto those Climes.
The dregs and puddle of all ages now
Like Rivers near their fall, on us do flow. 150
Ah happy *Daphnis*! who, while yet the streams
Ran clear & warm (though but with setting beams,)
Got through: and saw by that declining light
His toil's and journey's end before the Night.

Da. A night, where darkness lays her chains and Bars,
And feral fires appear instead of Stars.
But he along with the last looks of day
Went hence, and setting (Sun-like) past away.
What future storms our present sins do hatch
Some in the dark discern, and others watch; 160
Though foresight makes no Hurricane prove mild;
Fury that's long fermenting, is most wild.
But see, while thus our sorrows we discourse,
Phœbus hath finish't his diurnal course.
The shades prevail, each Bush seems bigger grown:
Darkness (like State,) makes small things swell and frown.
The Hills and Woods with Pipes and Sonnets round
And bleating sheep our Swains drive home, resound.

Men. What voice from yonder Lawn tends hither? heark
'Tis *Thyrsis* calls, I hear *Lycanthe* bark. 170

His Flocks left out so late, and weary grown
Are to the Thickets gone, and there laid down.

Da. Menalcas, haste to look them out, poor sheep
When day is done, go willingly to sleep.
And could bad Man his time spend, as they do,
He might go sleep, or die, as willing too.

Men. Farewel kind *Damon*! now the Shepheards Star
With beauteous looks smiles on us, though from far.
All creatures that were favourites of day
Are with the Sun retir'd and gone away. 180
While feral Birds send forth unpleasant notes,
And night (the Nurse of thoughts,) sad thoughts promotes.
But Joy will yet come with the morning-light,
Though sadly now we bid good night! *Da.* good night!

APPENDIX

TRANSLATIONS BY EDMUND BLUNDEN OF SEVEN LATIN POEMS

1. *To After Ages*

(See p. 34)

Time soon forgets; and yet I would not have
This present wholly mouldering in the grave.
Hear then, posterity; from Wales I drew
My life, and first its airy mountains knew,
And Usk below them winding; then I went
To learned Herbert's kind encouragement,
Herbert, the pride of our Latinity;
Six years with double gifts he guided me.
Method and love, and mind and hand conspired,
Nor ever flagged his mind, nor his hand tired. 10
This was my shaping season; but the times
In which it fell were torn with public crimes;
I lived when England against England waged
War, and the Church and State like furies raged.
Through happy fields went these demented foes,
And the coarse rush beat down the holy rose;
They fouled the fountains, peace died gasping there,
Glooms wept above and veiled heaven's glittering air.
But, Honour led me, and a pious heart;
In this great ravenous heat I had no part; 20
It was my faith, that guiltless blood will cry
Aloud, and has a power which does not die.
My mother's pure and patient pattern showed
How best with weeping I should bear my load;
So never with wild insult did I smite
The Holy down; my heart and hand were white.
Forbear, O friend, to ask me more than this;
Let the wise weigh my words; the fool may miss.

2. *To the River Usk*

(See p. 98)

Kind Usk, among thy flowers, whose wave
Golden pebbles still doth lave;

With dewy whisper making glad
The primrose and the bluebell sad;
While moons lead time his destined way
And men expire, yet day by day
In the sun the same as ever,
An unconquerable River,
So divine's thy murmuring hymn
To these woodlands tall and dim 10
That I think I hear on thee
Orpheus' deep-drawn melody,
His sweet strings resounding clear,
His ancient magic echoing here.

3. *To his old Schoolmaster and ever honoured Mr. Matthew Herbert*

(See p. 98)

Mere life, my Matthew, from my father came;
Soon it must vanish, and the giver's name.
Thy watchful wisdom did much more, and gave
My name (else dead) to bloom above my grave.
Share then your pupil! let this brief life be
My father's, and that future life for thee.

4. *To Echo*

(See p. 99)

O Nymph, that through the drowsy thicket fliest,
And boughs beloved, and sauntering there repliest
Out of the deeps; Spirit of this old grove,
Tongue of the venerable cliffs; whose love
None but our last few syllables attain,
Now, by Narcissus' dying voice, the pain
Of his last breaths, his life's extremity,
Broken attempts and sighs, I conjure thee,—
Show me the mystery of this tangled maze,
The happy secret of these hid green ways, 10
Thy home, thy walks!
So shall thy realms survive
For ever young and fine, thy copses thrive
With drinking of the Moon's unsullied tears,
And the brave morning's dew, and the warm airs
Of favouring heaven; so, discerned afar,
Like clustering stars, as constant as each star,

Elixired with eternal spring, may these
Green heads for ever shine! and every breeze
With scent of musk and cinnamon respire, 20
As air around the Phoenix' odorous pyre!

5. *The Flashing Flint*

(See p. 214)

O I confess, without a wound
Thou oft hast tried me,
And oft Thy Voice without a sound
Hath longed to guide me;
Thy zephyr circled me from heaven,
On a calm wing,
And murmuring sought t'allure me, given
To no such thing.

A Flint I was, both deaf and dumb,
But Thou, unceasing, 10
(So lov'st Thou all Thy tribe) didst come
To my releasing;
Thou hast tried all Thy powers, until
Thou show'st Thy love,
With whose vast Will my stubborn will
Thou dost remove.

Thy siege comes sharper; by Thy shock
My wall's o'erthrown;
Thou shatter'st even my breast of rock,
And what was stone 20
Is flesh and blood: O see, I bleed:
At last these Heaps
Burn with thy heaven, and, changed indeed!
The Marble weeps.

Thus in the world's first age Thy hand
Made fountains ripple
From Rocks, and Cliffs at Thy command
Refreshed Thy people;
Thy secret busy care, my Lord,
Hath here been plain: 30
My dying is my life restored;
My loss, my gain.

6. *The Fate of Servilius*
or
Divine Vengeance

(See p. 443)

As with the lyre, even so it is with life;
The harsh hand's answered with as harsh a strain;
See, one whose greedy looks so late glared strife,
Struck down into the common dust's disdain!
If violet, crocus warm and lily green
From just men's ashes and no others bloom,
What thorns and thistles, what a press unclean
Of weeds shall swarm, the offspring of this tomb!

Most noble heavens! grant to the saints here
Below the righteous stars a stubborn faith, 10
Till their last evening cloudless glow, and clear
As setting stars they stoop to a calm death.
O twofold death! for as a man hath made
Himself on earth, so must he face the shade.

7. *With a Salmon*
(*To his excellent friend*, *Dr. Thomas Powell*)

(See p. 443)

Accept this Salmon, that, when he had fought
From the deep sea to the hill stream, was caught
Amid the swiftest whirlpools. For his fate,
No more was needed than a seeming Gnat,
An empty Figure, a dissembled Fly,
Of feathers made, and dappled with bright dye.
The biter's bit! the eater's to be eaten,
The pirate by another pirate beaten.

O lovely peace, life's treasure! how would he
Have rested in deep pools' security,— 10
But even as through the roaring foam he tries
To reach that calm, he's hungry—and he dies;
In which I read, alas, the world's the spate,
Man is the salmon, falsehood the bright bait.

SELECT GLOSSARY OF UNCOMMON WORDS, FORMS, AND MEANINGS

Abear (327. 27). Behaviour.
Adopt (57. 13). Stand sponsor for.
Aire-monging (43. 21). Dealing in air.
Angel'd (48. 65). Governed by angels.

Back-side (67. 34). Obverse; (434. 15). Retrospect, backward view.
Bayle (58. 42). Defence.
Blew Aprons (48. 16). Tradesmen.
Bottome (65. 20). Skein of thread.

Canicular (42. 66). Pertaining to the dog-days.
Center'd (260. 5). Brought to rest; fixed.
Cere-cloth (55. 49). Surgical plaster.
Church'd (62. 36). Consecrated.
Church rents (181. 6). Schisms.
Cise (412. 46). Size.
Cypers (367. 9). Cypress lawn, a thin transparent material.

Decline (8. 23). Debase.

Eares (58. 33). The close-cropped Roundheads.

Fall (273. 15). Let fall.
Fense (437. 21). Fence; protection.
Forlorn (403. 86). Vanguard.

Geld (14. 33). Weaken (by adulteration).

Hin (113. 16). A Hebrew measure for liquid, *c.* 1 gallon.
Husbands (321. 11). Husbandmen.

Inch (57. 9). Eke out.
Influxe (12. 67 and 67. 32). Influence (astrological).
Interline (320. 38). Interpose itself.
Is (32. 485 and 277. 46). Yes.

Kelder (43. 2). Womb.
Key (64. 9). Mode, law. Cf. the verb (292. 36), put in tune.

Lapland-lease (56. 90). 'Lease' is perhaps a misprint for bease = baize, ? used in Lapland for clothing.
Leiguer (63. 10 &c.). Ambassador.

Line (260. 9 &c.). Boundary.
Lines (268. 54). Reaches to.
Luctual (346. 37). Sad; mournful.

Mancipated (133. 30). Enslaved.
Maze (3. 13). ? Metaphor for London or the Law.

Pistic Nard (344. 21). The aromatic ointment mentioned in Mark xix. 3. A.V., 'spikenard'.
Port-vein (451. 45). Portal vein; intestinal vein conveying blood to the liver.
Proine (180. 5). Preen; trim feathers.
Propension (395. 30). Favourable inclination, propensity.

Queer (377 title). Query.
Quist (97. 77). Ring-dove.

Reare (57. 8). Conclusion.
Relatives (219. 33). Narratives; relations.
Remonstrative (57. 2). Demonstrative; laudatory. Cf. remonstrances (58. 2).

Shag (55. 18). Nap (uneven).
Share (273. 4). Rend.
Signature (281. 41). Outward sign of an inward quality.
Snudge (307. 66). Lie close.
Span-extents (230. 14). Having only the extent of a span.
Stamps (407. 35). Coins.
Start (8. 23). Loosen.
Superstitie (172. 14). Power of survival.

Tiffanie (60. 16). A thin transparent silk.
Tinn'd (322. 12). Ignited.

Use (254. 1). Moral, application.

Voyders (68. 26). Receptacles for unwanted remains of food, &c.

Well (318. 23 &c.). Neighbourhood of a fountain.
White (88. 1, 249. 6 &c.). Innocent; holy.
Wrong (337. 39). Bent.

INDEX OF FIRST LINES

*The poems marked * are fragments and translations to be found among the prose works. Those marked † are commendatory poems addressed to Vaughan*

PRINTED IN GREAT BRITAIN
AT THE UNIVERSITY PRESS, OXFORD
BY VIVIAN RIDLER
PRINTER TO THE UNIVERSITY